What is Philosophy?

Anamnesis

Anamnesis means remembrance or reminiscence, the collection and re-collection of what has been lost, forgotten, or effaced. It is therefore a matter of the very old, of what has made us who we are. But *anamnesis* is also a work that transforms its subject, always producing something new. To recollect the old, to produce the new: that is the task of *Anamnesis*.

a re.press series

What is Philosophy?
Embodiment, Signification, Ideality

Jere O'Neill Surber

re.press Melbourne 2014

re.press

PO Box 40, Prahran, 3181, Melbourne, Australia
http://www.re-press.org

© re.press and Jere O'Neill Surber 2014

The moral rights of the author are automatically asserted and recognized under Australian law (*Copyright Amendment [Moral Rights] Act 2000*)
This work is 'Open Access', published under a creative commons license which means that you are free to copy, distribute, display, and perform the work as long as you clearly attribute the work to the authors, that you do not use this work for any commercial gain in any form whatsoever and that you in no way alter, transform or build on the work outside of its use in normal academic scholarship without express permission of the author (or their executors) *and* the publisher of this volume. For any reuse or distribution, you must make clear to others the license terms of this work. For more information see the details of the creative commons licence at this website: http://creativecommons.org/licenses/by-nc-nd/2.5/

National Library of Australia Cataloguing-in-Publication entry

O'Neill Surber, Jere, author.

What is philosophy? : embodiment, signification, ideality /
Jere O'Neill Surber.

9780992373405 (paperback)
Series: Anamnesis.

Philosophy.
Analysis (Philosophy)
Continental philosophy.
Philosophy, Modern.

101

Designed and Typeset by *A&R*
This book is produced sustainably using plantation timber, and printed in the destination market reducing wastage and excess transport.

Contents

Acknowledgements	vii
Preface	11
With What Must Philosophy Begin?	29
1. The Conditions Of Philosophy: An Informal Introduction	43
2. Kant's Fundamental Question and the Problem of Judgment	55
3. The Analytic *A Posteriori* and The Conditions of Philosophy	65
4. The Question About Philosophy: A Preliminary Response	77
5. Conditions and Principles	87
6. Limits, Excesses, and Consequences	107
7. Trajectories of the Conditions: Withdrawal, Reduction, Com-Prehension	139
8. Philosophy as Activity and Its Components	159
9. Philosophy as Texts and Their Elements	179
10. Philosophy as Ideality	213
11. Philosophy and Its 'Others'	255
12. The Contours and Partitions of Philosophy	285
Concluding Considerations and Questions	321

Acknowledgements

Many of the shards and fragments of ideas expressed in this work trace back to my earliest encounters, even before my university studies, with that enterprise called 'Philosophy'. However, these didn't begin forming a recognizable assemblage until I became the director of the Philosophy Colloquium in my university's Joint Doctoral Program. The Colloquium was typically held during the snowy Colorado Winter quarter, met in my 'back cabin' (well warmed by both the fire and good spirits), and usually consisted of no more than about a half dozen participants. It was mainly in preparing for and coordinating those meetings, and thanks to the intellectual honesty and generosity of now several 'generations' of those doctoral students, that this work assumed its present form. It is theirs almost as much as it is my own, and the blame for any errors or lapses of judgment that one may find in it I ascribe to them for not remaining at the meetings late enough, sharing one more round, and fully convincing me of the faults in my thinking. I would like especially to thank Drs. Rob Manzinger, Evgeny Pavlov, Jeff Scholes, and David Hale for, at different stages, serving as the Colloquium's ringleaders and provocateurs. Special gratitude goes to Jared Nieft, who patiently read and discussed the work with me as it was being written over about a two-year period. Also, much gratitude goes to my past and present GTAs, whose able assistance with my undergraduate teaching chores gave me a bit more time for research and writing.

Besides such active collaborators and critics, completing projects like this also tends to require fairly complex support networks. The University of Denver and especially my colleagues in its Department of Philosophy have long provided a stable, congenial, creative, and blessedly conflict-free environment. Over the years, I have especially benefited from (and thoroughly enjoyed) collaborative teaching ventures with Robert D. Richardson (English Literature), M. E. Warlick (Art History), Carl Raschke (Religious Studies), and Naomi Reshotko (Philosophy, and the World's Greatest Chair!) During my many stays in Germany, Achim Koeddermann and his wonderful family have provided a 'home away from home,' as has William Desmond and his family in Belgium.

My own household has born much of the brunt of the sort of absence, inconsideration, and occasional crankiness that accompanies the tunnel-vision necessary to complete a lengthy writing project. My extended household includes my partner Cheryl Ward, our twin daughters Tanya and Jennifer, Linda Kalyris, Stan Weddle, assorted Celtic musicians, and trans-species members Biggie (who attended more Philosophy Colloquium meetings than any student!), M-Cat, Midder, Macy, Hobbes, Ringo, and Victoria. I sincerely apologize to all for meals cooked for me that went cold, feline feeding times patiently awaited but delayed, and playtime curtailed while I was 'out back' working away. But do know that I'm ever grateful for all your patience, support, and love.

Preface

By the turn of the last century—which also ushered in a new millennium—the enterprise of philosophy had reached a point of what is called in chaos theory a 'phase transition.' It was, and thus far to some degree still remains, a point where things could follow, quite unpredictably, any one of a number of trajectories arising from the same set of 'initial conditions.' However, even if we can't predict which trajectory it will follow, we can describe, in broad terms, the trajectories (or sets of them) available to it. I see four possibilities.
1. Philosophy continues on as before—it would just continue doing what it's doing at present without any fundamental change.
2. Philosophy is absorbed and some, if not all, of its former activities assumed by some other discipline—mathematics, linguistics, cognitive science, psychoanalysis, art, poetry, or even religion.
3. Philosophy, in effect, hits the reset button, returning to some earlier state regarded as preferable to its present state.
4. Philosophy redefines and reinvents itself in a way that would make clear its fundamental differences from other human enterprises as well as its continuities and breaks with its own history and its present 'initial conditions.'

This work is both a wager on the fourth alternative as well as an effort to assist in promoting this outcome.

(1) As always, the 'initial conditions,' that is, the features of philosophy's present state, are sufficiently complex and sensitive to prevent any linear causal determination or predictive certainty. Still, we can cite a few of them.

A particularly conspicuous feature of the present state of philosophy is the persistence of a broad division of its field into what are typically called the 'analytic' and 'Continental' approaches. The reasons for this divide are as much cultural and political as they are intellectual. To see that this philosophical division was not *rooted* in any real intellectual divide, one need only recall that both branches grew from Kant's Critical Philosophy and that many of the seminal figures of the analytic tradition, like Frege, Mach,

Meinong, Wittgenstein, and Carnap, were fully formed products of the intellectual culture of the Continent. It is also the case that Continental philosophy would not have been defined in the way it came to be without its embrace and extension in the Anglophone world, especially after the Second World War. So, in some respects, attempts to bridge the gap between analytic and Continental philosophy from either side often end up in a situation of 'I met the other, and the other is me.'

Still, there has been an historically efficacious difference that had as its own initial condition the last great phase transition in philosophy: Kant's 'Copernican Revolution in philosophy.' Kant described his philosophical view as 'transcendental idealism.' Very roughly put, this involved two theses. One, the idealism part, asserted that human consciousness or subjectivity was the ultimate source of the structures constituting the 'world.' The other, the transcendental aspect, was that these structures were 'necessary and universal' for all experience and knowledge. We might, then, broadly say that the Continental trajectory following from Kant tended to assume as its foundation and starting-point consciousness or subjectivity, albeit in forms much more complex and ramified than that found in Kant, allowing questions about necessity and universality to assume their place in relation to this. The analytic tradition, by contrast, tended to take necessity and universality, whether interpreted in terms of logical or scientific 'laws,' as its primary concern and approached consciousness or subjectivity (when it did at all) in these terms.

This difference in basic assumptions and approaches was already in full play by the beginning of the 20th century and manifested itself most dramatically in the controversies between phenomenology (and its existentialist offshoots) and positivism, with American pragmatism (especially in Peirce and James), in a sense, splitting the difference. However, about a third of the way through the 20th century, a new element, almost wholly absent in Kant, appeared within these discussions, an event that has been described as 'the linguistic turn.' Though often associated almost solely with the analytic approach (especially with the post-*Tractatus* works of Wittgenstein), such a 'turn' also occurred within the Continental camp as well (particularly in hermeneutic and structuralist inflections of philosophy). It is important to realize, however, that the linguistic turn did not, in itself, represent any crucial phase shift for philosophy, since natural language continued to be treated either from the point of view of consciousness or subjectivity or from that of logic and linguistic science.

At about the same time, just after the First World War, that this linguistic turn was taking place, a remarkable development appeared on the scene that seems, in retrospect, to confirm Hegel's dictum that 'philosophy is its own culture reflected in thought.' Just as the entire world appeared to some observers like Freud and Thomas Mann to have attempted a mass suicide in the First World War and laid the groundwork for another attempt soon thereafter, so philosophy itself appeared to have become suicidal. On the analytic side, logical positivists, most famously Carnap and Ayer, proposed that, logically considered and employing some of Kant's own distinctions, all allegedly philosophical statements are 'meaningless' and hence possess no 'truth value,' since they are neither factual or empirical (in Kantianese, '*a posteriori*') nor logical ('*analytic a priori*'). More broadly, they claimed that there simply is no class of 'meaningful' and 'true' statements other than those of the natural sciences, on the one hand, and logic and mathematics, on the other. (They regarded Kant's claims on behalf of 'synthetic *a priori* judgments' simply as logically confused and unsupportable.) Later, Wittgenstein reached a similar conclusion with respect to philosophical statements by another route, claiming that all (alleged) distinctively philosophical statements were examples of 'language going on a holiday' by extracting them from the usages, contexts, and 'forms of life' required for any statement to be meaningful. Although philosophical statements possessed the same 'grammatical form' as 'ordinary' meaningful statements, they lacked the fundamental conditions necessary to be regarded as meaningful. In either case, the gesture was the same: *philosophical* reasons and arguments were adduced purporting to demonstrate that philosophy was, at best, a confused and, at worst, an ultimately impossible undertaking.

This deep suspicion about the enterprise of philosophy had its Continental counterpart. Also emerging from an explicit engagement with Kant, and inspired in part by certain themes in Nietzsche, Heidegger first called for a 'destructive recovery' of the 'history of metaphysics' and, gradually, came to a view that affirmed a sort of 'meditative thought' that would go beyond philosophy and its theory-driven 'technics.' Language (especially in poetic forms) played a crucial role here as well, as in Heidegger's famous claim that 'language is the house of Being.' Once again, we see a gesture in which, on *philosophical* grounds, philosophy's own 'end' was declared.

It was during the period following the Second World War, and, to some extent, due to political currents that it spawned, that the Continental and analytic approaches, despite their shared suicidal tendencies, became institutionalized and hardened into an explicit opposition. While the German and French universities (albeit with somewhat different emphases and styles) continued to study and teach Kant, though usually as interpreted through the lenses of Husserl's and Heidegger's phenomenology (and, in France, through structuralist spectacles as well), Anglophone philosophy departments doubled down on still recognizably Kantian themes such as logic, epistemology, and 'post-Critical' metaphysics. During the Cold War years, most Anglophone universities had, at most, a token Continental philosopher on their staffs (if they had any at all), just as universities on the Continent only rarely offered courses in analytic philosophy.

The gradual thawing of the Cold War witnessed a few calls for bridging the divide between Continental and analytic philosophy and a few, though widely scattered, points of intersection. Philosophers with analytic bona fides like Rorty, Putnam, Hintikka, Wilfred Sellars, and some of his students began reexamining some of the arguments and insights of Kant and Hegel, and Continental thinkers like Apel, Habermas, Ricoeur, and Dreyfus began considering and utilizing some of the insights of their Anglophone counterparts. However, these crossover episodes were, for the most part, the exceptions that proved the rule—or, rather, proved that, in actuality, there were no longer any rules. For what occurred within the last two or three decades of the 20th century can be described as a sort of exhaustion of possibilities within both images or paradigms of philosophy.

On the Continental side (and especially in France), poststructuralism represented a volatile mix of various doses of Nietzsche (via Heidegger), phenomenology (via Levinas and Merleau-Ponty), structuralism (via Barthes), psychoanalysis (on Lacan's reading), and assorted other more political currents such as Marxism and feminist theory. Most of its major representatives, such as Foucault, Derrida, Lyotard, and Baudrillard, rejected even the term 'poststructuralism,' agreeing mainly (though often not explicitly) that texts (mostly written) were the central focus of intellectual inquiry, that philosophy itself consisted primarily of a rather indefinite set of written texts, and that various strategies for the interpretation of these texts would reveal both their intrinsic instability, their ideological biases, and, ultimately, the impossibility of providing any more positive image of philosophy that would permit distinguishing it from other types of texts such as literary, scientific, or religious. While most of the poststructuralists had abandoned any frontal assault on philosophy in the form of a single *coup de grâce*, the strategy now seemed to be more a matter of 'death by a thousand cuts,' philosophy thus expiring with a whimper rather than a scream.

For its part, analytic philosophy seemed to have lost any sense of the direction and momentum that it had earlier possessed before the Second World War under the impetus of logical positivism, language-oriented critique, and various combined versions of them. In some quarters, it heeded what one might gloss as the Kantian dictum to 'do less but do it better,' that is, to formulate various more traditional philosophical issues (whether logical, epistemological, ethical, or metaphysical) ever more narrowly and apply increasingly sophisticated methods to their resolution. In other instances, it took up issues arising within fields other than philosophy, especially mathematics, linguistics, cybernetics, artificial intelligence, cognitive psychology, and neuro-biology, variously playing the role of project manager, arbitrator of disagreements, and sometimes critic of various empirical research programs and their working assumptions and conceptual foundations. In either case, 'philosophy' came to be pretty much whatever someone that still called himself or herself a 'philosopher' happened to be thinking about or doing whenever and wherever she or he did it. Under such a nominalist assumption about the meaning of "philosophy," neither another frontal attack nor a thousand cuts were necessary: as a distinctive enterprise, philosophy was in danger of quietly expiring in its own bed.

As the turn of the century and millennium approached, one began to notice references to what might have been two potentially hopeful developments: 'post-analytic' and 'post-Continental' philosophy. (See John Rajchman and Cornel West, *Post-Analytic Philosophy* and John Mullarkey, *Post-Continental Philosophy*.) The former moniker attempted to highlight certain developments within the broadly analytic tradition often regarded as beginning with Quine's critiques of logical positivism and 'ordinary language philosophy' through an infusion of certain elements of American pragmatism. Usually counted among the post-analytic thinkers were such figures as Rorty, Davidson, Putnam, and perhaps now Kripke. The somewhat later appearing term, 'post-Continental philosophy,' is usually regarded as beginning with the work of Deleuze (and his sometime collaborator Guattari) who, already in the late 60s, had come to reject the poststructuralist emphases upon texts, strategies of textual interpretation, and a general suspicion with respect to the philosophical tradition. For Deleuze, this involved more robust and, to some degree, sympathetic engagements with the history of philosophy and some of its central issues and, coupled with an outlook more realist, constructivist, and speculative, culminated in an explicit defense of philosophy as a distinctive enterprise in Deleuze's final work (co-authored with Guattari), *What is Philosophy?* Though often disagreeing with Deleuze on various topics, other figures often mentioned as 'post-Continental' included Badiou, Laruelle, and Žižek.

With respect to both 'post-analytic' and 'post-Continental' philosophy, however, several points are worth noting. First, adding the prefix "post-" to any term is an always problematic and relatively weak gesture. Doing so both assumes some broad agreement about the meaning of the original term and serves to indicate more what the new compound is not than what it in itself is or may become. It does not constitute any real 'naming of an event,' so to speak, but rather, at most, registers observations about certain usually fairly dispersed deviations from some assumed norm. Second, in both cases, what the term is usually taken to refer to is not really any very new or recent development but a gradual evolution over a quite long period of time—so long, in fact, that it is almost as if "post-" can't really mean something coming temporally or historically 'after' but, more accurately, something that had been developing within and, perhaps, alongside the referent of the dominant term. (Quine's work began to appear in the early 1950s, Deleuze's in the early 1960s). Third, and connected with this, is the fact that both 'post-analytic' and 'post-Continental' were terms that have appeared and gained traction mostly in the United States rather than in the UK or on the Continent. (With respect to the latter, it's important to remember that there was often a 10 or even as much as 20 year gap between many of the major works' original appearance and their translation into English.) So these terms are not only historically misleading but are somewhat geographically biased. Finally, and most importantly, although the employment of either term is often coupled with an anticipation of some *'rapprochement'* between analytic and Continental philosophy, the reality is that, in basic issues, approaches, and style, 'post-analytic' and 'post-Continental' philosophy still remain, for the most part, as foreign to each other as were their original counterparts: 'post-analytic' philosophers still don't study Deleuze or Badiou and proponents of the latter rarely mention Quine, Davidson, Kripke, or even Rorty.

Perhaps the most optimistic view, then, is that something has been stirring for a while in both camps and that at some future time something more unified and constructive may come of this. But, at this point in time, it would still be most accurate to say that, except in certain quite limited quarters, for the rank and file of those that still call themselves 'philosophers,' things remain business as usual. And, as I've tried to suggest, this business was disastrous for philosophy earlier in the last century and remains so today.

(2) In the concluding couple of decades of the 20th century, there was an ever-growing number of those who might once have called themselves philosophers but now either shied away from this or ceased doing so entirely. Generally speaking, those who have abandoned the field of philosophy have moved in one of three directions: either toward science, art, or religion. In each case, there have been two important forces at work impelling them in these directions.

On the one hand, as we've already seen, the enterprise of philosophy itself had become so dispersed, vague, and indefinite that it lacked any discernible boundaries that might allow it to differentiate itself from these other areas of human endeavor. That is, it became impossible to defend philosophy simply because it became difficult, if not impossible, to say what one was attempting to secure.

On the other hand, in all three of the areas mentioned above, there have been long-developing tendencies to incorporate in their own activities and projects elements that might earlier have been regarded as distinctively philosophical. In the case of the natural sciences, Newton still regarded himself as a 'natural philosopher.' (See the title of his great work, *Philosophiae Naturalis Principia Mathematica*.) However, over the next hundred years or so, natural science came to distinguish itself from and oppose itself to philosophy, a development that provoked Kant's own philosophical phase shift, the 'Copernican Revolution in philosophy.' Since the time of Kant, the expansion of the field of science to include the social or human sciences, as well as advances within mathematics (alternative 'geometries,' mathematical logic, and set theory, for example) and the natural sciences (relativity theory, quantum theory, cybernetics, artificial intelligence, and cognitive science, among others) have appeared to many to harbor the capacity to finally answer questions that, for Kant, remained the distinctive province of philosophy. In the process, the enterprise of philosophy moved from, to paraphrase Locke, 'clearing away the metaphysical rubble obstructing the path of science' to serving as an active collaborator in scientific research (for example, in cognitive science) or, ultimately, simply abandoning the field of philosophy entirely and merging itself with scientific research programs.

The field of art, especially with the rise of 'Modernism' early in the 20th century, manifested a similar dynamic. Such figures as Mallarmé, Breton, Duchamp, Kandinsky, and Schoenberg, in their extensive theoretical writings, were explicit in claiming for art the capacity of expressing in concrete, sensory forms what would previously have been regarded as philosophical ideas. In doing so, they were extending and accelerating a process that had already begun within philosophy itself with such figures as Schelling, Schopenhauer, and Nietzsche that extended to the later Heidegger and some of his poststructuralist progeny. By the late 20th century, radically novel media, extending from photography and film to digital art, multi-media installations, and video games, had so expanded the former realm of art that 'theory' had become an essential and ever-present feature of art itself. Art, that is, had become both a vehicle for and primary object of philosophical activity. Except in isolated cases like that of Max Ernst, who earned a degree in philosophy early in his career, or the philosophically trained filmmaker Terence Malick, we will never know how many initially attracted to philosophy opted in favor of careers as artists. But, given how the realm of art developed in the 20th century and the inchoate condition of philosophy, the force of its attraction should not be surprising.

Developments in religion and theology also exerted their own attractive forces. Already early in the 19th century, Kant's philosophy, as interpreted by such figures as Schleiermacher and Hegel, had provided the basis for what came to be called 'liberal theology,' a movement that dominated religious and theological discourse for much of the 20th century. In fact, it would not be inaccurate to describe much of the theology of the 20th century as proceeding by a series of deliberate appropriations of philosophical developments, both analytic and Continental. More than any other figure, it was probably Heidegger who played a pivotal role in the 'theologizing' of philosophy, first, in his early 'existential hermeneutic' thought, by introducing key insights of Kierkegaard and, later, by developing a 'post-philosophical' view that represented for many a wholesale convergence of religious and philosophical concerns. By the post-war era, figures such as Tillich, Ricoeur, Levinas, Henry, Moltmann, Pannenberg, Altizer, Lonergan, Kung, and

Marion appeared to have wholly absorbed philosophy as an independent enterprise and deployed it in the service of self-confessed theological reflection and religious apologetics. In so doing, not only were the boundaries between philosophy and religion, so carefully erected by Kant, dismantled, but this was accomplished very much in favor of theology and more generally religious viewpoints.

It is worth observing that in none of these cases—science, art, and religion—was it merely a matter of philosophy's 'suturing itself' to another field or domain, as Badiou has described it. Rather, what occurred was something considerably more radical than this. It was not as if these developments represented merely some temporary weakness or momentary lapse on the part of philosophy, from which it could, with a sufficient effort of self-assertion, recover. Rather, on the one hand, philosophy, already weakened by its own suicidal episodes and disoriented by its dispersion of aim and momentum, lacked the capacity to resist such absorptions, to 'unsuture' itself from that to which it had become attached. On the other, these other domains had not, since the time of Kant, developed entirely independently of philosophy, such that philosophy might be regarded as able to 'suture' and 'unsuture' itself from them at will. Rather, as I've been suggesting, the appropriate metaphor would be one of 'absorption' rather than mere 'suturing.' In the case of this second possible trajectory, then, the crucial issue is not one of being able to disentangle philosophy from unfortunate liaisons but of the wholesale disappearance of philosophy itself as a viable enterprise.

(3) Earlier, I described the third possible trajectory that philosophy might take as 'hitting the reset button,' that is, returning to some earlier point before the travails that I have catalogued commenced and beginning again, now cognizant of what must, at all costs, be avoided. Such a temptation can be found throughout philosophy's history and, if we trust the insights of literature and psychoanalysis, it may well be the expression some deep-seated feature of human desire itself. But such insights are often accompanied by the warning that 'you can't go home again,' and this, I think, should be born in mind by such philosophical attempts as well. Whether the return is to the pre-Socratics, Plato, Aristotle, Aquinas, Kant, Hegel, Frege, Nietzsche, or the early Heidegger (to name a few of the 'reset destinations' that have enjoyed some currency), the basic problems remain the same. We might summarize them in forensic terms as diagnosis, treatment, and prophylaxis (or the prevention of relapse). For such a reset to succeed, it is first necessary to identify and describe the symptoms to be alleviated and trace them to some underlying cause or condition. With respect the present state of philosophy, we would need an account that suggests what is problematic about the present situation, specifies the underlying viewpoint, thesis, or set of assumptions that produced it, and identifies their point of origin. Second, we must specify the conditions antecedent to the 'onset of symptoms,' that

is, prior to the point of origin, that we wish to reinstate in some form and we must reformulate them in a way that suggests the potential for addressing the problems of the current situation. Finally, we must apply prophylaxis to ensure that no 'relapse' occurs, that we do not merely recapitulate the process by which the antecedent conditions originally produced the trajectory that we are trying to avoid.

In the present situation of philosophy, the 'reset gesture' with which I am principally concerned is that rather diverse set of views sometimes (though often controversially) called 'speculative realism,' 'speculative materialism,' or, more broadly, 'the speculative turn' (the latter being the title of a recent anthology of representative essays available both online and in hardcopy from the publisher 're.press.') Though these terms embrace a quite diverse set of figures, projects, and viewpoints, there seems to be enough broad agreement on a few basic issues among them that we can consider them collectively at least as a tendency or movement, if not yet an articulated position or school. Viewing them in terms of the forensic conditions I mentioned above should make clear why I have characterized them as representing a 'reset gesture.'

(A) DIAGNOSIS

It seems generally agreed among them that Quentin Meillassoux's *After Finitude* (published in French in 2006, English translation in 2008) is a seminal work for this new trajectory. While this essay, in its details, has been the target of quite vigorous criticism even from within this group itself, Meillassoux makes several broad 'diagnostic' points with which most seem to agree. The first is that Kant's Critical Philosophy and its transcendental idealism initiated a new trajectory that produced the problems besetting subsequent philosophy up to the present time. In particular, Meillassoux introduces the term 'correlationism' to specify the underlying problem. He explains,

> By 'correlation' we mean the idea according to which we only ever have access to the correlation between thinking and being, and never to either term considered apart from the other. We will henceforth call *correlationism* any current of thought which maintains the unsurpassable character of the correlation so defined. Consequently, it becomes possible to say that every philosophy which disavows naïve realism has become a variant of correlationism. (p. 5)

While there is much in this passage alone deserving critical scrutiny, both with respect to the terms in which it is expressed and the very broad scope of application that Meillassoux wishes to give it, we can at least take it as expressing a general opposition to any philosophical view that regards the relation between thought or knowledge and its 'objects' (or, more generally, 'reality') as mediated, whether this be through transcendental structures of consciousness, phenomena (in the Kantian sense), dialectic (in Hegel's sense), a theory of intentionality, sense data, language, or cultural formations. Although important parts of the analytic tradition may be more problematic for such a characterization, his claim harmonizes with others, more concerned with Continental approaches, such as Lee Braver's *A Thing of This World: A History of Continental Anti-Realism* (2007), another work often cited by figures falling under the 'speculative realist' designation.

We can summarize the general diagnosis offered by 'speculative realism' in this way. Kant's Critical Philosophy represented the last major phase transition in philosophy. In order to counter the 'pretensions of metaphysics' to know 'being' or 'reality' as it is in itself, which resulted in long-standing though irresolvable controversies, and, at the same time, to rescue the natural sciences from Humean skepticism, Kant denied that it was possible to experience or know 'things as they are in themselves.' Instead, he proposed that what we call 'objects' (and the assemblage of them that we call 'reality') are products of the 'synthetic processes' of consciousness, hence 'no consciousness, no object.' Read in this way, Kant's 'correlationist' philosophical view was the origin of both later 'anti-realism' as well as the modern tradition's antipathy to 'speculative thought' (which presumably requires some direct access to 'things as they really are').

(B) TREATMENT

The antidote offered is threefold. First, most participants in this trajectory obviously support some version of a realist ontology, though there is some disagreement as to whether the preferred version of realism is, more specifically, materialism (an important question I'll return to later). Second, they tend to regard Kant's transcendental idealist critique of metaphysics as misguided and wish to rehabilitate 'speculative' thought that deals with objects or 'the real' in some direct and unmediated way free of the doctrine of 'correlationism.' Finally, as the title of Meillassoux's book suggests, they tend to reject any view that would amount to a 'philosophy of finitude,' to the idea that there are any intrinsic limits to our knowledge or discourse about 'reality.'

It is this triple gesture that represents what I've called the 'reset': it returns us to the situation of classical metaphysics prior to Kant (since, on their account, most of what came after Kant, with perhaps a few exceptions like Bergson, Whitehead, and perhaps Marx and the early Heidegger, was fatally tainted by 'correlationism' and 'anti-realism'). Now Meillassoux is clear that the view he, at least, is after is different from any of the specific forms of 'pre-critical metaphysics,' but his central and sustained attempt to reconfigure such terms as possibility, contingency, and necessity (with the help of quite un-Kantian readings of Locke and Hume) serves to situate his view squarely within the philosophical conversation of the late, 'pre-critical' Enlightenment. Other members of this group variously bring further elements into this discussion (especially Schelling's philosophy of nature, the 'post-Hegelian' Marx, and parts of the early Heidegger), but the underlying 'pre-critical' orientation remains, for the most part, the same. It is that 'speculative' thought or philosophy is capable of making demonstrably true statements about reality as it is in itself, even if it is unlimited or infinite.

(C) PROPHYLAXIS

It is at this point that 'speculative realism' (or 'materialism') seems weakest. There may be several available options open for preventing a relapse into 'correlationism,' but none of them seem to have much chance of success. Of course, we can declare by fiat that we are done with 'correlationism' and proceed to some direct description, mathematical modeling, or 'speculative' theorizing about 'the things themselves.' But do not all of these, in fact, constitute mediations between 'the things themselves' and the 'speculative theorizer'? Or, we might attempt to formulate a realist epistemology to counter that of Kant. But even a realist epistemology is still an epistemology and, as such, begins with the very 'correlationist' question that this trajectory finds problematic, namely, what is the relation between a 'knower' and its 'object' such that 'knowledge' (or 'truth,' or 'justified true belief') is possible? Finally, we might (like a few members of this group) invoke mathematics or cognitive science as possessing the potential for avoiding a relapse into 'correlationism.' But won't precisely Kantian 'correlationist' questions still arise regarding the 'grounds for the possibility' of the application of a mathematical system to 'nature' or 'the real,' or the soundness and potential limits of the theoretical framework of cognitive science? The point, then, is that, starting with a realist ontology and an affirmation of the 'speculative' mission of philosophy, all roads still seem to lead back to Kant and the 'correlationist' questions that he posed. While this attempt to confront a major tendency in recent philosophy, trace it back to its origins, identify the root of the problem, and 'reset' philosophy at a point before things jumped the track constitutes a breath of fresh air in the current situation, it cannot, in the end, serve as an adequate response to the current state of philosophy.

(4) Where I do agree with Meillassoux and his trajectory is that an engagement with Kant's transcendental idealism is the proper starting-point and that a crucial issue concerns affirming some version of 'realism' against Kant's 'idealism.' However, as I've just indicated, I do not think that the Kantian citadel (nor 'correlationism,' which may prove to be an ancillary issue) can be conquered by a frontal assault that returns us to some *status quo ante*. Nor do I think any 'deconstruction' of transcendental Idealism without

further issue will ultimately succeed as a philosophical response. Rather, a different strategy is required, one that acknowledges the weight of Kant's achievements while placing them in a broader context. The key to this lies in seeing that any response to Kant's principal philosophical question, 'What are the grounds for the possibility of experience and knowledge?,' assumes some response to another even more fundamental question that Kant himself did not formulate, namely, 'What are the grounds for the possibility of philosophy itself?' or, more succinctly, 'What is philosophy?'

I begin my approach to this question with two preliminary discussions. The first considers some of the typical responses, familiar from the tradition, to how one might begin such a project and concludes by suggesting that the only adequate beginning must involve an account of the fundamental *conditions* that must obtain for something like philosophy to exist in the concrete and familiar forms to which the term is typically applied: a distinctive type of activity, a body of texts, and a set of ideas (or 'viewpoint' or 'position').

The second section, a sort of informal orientational discussion about how and why philosophy is a peculiarly human enterprise, is designed to suggest certain features of philosophy that must be accounted for by any more systematic treatment. It is also a sort of informal response to views that reject 'finitist' notions of philosophy. There I suggest that it is precisely the fact that human beings and their capacities *are* limited and that they *know* this to be so that provokes philosophical reflection in the first place. And, I might add, the fact that we can *conceive* of some 'absolute' or develop a mathematical theory of the 'transfinite' does not change this basic human condition.

It is the subsequent insistence, throughout this essay, upon these basic conditions of philosophy as 'actual' and 'excessive' to the enterprise of philosophy defined by them that makes this view 'realist' and, up to a point, 'materialist,' though in somewhat different senses than these terms are often used. It is 'materialist' in the quite straightforward and brute sense that no human enterprises, including that of philosophy, would exist without the existence of embodied human beings and the material conditions that have led to this and support it. However, at least two other conditions, emergent from the first but irreducible to it (or to each other), are required, more specifically, for the existence of the enterprise of philosophy: I call them 'signification' and 'ideality.' Both significative communication and conceptual thought also have, without a doubt, material substrata, both in the sense that they would not exist without the material existence of embodied conscious beings and in more specific senses such as 'signifying objects' and 'acts' in the former case and neural networks of the brain in the latter. But I attempt to show that the enterprise of philosophy must assume that the 'actual condition of signification' and that of 'ideality' also involve elements and dimensions not reducible to exclusively material processes. In this sense, although

I regard 'signification' and 'ideality' as 'real' in that, as 'ontological presuppositions' of philosophy generically considered, they both exceed the enterprise itself in characteristic ways, neither can be regarded as wholly 'material.' So the philosophical position I am attempting to formulate is, at once, 'realist,' in part 'materialist,' and 'ontologically pluralist' (in that it acknowledges three irreducible 'actual' conditions). However (perhaps *pace* Deleuze and Meillassoux), it does affirm the 'ancestral' claim that conscious embodied beings, and hence the enterprise of philosophy, did not exist in past times as well as the possibility that they may not exist at some future point, that is, that the existence of all three of the actual conditions of philosophy are contingent.

A response to the issue of 'correlationism' and the possibility of 'speculative thought' is yet more complicated and must be formulated within the framework of these 'actual conditions' of philosophy. On the one hand, as an activity of embodied beings deploying significational communication to express ideas or concepts, there will always be a sense (if not exactly in the epistemological terms that Kant framed it) that any philosophical view or position, however 'scientific,' 'mathematical,' or 'speculative' it might be, will involve some determination, and hence limitation, by the reflective capacities of embodied beings, the significative complexes deployed for their articulation, and the concepts that they express. The actual conditions are, *in reality*, unsurpassable and, to this extent, every philosophy involves an element of 'correlation' (or perhaps set of 'correlations'). However, while there is no fixed limit dividing any of the actual conditions from the ways in which they are excessive to philosophy, either regarded generically or as a particular philosophical view, there will always be a way in which each is excessive to it and therefore beyond the reach of any 'correlation.' In this sense, the possibility of 'speculative thought' depends both upon an antecedent 'correlation' and the process by which this 'correlation' is questioned and, in part, undermined in the attempt to engage excess by 'thinking beyond' the terms of any 'correlation.' The point, then, is that it's mistaken to think that jettisoning 'correlationism' will, of itself, open up some infinite domain for speculative thought; rather, what this produces (if it is even possible) would be something like the Buddhist notion of 'egoless' and 'non-conceptual contemplation.' Rather, genuinely 'speculative thought' always presupposes some conditioned 'correlationist' framework beyond which it attempts to move by tracing the various trajectories of the ways in which the framework's own conditions exceed it. So I agree that a 'speculative turn' is a vital and necessary aspect of the enterprise of philosophy, but not with the thesis that its generic and primary obstacle is 'correlationism,' which is equally a feature dictated by the 'actual conditions' of philosophy.

The more 'systematic' exposition begins, as I have suggested it must, with Kant and his transcendental idealism. However, it approaches this in a way not involving some frontal assault or wholesale rejection but, rather, through creating a specific opening in Kant's view that he himself had regarded as foreclosed. Specifically, it focuses upon that class of judgments that Kant called *'analytic a posteriori'* and which he regarded as empty, presumably because the notion itself would be contradictory (although, as we will see, Kant himself never said exactly this, whatever many later commentators may have inferred). Reflecting on this theme, I suggest that there are, in fact, at least three judgments or statements that share the unique property of being at once 'analytic' (in the sense that their denial or negation entails a 'performative contradiction') and *'a posteriori'* (in the sense that they involve contingent 'existential claims'). This then amounts to a sort of 'deduction' (in something like Kant's own sense) of what I call the three 'actual conditions' of philosophy: embodied being, signification, and ideality.

The sections immediately following, 'speculative' in their way, consider certain general aspects of these actual conditions that, in their interrelations with one another, serve to constitute the 'field of philosophy.' Three points deserve special mention. First, as actual conditions of philosophy, each of them are both operative as constituent elements *within* philosophy, regarded either generically or as some particular position or view, and, at the same time, *exceed* it in their own distinctive ways. Second, it is possible to formulate certain general principles concerning some of the ways in which these actual conditions interact in constituting the 'field of philosophy' and hence in determining any more particular 'position' within it. Finally, without claiming to know, comprehend, or articulate their excesses as some totality, it is nonetheless possible to indicate some of the 'traces' of these excesses within and the effects of their operations (or the 'forces' they exert) upon the field and upon specific positions within it.

The three chapters comprising the next major section of the work consider each of the actual conditions and their excesses from 'its own perspective.' Although it turns out, in each case, that the other conditions and their excesses are reflected within it in distinctive ways, it is nonetheless possible to focus upon a condition and articulate some of the fundamental structures, processes, and broader issues involved with it. In particular, an approach that, at once, affirms the reality of the conditions of philosophy, the excessiveness of each to any philosophical attempt to articulate it, and the 'forces' exerted by the other conditions upon it allow a number of familiar philosophical issues to be reformulated in novel ways. For example, with respect to embodied being, it highlights the crucial role played by desire in what are typically treated as epistemological questions; for signification, it suggests how formal logic (and its key notion of 'logical necessity') can be preserved while maintaining the contingencies of natural language and other significational systems; and it proposes a 'speculative image' of thought and its conceptual elements that acknowledges its 'evental' and processive aspects in addition to its more typically emphasized structural features. (This latter discussion, by the way, situates the view I am developing in relation to Hegel, and, by extension, his poststructuralist critics, rounding out that of my earlier engagement with Kant and transcendental idealism.)

The two chapters of the final major section of the work address issues that figured prominently in my own 'diagnosis' of the current state of philosophy. Earlier in this Preface, I suggested that part of the problem facing philosophy today was the gradual erosion, over the last century or so, of the traditional boundaries separating the enterprise of philosophy from other areas contiguous with it. Part of the problem was the lack of any positive answer to the question, "What is philosophy?" The bulk of this work attempts to provide such a response in terms of the configuration of philosophy's actual conditions and their interrelations. However, these actual conditions are also fundamental for other non-philosophical enterprises as well—especially religion, science, and art—but they are differently configured in each case. In the first of these chapters, I suggest that the 'field' of philosophy can be both distinguished from and related to those of its 'others' on the basis of the different ways in which the actual conditions are configured within each. That is, it attempts to articulate what the enterprise of philosophy is not and why. The second of these chapters then proposes, in an anticipatory way, a sketch of a new 'partitioning' of philosophy's own field based upon an account of its actual conditions and their distinctive excesses and interrelations among one another. That is, it represents a first attempt to envision a new 'division of labor' of the enterprise of philosophy that would, at once, displace that inherited, in large part, from Kant, provide a home for certain questions currently left 'orphaned' in the present framework (which may well turn out to be central philosophical concerns in the future), and provide arenas of productive engagement for diverse philosophical approaches currently divided or opposed due, at least in part, to the (usually unquestioned) way in which the field of philosophy has been segmented over the last century or two.

One especially important aspect of this 'repartitioning' of the field of philosophy involves a very preliminary pass at rethinking and remapping what, since Aristotle but by way of Kant, has been referred to as the relation between 'theory' and 'practice.' Certainly Fichte, Hegel, Marx, Heidegger, the 'Frankfurt School,' and many others have been right to point out the deficiencies of any view that would segregate such 'areas' of philosophy as ethics, politics, and ideology critique from those of logic, epistemology, and metaphysics. But it will also not suffice simply to subordinate one to the other, whichever one chooses as 'superordinate.' My response involves, first, a general 'repartitioning' of the field of philosophy and, then, an attempt to show that one and the same 'partition' can be approached either from an 'engaged' or 'disengaged attitude,' while allowing that these 'attitudes' are always 'metastable' and freely convert one into the other. I emphasize that this section is very provisional and, at most, suggests some directions that a future work might take.

The work concludes with an epilogue that reflects upon some of the broader consequences of the account I've offered for philosophy generically considered and attempts to respond to some of the more important and pointed questions that my view has provoked over the years of its gestation.

Two final comments about certain features of the text are in order. First, I have deliberately avoided (though not without considerable temptation) the common practice (perhaps not purely coincidentally beginning, at least in philosophy, with Kant) of deploying footnotes as a 'mixed subtext' involving textual references, critical responses to the texts cited, and sometimes even a 'meta-commentary' on the text to which they are appended. Rather, where references to other texts are not immediately clear, I've incorporated them into the body of the text itself, thereby resisting altogether any temptation to create an 'internally doubled' text. While I do argue that 'texts' constitute an essential part of the enterprise of philosophy (though certainly not the whole of it, as some poststructuralists seemed to suggest), I believe that their value and force become diminished to the degree that they internally double and proliferate without limit.

In another direction, while I don't entirely agree with Deleuze and some others (see the final chapter of John Mullarkey's *Post-Continental Philosophy*) that thinking can or should take the form of a 'diagrammatics,' I do think that diagrams can play a more important and productive role than many philosophers (especially Hegel, who rejected them entirely) have countenanced. Their advantages for philosophy are twofold. First, they permit relations among terms and their corresponding concepts to be directly presented in ways that the complexities of natural languages may unnecessarily complicate and obscure. Second, they can be suggestive of further relations and connections that may have otherwise gone unnoticed; that is, they can, at times, serve to suggest new or unsuspected trajectories for thought itself. However, these are counterbalanced by two disadvantages. One is that diagrams tend to emphasize the 'structural' aspect of thought and suppress its 'processive' nature (a feature that I have emphasized in Chap. X of this work). The other is that their very simplicity and clarity (in relation to spoken or written expositions in natural language) tends to obscure other crucial aspects (especially 'excessive' ones) and eliminate nuance. In this work, I offer several diagrams, along with the warning that these points be born in mind when considering them. It should in no way be assumed that the view I am proposing can be 'read off' of or reduced to the diagrams that I have provided, but they can provide (in a sort of post-Kantian sense) general schemas for interpreting the written text. Therefore, I would propose the principle: "Use, but use critically and with caution."

Overall, then, this work represents an attempt to outline what might count as part of a fourth possible trajectory that the current phase transition of philosophy might take. To borrow a term from Deleuze, I am proposing a new 'image of thought,' or, rather, 'image of philosophy.' Generally speaking, it is at once (in the specific senses of these terms that I discussed earlier) finitist, realist, and speculative and, more specifically, constructivist and pluralist. It is connected throughout with the history of philosophy, though it does not seek any return to some earlier situation or view. It affirms both the importance and integrity of the enterprise of philosophy, both as fundamentally different from and yet related in important ways to other contiguous areas of human experience and activity. It attempts to envision a productive future for philosophy when 'repartitioned' in a way that ameliorates the arbitrary historical divisions that currently characterize it, and to provide a home for important questions that have so far 'fallen between the cracks.' And it maintains, in the end, a deep commonality between the fate of philosophy and the fate of embodied sentient beings upon this planet. But like any such attempt, it's a 'roll of the dice' and, in this case, the 'die are still rolling' and who can anticipate how they will land. If it even begins to initiate a new trajectory, it will have more than served the purpose that I've intended.

With What Must Philosophy Begin?

Throughout its history, the principal philosophical question has, in one form or another, always been, "What is philosophy?" From Socrates' and Plato's personal and intellectual struggles to convince the suspicious Athenians of the difference between philosophy and sophistry, to current debates about how, or even whether, philosophy can exist as a distinctive enterprise or discourse, the central question remains the same.

In an important way, it's the very fact that every philosopher must, at some point, confront the question of what it is that he or she is pursuing (and, of course, why) that most distinguishes philosophy from other types of human activity. Artists, for instance, need not ask "What is art?" as part of their creative process (and, when they do, they themselves enter the realm of philosophical questions). Such a question as "What is science?" seems rarely to occur to the natural scientist and some can become outright irritated when such questions are posed to them. Religious practitioners can immediately invoke their faith in revealed doctrine, the totality of which serves as a ready-made answer to the question of "What is religion?" Likewise, carpenters, athletes, merchants, and even politicians can merely point to what they, and others like them, do as a response to questions about what the activity in which they are involved is. But not the philosopher.

Why, then, this peculiar feature of philosophy among all the many other types of human activity? Why is the philosopher in the unique (and sometimes disconcerting) position of continually having to articulate, justify, and often defend his or her own form of activity, when virtually all others enjoy the luxury of doing what they have chosen without such difficulties and complications? What follows in this section concerns how one might begin to respond to these questions.

I. THE MEANINGS OF 'PHILOSOPHY' AND THE QUESTION OF BEGINNING

Beginnings are almost always painful and unsettling; often they are the most difficult part of any project. This is especially true if the topic is philosophical. Persons who have fought their way through this intellectual birth-trauma to finally produce some form of written philosophical document have often reflected on this moment and its significance. Sometimes, they have done so at a later point in the text itself, sometimes in a 'preface' or 'introduction,' sometimes even in a separate essay on the topic (which, of course, must have its own beginning). And occasionally, there are those who manage to just start writing and see where it takes them (though these, at least the ones we still remember as philosophers, are considerably rarer.)

Part of the difficulty of thinking about beginnings in philosophy has to do with the fact that there are three different, but closely related, things that one might have in mind in speaking about 'philosophy.' One way of regarding philosophy emphasizes the fact that it is a particular sort of activity. Some philosophers themselves even speak of 'doing philosophy.' Approached in this way, philosophy is regarded as a sort of ongoing activity than can be pursued as well in conversations or dialogues, written works, in our own 'interior monologue,' or even as part of one's daily life. Another sense of philosophy emphasizes the products of such activities, which are typically written works. There are, for instance, 'philosophy sections' of libraries and bookstores and now philosophy websites and blogs. Yet a third meaning of philosophy emphasizes the 'content' of philosophy, the more abstract thoughts or ideas with which we are engaged in 'doing philosophy' and which are articulated in its written products. In this sense, we often speak of the 'philosophy of Plato,' or the 'philosophy of art,' or 'materialist philosophy.'

These differences in the meaning of 'philosophy' immediately suggest three quite different ideas of what it means to begin in philosophy.

If we emphasize the active aspect of philosophy, then the beginning of philosophy will be viewed as some point (or points) in time where an individual commences to pose philosophical questions and develop responses to them. In this sense, there are as many beginnings to philosophy as there are persons who become engaged in 'doing philosophy.' Part of the truth of saying that, in philosophy, one always has 'to begin anew' (as Socrates frequently reminded his interlocutors), or that 'philosophy begins in wonder,' another view found in Plato's dialogues, is that any individual who engages in this activity must, at some point (or points) in his or her experience, be gripped by the force and seriousness of the sort of questions that philosophy raises. Such a beginning will always be, in a sense, singular and idiosyncratic and there will be a limitless number of such beginnings.

If, however, one has in mind the products of this activity, then the beginning of philosophy will mean something a bit more complicated. On the one hand, every work of philosophy, as it stands before us, will contain a first word, sentence, paragraph, and so on. On the other, that it exists as a written linguistic product means that the more open and free activity of pursuing certain questions has been submitted to and formed by the significational resources of a linguistic medium, with all the possibilities that these open as well as the limitations that they impose. Most important, to produce a work of philosophy is already to have entered the sphere of intersubjective discourse, of a preexistant and shared language that makes mutual recognition and communication among human beings possible. This can never be regarded as some singular, individual, or subjective event, however unique the resulting work itself may be, but always involves the sort of significational commonalities constituting an intersubjective world. Further, even if the beginning of a given work seems idiosyncratic, this can itself be misleading, since, once some version or draft of a written work is produced, it confronts its author as an artifact just as much as it does another reader, and is subject to revision and rewriting. For most works of philosophy, the 'first word' is rarely *really* the first word but some product of rewriting that has erased the original 'first word' and substituted for it another (sometimes many times over). We might say, then, that the actual beginning of any work of philosophy is language itself, borrowed, refined, worked over, and finally set down in what always remains a sort of provisional form. Such a beginning, then, can never be entirely idiosyncratic but is, rather, a sort of intersubjective generality delimited by the resources of a shared language. Viewed in this way, philosophy never completely begins anew or in some idiosyncratic experience of wonder, but in our immersion in a broader intersubjective and linguistic world—in, for example, the *agora* of ancient Athens, the salons of 18th century Paris, or the seminar rooms of modern universities.

Finally, if it is the 'content' or 'object' of philosophy that is emphasized, then the question of the beginning of philosophy becomes almost impossible to pose in any clear or unambiguous way. In this sense, philosophy is viewed neither as some sort of activity in which an individual can engage nor some particular artifact that has been produced. Rather, it is something like the overall viewpoint or interrelated set of ideas aimed at by individual activities or articulated within the specific linguistic resources deployed by a particular work or set of works. At least in the spatio-temporal sense in which we can say that a particular activity has commenced or a particular work has been written, such 'content' exists neither in a particular space nor at any specific time. Of course, we can associate philosophical ideas or viewpoints with some particular philosopher or historical epoch, but 'Plato's Theory of Ideas' or 'The Enlightenment Idea of Freedom' are neither completely reducible to what some individual thought or wrote nor to what viewpoint might have been prevalent in some historical period of time. One way that this irreducibility of an idea or viewpoint to some individual or time-period has been characterized is to say that it is 'universal,' meaning, at least, that it is non-spatial and atemporal, hence (at least in principle) available to anyone at any time and linguistically expressible in a variety of ways. Most philosophers have gone even further, claiming that the ideas or viewpoints that they have pursued and attempted to express are somehow valid for or trump those of all other philosophers. But whatever 'universal' may further mean, at least with respect to the question about beginnings when the 'content' of philosophy is emphasized, we can say that, in this sense, philosophy has no beginning. The heart of philosophy is that which is 'universal' and the 'universal' is precisely that which has no beginning locatable in space, time, or language.

In a way, however, this returns us to the beginning of our discussion, since, clearly, the meaning of philosophy is no more exhausted by viewing it in terms of its aim or 'content' than it is by viewing it as an activity or a product of that activity. All three views have full rights to be considered as part of the meaning of philosophy. Consequently, our question about the beginning of philosophy has to accommodate the paradoxical-seeming fact that the beginning of philosophy is at once personal and idiosyncratic, intersubjective and linguistic, and universal. Given the difficulty of such a question, it will be helpful to turn briefly to some of the ways in which those whom we've come to call philosophers have approached this question.

II. SOME RESPONSES TO THE QUESTION OF BEGINNING IN PHILOSOPHY

How philosophers have historically dealt with the problem of beginning philosophy would itself make a revealing and likely quite complicated philosophical work, especially if we were able to compare what they said about philosophical beginnings with how they actually began and where this led them. And, of course, such a work would likely also eventually have itself to consider how to begin dealing with philosophical beginnings. Whatever might come of such a project, two things at least are certain. However an activity or work begins, if it is philosophy, the way in which it begins will propel the work along a certain trajectory and reverberate throughout the work. Different initial experiences will give rise to different sorts of activities, and different beginning points, even for different works by the same author, will issue in rather different products. The point is that choosing a beginning point for a work of philosophy is itself a crucial philosophical issue and one that deserves some serious reflection. The second point is that, for the most part, philosophers have, in fact, eventually returned, at some point in their trajectory, to the question of beginnings. They have, at some later point of their trajectory, reflected back upon its own beginning. However, we must remember that such a return is never 'innocent,' but is always informed by the trajectory of thought that they are already upon. In fact, our earlier discussion seems to agree with some of the poststructuralists that there can never be some account of a 'pristine origin'; with philosophy, like many other human enterprises, we will have 'always already' begun before the question about beginnings ever arises, and then it is, so to speak, too late. Even so, it may be helpful to review some of the ways that philosophers have addressed this issue as a way of access to our own question.

If we look at how historical philosophers have treated the question of beginnings, we can discern at least three main approaches. These turn out to be related in some interesting ways to the more general issues we've already discussed. In particular, I'll suggest, as we proceed, that each approach turns out to adopt a particular viewpoint on the three meanings of philosophy and their associated senses of beginning. That is, they will, in effect, accommodate all of these, but from the point of view of a particular approach.

1. Ontological Approaches

The first approach is 'ontological.' I call this approach 'ontological' because 'being,' beginning in classical times, has most often been cited as the ultimate concern of philosophy. There have, of course, been other candidates for this—'truth,' 'the Good,' 'the Whole,' 'God,' 'nature,' and so forth—but philosophers have generally regarded 'being' as, in some way, prior to all others. Aristotle, for instance, claims that the 'highest knowledge' or 'science' is 'metaphysics,' and metaphysics is, itself, the 'science' of 'being qua being.' On this approach, philosophy has a sort of dual beginning. On the one hand, 'being' is regarded as the universal ground for any knowledge or activity whatever, and philosophy arises as the activity initiated by a human being's questioning response to what being is or what it means to be. Parmenides, at the very beginning of the historical tradition of philosophy, makes his powerful and portentous assertion of the absolute primacy of Being within an account of his own philosophical quest. Leibniz claimed that the most fundamental philosophical question is, "Why are there beings rather than nothing at all?" In more recent times, Heidegger, especially in his earlier works, has reminded us both that the 'question of Being' is the most fundamental issue of philosophy and that it can only be authentically approached from the singularity of one's own *'Dasein'* or 'There-Being.' In the terms we used earlier, the ontological approach to beginnings starts with 'being' or some other suitably universal cognate and tends to immediately implicate the individual's activity of raising this as a question and seeking its meaning.

There are, however, several limitations with this type of beginning. For one thing, actual works of philosophy that begin ontologically usually don't, in fact, begin with the notion of 'being.' Rather, they tend to begin with discussions of a variety of other matters which eventually lead to the point of asserting that 'being' or some other particular concept is the 'true beginning' of philosophy and from there move on to showing what follows from this. They therefore end up erasing the event of the work's actual beginning by, so to speak, retrojecting the 'ontological beginning' to the actual beginning of the work and inviting the reader to see that, somehow, the concept was always there but initially unnoticed or obscured until later clarified in the work itself. More generally, the ontological approach to beginnings tends to suppress or underemphasize the intersubjective and significational element of philosophical beginnings. For one thing, language must already be available to the individual if any question whatever, including the 'question of Being,' is to be articulated in a way that would initiate the activity of philosophy. Further, 'being itself,' whatever else that phrase might serve to indicate, is itself a linguistic artifact, with all the possibilities and limitations that this implies. Finally, if posing the 'question of Being' is, at least minimally, a linguistic act, then this further implies an intersubjective sphere, other persons to whom such a question can be posed and for whom, too, it can be meaningful. If, as Plato suggested, philosophy begins in wonder (about the meaning of Being, Heidegger might add), philosophy will not commence unless this experience can be expressed in a way accessible to others. Just as Wittgenstein argued that there can be no 'private language,' we might also extend this by saying that there can be no 'private philosophy.' While my own beginning in philosophy may be my idiosyncratic experience of the 'wonder of Being,' it will not issue in the activity of 'philosophizing' without the mediation of language, which immediately opens the possibility of its being communicatively shared with others.

2. Methodological Approaches

The second approach that historical philosophers have adopted toward the question of beginnings in philosophy is the 'methodological.' Rather than highlighting the concrete individual's response to something that is universal and all-encompassing, this approach views the beginning of philosophy as the attempt to articulate some general method that would channel the activity of philosophy in the direction of universal claims and guarantee the validity of its results. Again, there is a sort of duality of beginning for such an approach. On the one hand, methodological approaches tend to start with conflicts among the many linguistic claims that we confront on a daily basis. On the other, it proceeds from a conviction that only some of these claims can be accepted as valid or true and that there is a non-idiosyncratic procedure or method for determining this. Rather than 'being,' 'truth' usually becomes the relevant universal for methodological approaches and method becomes the procedure linking the universal with the intersubjective world of competing claims. Socrates, for example, often begins by noting that there is a crucial difference between belief (*doxa*) and knowledge (*episteme*) and then proposes a methodical way of proceeding (sometimes later called 'dialectic') by which claims that only qualify as the former can be separated from others that can count as the latter. Other parallels can be found in such diverse figures as Aristotle (in part), Descartes, Fichte, and Husserl, not to mention many modern 'logicist' positions. Whatever wonder or confusion may have preceded it, philosophy, then, commences in earnest with the search for and articulation of a method that will guarantee the truth of its results. From there, the activity of philosophy need only follow the procedures dictated by the method in order to arrive at and connect with the 'truth' that it guarantees.

The thrust (and, to its advocates, the major strength) of the methodological approach is to eliminate, so far as possible, idiosyncratic and potentially relativistic aspects of the other approaches. As an account of the beginning of philosophy, however, the methodological approach is probably the most problematic of the three, as has been often pointed out in the philosophical tradition. Major problems arise both with respect to the manner in which it defines its aim (the universal, usually viewed as 'truth') and the way it presents its central idea of a 'truth-guaranteeing method.' In both cases, there is an inescapable circularity in its procedure that tends to conflict with the method that it presents.

To take the first case, methodological approaches actually begin with an assumption that 'truth' is a sort of 'primitive concept' indicating an immediate relation between 'the way things are' or the 'world' and what we say about such things. In the form that Tarski famously put it, "The proposition, 'It is raining,' is true if and only it is raining." However, 'truth' is also regarded exclusively as the outcome of some methodological procedure, so that it is not possible to know 'the truth' prior to the establishment of the method. The result is the clearly circular view that, on the one hand, we can't formulate a 'truth-guaranteeing method' without first knowing the nature of the sort of truth that it is supposed to guarantee, and, on the other, that we can't know 'the truth' prior to having available the method by which truth is guaranteed. As an account of beginnings, it thus remains unclear whether we are to begin with a universal concept of 'truth' and formulate a method that guarantees it, or begin with a method which then generates 'truths' as the result of its operation.

Viewed from a different, more textual, perspective, most methodological approaches in fact begin with an account of conflicting 'truth-claims' (for example, Plato's 'opinions of the marketplace,' Descartes' dissatisfaction with the different branches of learning of his day, or Husserl's idea of the 'crises of the sciences') and then claim that philosophy begins in earnest with the formulation of the method itself. The question then arises, "Which is the actual beginning of philosophy?" Is philosophical reflection already underway when we become perplexed about conflicting claims or only when we possess a method that allows us to sort out such claims? Again, there is a sort of circular process involved in reading such texts. We must first become aware of such conflicts of opinion and convince ourselves that some method is needed to resolve them before we commence with the quest for a method. However, only after formulating the method are we able to see that there are conflicting claims that are capable of being resolved (since it's always at least possible that human beings simply have differing opinions and that establishing one over another is a matter of sophistic skills, political power, or 'public opinion.')

Because of such circularities at the heart of an approach that is supposed to directly connect what is asserted within intersubjective discourse with some more 'universal truth' through the intermediary of a method, such approaches have a marked tendency toward what has later been called 'foundationalism,' the idea that there are certain 'necessary truths' already known prior to the formulation of any method. Whether this move succeeds in breaking the 'circles' remains a matter of dispute among advocates of this approach (and, of course, its critics as well). But what seems clear from such discussions is that the very idea of a 'necessary truth' is itself a quite complex philosophical notion requiring considerable philosophical discussion and elaboration. For the question of beginnings, this means that the 'foundationalist move' merely adds yet another candidate, some immediate or intuitive knowledge of 'necessary truths,' for the beginning of philosophy to the original 'double-beginning' already indicated.

3. Dialogical Approaches

This type of approach, already visible in Plato's more 'Socratic dialogues,' presents the beginning of philosophy, not in some idiosyncratic experience of being or as some quest for a truth-guaranteeing method, but in the realm of intersubjective and, most importantly, significational (especially linguistic) activity. Socrates, for instance, in a sort of autobiographical digression in the *Phaedo*, documents his apparent 'conversion' from an ontological approach, looking directly at things (beings), to an intersubjective one, seeing how they are reflected in human discourse (*logoi*). This new departure emphasizes that the beginning of philosophy is to be sought in the individual's linguistically mediated engagement with others. Philosophy, on this approach, arises as the result of competing linguistic claims to knowledge or truth within intersubjective contexts requiring their adjudication and unfolds (as in the Platonic texts) as a sort of open-ended, more or less cooperative and dialogical effort to determine on what basis such an adjudication can be made. To initiate the process of determining where commonalities lie and distinguishing them from points of disagreement is thus the real beginning of philosophy. More exactly, it is the human capacity to signify to others possessing the same ability that both provokes philosophical reflection and provides the essential vehicle by which this can be pursued. Later on, this 'dialogical process' will be rendered in much larger brushstrokes when history becomes viewed as the broad process within which such dialogue unfolds. Even later, it invokes 'ordinary language' and the permutations of which it is capable as giving rise to specifically 'philosophical problems.' In relation to the other two approaches to beginnings, this approach tends to suppress idiosyncratic elements in favor of shared communicative commonalities, but it tends to reject the idea that it is possible, within language, to formulate some privileged method that can serve to resolve all conflicting claims arising therein.

Dialogical approaches to the question of beginning can accommodate the idiosyncratic element of ontological approaches, but with the important proviso that this finds expression within the intersubjective realm of signification, thus bringing the singularity implicit in such approaches under the more general structures of a shared language or significational system. On the other hand, dialogical approaches tend to view others that emphasize methods or foundations with suspicion (though usually not outright rejection) on the grounds that the formulation of a method or set of foundational claims is one discursive possibility that, nonetheless, must itself be submitted to the open possibilities of further communicative and critical exchange.

There are two related problems that any dialogical approach to the question of beginnings has to confront. First, dialogical approaches must assume or posit the prior existence and on-going functioning of some system of intersubjective signification. It is as if there is always already a conversation underway to which, at some point, an individual becomes a party. However, the mere entry of an individual into a conversation neither requires that the conversation be philosophical nor that the individual commence philosophizing upon entry. Rather, something else beyond a significational system and individuals capable of deploying it seems needed in order to speak of a philosophical beginning. This problem is well illustrated in some of the Platonic dialogues that seem to begin in the middle of a discussion that requires the intervention of Socrates, serving as a 'midwife' to assist in the birth of a specifically philosophical exchange.

Such an intervention by someone who is presumably already engaged in the activity of philosophy leads to the second problem, also well illustrated by a characteristic Socratic move. If the conversation is not to remain mere talk or perhaps an exchange of various more or less random opinions, then the interlocutors must somehow be brought to see that some opinions conflict with others, that not all opinions are equally valid or plausible, and that there must be some extra-discursive criteria for adjudicating among them. If philosophy, then, is somehow to begin within such a context, it can only occur when at least some of the interlocutors come to acknowledge an extra-discursive dimension that can serve as a basis for adjudicating among particular discursive claims. But herein lies the problem, in the form of a dilemma. On the one hand, if the criteria are 'extra-discursive,' then it is impossible to state them or certify within discourse that they are in fact shared among the interlocutors; on the other hand, if they can be articulated in discourse, then they require, in turn, further criteria that would allow us to judge whether they are, in fact, valid criteria, since they will themselves have become further discourses.

Readers of Plato will immediately recognize in this dilemma the main problem of the Socratic invocation of the 'forms': if they are to serve as the criteria for determining whether a particular opinion (*doxa*) can qualify as knowledge (*episteme*), then, strictly speaking, they themselves can't be known or at least articulated in language. If, however, one insists (as Socrates often does) that the forms are that which is 'most knowable' (in opposition to discursively articulated opinions), then the meaning of 'knowing' has shifted from that which is expressed in statements (*logoi*) to that which can only be seen or intuited but not articulated in language.

Just as the shadow of idiosyncrasy darkens ontological approaches to the question of beginnings and that of circularity accompanies methodological or foundationalist approaches, so the specter of relativism haunts dialogical approaches. If the beginning of philosophy is to be sought in the intercourse of the marketplace (or the much more extended conversation constituting history), then it always remains possible (and, depending on one's viewpoint, is even likely) that there are only opinions lacking any further criteria for adjudicating among them. It is possible, that is, that philosophy never actually begins, that Socrates was (as some Athenians apparently thought) just another sophist (albeit an eccentric one), and that Wittgenstein was right in claiming that philosophy is just a sort of illusion produced by certain anomalous aspects of 'ordinary language.'

III. PHILOSOPHY AND ITS CONDITIONS

If there is a single conclusion to be drawn from the preceding discussion, it is that there is no unambiguous or entirely coherent answer forthcoming to the question of the beginning of philosophy. Viewed in one way, this is because philosophy itself can mean several very different things: an activity, a linguistic artifact, and a universal idea or viewpoint.

Viewed in another way, our discussion of philosophical accounts of beginnings suggests that philosophy always involves some particular configuration of all three elements. Most fundamentally, however, the underlying problem is that all accounts of the beginning of philosophy are attempts, *from some given philosophical perspective*, to locate or posit the beginning of philosophy outside of philosophy itself. Being, method, and language are all posited as pre- or extra-philosophical and, only as such, are regarded as the beginning or origin of philosophy.

Approached in yet another way, we might observe that the question of the 'beginning of philosophy' is itself biased in a certain direction. The concept of 'beginning' is itself a temporal notion and in the very asking of such a question we are, in fact, assuming that any adequate answer will take the form of citing some particular point in time before which there was no philosophy and after which philosophy can be said somehow to be present. Clearly, 'beginning' is a notion most at home in the realm of the experience of concrete individuals and is therefore biased toward the view of philosophy as a particular sort of activity. But, even if we can locate some point in experience where we might say that we begin to philosophize, this still leaves obscure what other elements may have been required for philosophy to begin. We've already seen how approaches based upon other meanings of 'philosophy' issue in either hopelessly ambiguous or incoherent responses to the question of beginnings. What this shows, I suggest, is that, while any view of philosophy must eventually confront the question of the beginning of philosophy, the only relatively unambiguous and coherent answer can be in terms of a particular view of the meaning of philosophy, though one which is itself incomplete and requires supplementation by other meanings. In an odd way, then, the question of the beginning of philosophy *can*, in fact, receive a cogent answer, but the answer will not accommodate other crucial views or aspects of what philosophy is and hence will necessarily be incomplete. Yes, we might say, philosophy does begin at some point in the experience of individuals, but this leaves obscure other elements required to account for why this particular experiential point issues specifically in philosophy. The problem, then, is that the temporal concept of 'beginning' is not really applicable within the other views, since speaking of the 'beginning' of language or ideas always misrepresents what is most distinctive about them.

As I've already suggested, if there is a single question common to everything that we call 'philosophy,' it is 'What is philosophy?' We have seen that approaching this question by asking about the beginning of philosophy is beset with serious problems, though the discussion offers some clues that will later prove helpful. But it does appear that a different approach is needed if we are to make headway in addressing the main question. In this work, I want to adopt an approach that asks, "What conditions must be satisfied for there to be such a thing as philosophy?"

Putting the question this way assumes rather straightforwardly that there is something called philosophy, however else we may further characterize it. In fact, in addition to the three senses that the term may have as noted above, there is a tradition of over 2000 years, offering a wide variety of instances that are commonly referred to as 'philosophy.' Even those who have attempted to argue that philosophy is a form of delusion or that the term is logically vacuous have, nonetheless, pointed to the same instances that those who reject their views typically refer to as 'philosophy.' In fact, such "a/philosophers" themselves deploy distinctively philosophical arguments and have, despite their protestations, been regarded by others (and usually have also regarded themselves) as philosophers, so there seems no major obstacle to assuming that there is something called 'philosophy' about which we can inquire.

Clearly, the term that carries the most freight in the question posed above is that of 'conditions,' and this deserves some more detailed discussion. When we speak about 'conditions,' the most straightforward interpretation would be factors or elements that must be present in order to refer to something as philosophy at all. We might refine this a bit by saying that the sort of conditions we have in mind are, taken individually, 'necessary,' that is, that if any one is lacking, we will not be referring to philosophy or an instance of it but, perhaps, something else.

Notice, however, that I'm not claiming that the conditions, taken together, should be regarded as 'necessary and sufficient' for us to speak of philosophy, since there's no reason to close off the possibility of there being further necessary conditions not included in our account. Likewise, I'm not claiming that the conditions we're seeking are somehow 'uniquely sufficient' to refer to something as philosophy, as if other sets of conditions can't accomplish the same thing. Rather, the simplest way to put it is that we're seeking the 'minimal necessary conditions' for referring to something as philosophy. Perhaps there are other conditions, but any set of conditions that would be involved in calling something philosophy will include at least the ones we're seeking.

Although I've clearly borrowed the term 'necessary' (and 'sufficient,' for that matter) from logic, I do not say that the conditions I'm after are *'logically* necessary,' since this would seem (at least on some, probably even most, interpretations of logic) to rule out some other dimensions of them that I wish to highlight. For one thing, we are not just seeking some logical definition of 'philosophy' but are interested in what conditions are necessary for philosophy *actually to exist* as an historical phenomenon and as existing complexes of practices, texts, and viewpoints. The conditions don't concern only what we *mean* by 'philosophy' but what it, in fact, *is* as an historical and present 'reality.' For another, the usual way of understanding a 'logical condition' would be in terms of those logical entities called 'propositions.' However, the conditions we're seeking cannot be adequately or fully expressed in any limited 'propositional form,' but are, in various ways, more basic than the 'propositional content' of the logician.

For related reasons, they should also not be understood as some Kantian-like 'transcendental grounds for the possibility of philosophy.' Transcendental approaches like that of Kant or Husserl typically make a firm distinction between 'transcendental' and 'empirical' grounds. However, the conditions we are after will prove to have certain 'empirical' aspects, thus excluding them from qualifying as 'transcendental conditions' as Kantians usually understand this phrase. We might say that the conditions for philosophy are 'prior to' or, perhaps better, occupy the region anterior to the subsequent philosophical differentiation of the empirical and the transcendental. They are, in a sense, 'facts' but of a very specific kind that one would hesitate to call 'empirical' in any of the usual senses of this term. At the risk of unnecessarily complicating matters, we might say that these 'necessary conditions' inhabit the region of the 'analytic *a posteriori*' that Kant regarded as empty, at least in the sense that they have an empirical aspect that is, nonetheless, 'necessary' at least with respect to the existence of philosophy. But before we come to this, another discussion is necessary regarding philosophy as a distinctively human enterprise.

DIAGRAM 1: The Order of Precedence of the Three Conditions

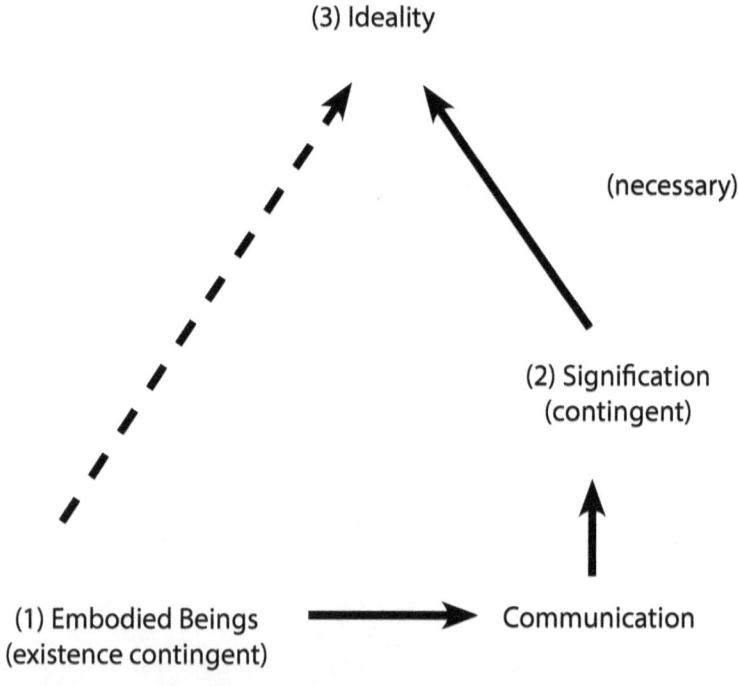

(1) The existence of embodied beings is contingent
(2) That their communication becomes significative is contingent
(3) If (1) and (2) obtain, then ideality necessarily obtains

I

The Conditions of Philosophy: An Informal Introduction

1. GODS, ANIMALS, AND HUMAN BEINGS

To extend an observation of Aristotle, philosophy is an enterprise foreign to gods and beasts. Gods, one might assume, have no desire for such a difficult and contentious undertaking and animals lack the capacities necessary for engaging in it.

While we humans can never really know or say what it would be like to be divine, we can make a few conjectures. First of all, a god such as Plato or Aristotle might have imagined would be immortal. The sense of temporal finitude, of having a limited lifespan confined to the period between birth and death, would not be a feature of the 'experience' of a god (whatever else this might involve). Because of this, a god would lack many of the concerns, moods, and emotions that so often burden our own human lives. For instance, they would experience no anxiety about having sufficient time to realize their projects and goals (assuming that they even had such things). They would be spared the depressing sense of missed opportunity, the leaden weight of limited ability, the disturbing possibility that their lives may remain unfulfilled, and the fearsome thought of ultimate annihilation and non-existence. Lacking these, any question about some ultimate 'meaning of life' would itself be meaningless or pointless to them, since the verdict would always be outstanding. Aristotle said, "Judge no man happy until he dies." In the case of an immortal, no such judgment would be either possible or meaningful, since there would always be 'more time' to set matters straight (if they were not already).

Similarly, a god would presumably be disembodied (at least in comparison to us corporeal beings). A god would not experience the painful process of growth or the inevitable deterioration of its body and faculties. It would know neither the restrictions of physical limitations or infirmity, nor the suffocating sense that it was confined to a single physical form. (The Greek gods seemed especially fond of shape-shifting and sometimes even gender-bending.) Lacking a physical body, a god could not be confined to a prison, spatially separated from its objects of desire, or restricted in its movements. It would, then, likely lack any clear sense of a spatial distinction between itself and a world beyond it.

Lacking any clear temporal and spatial limits itself, a god would seem to be exempt from the sort of alienation from and conflict with its peers so familiar to us humans (though Greek mythology is not as clear on this point). Gods, according to one of Aristotle's observations, would have no need for politics or any other intersubjective devices that would establish either the bonds of friendship or the repulsions of enmity. Though the Greek gods (quite different, admittedly, from Aristotle's own idea of a 'divine being') could be loquacious at times, this usually occurred only in their dealings with human beings, not other immortals. Their employment of language was merely convenient or adventitious, not a necessity for them.

Because they would have no need to communicate, they would also have no need to think about what they might say. If, as Aristotle sometimes suggests, they did think, it would only be a case of 'thought thinking itself.' That is, it would be a case of an action whose 'content' is nothing but its own activity, self-contained, complete, and in need of nothing beyond itself. Neither would such a god likely desire to communicate its thought to another being nor would it likely be capable of doing so. Its own thinking would be its sole object and that object would be fully lucid to its own thinking. The thinker and the thought would be identical, there would be nothing beyond this identity, and hence neither anything more determinate to say nor anyone to whom it needed to be said. To revert to the speech of mere mortals, for a god, there would be no desire for philosophy, no love of wisdom, because they would already be wise and any further attempt to articulate this would only deform it.

If the gods have no desire for philosophy (if such a term were even meaningful for them), the 'beasts' lack the capacity for it. While we should probably be careful about assuming that we know more about the experience of animals than we do about that of gods, and while the case of animals may be more complex since they exist in such a wide variety of physical forms, some parallel speculations are possible. Like ourselves, the lives of animals occur within definite limits, often (but not in all respects) more limited than our own. But, so far as we know, animals lack any capacity for being aware of their own temporal limitations. Living in a sort of 'extended present' and in whatever states they enter when they sleep, and assisted by their instincts and the biorhythms of their bodies, they do have some rudimentary sense of time, but it seems to be quite circumscribed and episodic. In particular, it includes no sense of the animal's own continuity from birth to the present nor some awareness of the finality of its future death. In other words, while an animal can certainly be aware of certain parts or areas of its life (its food supply, sexual urges, feelings of energy or exhaustion, pains and pleasures, etc.), it lacks the capacity to view such elements as parts of a temporal whole circumscribed by its birth and death, a sense of a life that could be regarded as meaningful or not.

Again, unlike gods, animals are embodied, confined to a definite spatial location, restricted in their movements, and subject to the same processes of physical growth and deterioration as ourselves. We even say of some animals that they are 'territorial,' that they have a sense of certain spatial areas proper to them and sometimes even employ (often noxious!) devices for marking these off. Animals, then, exist in and have a sense of their 'immediate environments,' their hives, nests, dens, yards, and, in the case of my cats, chairs, beds, and desks. But they lack the capacity to see their own bodies and their immediate environments as forming parts of a larger spatial whole that would include their own immediate environments as well as those of other spatial beings. For animals, their growth passes unnoticed and their physical deterioration is registered only by the pains accompanying it. They are clearly capable of responding to absences of accustomed objects in their immediate environment (food, warmth, their favorite toy, even their human 'support systems'), but they lack the human capacity to imagine being somewhere else (most animals seem to dislike traveling, as many of us have noted), to realize that their physical constitution bars them from certain activities, and to grasp that their bodies will gradually deteriorate and die, leaving many possibilities unrealized.

Further, the temporal, spatial, and physical limitations of animals work together to render them incapable of creating or utilizing anything that would qualify as a language in the human sense of the term. Of course, animals can and do communicate with one another (and sometimes even with us) in many ways, but communication should not be confused with linguistic activity, however much language is also used for that purpose. Communication, rather, is merely one function among others of language. To borrow for a moment from structuralist theory, language itself is a form of signification. This involves 'signs,' which are (more or less) stable relations between 'signifiers' and 'signifieds.' While signifiers can be almost any sensory phenomenon that can attract the attention of or be presented to another sentient being, signifieds are 'mental images' or, in a more developed form, 'concepts' connected with and provoked by the signifier's occurrence. From this perspective, we can say that an animal is capable of producing, utilizing, and responding to certain physical stimuli that, for humans, would be capable of being signifiers standing in a 'sign-relation.' To this extent, they can be said to communicate, but they are not capable of 'signifying' in the sense that human languages do.

There are several reasons for this. Limited in their sense of past and future time to their local environment, they lack the sort of longer-term memory needed to form relations between signifiers and their corresponding signifieds that would be sufficient to constitute any even rudimentary linguistic formation. Further, while we can only conjecture about the 'mental content' of the animal mind, there seems little basis for assuming that it employs repeatable mental images, much less concepts. In other words, it's by no means clear that there is anything corresponding to a 'signified' in the mental experience of animals. Lacking both signifieds and memory sufficient to establish the longer-term iterable relations that make up 'signs,' we can say, at most, that animals are capable of communication through the employment of 'signifier-like' sensory phenomena. This, however, is qualitatively different than human language, however proficient and complex animal behavior may be in its communicative activities.

Heidegger, in *The Fundamental Concepts of Metaphysics*, has very suggestively summarized the condition of the animal as being 'poor in world,' contrasting it to the human condition of being 'world-forming.' In his discussion, he also proposes that such inanimate objects as stones are 'worldless,' though he doesn't mention gods (that comes later on in the development of his thinking). But we might now say that gods have an 'excess of world.' In terms of our discussion, this reinforces and helps clarify the point that while gods have no desire for philosophy, animals have no capacity for it.

To say that gods have an 'excess of world' means, in essence, that they lack the sort of awareness of temporal and spatial limits that would provoke them to imagine or think beyond those limitations. Depending on which notion of god one has in mind, either the gods have no desire to pursue philosophy because no serious questions occur to them or, if they do, they have unlimited time and resources for addressing them; alternatively, they already possess the answers to all possible mortal questions and there is nothing further to pursue. On either version of an 'excess of world,' the gods will have no desire of philosophy precisely because the sense of limitations that would provoke the desire for such an enterprise is lacking. Put the other way around, human beings experience a desire for philosophy precisely because of their spatial and temporal limitations, because the 'world' formed by embodied humans is never the 'forever' or the 'all-encompassing.' Were humans not embodied, spatially and temporally limited beings, there would be no motivation to pursue philosophy.

Beings 'poor in world' could also be said to have no desire for philosophy, but for the opposite reason. Animals don't desire philosophy because they lack the capacity to identify it as an object of desire. To adapt an old saying, animals desire philosophy like a fish needs a bicycle. Being incapable of pursuing it or of benefitting from it if they even could, it is simply not something that figures among the possibilities of their limited world, so, strictly speaking, we can't even say that they have no desire for it (as if they might, but happen not to); rather, philosophy is simply not a possible object for them.

It is, then, only in the case of a being that is 'world-forming' that philosophy can be both desired and capable of being pursued. However counterintuitive it may seem, especially considering the rather 'cerebral' way that philosophy is often represented, philosophy is intimately connected with the fact that we are embodied beings, temporally limited in the scope of our lifespans and spatially limited in the range of our experience and abilities. To say that we are embodied beings is to emphasize the limitations that provoke us to pursue something like philosophy and that lie at the basis of our desire for it. On the other hand, to say that we are 'world-forming' beings emphasizes, rather, our capacity for engaging in philosophy. Part of what Heidegger meant by 'world forming' is the projection of various possibilities upon the horizon formed by our limitations; one of these possibilities is philosophy. Because we are not limited solely to our immediate temporal and spatial environments, the sort of 'extended now' in which animals live, and because we are capable of signifying rather than merely communicating, we are able to pose questions about where we are, what it might be like to be elsewhere, what we have or ought to have accomplished at the point in life at which we find ourselves, what we might accomplish in future time, what roles other beings and our relations to them play in this process, and many other questions.

Gods, then, have no desire for philosophy; animals have no capacity for it. We human beings can, as embodied and hence limited in space and time, desire philosophy and, as 'world-forming beings,' we possess the capacity to pursue it. Already, we can now point to two fundamental conditions for philosophy that have continually figured in our discussion up to this point. The first is that there be embodied, limited beings; the second is that these beings be capable of signification and not merely communication. We could, so far, say that philosophy is a type of activity that can be pursued by embodied beings capable of signification or possessing language.

II. A WORLD WITHOUT PHILOSOPHY?

But suppose that both of these conditions are met. Could we nonetheless imagine a 'world' in which philosophy failed to arise or does not exist? Put differently, even if we can, in some sense, desire philosophy and are capable of realizing it as a possibility, is there any reason to think that this particular desire can or must be satisfied? Human beings, after all, can desire and pursue many things; why would something like philosophy be among them? To ask this in a different way, is there anything about either our embodied and limited condition, our ability to signify, or maybe the relation between the two, that could serve to make a possible desire into an actual need or a necessary practice?

In order to approach this question, we might try to imagine a world without philosophy and what it would be like. One way to do this would be to imagine a world in which human beings failed to evolve, one, for example, still dominated by dinosaurs, or chimpanzees, or insects. Another would be to imagine a world in which the species 'homo sapiens' emerged, its members able to communicate (through, say, simple gestures or sounds) but without developing a capacity for signification in the sense of a relatively stable system of verbal or written signs. Both are certainly logically possible worlds that, in fact, existed at some time in the past.

The more difficult and instructive case would be one in which human beings evolved, succeeded in creating verbal or written signifying systems, and yet did not develop any distinctive practice or bodies of discourse that could be recognized as philosophy. Our initial reaction might be that such a world should be just as 'logically possible' as the first two mentioned above. But in what follows, I want to suggest that we would be wrong on this account, that the very conception of a world of embodied human beings mutually interacting through relatively stable processes of signification but lacking any sense or practice of philosophy would be inconsistent and unthinkable. More specifically, I want to claim that what I will call 'ideality,' which I take to be a third condition for philosophy, is implicit in the existence of embodied human beings who have developed systems of signification and that the explicit registering of this in discourse opens the 'space' within which philosophy emerges and can develop.

One way, then, to try to imagine a world without philosophy along these lines would be that often suggested in the Platonic dialogues through the figure of the sophist. For Plato, 'sophism' is precisely the view that acknowledges embodied human beings engaged in discursive interaction, while denying any ideality as implicit in or regulating for these activities. Through the figure of Socrates, Plato presents a rich variety of arguments against sophism, but the nerve of all of them is the demonstration that sophism cannot be consistently stated without reference to some third condition, some ideality, that would immediately compromise its opposition to philosophy. For instance, in response to Thrasymachus's famous claim, in the *Republic*, that "might makes right," Socrates suggests that even someone who holds this view must distinguish between more and less effective practices for achieving and maintaining power. However, to grant this, as Thrasymachus does, is immediately to have acknowledged a criterion—a rudimentary form of ideality—in addition to and other than his own desire and its discursive expressions. Other Platonic arguments for the 'ideas' function in broadly similar ways, demonstrating that, ultimately, it is not possible for human beings to engage in meaningful discursive interaction without the assumption of some structure of ideality as its basis. Whether we explicitly admit it or not, to enter the realm of *logos* is 'always already' to have entered the space of philosophy opened by *eidos*.

Descartes offers another way of trying to imagine a world without philosophy. He recounts, and recommends to his reader, an extended thought experiment of what he himself calls 'hyperbolic doubt,' or, as we might otherwise say, 'extreme skepticism.' Of course, he gives grounds for doubting any particular judgment about sense experience and goes so far as to suggest that there is no final criteria that would allow us determine whether we are, at any moment, undergoing the systematic deception of dreams. The crux comes, however, when he conjures up the 'evil genius' as a universal deceiver and then 'discovers' that there is one thing about which this entity, however powerful, cannot deceive us: the fact that I must exist in order even to be deceived. He goes on, as well, to suggest (though less explicitly) another condition for deception: that in order for the 'evil genius' to do its work, we must also make judgments capable of being false. A Cartesian 'world without philosophy,' then, would be one in which we exist (at least as *res cogitans*, but, we soon learn, problematically associated with the *res extensa* of our bodies) involved in articulating judgments about which we are continually deceived thanks to the work of the 'evil genius.' But the trajectory of his thought experiment is finally designed to show, in a quite overdetermined way, that this situation cannot be consistently thought due to the intervention of 'idealities' that not even an 'evil genius' can thwart. In fact, Descartes offers us a series of idealities, beginning with the *res cogitans*, which, since it is a 'clear and distinct' (necessary) concept, opens the way, via a version of the ontological argument, to the concept of God as a 'perfect being,' and thence to the realm of the 'clear and distinct' ideas of mathematics, all exempt from the deceptive powers of the 'evil genius.' Again, the intervention of ideality renders the attempt to imagine a 'world without philosophy' incoherent and impossible.

A third example of such a demonstration can be found in Kant's 'transcendental deduction.' Hume's skepticism, which famously awakened Kant from his 'dogmatic slumber,' might be read as yet another attempt to imagine and describe a 'world without philosophy.' Hume grants that, as embodied human beings, our experience consists only of sensory impressions and, as a result of memory, language, and the 'laws of association,' of 'relations of ideas.' However, since our impressions are otherwise inexplicable and radically contingent, all that is derived from them, including our 'ideas,' possess this same character. Kant's response, most compactly and directly articulated in the 'transcendental deduction,' is to argue, in effect, that Hume's description of human experience must already presuppose at least three types of idealities: a unity of consciousness (the 'transcendental unity of apperception') whereby impressions must necessarily be recognized as 'mine'; a unity of judgment, whereby impressions can be joined and articulated in determinate and not merely random ways; and conceptual unities, those fundamental 'constitutive principles' which both ground and are articulated in judgments. Another way of expressing Kant's argument would be to say that we cannot imagine or conceive of embodied, spatio-temporal beings capable of articulating judgments without also acknowledging a realm of ideality (ultimately, the 'categories') irreducible to our own idiosyncratic sensory experiences or their expression in judgments.

As a final example, we can consider one of the most radical modern attempts to imagine a 'world without philosophy,' that presented by Wittgenstein in the *Philosophical Investigations*. Wittgenstein's quite complex description of such a world is deliberately designed to undermine any claim about the irreducibility of ideality to embodied human beings interacting linguistically. The heart of his description involves his notion of 'language games.' On his account, linguistic entities (words, phrases, etc.) can and do have meanings, but such meanings are always relative to contexts of significational interaction among human beings (what he calls *Lebensformen*, forms of life). More specifically, the 'meaning' of a word or phrase is just the way it is used in a particular context. Wittgenstein suggests that the significational aspect of such contexts can be viewed on the analogy of 'games.' Just as there is no single feature (or set of them) defining for games, but only a set of 'family resemblances' among them, so there is neither some single 'ideal' meaning of any word or phrase nor, more generally, some extra-linguistic idea of what language in general might be.

For Wittgenstein, it follows directly from this that there can be no distinctively philosophical space or field. As he famously puts it, philosophy arises only "when language has gone on a holiday," that is, when the necessarily context-bound condition of language is forgotten or put out of play. Philosophical statements are thus meaningless because they lack any concrete context within which their 'proper use' (and hence their meaning) could be determined. Philosophy, then, is a sort of linguistic illusion or, as Wittgenstein puts it, 'bewitchment,' the antidote to which is showing exactly how philosophical statements have, in any given case, become detached from their 'normal functioning' in ordinary contexts.

Put in the terms we've been employing, this amounts to a description of a world of embodied human beings involved in significational interaction but lacking anything like the idealities that would be required to open the space of philosophy. There is a good deal deserving more detailed discussion in such an account, but for present purposes, we can simply observe two features of Wittgenstein's general discussion. First, in order to describe a 'world without philosophy,' Wittgenstein begins within a 'world' in which philosophy already exists as a discursive fact and tradition. This is equivalent to saying that philosophy is itself already at least a sort of 'language game,' the statements of which have implicit rules for 'correct usage' within this context. (It would be false, for instance, to claim that "Hume introduced the idea of 'synthetic *a priori* judgments'" or that "Synthetic *a priori* judgments are statements of fact.") To reply that philosophy does not constitute a 'language game' because its statements have no proper use in 'ordinary contexts' would, however, assume that we (or at least Wittgenstein) already somehow know what 'ordinary contexts' are and hence know the general meaning (an ideality!) of the phrase 'ordinary contexts.' Second, Wittgenstein's critical procedure shares with that of other 'transcendental minded' philosophers the feature of assuming an existing framework or set of conditions and deploying that set of conditions in order to, in effect, erase or foreclose one of them, in this case ideality. I'll discuss such procedures in more detail later, but for now it will suffice to observe that Wittgenstein, like others before him, ultimately fails in imagining and describing a 'world without philosophy' precisely because the basic of conditions of philosophy, including ideality, had to obtain in order for such an enterprise as his to be meaningful or possible.

At this point in the discussion, I'm not concerned about the validity of arguments such as the ones we've reviewed or their specific accounts of ideality, but rather with their force and general trajectory. The main point is to see that, so long as there are embodied beings capable of signification, ideality immediately and necessarily intervenes and thereby opens the space or field for philosophy, whether it be regarded as a practice, body of discourse, or a structure of thoughts, ideas, or doctrines. Another way of putting this is to say that, while the existence of philosophy in any of these senses is dependent upon there being embodied human beings capable of signification, and is thereby contingent in the sense that such conditions have not always and well might never have obtained, it is necessarily implied once they have developed. Philosophy itself (or 'philosophical truth') is not absolute or necessary in some universal sense, as if the universe must have developed in a way that produced the basic conditions of human beings capable of signification. But once these conditions are present, philosophy becomes a necessary feature of such a world as a space within which further 'necessities' can be recognized and articulated.

Therefore, although we are not, in some universal sense, 'condemned to be' (and may elect to cease being at any time), and although, if we do exist, we may yet not be able to engage in signifying activities (or, perhaps, choose not to, though this is more problematic), we cannot exist as embodied signifying beings without entering the space of philosophy. What Aristotle failed to capture, in defining a human being as '*zoon echon logon*' (an animal possessing speech), was that such an 'animal' would also necessarily be 'philosophical.' A human, discursive world lacking philosophy (whether it is explicitly so called or not) is not an option.

III. IMPLICATIONS AND ANTICIPATIONS

In this informal presentation, we began with the assumption that philosophy is an existing, on-going enterprise that encompasses both a distinctive type of human activity, the production of significational artifacts (usually texts), and certain complexes of ideas or concepts not reducible either to individual and idiosyncratic activities of 'philosophers' or to the texts in which they are articulated. It should now be clear that the various modalities under which philosophy presents itself are closely related to and, in fact, grounded in what I have called the three basic conditions of philosophy: embodied human being, signification, and ideality. Together, these three conditions open a space or field within which further philosophical activity or thought can occur and develop.

I've also suggested that these conditions, though distinguishable, are not independent of one another. Viewed in one way, there is an order of precedence among them (see Diagram 1). Without the emergence of embodied human beings, there would be no signification; without these two together, there would be no ideality. Viewed in another way, however, there are important asymmetries among them. The fact that embodied human beings exist is entirely contingent: such a species may just as well have evolved as not. Signification, too, is, in a sense, contingent, but in a more restricted sense: embodied human beings might well have been able to communicate without this developing into independent and relatively stable significational complexes or systems. Signification, that is, is a 'contingency of a contingency.' Ideality, however, while, in a sense, contingent upon the *occurrence* of the first two, is, at the same time, a necessary and irreducible feature of their co-occurrence, as was suggested by the inability to imagine or describe a world of embodied human beings involved in significational activities but lacking the ideality necessary to open the space of philosophy.

Clearly, the sorts of 'contingency' and 'necessity' involved here are both more complex than and rather far removed from the meaning of such terms as usually treated in formal logic. In fact, it will turn out that the logical meanings of such terms are at once parasitic, simplified, and often distorted versions of their much richer and more complex philosophical meanings (as logic in general is in relation to the field of philosophy itself).

In this chapter, I've tried to offer a more informal and intuitive approach to the question, 'What is philosophy?,' based upon a consideration of the 'conditions' of philosophy. The next chapter will begin to provide a more systematic account of these conditions and their relations, one that will further clarify the nature of these conditions, their interrelations among one another, and the field of forces and trajectories that they open.

2

Kant's Fundamental Question and the Problem of Judgment

The contemporary philosopher Hilary Putnam once said that "almost all the problems of philosophy attain the form in which they are of real interest only with the work of Kant." Perhaps this somewhat overstates the case, but it does call attention to the undeniable importance of Kant's thought for virtually all views of philosophy that have emerged over the last two hundred years. In particular, Kant's Critical Philosophy represented a watershed in the history of philosophy, not only providing a new language and set of methods for formulating and approaching traditional philosophical issues but, in the process, developing a novel and unprecedented conception of philosophy that set the agenda for much that would follow. One could fairly say that any current attempt to explore the question "What is Philosophy?" must either start with or pass through Kant. This is especially true if our response to this question involves exploring the limits and conditions of philosophy, for it was Kant who first suggested that philosophy might be an inherently limited enterprise and that its limits could be determined only by asking about its fundamental conditions, the 'grounds for its possibility.' To understand Kant's conception of philosophy is to learn something crucial about the nature of philosophy itself, and to discern its underlying difficulties is to gain a perspective on the direction in which we must proceed in attempting to answer the same questions for ourselves.

I. 'SYNTHETIC *A PRIORI* JUDGMENTS' AND THE POSSIBILITY OF PHILOSOPHY

Kant famously claimed in the Introduction to the *Critique of Pure Reason* that "the proper problem of pure reason is contained in the question: How are *a priori* synthetic judgments possible?" (KdrV, B19, KS 55) A highly technical, even arcane sounding question, to be sure. But Kant believed that the very possibility of philosophy and its fate in the future depended upon whether a convincing answer to this question could be articulated. The failure to answer this question would be to admit the possibility and, ultimately, the actuality of a 'world without philosophy.' On the other hand, a successful answer to this question would be tantamount to opening and securing henceforth a proper space or field for philosophy. It would, that is, be nothing less than an account of what we've been calling the conditions of philosophy.

Kant, who himself frequently invoked topographical metaphors, saw the space or region of philosophical discourse bounded on either side by two 'realms.' On the one side is the realm expressed in analytic *a priori* judgments. These are judgments whose truth can be known independently of experience (*a priori*) and which are necessarily and universally true because the concept expressed in the predicate of the judgment is already 'contained' in that expressed in the subject (analytic). They are necessarily true (or false, in the case of contradictions) because, in thinking or knowing the subject term, we must already know or think the predicate. For instance, consider the judgment, "The triangle is a three-sided figure." If you think of a triangle (the subject), you are immediately and necessarily also thinking of a figure with three sides. Since the predicate concept is already 'contained in' the subject concept, no further appeal to experience is needed; we know that it is true simply because we understand the subject concept and all that it 'contains.' What such judgments do not do is tell us anything about the 'way the world is'; rather, they concern solely the various relations among our concepts or ideas.

On the other side is the realm expressed in synthetic *a posteriori* judgments. The truth of such judgments can be determined *only* on the basis of experience *(a posteriori)* and are always variable and contingent because the concept expressed in the predicate of the judgment is not already 'contained' in that of the subject but has to be imported from elsewhere (synthetic). Experience, that is, serves as the ground for the linkage (synthesis) between the subject and predicate of synthetic *a posteriori* judgments. For instance, we can determine whether the judgment "This cat is black" is true only by consulting our sensory experience of this cat, since there's nothing about the mere concept of a cat that tells us what color it is. Such judgments are the form in which all of our ordinary knowledge about the 'world' is expressed. However, unlike analytic *a priori* judgments, which are necessarily true (or false), the truths expressed by synthetic *a posteriori* judgments are contingent, that is, their truth-value varies as our experience itself changes.

Kant's pivotal question about synthetic *a priori* judgments asks whether there is an additional realm lying between that expressed in judgments of which we can be certain but which tell us nothing about the world as experienced, and that expressed in judgments the truth of which is contingent and variable but which do provide us with our knowledge of the world of experience. On the one hand, as *a priori*, such judgments would have to be knowable independently of experience, that is, they would be necessarily, not merely contingently, true. On the other hand, as synthetic, their necessity would not be based upon the fact that the meaning of the predicate was already contained in the meaning of the subject; their necessity, that is, could not be determined through a mere analysis of concepts but in some other way. Further, as synthetic, such judgments should also be able to express true statements capable of expanding our knowledge of 'the way things are,' of linking concepts in ways not already implicit in the concepts themselves.

We can now understand why Kant thought that the possibility and fate of philosophy turned upon our ability to successfully answer his original question. On the one hand, Kant viewed the conceptual realm invoked in analytic *a priori* judgments as that of formal logic and perhaps other formal systems of conceptual manipulation like algebra (he called these '*Kombinatorics*'). On the other hand, he viewed the experiential realm expressed in synthetic *a posteriori* judgments as the proper field of the natural sciences. His question, then, ultimately concerned whether there was a space or domain lying between those of formal logic and natural science where judgments could be formulated that would at once possess the certainty and necessity of logic and yet inform us of aspects of experience not accessible merely through the analysis of concepts. On Kant's view, such a realm would be none other than that of philosophy, which had always traditionally expressed itself in judgments purporting both to be 'necessarily true' (and not mere idiosyncratic opinion) and yet in some way informative about being, experience, or 'the way the world is' (and not merely the clever manipulation of concepts). Thus, for Kant, to answer the question of how synthetic judgments are possible *a priori* would ultimately be to answer the broader question of how philosophy itself is possible. Kant's question, then, finally concerns whether, between logic and natural science, there is a proper space for philosophy and, if so, how this might be further articulated.

II. KANT'S 'STRANGE QUESTION'

Kant believed, as we know, that he could and did produce a cogent answer to both the more technical and the broader questions, though we also know that this was hotly disputed beginning in his own lifetime and continuing ever since. But rather than pursuing this straightaway, we first need to look more closely at the seemingly direct, if technical, question Kant was asking in order to appreciate some of the intricacies, nuances, and difficulties that it conceals.

To begin with, we should note that Kant, from the very start, admits (see *Prolegomena* 4:276; Zöller translation, 81) that the main question was never whether there *are*, in fact, synthetic *a priori* judgments (there are 'plenty of them,' he says), nor whether they *are* possible, since if they are actual, they must likewise be possible. Later on in the same work, as well as in the *Critique of Pure Reason*, he explicitly cites mathematics (geometry and arithmetic) and the basic principles of natural science (Newton's laws of thermodynamics, for instance) as offering abundant, actual, and indisputable examples. Likewise, Kant assumes that philosophy is an actual discipline, perhaps not yet a 'science' but at least a long-standing body of practices, texts, and doctrines. (For Kant's most explicit discussion of 'philosophy,' see the final section of the KdrV, 'The Transcendental Doctrine of Method,' A838/B806, KS 657 ff.) In neither case, then, is the very possibility of synthetic *a prior* judgments or philosophy itself in question for Kant.

Rather, the gravamen of Kant's original question concerns the 'how'—*How* are synthetic *a priori* judgments possible? But what sort of answer would suffice as a response to this question? In the Introduction to the KdrV (A6/B10, KS 48 ff.), Kant offers a formula for such an answer in terms of a 'something = X' which grounds the connection between subjects and predicates in any judgment. In the case of synthetic *a posteriori* judgments (which are undisputedly both actual and possible), Kant assures us that nothing more than consulting experience is necessary in order to explain how one experiential concept is connected with another: experience itself provides the ground (= X) for joining the subject and predicate in such judgments. Similarly, in the case of analytic *a priori* judgments, the 'containment' (= X) of the predicate concept in the subject concept grounds these (both actual and possible) judgments. These types of judgments Kant views as unproblematic in that the answer to the question 'how' is immediately and straightforwardly available. Both types of judgments are both actual, hence possible, and 'how' they are possible is immediately obvious (perhaps even 'analytically contained' in our very concepts of them).

It is only in the case of synthetic *a priori* judgments that the answer to the question of 'how' seems problematic, since that 'something = X' must suffice both to join two disparate concepts and yet, at the same time, do so with the force of necessity. We know, of course, that the answer will turn out to be the 'categories,' together with all the other 'transcendental machinery' that Kant musters to explain their operation. But, since Kant maintains that they are just as actual, hence possible, as the other two types, just as 'natural to us,' so to speak, one might still wonder why their ground is not equally obvious. Why should this question be so difficult when the answers to the others are so straightforward? Why does joining two disparate concepts with necessity (which, Kant admits, we do easily and often) pose such a philosophical difficulty and require such a complicated response?

III. JUDGMENTS AND THEIR CONDITIONS

This seeming asymmetry among judgments that are all equally actual and possible might suggest that, in fact, Kant was wrong in viewing the first two types of judgments as unproblematic; perhaps something philosophically significant about them escaped Kant's notice in formulating his fundamental question.

In order to see this, we can begin with their common denominator: they are all judgments, which Kant understands as the linking of a subject and predicate by the copula 'is.' It is not difficult to see that Kant's notion of judgment is already ambiguous. In fact, judgment, as Kant uses the term, can mean any of three things. In one sense, he uses the term 'judgment' to indicate a logical relation between or among concepts. (Later thinkers will introduce the term 'proposition' to indicate the 'logical meaning' or 'logical force' of 'judgment.') In a second sense, 'judgment' refers to the mental or psychological act that a person performs in linking two concepts together in thought. Finally, 'judgment' can also mean the linguistic expression of some 'conceptual relation' or the psychological act that grasps it (later thinkers introduced the term 'statement' for this sense of 'judgment.') The main point, here, is that this ambiguity in Kant's use of the term 'judgment' pertains to all three types of judgment that he wishes to distinguish.

Kant's original question about the 'how possible' of synthetic *a priori* judgments, then, cannot really be addressed until we consider the prior question, "How are judgments in general possible?," and, due to the systematic ambiguity just noted, the answer to this question is by no means obvious or straightforward. Of course, we can easily grant, along the lines indicated earlier, that judgments, understood in any of the three senses of this term, are actual and therefore possible. But this forces us back on a more basic question: How, that is, under what conditions or assumptions, is judgment in general possible?

Notice that all three senses of judgment—the conceptual, the cognitive, and the linguistic—seem necessary for a full understanding of a judgment. That is, any judgment must have some 'conceptual content' that can be grasped in a cognitional act that is capable of being linguistically expressed. Denying any one of these elements would be tantamount to logically evacuating the very idea of 'judgment.' (What, indeed, would we call a 'judgment without content,' or a 'judgment that could not be thought or understood,' or one that 'cannot be expressed'?)

This already suggests the beginning to an answer to the question, "How are judgments in general possible?' To answer this in terms with which we're already familiar, judgments in general are possible only if we assume the existence of human beings capable of cognizing idealities, idealities providing the 'content' of such cognition, and a significational system in which to express their cognition of this content. It should not be surprising by now that these three conditions for the possibility of judgments (as Kant employs this term) are exactly what I've called the 'conditions of philosophy.'

IV. REVISITING KANT'S CLASSIFICATION OF JUDGMENTS

As we've seen, Kant himself was focused upon a much narrower question than that about the possibility of judgments in general. We now need to explore both how Kant accommodated these conditions in his original classification of judgments and yet why he failed to raise the question that might ultimately link the fate of philosophy with that of the answer to his own question about the 'how possible' of synthetic *a priori* judgments. We'll especially be interested in how Kant's framing of his basic question led him directly into a type of 'idealism' (he called it 'critical' or 'transcendental idealism') that has created so many difficulties for thinkers following him.

Kant sometimes refers to synthetic *a posteriori* judgments as 'judgments of experience.' As the empiricists of the 18th century described in detail, such judgments arise from our sensory experience, from the fact that we are embodied beings with organs that register various aspects of the physical world around us. Kant's response to the question of how such experiential judgments are possible is entirely 'mentalistic.' That is, like the empiricists, he merely points to the fact that, given such 'sensory input,' human beings are capable of associating one example of such input with another and sometimes observing repeated patterns of association. Synthetic *a posteriori* judgments, then, are merely the expressions of such idiosyncratic cognitive activities. Of course, viewed from Kant's own 'transcendental perspective,' this is a sufficient account of such judgments, but this approach leaves entirely unobserved the principal (though not, in Kant's sense, 'transcendental') assumption for the possibility of such judgments: that embodied beings capable of such sensory experience and cognitive activity exist in order for there to be such judgments at all.

Following such rationalist thinkers as Leibniz, Kant also sometimes refers to analytic *a priori* judgments as 'truths of Reason' or 'logical truths.' In general, such judgments articulate the (logically necessary) relations among concepts. Kant is clear in holding that such 'conceptual content' is not dependent upon the subjective idiosyncrasies of experience but, rather, is 'objective,' possessing its own autonomy independently of any particular cognitive act within which it might be given. But, once again, Kant assumes without argument that there can be such things as concepts or, more broadly, idealities. Because he assumes the existence of concepts and their relations, he again finds the question of how such judgments are possible unproblematic.

For Kant, it is synthetic *a priori* judgments that present the major problem. In his attempt to explain the 'how possible' of these, he develops his 'transcendental method' and offers a 'transcendental deduction' and its associated doctrine of Categories and Schematism. In the end, Kant explains how we can have knowledge that is both necessary but in some sense informative about features of the world by invoking what we might call the underlying or transcendental 'structure of experience.' Just as synthetic *a posteriori* judgments are 'about' sensory or embodied experience and analytic *a priori* judgments are 'about' concepts or idealities, synthetic *a priori* judgments describe the basic underlying structures of experience. Because these structures constitute what can even count as experience (i.e. they constitute 'all possible experience'), they are knowable independently of any particular experience; but because they are not mere logical concepts or idealities but involve a 'synthesis' of diverse elements, they inform us of something about 'the world' (i.e. about its basic underlying structure, though not any specific 'facts' about it).

This, however, is exactly the same function that signifying systems serve. As various linguists (especially the structuralists) have insisted, signifying systems (and especially language) define the conditions for anything that can be expressed. It is instructive to observe that Kant himself derived his 'Table of Categories' from the basic forms of logical judgment. In fact, his categories just *were* the forms of logical judgment restricted to objects capable of appearing under the conditions of space and time. Just as Kant regarded the categories as forming a universally valid 'conceptual structure' constitutive for human experience, the structures of signifying systems prescribe the limits of what can be expressed within them.

Kant, of course, would insist that the categories, taken together, are not just one among other 'conceptual structures'; and he explicitly denied that the most fundamental 'conceptual structure' of human experience could ever be discovered by analyzing existing languages on the grounds that such empirical procedures can never resolve the sort of logical question that he was posing. (See Prolegomena, Sec. 39) But such assertions on Kant's part were symptoms of his failure to ask the more fundamental question: How is it possible to express or articulate judgments at all? Even the most sympathetic readers of Kant have been disinclined to defend Kant's derivation of his 'Table of Categories' from the traditional catalogue of logical judgments, even if they have accepted his 'transcendental deduction' as demonstrating that all judgments must be based on *some* categorial structure.

The more fundamental question Kant did not ask, then, was how a significational system is possible at all, granted that his own articulation of a set of categories would certainly qualify as one. But, again, this is not a question that can be resolved (or perhaps even posed) within Kant's 'transcendental approach,' which merely assumes the existence of certain types of judgments and then attempts to account for them in terms of a combination of epistemic and logical considerations. In fact, Kant's own 'transcendental account' is a particular deployment of a broader signifying system (or perhaps set of them) and it is the possibility of this that must first be explained.

V. DESTABILIZING KANTIAN JUDGMENTS: THE 'ANALYTIC *A POSTERIORI*'

Structurally viewed, there should clearly be a fourth possible type of judgment in addition to the three that Kant explicitly recognizes: the analytic *a posteriori* judgment. Kant himself curtly dismisses this possibility by remarking that "it would be absurd (*ungereimt*) to found an analytic judgment on experience." (KdrV B11, KS 49) But Kant's choice of terms here should alert us to the fact that something is amiss. We might have expected Kant to say that the very idea of an analytic *a posteriori* judgment is contradictory (*widerspruchlich*), but in fact he uses a weaker term that literally means 'unrhymed' or perhaps, more generally, 'terminologically inappropriate.'

We can put Kant's problem here in this way. If Kant were to admit that the concept of an analytic *a posteriori* judgment is contradictory, this would call his whole schema of classifying judgments into question by suggesting that one of the possible types of judgment that it projects is empty or a null set. But this would mean that the analytic/synthetic distinction doesn't really intersect with the *a priori/a posteriori* distinction as Kant's overall approach seems to suggest and that he, in fact, merely believed ('dogmatically'?) that there were only three types of judgments without any clear way of explaining why there were just these three. On the other hand, to admit that there are analytic *a posteriori* judgments would require an account that could not be provided from within the transcendental approach that Kant adopted. Kant, in effect, sidesteps this crucial dilemma by suggesting that to talk about analytic *a posteriori* judgments is somehow inappropriate, though he offers no real explanation as to why this might be the case.

I want to suggest that, for our discussion, which will affirm the meaningfulness and importance of analytic *a posteriori* judgments, the crucial issue is understanding why the question of how analytic *a posteriori* judgments are possible *cannot* be answered from the perspective of Kant's transcendental approach. Let's begin by asking what sort of thing an analytic *a posteriori* judgment would have to be. As analytic, it would have to express a 'universal and necessary truth,' that is, it would have to be 'true without exception' and, somehow, the concepts expressed by the terms occurring in it would have to stand in some sort of direct or strict logical relation. As *a posteriori*, however, its truth would have to be the result of and knowable upon the basis of certain experiential facts or observations that are themselves contingent.

Now a transcendental approach, as Kant often tells us, inquires about the 'grounds for the possibility' of certain sorts of experience and the judgments expressing them and responds in terms of certain underlying formal (logical or 'transcendental logical') determinations. Because all judgments (even analytic ones) are, in a broader sense, 'syntheses' of concepts or their linguistic terms (subject and predicate), Kant's transcendental approach assumes that all judgments require some act of consciousness joining the subject and predicate in the unity of the judgment (this is one way of expressing the heart of his 'Transcendental Deduction'). For the three types of judgments that Kant discusses, such an assumption seems warranted, since the determinations involved in all three are 'mental contents' or 'representations' (sensory experience, 'the pure forms of intuition,' and concepts).

But, in the case of analytic *a posteriori* judgments, it's not clear either what their 'content' would be or whether some 'synthesizing' act of consciousness would suffice to account for their being joined in a judgment. They might, that is, qualify as 'universal and necessary' (in Kant's logical sense), but for reasons, themselves *a posteriori* and contingent, that cannot be traced to the formal operations of consciousness itself. Were this the case, then 'the ground of the possibility' of analytic *a posteriori* judgments would lie outside the reach of the sort of formal and consciousness-based ('correlationist'?) procedures employed by Kant's transcendental approach.

To describe the situation we now have before us, Kant's transcendental philosophy is developed in response to a question formulated in reliance on a specific classification of judgments. This classificatory schema projects four types of judgments, one of which is thoroughly problematic and the possibility of which Kant forecloses without further explanation. This foreclosure thus constitutes analytic *a posteriori* judgments as a sort of 'possible impossibility'—on Kant's schema of judgments, they should be possible, and yet he seems to regard them as impossible. As far as the realm of transcendental philosophy goes, they *are* impossible, but they remain nonetheless possible if we are willing to abandon Kant's transcendental perspective. But if we do so, if we choose to explore the question of the 'grounds for the possibility' of analytic *a posteriori* judgments, then we will also have to rethink Kant's basic questions and the sort of answers that he offers for them. By thinking further about analytic *a posteriori* judgments, we will have destabilized Kant's entire way of questioning and the sort of answers that those questions anticipate. In the end, we will then be asking another, more fundamental, question: How is something like 'transcendental philosophy' itself possible?

At this point, however, it's important to note that raising this question does not mean that Kant's transcendental philosophy has somehow been refuted, superseded, or (as Hegel would say) '*aufgehoben*.' Rather, within the contours of the philosophical space opened by Kant's transcendental approach to philosophy, both the questions he posed and the sort of answers he suggested provide a still profound answer to the question, "What is philosophy?" To acknowledge the philosophical significance of the analytic *a posteriori* or the fact that this destabilizes Kant's basic schema and requires a thorough rethinking of such a fundamental concept as judgment does not mean that, *within the scope of transcendental philosophy*, what Kant regarded as necessary judgments thereby become contingent or that contingent judgments are actually necessary. Rather, I want to say that, within a framework that assumes that the most fundamental questions of philosophy can only be formulated and receive answers guided by the laws of logic interpreted from the point of view of limited human experience, then Kant's Critical Philosophy represents a viable response and one that should be taken with utmost seriousness. But, like all philosophers, in order to construct the space for his own project, Kant foreclosed others that the question, "What is philosophy?," requires us to keep open.

3

The Analytic *A Posteriori* and The Conditions of Philosophy

So far, I've suggested that the question, "How are analytic *a posteriori* judgments possible?," might provide a beginning for thinking beyond any transcendental approach to philosophy (which, I'll just assert here without argument, characterizes most post-Kantian philosophy of the last 200 years). We now need to investigate in more detail the implications of this new and 'trans-Critical' question for our understanding of the conditions for philosophy.

I. THE CONTINGENCY OF ANALYTIC *A POSTERIORI* JUDGMENTS

The first and most obvious consideration is, "Are there any actual (and therefore possible) analytic *a posteriori* judgments?" Within the context of the question, "What is philosophy?," I want to claim that there are three principal ones. (I leave it open whether there are others.)

Put in the most straightforward form, they are:
1. "There are embodied human beings."
2. "There are significational systems."
3. "There are idealities."

This way of stating them makes clear one important feature of analytic *a posteriori* judgments: they make explicit existential claims, which we know from Kant's discussion of the categories of modality as well as his famous 'refutation' of the ontological argument, can only be based on experience and hence must be *a posteriori*. This means that they would also be logically contingent.

To elaborate, we know that there was a time, not so long ago in cosmic terms, when human beings had not yet evolved and did not exist. Since significational systems are functions of human interaction, there was also a time when they also did not exist. Though we might hesitate in the case of idealities (since, beginning with Plato, many philosophers have tended to characterize them as 'eternal'), I've suggested above that, on good Kantian grounds, we'd likely be inclined to say that idealities are also, in some important way, a function of human consciousness and its capacity for judgment. Even if one were a die-hard Platonist, it seems contradictory or at least highly paradoxical to maintain that there are idealities that have never or cannot be cognized or expressed (and there's evidence scattered in the Platonic *Dialogues* that Plato himself was hesitant about this). On this, Kant himself is clear: his entire 'transcendental idealist' position is designed to show that the categories and even space and time are functions of reason employed by embodied human beings. So there seem to be good grounds for thinking that all three of the statements above are *a posteriori* and contingent.

One further observation follows from this. It's fair to say that Kant's treatment of the other three types of judgment is strongly oriented toward possibility and is formulated in terms of the modal category of possibility, not actuality. As we've seen, Kant's 'transcendental inquiry' always asks about the 'grounds for the possibility' of the other three types of judgment upon the assumption that they are all actual (there's 'plenty of all of them,' to borrow Kant's own phrase). In fact, immediately following his presentation of the 'Table of Categories' (KdrV A80/B106, KS 113), Kant notes some 'nice points' about the Table that omit any explicit mention of the modal categories, which, until much later in the work, he seems to view as self-explanatory. And even when he does take them up (e.g. in the Postulates, cf. KdrV A232/B285, KS 251), his discussion of 'actuality' is framed mainly in terms of the relation of possibility and necessity as sort of a 'middle ground' between the broader field of what is possible and the narrower one of what is necessary. I suggest that, had Kant focused more explicitly on the category of actuality, he would have had to consider the issue of analytic *a posteriori* judgments and ultimately the conditions of philosophy. That he did not leaves his philosophy a prisoner of his transcendental idealist assumptions and subject to all the critiques involving the internal difficulties and the philosophical incompleteness of this view that followed his Critical Philosophy. To go where Kant did not, however, brings us face to face with contingent existential judgments, the question of 'actuality,' and its relation to necessity.

II. THE NECESSITY OF ANALYTIC *A POSTERIORI* JUDGMENTS

Since the analytic *a posteriori* judgments I've noted above make existential claims which must be contingent, it may at first be difficult to see how they can, at the same time, be necessary judgments. I've suggested, however, that they direct us to what Kant called the category of 'actuality' as the proper point of departure, which might lead us to suspect that 'possibility' and 'necessity' stand in rather different relations than those that Kant seemed to assume, at least as they function within a discussion of analytic *a posteriori* judgments. As we will see, this is indeed the case.

We can begin by reformulating the above statements in a way that looks more like Kantian judgments. We can put them in this way:

1. "The universe contains embodied human beings."
2. "The universe contains significational systems."
3. "The universe contains idealities."

(In fact, if we wanted to be more precise, we could formulate the first statement, for example, as something like, "The universe possesses the property of 'containing embodied human beings'," but such complication isn't really needed for the point I wish to make.)

Now we know that Kant himself would immediately have problems with the concept of 'the universe' as I'm using it here. He would likely say that this term could mean only one of two things on his transcendental idealist view. Either it means something like his term 'nature,' which he regards as a construct based on the (synthetic *a priori*) 'transcendental principles' underlying the operations of consciousness. Or it has the logical meaning of 'totality' that he shows, in the Transcendental Dialectic, to be systematically ambiguous and antinomic. But, if we focus on the question of analytic *a posteriori* judgments, then a third meaning of the term emerges. 'The universe,' in this context, is actually closer to the way we ordinarily use this term than either of the options provided by Kant himself. On the one hand, it serves to indicate the actual existence of all that is, of which embodied human being is only a part. That is, it indicates something beyond 'nature' viewed as a construct of human consciousness. On the other, while our human knowledge or further discourse about it may be factually limited and, at points, logically problematic, its existence and the dependency of embodied human beings upon it is by no means contradictory or antinomic.

If the issue is neither one of 'synthetic *a priori* construction' or 'analytic contradiction,' what sort of necessity is expressed in such judgments involving terms like 'the universe'? A simplistic answer would be to say that it is merely a matter of 'physical necessity,' that, given the laws of causality (or, more grandly, a 'law of sufficient reason') operating through something like a 'scientific theory of evolution,' the actuality of the conditions expressed in the three judgments stated above is a sort of 'physical necessity' produced by the universe's own operations. This might well turn out to be true, but such a reading could still be countenanced by Kant's own transcendental idealism, since 'physical necessity' is not the same as the strict logical necessity that

Kant attributes to all analytic judgments. Specifically, one of the characteristics of analytic judgments that Kant cites (following Leibniz) is that their logical negation results in a contradiction. On this score, 'physical necessity' would turn out to be a misleading term for the sort of 'transcendental necessity' involved in synthetic *a priori* judgments, the negation of which does not result in a *logical* contradiction.

I want to suggest, however, that there is a stronger sense of necessity involved in analytic *a posteriori* judgments that *does* have this feature of their denial resulting in a type of logical contradiction (though not exactly what Kant probably had in mind by this). Let's begin with the first judgment:

"The universe contains embodied human beings."

Its negation would read:

"The universe does not contain embodied human beings."

But such a judgment is itself 'self-negating' in the sense that its very occurrence as a judgment assumes, as its condition, the existence of a being capable of cognizing and articulating such a judgment, which condition the 'content' of the judgment itself explicitly denies. Inasmuch as the existence of this judgment presupposes a condition that the judgment itself denies, then such a judgment is self-contradictory, at least in the sense of generating a logical paradox. Even more to the point, whether we assert the first judgment or its negation, both, as judgments, presuppose as their condition the existence or actuality of a being capable of expressing them.

It should be relatively easy to see that a similar sort of argument would apply in the case of the judgment, "The universe contains signifying systems." If it (or its negation) can be formulated as a judgment, then a signifying system must exist in which it is articulated. It would be contradictory, or at least paradoxical, to assert an actual judgment (at least as Kant understands it) that claims that no language exists in which to articulate it. I conclude, then, that at least the first two judgments, while stating contingent *a posteriori* claims, are nonetheless analytic in the sense that any attempt to negate them produces a logical contradiction or paradox. That is, they express contingent facts that possess, nonetheless, a sort of logical necessity, at least in the sense that their denial involves a contradiction.

Somewhat similar seeming arguments are, of course, familiar within the philosophical tradition, but they also differ from the above in important ways. For example, Descartes' "Cogito argument" purports to demonstrate the necessary existence of the '*res cogitans*' on the grounds that any attempt to doubt one's own existence as a 'thinker' will, in fact, prove its existence on every occasion that one attempts to doubt it (since doubting is a type of thinking, as Descartes explicitly notes). However, such an argument is itself paradigmatically 'idealist' (it concerns only 'mental' operations) and it succeeds only on the condition that there is a 'thinker' and only on those occasions when the 'thinker' actually undertakes to doubt its own existence. By contrast, the sort of necessity involved in analytic *a posteriori* judgments as we're exploring them is neither merely a function of a mental act nor dependent upon some occasional 'event' of thinking, even though the 'Cogito argument' does capture one aspect of what is involved in analytic *a posteriori* judgments.

The 'Liar's Paradox' presents another well-known case that, perhaps, captures an aspect absent from the Cartesian argument. The statement, "This statement is false," is paradoxical because, if the statement is true, then it must be false; if false, then it must be true. As usually analyzed, this paradox turns upon a linguistic mistake, the failure to make a distinction between the 'propositional content' of a statement and the statement in which this 'content' is expressed. (Or an 'object language' and a 'metalanguage' as this is also sometimes expressed). Another way of putting this is that the statement is 'self-referential,' that it is a statement that seems to refer to itself. But this seeming paradox can be remedied by simply explaining the logical difference between making statements (without quotes) and referring to statements (in quotes) or, alternatively, banning self-reference with the help of an hierarchical 'theory of types' (as Russell early on proposed with respect to set theory). Analytic *a posteriori* judgments, however, involve neither a mere linguistic confusion nor complete self-reference. The negation of 'The universe contains embodied beings' (or 'signifying systems') is false not because it confuses or collapses its 'content' with the linguistic expression of that content, but because it could not exist as a statement without presupposing the actual condition for making statements at all, whatever they may be. And, while to utter the negated statement involves a contradiction, it is 'necessarily false' not because of its self-referentiality but because the statement denies an actual condition for statements in general. That is, it immediately instantiates what it appears to deny.

III. IDEALITY AND THE ANALYTIC *A POSTERIORI*

So far, I've only indicated how the first two types of analytic *a posteriori* judgments make contingent, existential claims that must yet be regarded as logically necessary. I've also tried to suggest why we should not regard them merely as paradoxes (which seemed to be Kant's view of them). On the view of ideality that I am proposing, my third example requires some additional explanation, though I think that, in the end, the structure of the basic arguments turn out to be parallel to that of the first two. Here, however, I want, in the end, to concede something to Kant and, more generally, 'idealism,' that my discussion thus far appears to have discarded.

I have suggested that 'idealities' are, in a sense, 'doubly contingent.' On the one hand, their possibility depends on the existence of embodied human beings capable of cognizing them and upon those beings employing signifying systems in order to express them. Were there no human beings, or human beings who could communicate but did not develop the capacity for signification, then there would be no idealities. On the other hand, as we have seen, the existence of human beings and signifying systems is itself contingent, and idealities are dependent in turn upon these latter contingencies.

Still, I've also suggested that, once embodied human beings and signifying systems are actual, then it is logically necessary to acknowledge the 'existence' (perhaps in a somewhat different sense than the first two) of idealities. What I am suggesting, that is, is that idealities be regarded as logically necessary features of the (contingent) existence of embodied human beings engaged in significational activities. While human beings might not have evolved, or may have evolved but failed to develop significational systems, once these two are in place, the structured activities of human signification necessarily imply the influence and possibility of the explicit recognition of idealities. In fact, both embodied being and signification, in different though complementary ways, point toward and are governed by idealities.

1. Ideality and Embodied Being

If we begin from the side of embodied human beings, ideality indicates, in the most general sense, the manner or modality in which whatever is other, different than, or beyond the limitations implied by embodiment is disclosed and registered. To realize that we are embodied, finite, and limited is also to recognize that there is some greater whole of which we are a part. Western philosophy has typically employed the notion of 'being' as the 'primary ideality' which includes all other 'beings,' both actual and possible, (including ourselves) as parts. 'Nature' (in the sense indicated above) also functions as a basic ideality when the emphasis falls upon the 'actuality' of embodied human being in the larger context of other actual, existing beings. 'God' has also functioned as an ideality when the emphasis falls upon the contrast between the contingency of our own embodied existence in relation to 'necessity.' (It is because all three—Being, Nature, and God—are alternative expressions of ideality, of the 'other than' or the 'beyond' of embodied human being, that they have been so closely interrelated in the history of Western philosophy and theology.)

Beyond this general relation between embodied human being and whatever manner the ideality that expresses its limitations is named or registered, desire also plays a decisive role in forming and further specifying ideality. Desire presupposes a lack or absence in our embodied condition of something that lies (sometimes only temporarily) beyond it. The objects or ends of desire thus function as more specific idealities with respect to our finite embodied existence. When we are hungry, we desire food in general, which thus functions as an ideality with respect to our bodily desire for nourishment or satisfaction. We can, of course, desire something more specific, like a taco or a Big Mac, which then functions as a more specific ideality in relation to our desire. Even when our desire is for something singular, like my friend's car or a family heirloom, the object of desire takes on the aura of and functions as an ideality. And for philosophy itself, wisdom (*sophia*) is an ideality with respect to a sort of human desire (*philos*). From the point of view of embodied human existence, then, idealities can be, but are not necessarily, universals (as the philosophical tradition has tended to treat them); rather, they can just as well be types, particulars, or even singularities. The crucial point is that whatever is taken to be the object of desire is an ideality with respect to that desire; it is something lacking to embodied existence that marks it limitation from whatever lies beyond itself.

Are there, then, from the perspective of embodied existence, logical difficulties in denying or negating our analytic *a posteriori* claim that "The universe contains idealities"? Now, we've argued that this claim presupposes the existence of embodied human beings. So to deny this claim would be to presuppose that there are embodied beings at the same time as denying the most fundamental condition of embodiment: that such beings are a limited part of a greater whole (however this is conceived). To deny that, with respect to embodied beings, there are idealities is, in effect, to deny that there is any difference between (in the present way of formulating this) embodied being and 'nature' of which it is a part. That is, denying that there are idealities ultimately contradicts the assumption on which the statement itself is based, that is, that there are embodied beings as part of some greater whole. But we have seen that we can't consistently deny this claim, so any statement that entails such a denial must also be logically inconsistent. Put more positively, if there are finite embodied beings, then there must be idealities that correspond to the ways in which embodied beings are finite and limited.

A somewhat different argument emerges from a consideration of desire. The negation of "The universe contains idealities" is itself a judgment and we've seen that the existence of judgments implies the existence of embodied beings capable of articulating them. As a human action, the articulation of a judgment must have some sort of motivation, that is, it must result from some desire—for communication, clarity, persuasion, whatever. In this case, the ideality aimed at by the desire is the articulated judgment itself and to deny that ideality exists is, in effect, to deny the grounds for articulating any judgment. In other words, denying the existence of ideality here is equivalent to denying the possibility of judgment, which contradicts the judgment itself which expresses this denial. Put in other terms, to deny the existence of ideality is to deny the existence of desire which is, in turn, to deny the existence of finite embodied human beings. So it turns out that, beginning from the existence of embodied human beings, we can't consistently deny the existence of idealities, at least as forms of its limiting 'others.'

Most philosophers, however, will likely reply that I've purchased these arguments at the cost of watering down the usual meaning of 'ideality' into something unrecognizable to them. They might well say that, in the sense I've given the term, 'ideality' turns out to mean most anything other than the mere condition of embodiment itself. At least, it seems to have little to do with the sort of 'universals' or 'ideas' figuring in most traditional philosophical discussions. I would, in fact, agree with them, but I would add two crucial points. First, the arguments I've presented adopt only the point of view of embodied existence and are meant to function, as much as possible, without importing considerations of signification. Second, I do mean to claim that, simply from the point of view of embodiment, ideality does not either in the first instance or generally appear in the guise of universality. As embodied and desiring beings, we do recognize lacks that arise from limitations in our finite condition and we variously project or fixate on things other than ourselves as the objects of our desires. Typically, these 'others' are not 'universals' but either more than them (the total context from which we are delimited as a only a part) or less (determinate objects). Embodied desires, that is, intend something beyond our own embodied condition and, in so doing, enact and remind us of our own limitations. But idealities in the form of concepts or universals come from elsewhere, from the condition of signification. In a sense, while embodied desire opens the space of 'otherness' and constitutes a force that places us on a trajectory beyond our embodied condition, it is signification that first structures this space in terms of concepts or universals and provides it with a more stable structure than that implicit in desire.

2. Ideality and Signification

That the functioning of signification necessarily requires idealities is a recurrent theme in the philosophical tradition and there are numerous examples of arguments on behalf of this claim (sometimes several in a single thinker like Plato). Here, what I am generically calling 'idealities' can assume multiple forms. When viewed from the perspective of their relative independence from concrete instances of signification, they can range from minimalist, such as meanings of words or rules governing speech acts, to robust, like certain versions of Platonic 'forms.' The common denominator of arguments for idealities based upon signification is the claim that something can count as an instance of signification or language only if something else beyond its mere occurrence is assumed. What is assumed about that 'something else' or how it is described is (perhaps among other things) a function

The Analytic A Posteriori and The Conditions of Philosophy 73

of the argument(s) deployed on its behalf. That is, different arguments for idealities tend to make different assumptions about what is being argued for and result in different descriptions of the idealities involved.

Paralleling our earlier discussions of embodied being and significational systems, we might look to the view often called 'nominalism' for a formulation of the negation of the claim that there are idealities. But this is somewhat problematic, since the tradition offers numerous versions of nominalism, each of which tends to assume a particular version of ideality that it is concerned to deny. For instance, the 'nominalism' of medieval thought, designed to deny the existence of Platonic 'forms' or 'essences,' is quite different than that of the early modern period, which was directed, as in Hume, against 'innate ideas' (and similarly for more recent versions like that of Quine or Goodman). Even if, as is sometimes suggested, we think of idealities as 'abstract objects' and regard nominalism as a denial of the existence of these, we might still claim that idealities need not take the form of 'objects' at all, leaving other candidates for idealities (such as linguistic rules, 'possible worlds,' or even the entirety of a significational system, such as the structuralists' '*langue*') as options. So just to begin with nominalism straightaway will not be of much help here, since what the various versions of nominalism explicitly intend to deny will usually leave open the possibility of admitting other forms or descriptions of idealities not covered by what they oppose. This means that there can be no *general* 'refutation' of nominalism because there is no single or universally applicable form in which the view can be stated.

Rather, the denial of idealities altogether is a stronger claim than most (if not all) traditional forms of nominalism. This would be the claim, rather, that signification is possible without recourse to anything beyond the mere occurrence of significational acts or instances of their expression. But it is exactly this claim, I want to argue, that cannot be consistently asserted, that is, that is necessarily false (and hence that its opposite, that there are idealities, is necessarily true).

To see that this is the case, consider the claim, "There are no idealities." In order for it to be meaningful and not just mere random sounds or inscriptions, at least three minimal conditions must be met. First, it must, as an instance or occurrence of signification, appear against a background or field. If it is spoken, it will occur at a specific point in time against the broader background of, so to speak, the flow of time itself. If it is written, it will exist as a limited segmentation or area of differentiation within the broader spatial field that constitutes its background. Therefore, to occur as an instance of signification at all, the statement must presuppose something beyond its mere occurrence, that is, the broader fields of time and/or space. But these function here precisely as idealities, fundamental and necessary conditions for the occurrence of any instance of signification whatever.

Second, to be meaningful as an instance of signification, it must be internally differentiated within itself. Statements typically are differentiated into discrete units (words) and these units are further differentiated into smaller units (syllables), which may in turn be differentiated into sound differences (phonemes) or written units (letters or lexemes). As we have learned from the structuralists (as well as even their opponents such as Derrida and Lyotard), 'difference' is a fundamental condition for the existence of signifying systems and any instance of their functioning. But 'difference,' in the sense of a basic condition, is also something beyond the mere occurrence of the statement itself and hence functions as another sort of ideality.

Third, the units of the statement thus differentiated must be iterable and recognizable as such. That is, all the words in the statement (as well as their sub-units) must be capable of being repeated and recognized as the same in other or multiple occurrences. For instance, though few (if anyone) would argue that the word 'there' requires the existence of some corresponding 'idea' in order for it to function or be understood as part of a sentence, it must at least be capable of being repeated in other sentences or referred to in quotation marks as a verbal unit of the present sentence. But to recognize a word (or other unit) as the same across different occurrences assumes that there is something beyond its single occurrence (call it its 'field of iteration') that makes it recognizable as just this word or unit and not some other. This 'something other' than its singular occurrence need not be regarded (though it often has) as an 'abstract object,' universal, or Platonic form, or even the mere 'meaning' of the term. But however else one might try to describe it, it is clear that something more is required than its mere singular occurrence within a specific statement. To use the term above, any unit's 'field of iteration' thus constitutes another type of ideality as a condition for the meaningful assertion of a statement.

The conclusion, then, is that the statement, "There are no idealities," contradicts the fundamental conditions of its own existence as a statement. In order to signify at all, it must at least be temporal and/or spatial, involve the more general operation of differentiation, and operate within various fields of differentiation. All of these go well beyond its mere occurrence (as well as the occurrence of any and all units within it). I will immediately add that these conditions are, of course, minimal and other thinkers who have argued for idealities have elaborated them in various directions, often indicating the need for more robust views of idealities such as abstract objects or universals. But I hope to have indicated that such further elaborations are not necessary in order to make the point that the statement, "There are idealities," possesses a sort of logical necessity and is, as I've been suggesting, another example of an analytic *a posteriori* statement.

IV. THE ANALYTIC *A POSTERIORI*: THE CONTINGENT EXISTENCE AND LOGICAL NECESSITY OF THE CONDITIONS OF PHILOSOPHY

The above considerations indicate that we must recognize a certain class of judgments that have the peculiarity that, while they make contingent existential claims, any attempt to deny these claims turns out to be self-contradictory. Since any existential judgment is contingent, that is, is 'knowable' only on the basis of experience, and implies that it is possible that whatever it concerns might not have existed, then it must be, following Kant, '*a posteriori*.' However, since any attempt to deny such judgments results in logical contradiction (or a paradox, which entails a contradiction), then they must also be regarded as logically necessary, that is, 'analytic.' We've further suggested that what we've been calling the 'conditions of philosophy' all have this quality of being 'analytic *a posteriori*.'

It is, of course, true that such an account does considerable violence to the way in which Kantian transcendental Idealism deployed such terms as 'contingency' (or 'possibility') and 'necessity.' But we've suggested that a consideration of analytic *a posteriori* judgments forces us beyond the scope of transcendental idealism's dual concerns with the 'possibility' of objects of experience and the 'necessity' of that upon which they are grounded. It suggests, that is, that such terms must be rethought beginning from 'actuality,' a category that Kant acknowledges but treats as a sort of 'vanishing midpoint' between possibility and necessity. In fact, it is precisely 'actuality,' in the form of the conditions of philosophy, that must be privileged in order to address the question, "What is philosophy?"

If the Kantian Critical Philosophy was designed to question the limits of Reason and proposed transcendental idealism as the answer to this question, then asking about the limits of transcendental idealism must lead us directly into the broader question of what philosophy itself is and the actual conditions that make it possible. But to do this requires that we be willing to think beyond the relatively straightforward logical relations that transcendental idealism attributed to such terms as 'contingency,' 'possibility' and 'necessity.' The meanings of such terms are, after all, by no means fixed or self-evident but are themselves legitimate themes for philosophical reflection. It is, then, only to be expected that, outside of their deployment within some specific philosophical position (such as transcendental idealism), they will turn out to function in rather different ways than they do within its scope. That they do will, then, serve as one indication that we have transgressed the limits of a particular philosophical viewpoint, which is precisely what the answer to the broader question about philosophy requires.

4

The Question About Philosophy: A Preliminary Response

At this point, I want to take a step back from the details of the discussion thus far and summarize where this has led us. We began with a question posed by Kant. As any such beginning, it was arbitrary in the sense that we could have begun with many other philosophers or a particular question that they raised. However, because Kant, in his Critical Philosophy, attempted to provide a comprehensive answer—in fact, perhaps *the* major comprehensive answer of modernity—to the question, "What is philosophy?," any further attempt to address this question must eventually have to confront his own. So, in another sense, given our own initial question, beginning with Kant was perhaps necessary for my project. In reviewing Kant's view of judgment and its various types, we found that Kant structured the space of judgment in a way that both opened and immediately foreclosed the possibility of a fourth type of judgment (the analytic *a posteriori*) in addition to the three that he treated in detail. In exploring this possibility foreclosed by Kant, I suggested not only that it was not 'absurd' but, in fact, crucial to understanding the limits of Kant's own view of philosophy. In particular, I proposed that the realm of the analytic *a posteriori* involves exactly the very conditions of philosophy, the 'grounds for the possibility' as well as the 'actuality' of philosophy itself, Kantian or otherwise. However, the price to be paid for this 'defore-closure' was a sort of destabilization of Kant's own project, since it involved reformulating his own basic question about synthetic *a priori* judgments and reinterpreting his view of this as well as of the other two types of judgments involved in his framing of this question. I said earlier that, having done this, I wanted to grant something back to Kant after all and I turn to this now as a step on the way to considering the central question of how our discussion of the analytic *a posteriori* leads into the question of the 'field of philosophy' as constituted by its actual conditions.

I. THE ANALYTIC *A POSTERIORI* AND KANT'S TRANSCENDENTAL IDEALISM

Kant characterized his thought as a 'Copernican Revolution' in philosophy. Overlooking some of the difficulties or, perhaps, unintended implications of this metaphor, we can say, in a general way, that Kant invoked it to emphasize the fundamental role that he attributed to human consciousness and its activities in structuring what we ordinarily take to be 'reality,' 'the world,' or 'nature.' To develop this insight, he asserted, as we know, that 'things as they are in themselves' are unknowable; rather, all knowledge can only be of appearance. However, he was equally insistent that the activity of consciousness in structuring 'reality' and the unknowability of things as they are in themselves did not imply any type of skepticism or 'subjective idealism,' a view (which Kant attributes to Berkeley) that reality or the 'world' just is whatever we perceive it or imagine it to be and might therefore be wholly arbitrary and contingent. Rather, he wanted to claim that, although the 'world' or 'reality' depends upon the activity of consciousness for its form or structure, the basic features of this structure are logically necessary and invariable for human beings. He wanted, that is, to claim that what we take to be 'reality' is mind-dependent but not, in its basic structure, contingent or arbitrary.

In the course of his discussion, Kant devised a precise way of putting this. He characterized his thought as both (and equally) a 'transcendental idealism' and an 'empirical realism.' The former served to emphasize the mind- or consciousness-dependent aspect of his view: that the 'grounds for the possibility' of experience or what we take to be the fundamental structural features of 'reality' are to be discovered in the activities of consciousness. The latter served to indicate the other, and equally important, aspect of his view: that what we take to be the world of experience is fully 'real,' in the sense of being the same (at least structurally) for all conscious beings. Put more simply, while the structure of reality is necessary and invariable, the empirical objects that make up the 'content' of the world exist, possess all the properties (including spatial and temporal features) attributed to them by 'realists,' and are contingent in their existence and properties. The 'world,' that is, is 'transcendentally necessary' and 'empirically contingent' (which is, in fact, a concise way of stating the answer to his basic question about synthetic *a priori* judgments).

An exploration of the foreclosed analytic *a posteriori* judgments, however, seems immediately to call into question Kant's entire view. With respect to his 'transcendental idealism,' analytic *a posteriori* judgments imply that there are 'real' grounds that must necessarily be presupposed by any articulation of transcendental idealist claims. That is, they imply that consciousness and its synthesizing activities are based upon the actual occurrence of certain extra-mental conditions, which are themselves in some sense contingent. With respect to his 'empirical realism,' such judgments imply that the contingent 'content' of appearances and the 'phenomenal world' formed from them cannot be immediately identified with the more fundamental 'real' conditions that make consciousness and signification possible in the first place.

There are two other important results that follow from this. First, the 'thing-in-itself' cannot be regarded merely as a 'limit concept' (as Kant himself later suggested and Fichte developed more fully). The reason is that the fundamental conditions underlying Kant's transcendental idealism (and indeed any philosophy) cannot merely be concepts (however much they may be articulated through concepts) but must necessarily be real counterparts or referents of any concept that we may frame of them. The second is that 'nature' cannot be understood merely as a categorial construct of consciousness as Kant viewed it (however much this might also be involved) but must also include the 'real,' extra-mental conditions only on the basis of which consciousness and its signifying activities can exist in the first place.

What, then, if we admit the possibility (and actuality) of analytic *a posteriori* judgments, can be granted back to Kantian transcendental idealism? I want to claim that, although the occurrence or existence of these conditions are contingent—that neither embodied conscious being, nor signification, nor therefore idealities had to develop or exist—once they do exist, then the sort of logical (and 'transcendental logical') necessity that Kant so emphasized and articulated must be acknowledged with much of the weight that Kant attributed to it. That is, we can accept Kant's transcendental idealism as a philosophically cogent and fecund account of the necessary structures governing *conscious* activity, with the proviso that we understand consciousness and its activities (including signification) as themselves contingent in their existence and dependent upon actual, extra-conscious conditions. Consciousness and its signifying activities might not have developed or existed, but, once they do, then a field of necessary structures opens for further philosophical exploration along the lines (among others) that Kant's transcendental method traverses.

II. THE FIELD OF PHILOSOPHY AND ITS CONDITIONS

What is true of Kantian transcendental philosophy is, in fact, true of philosophy in general. That is, the conditions pointed to by analytic *a posteriori* judgments are not merely conditions for Kantian transcendental philosophy but must be assumed as actual by any philosophy whatever. Viewed in this way, analytic *a posteriori* judgments serve simultaneously as the exit point from transcendental idealist philosophy and the entryway into the broader field of philosophy itself and the access to our original question, "What is philosophy?"

We are now in a position to suggest a preliminary answer to this question. Philosophy—whether viewed as an act, a set of texts, or a general position—is, at the most fundamental level, a contingent enterprise. There is no 'eternal wisdom' or '*sophia*' that we might somehow attain only if we could desire it enough, think more deeply, or express our thoughts more completely. In fact, had embodied conscious beings not evolved or developed, or had they not developed systems of signification capable of recognizing and expressing idealities, neither philosophy nor its '*telos*' would have existed at all. However, once these conditions occur, a field for activity, thought, and discourse opens that can be occupied in many different ways. That is, there is a certain empirical fragility to philosophy that, however much it may be repressed or foreclosed, must ultimately be acknowledged.

The various possible ways in which this field is traversed, territorialized, and occupied (that is, various 'philosophical positions,' which phrase turns out to be a quite apt for what I am trying to describe) depend upon and assume their specific forms from the determinate ways in which they interpret, negotiate among, and bring the fundamental conditions into a concrete unity. At the most basic level, every undertaking that can be regarded as philosophical enacts and instances a set of particular interpretations of philosophy's basic conditions and, implicitly or explicitly, configures them in specific ways. That is, *every philosophy, whatever else it may be, adopts a position, either implicitly or more or less explicitly, with respect to the relations among embodied being, signification, and ideality.*

Particular philosophies differ from one another with respect both to the degree to which they make their positions with respect to these conditions explicit and the degree to which they tend to privilege one of the conditions over others or, alternatively, suppress one or more conditions in favor of others. As a rough illustration of this, we might distinguish among philosophies that privilege embodied human being (e.g. most forms of empiricism and certain strands of modern existentialism and poststructuralism), signification (e.g. structuralism, hermeneutics, and generally any 'linguistic philosophy'), and ideality (e.g. most of the 'metaphysical' tradition). And in each case, a philosophy can be more or less explicit in recognizing its own commitments and position *vis a vis* other philosophies and the manner in which they configure the basic conditions.

Of course, the most powerful and fecund philosophies will be those that territorialize the field of philosophy in a way that both does justice to all the basic conditions and makes explicit the multiple ways in which the conditions interact to form, we might say, a specifically configured set of 'forces' that constitute the field of philosophy as territorialized and occupied by them. It is because of this that some philosophers, like Plato, Aristotle, Kant, Hegel, and Heidegger, become recognized as canonical, while others, though perhaps providing an important insight or argument, remain as footnotes to the tradition.

This approach also suggests a potentially important way of distinguishing philosophy from its 'others' as well as seeing how they are related to it (more on this in a later chapter). If one of the three conditions is foreclosed or collapsed into another, the enterprise thus generated will not be philosophy but something else, though we will also be able to say, in a general way, what would be required to recover its philosophical core or relevance. As a brief preliminary overview, we can say that formal logic, mathematics, and natural science, in their emphases on 'objective discourse' about law-like idealities, tend to foreclose the condition of embodied conscious human being. Of course, it remains implicit as a theme, but is foreclosed by functioning as an unacknowledged element of the discourse itself. The field of religion and 'spirituality' tends to suppress the element of signification in favor of some direct relation between embodied human being and an absolute ideality. Signification, of course, remains present, but in the form, not of independent logical discourse, but as sacred texts that serve only as a mediation between finite embodied being and an infinite ideality or state of being. Finally, the realm of art emphasizes the expressive or significative activities of embodied being, free in important ways from the constraints imposed by logical or epistemological versions of ideality. Again, idealities may remain (for example, as a general idea such as beauty or sublimity), but these occur more as side-effects of expressive or significational activities and their products rather than as conditions directly determining them. For any of these, then, the first step toward bringing out their philosophical force or relevance will be to thematize and restore the condition that each has suppressed or foreclosed.

Still, an important point remains to be added. Although the existence of philosophy itself (and any particular philosophy) is contingent and the possibilities for territorializing and occupying the field of philosophy formed by the conditions open, every philosophy constitutes a specific configuration of the basic conditions which then necessarily governs the form of that philosophy. That is, given a specific configuration of the conditions, a philosophy cannot proceed arbitrarily but is constrained by a sort of necessity dictated by the specific configuration of the conditions that it assumes and instantiates. In a sense, then, every philosophy is bound by the 'logic' of its own interpretation and configuration of the basic conditions. This is why, having adopted a particular position within the space opened by the conditions, a philosopher can 'learn more' about his or her own position in the process of developing and articulating it and may even, by following its trajectories, come to reterritorialize the original space that it occupied. This also explains the claim, so emphasized by Kant and the German Idealists, that any genuine philosophy must ultimately be systematic (whatever its attitude to 'systems' might otherwise be). Philosophy, that is, cannot ultimately be some random collection of idiosyncratic intuitions or insights but must develop and be articulated in a way that both respects and conforms to the internal logic of the specific configuration of the basic conditions that it assumes and instantiates.

However, while philosophy necessarily possesses an inner drive toward systematic articulation, our discussion of the analytic *a posteriori* and the conditions of philosophy that it discloses also implies that there can be no final, complete, or closed philosophical system. Put differently, there can be no fully self-reflexive account of the basic conditions. All of the conditions necessarily figure in the construction of the space of philosophy and the specific ways this is territorialized and occupied by specific philosophies, but each condition also, and necessarily, involves an excess and withholds its own sort of remainder that resists any philosophical effort to include it within the field of philosophy. It is these excesses or remainders inherent in the conditions, and thus the essentially incomplete and necessarily open nature of philosophy, that will be the theme of some later chapters.

III. PHILOSOPHY, 'METAPHILOSOPHY,' AND 'TRANS-CRITICAL ACTUALISM'

Such an answer to the question, 'What is Philosophy?,' must seem, in a sense, 'metaphilosophical,' but this is true of any answer to this question. Still, any philosopher should immediately be suspicious of the very idea of 'metaphilosophy' since it seems to presuppose some stance 'outside philosophy' from which a presumably 'extra-philosophical' answer to the question can be given, an answer that nonetheless will itself also count as an instance of philosophy. Put in other terms, we might ask whether the present (though preliminary) answer to the question 'What is Philosophy?' is not just one more among other philosophical views about philosophy, perhaps containing its own specific emphases and limitations? Does philosophy, that is, ultimately turn out to be an 'impossible possibility,' in the sense that, while it can and must address the fundamental question about its own nature, any answer that it offers will, like some of Socrates' interlocutors, only provide merely another instance of what the question intends without actually addressing the question itself?

To begin with, notice that formulating the issue in this way is very much implicated in a 'logic' dominated by possibility. It presupposes, that is, that philosophy might, after all, not be possible or at least that what has been called 'philosophy' is merely a delusion. But to pose the issue in this way is, following Kant's 'idealist' lead, both to confuse or conflate two ideas, those of possibility and of contingency, to foreclose actuality as an operative element, and to misconstrue the idea of 'limit.'

To claim that the existence of philosophy is contingent upon the occurrence of non- or pre-philosophical conditions is not the same as to claim that philosophy is a 'mere possibility' (which, perhaps, might exist in some 'possible worlds' and not others, as certain modern logical approaches might understand this). The former takes it as a fact that philosophy is actual, that it exists, and observes that, lacking certain conditions, it might never have existed; the latter, in effect, 'suspends actuality' and proceeds as if it is somehow an open question whether philosophy exists or not. The problem with the latter view, of course, replicates, in its structure, the sort of arguments we've already considered in connection with the conditions of philosophy. That is, it tacitly begins with the actuality of philosophy, then forecloses its beginning in absorbing actuality into the dyad of 'possible' or 'impossible,' the latter indicating, on such a logic, a type of necessity (if it is 'impossible,' then it must necessarily be so). But this is precisely the situation of the sort of 'metaphilosophical' account (the Logical Empiricists and Wittgenstein come most readily to mind) that seeks to establish the logical 'impossibility' of philosophy. It is, in fact, a deep-seated flaw of all 'idealisms' following in the wake of Kant.

Kant himself, of course, famously claimed to have 'rationally' assayed the 'limits of pure Reason.' Of course, he never questioned and always assumed the actuality of Reason (and philosophy), but he immediately translated this into the question of the 'limits' of Reason and sought these limits in the 'transcendental conditions' of experience and consciousness. In dividing his response into the (transcendental logical) necessity of the formal structures underlying experience and the (transcendental logical) possibilities presented by the empirical content of experience, he foreclosed (along with the analytic *a posteriori*) any further thematization of the *actual* conditions underlying philosophy itself. Although it would seem to follow from Kant's claim about the limits of Reason that philosophy itself would be limited (since he seems to have equated the 'work of philosophy' with rational activity itself), nowhere does he seem to draw this conclusion. The problem, of course, was that the limits of Reason, when viewed from the perspective of his transcendental idealism, were understood solely in terms of possibility and necessity. That philosophy itself might have *actual* limits or conditions was a question foreclosed along with the analytic *a posteriori*.

If we lift this Kantian foreclosure (as I have argued we must), then we must begin with the actuality of philosophy and therefore the actuality of its basic conditions, to deny which, as we've already seen, results in logical contradiction even on Kantian terms. Is doing so thus to adopt a 'metaphilosophical' position? In the sense that these actual conditions constitute the limits of any philosophy, it is. It does, that is, make claims applicable to any and all instances of philosophy. However, once we begin with actuality, this requires no step into some 'extra-' or 'non-philosophical' space but rather enlarges the 'space of philosophy' beyond the limits imposed upon it by Kantian transcendental philosophy and its successors. However, this view itself also unfolds under the same actual conditions as all other philosophical views, with the difference that it explicitly acknowledges them while others often do not.

What might such a view be called? On the one hand, it suggests that all philosophies fully occupy the field constituted by the basic conditions and do so each in its own unique way (somewhat analogous, perhaps, to 'cultures,' where each is a unique 'functional totality' with respect to the basic conditions of physical and social life which they must accommodate.) In this sense, its outlook is markedly pluralistic. On the other hand, various philosophies territorialize the space constituted by the conditions in ways that tend to intensify certain regions while muting, occluding, or suppressing others. There are, that is, more and less forceful, rich, and nuanced ways in which the field of philosophy can be occupied.

Four important considerations in this connection have already been mentioned. The first is that every philosophy possesses its own 'internal logic' which can sometimes be violated. (I remember Paul Weiss once claiming, in response to a question about his reading of Aristotle, that "if Aristotle didn't say that, he should have.") That is, philosophers can and do sometimes violate the 'internal logic' of their own views, creating a gap or rupture within their own territorialization of the space of philosophy. This need not be grounds for discrediting an entire view, but it may also lead to a re-territorialization and a revised or even new philosophical view. Second, although (for reasons we'll take up in a later chapter) there can be no view in which any or all of the conditions are fully and explicitly reflected, philosophies differ in the degree to which partial reflections occur. In general, the degree to which a philosophy reflects upon the basic conditions enhances its force and fecundity as a philosophy. Third, every philosophy shares the field with others that have territorialized it with different regional emphases and intensities. This opens the possibility for productive exchanges among positions which both serve to clarify the contours of given positions and suggest areas of limitation or lack of sufficient intensity. Finally, all philosophies unfold in a space bounded by other spaces or fields that are 'non-' or 'extra-philosophical.' A philosophy gains in intensity, richness, and nuance to the degree that it succeeds in articulating the limits separating philosophy itself from its 'others.' A philosophy, that is, must, at its most forceful, be capable of differentiating itself from other such fields as science, art, and religion.

If one must name the present view, then, I would suggest that it be called 'trans-critical actualism.' The first part should be clear enough: it is 'trans-critical' because it begins with Kant's Critical Philosophy and arrives, via a consideration of analytic *a posteriori* judgments, at the fundamental conditions of philosophy itself. This also, perhaps, retains at least some connection with Kant's insistence on the necessary character of the 'grounds' or structures involved. 'Actualism' may be more problematic, since it might naturally be taken as synonymous with 'realism.' To equate it with realism, however, would be problematic for two reasons. First, 'realism' usually functions as the opposite of 'idealism,' and, second, 'idealism' itself can be understood either as a metaphysical position (such as some forms of Platonism) or an epistemological position (as in the cases of such thinkers as Kant, Hegel, and early Husserl). I want to claim, however, that, within the field constituted by the basic conditions, 'idealism' of any of these varieties is, in fact, a viable option as a particular sort of configuration of the basic conditions (as, therefore, is 'realism'). By calling my view 'actualism,' I want to emphasize that it is neither, *per se*, a metaphysical nor an epistemological position, either of which would be an element of a particular territorialization of the field of philosophy. Rather, by this term, I want to indicate that the conditions of philosophy are neither entirely 'mind-' or 'consciousness-dependent' but 'actual' and that they intrude upon the enterprise of philosophy in ways that can neither be entirely controlled by nor fully reflected within philosophy itself. I want, that is, to emphasize that philosophy, as either a practice, a set of texts, or a particular set of ideas or views, is actual and is based on certain actual conditions; that, as any actuality, it is contingent; and that, as any contingency, it is limited in its scope or field. Nonetheless, I want immediately to add that, once constituted, there are senses of necessity (including the logical) that play important philosophical roles both within philosophy generically considered and within particular philosophical positions.

5

Conditions and Principles

I've suggested thus far that there are three basic actual conditions for philosophy—embodied human being, signification, and ideality—and that, though their existence is contingent, they nonetheless involve a certain logical necessity within the field that they constitute. The next task is to explore some of the relations among them, which can then also be regarded as necessary in a similar sense. Formulating these necessary relations among them should result in a set of principles that can be taken as further delineations of the field of philosophy. Alternatively, employing the spatial metaphors that I've sometimes used, these principles can be viewed as a more precise mapping of the space or field of philosophy bounded by the relations among the basic conditions. Viewed in yet another way, one could regard the principles as a further elaboration of the 'content' of some fundamental analytic *a posteriori* judgments and the relations obtaining among them.

I. THE PRINCIPLE OF ASYMMETRY

We have already seen that there is a certain 'order of precedence' among the conditions. In terms of 'actual existence,' embodied human being has a certain priority. Were there no embodied human beings, philosophy would exist neither as an activity, a body of texts, or a general view or set of ideas. Once embodied human beings exist, it remains possible that, while they might be able to communicate in some rudimentary sense, they might not have developed the more complex structures that permit genuine signification. However, we also argued that once these two are (jointly) in place, the recognition of ideality is immediately necessary. So, even in this 'order of precedence,' the relations among the conditions are not logically symmetrical, since, while signification presupposes but is contingent with respect to embodied human being, ideality both presupposes the other two conditions but necessarily results when both obtain.

At least part of the reason for this logical asymmetry even in the order of precedence lies in the fact that the three conditions 'exist' in different ways. That is, while all three are 'actualities' (are, in a special sense of the term, 'real'), they constitute different 'types' of actualities.

Embodied human being is (among other things) physical. It requires a material form for its existence that depends upon other material beings and processes beyond itself. Ultimately, it is a product of forces—physical, chemical, and biological—that, working together, also constitute the mechanisms of cosmic and terrestrial evolution. As such, embodied human being is a part (indeed a quite minuscule one) of the much greater and unbounded physical whole that we ordinarily call 'nature' or 'the universe.' Embodied human being shares, at least in part, in the materiality of the universe itself and continually registers this in its very being. Embodied human being is, then, a 'contingent actuality,' in the sense that it does exist but might not have, and yet its actuality involves and, at least in part, is defined and constrained by the same physical structures governing 'nature' or 'the universe' itself. It is, so to speak, the principle point of contact and continuity with the broader physical whole of which it is a part.

Signification is a very different type of actuality. Although significational systems utilize various material means for expression and articulation, they are not essentially physical or material, as mere communication through physical gestures or sounds drawing attention to some element of the immediate physical environment would be. Often significational systems are regarded as either the primary element of or even coextensive with 'culture,' which though it can be viewed as 'material' (in a particular sense of this term), involves much more in its 'essential being.' Nonetheless, like culture itself, significational systems are very much actual, directly affecting, in their operation, material beings and processes, especially embodied human beings. In a sense, they are 'doubly contingent actualities,' since they depend for their own existence on the existence of embodied human beings and, even when this condition is met, can assume a variety of different, contingent forms. However, in their own actuality, they possess a kind of 'inner necessity' by virtue of the regularities that permit their operation as signifying systems. These regularities (which structuralists explain in terms of the fixed linkages between 'signifiers' and 'signifieds' which constitute 'signs') are themselves neither physical (or material) nor ideal, but exist more as stable relations among elements that can be physically manifested (for instance, in the form of sounds or inscriptions). A signifying system, that is, can be reduced neither to a mere set of physical elements nor to some idea (or set of them), the expression for or representation of which they are merely means. Rather, every signifying system, by virtue of its own 'internal necessity,' possesses a distinctive and actual insistence or force of its own beyond any other connection it might have to physical elements or idealities such a 'meanings' or thoughts. They are also, then, 'contingent actualities' but exist in a different mode than embodied being or ideality.

Idealities are also 'contingent actualities' but exist in yet a different mode than embodied human beings or significational systems. Like significational systems, they are 'doubly contingent,' but in an even more complex manner, since they too might not have existed but depend for their actuality on the existence of both embodied human beings *and* significational systems. However, once these two conditions obtain, their existence is itself necessary (which is not the case for significational systems in relation to embodied being). Their distinctive mode of actuality is neither physical or material nor *essentially* relational. Although idealities can and do have relations among themselves (and also to embodied beings and signficational systems), in themselves they possess a certain 'eidetic autonomy.' Consider, for example, 'meaning' in a fairly ordinary sense. While words, in the form of auditory sounds or visible inscriptions, can 'have meaning,' their 'meaning' is, in an important sense, autonomous of any particular physical sound or manner of inscription. 'Book,' 'Buch,' 'livre,' etc. all 'mean' the same thing. Likewise, while these words stand in somewhat different relations within their respective signifying systems (the English, German, and French 'natural languages'), the words are 'intertranslateable' not simply because of the relations in which each stands within its own signifying system but because they all intend a common ideality. It makes no difference if one responds that such an ideality is in turn based upon the physical processes of perception or the operations of a signifying system. There can certainly be various alternative accounts of the genesis of idealities, but the point is that their actuality is *already* recognized as different and other than the starting-points of such accounts.

It is worth noting that, while the philosophical tradition has often attributed to idealities many other properties than I do here—universality, eternality, stability, etc.—these are not essential to recognizing the fundamental difference between the type of actuality possessed by idealities and that of the other conditions. On the minimal view presented here, idealities are neither material nor essentially relational. Rather, we can say that they are necessary results of embodied human being employing a significational system, though irreducible to being a mere function of one, the other, or both together. If we want to claim that they 'arise' or 'emerge' from the other two conditions, we must also add that, once arisen or emerged, they possess their own autonomy and 'internal necessity' (i.e. are 'actual') that can have affects on their 'origins.' As an example, think of the idea of 'human rights.' Certainly there was time, even in the relatively brief span of human history, when such an ideality did not exist; certainly we can identify key authors who gave the words representing this idea a place in the lexicons of signifying systems; certainly this idea may have become linked to others (e.g. 'legality' and 'democracy') over time; there will likely even be a time when this ideality no longer exists (e.g. when the human race has perished as a species). But, so long as this idea has existed, its own 'inner logic' has exerted a distinctive force on and indeed changed both the material conditions of embodied human beings and the significational systems that they have employed.

To summarize, then, the three basic conditions of philosophy are asymmetrical at least in part because, although they are all, in some sense, 'contingent actualities,' they exist in different ways or modalities. Embodied human being's mode of existence is essentially bound up with physical and material processes. Significational systems exist as relations among elements that may be material or physical, without the systems thereby themselves being physical or material. Idealities exist as immaterial termini of other processes (which can be material and relational) but then possess an autonomy (in the form of their own 'inner logic') which permits them to affect and influence physical and significational processes.

This means that the field of philosophy cannot be regarded as a unidimensional or homogenous 'space.' It is not as if the three basic conditions represent three points on a plane defining a homogenous space bounded by the lines connecting them. Rather, each condition possesses its own distinctive sort of actuality and, so to speak, exerts its particular sort of force across the space. Or, more accurately, the space itself is constituted by three different types of forces, that is, distinctive ways in which the conditions 'actualize themselves' and interact with one another. However, this is not to say that the space so formed is somehow discontinuous, as if within it there were natural boundaries between the region of one force and another. Rather, it means that any 'point' in the space will always possess some 'degree' of all three forces. So, to speak in this way, 'points' that lack one or more of the coordinates no longer occupy the 'space' of philosophy; they will constitute a 'position' in some space or field other than philosophy.

There are two important practical implications of this for philosophy. Every philosophy either implies or explicitly adopts a position with respect to embodied human being, signification, and ideality. That is, every philosophy at least exemplifies a stance with respect to our finite and fragile embodied condition; whether it states this explicitly or not, it implies something about the status of human life and experience (though in some cases we may have to work quite hard to see what this is). Further, every philosophy at least stands as an example of a particular relation to language and signification, of what it means to interact meaningfully with other human beings. Though what a philosopher says about signification and how she articulates this might sometimes be at odds, this too represents a particular way of 'relating to language.' Finally, as Hegel said, every philosophy is, at base, an idealism, at least in the sense that if it is linguistically articulated by an embodied being it will, so to speak, generate 'idealities.' Even the most committed 'anti-idealist' or 'eliminative materialist' will be an embodied finite being that articulates a view (an ideality!) that states something both beyond a description of her idiosyncratic embodied condition and the particular signifying system that she is employing.

This also implies that, since all the conditions are necessary to define the field of philosophy but each possesses a distinct and irreducible sort of actuality, it is not possible to account for the others by exclusively addressing just one. True, every philosophy adopts a particular position or standpoint that may locate it relatively closer to one condition than to others (see the later point following). But, due to the differences among the conditions, it is a delusion to think, for example, that a philosophy can 'resolve all problems' about embodied existence or ideality solely through the analysis of significational systems or language. The same goes for views that proceed from the other conditions.

II. THE PRINCIPLE OF INTERNAL COMPLEXITY

While each condition of philosophy is a 'contingent actuality' with its own distinctive type of existence, each also, considered in itself (to the degree that this is possible), is internally complex. By this, I mean that such actualities are not themselves like simple 'points' or inert 'objects.' Rather, each possesses its own internal dynamic; to say that it is an 'actuality' rather than just an 'existent' is to emphasize its own set of internal forces and their inter-*actions*.

Embodied human being provides a ready example. What we call our 'bodies' are not just inert things like mathematical points or simple units, but involve a number of complex processes—digestion, circulation, excretion, cell multiplication, reproduction, nerve transmission, and so on. While most of these remain unconscious in the course of our performing ordinary conscious actions, they are nonetheless real and continue on their own courses as we sit, walk, perform tasks, and interact with others. Indeed, they continually exert their own characteristic forces upon the larger scale intentional actions that we perform. So, although we can speak of our 'body' as a single entity, we realize at the same time that its actuality consists of multiple structures and processes, each continually contributing its characteristic force to the whole.

Significational systems have a similar character. Despite certain structuralist accounts that appear to suggest otherwise, significational systems are actualities involving their own distinctive type of structures and processes. Although these can appear to be only fixed structures when described or analyzed, their actual mode of existence consists in their active deployment. Every structure, that is, whether syntactic, semantic, pragmatic, or otherwise, is the 'abstract' or 'ideal' aspect of what is essentially a sort of act or event. A significational system is not, then, merely a set of structural relations but rather a set of acts or processes structured in certain necessary ways. Like embodied beings, significational systems, as actualities, involve a complex array of (also often unconscious) processes or forces, interacting in specific ways to produce 'acts of signification.' Phonemes must be formed into words, words must be 'selected' from a 'lexicon,' they must be ordered into phrases and sentences, these must be accommodated to contexts, and so on. It is neither the case that we construct and use signifying systems nor that they somehow deploy or 'bespeak' us, but that all signification requires the cooperative coming together of significational structure and the act or event that mobilizes it and constitutes it as an actuality.

Finally, idealities also possess complex internal structures. Deleuze and Guattari, in *What is Philosophy?*, claimed that all concepts are internally complex and, on this, I think, they are right. Every concept (which is a kind of ideality) is a sort of 'force field' that possesses its own internal contours. To employ their example, Descartes' 'Cogito,' when regarded as a fundamental philosophical concept, is not a mere geometrical point or simple 'existent,' but lays out and occupies its own 'plane of immanence' (as they put it) with a set of 'intensities' different, for example, than Leibniz's 'monadic souls' or Kant's 'transcendental unity of apperception.' The internal dynamics of each of these then extend their trajectories in multiple directions that link them with other concepts, thus forming a network of concepts that, together, constitute a view or position that we can call 'Cartesian,' 'Leibnizian,' or 'Kantian.'

The upshot is that, in all three cases, the contingent actualities that make up the conditions for philosophy are internally complex. Further, each possesses its own distinctive 'inner logic,' its own characteristic type of 'necessity.' This, too, has important practical implications for understanding the nature of philosophy. Philosophers have often been tempted to posit some single common element or constituent of one of its conditions—often an ideality—as its basic ground or end. (One thinks immediately of Plato's 'Good,' the medieval conception of God, Spinoza's 'Substance,' and Hegel's 'Absolute Concept.') But invariably and necessarily, such a philosophical 'One' proves to be so internally complex that its intended unity is undermined by a virtually limitless multiplicity of concepts (further idealities) produced by its articulation as well as by the limitations of any embodied finite being to comprehend it. As Plato early on showed in the *Parmenides*, if 'Being is One,' then not only can we not express it (since any statement that we make about it will generate an 'Other') but it can't even be thought by finite beings (since, in fact, they can't themselves be 'beings' on such a supposition). We might, then, say that 'philosophical monism' is only a 'virtual position,' an 'impossible possibility' that is undermined by the actual conditions of its own articulation. Although one might try to maintain a monism by a hyper-emphasis on ideality, this will mean suppressing embodied being and signification to the point where, under their forces, it will either break apart or land us in a space other than philosophy—mysticism, perhaps. To call a philosophy 'monistic,' then, can only indicate something relative, perhaps to other philosophies that are 'less so.' But it cannot occur as an actual philosophical position. The same considerations apply to 'univocity,' which is simply 'monism' translated to the register of signification.

The same, however, can be said of 'pluralism,' at least if this indicates the possibility (or actuality) of an unlimited number of beings, types of beings (or ways of speaking of them). To claim that 'being is many' or is 'predicated in many ways' already implies some specific, unitary standpoint from which such a claim is made, a standpoint capable of surveying beings or their various types and concluding that they are 'many.' But the standpoint is itself a 'one' capable of 'gazing' over the rest of 'being' and concluding that it is multiple. Every 'pluralism' therefore assumes a 'monism' at its basis, just as every 'monism' introduces a 'pluralism' in its articulation.

The real practical implication for philosophy is that terms like 'monism' and 'pluralism,' 'univocity' and 'pluravocity,' and 'idealism' and 'realism,' not only fail effectively to sort or distinguish philosophies from one another but serve to reduce the actual internal complexities involved in any philosophical position and ultimately obscure our view of the unique ways in which every philosophy constitutes and occupies the field opened by philosophy's basic conditions. That is, every philosophy is, necessarily, both a 'monism' and a 'pluralism,' is both 'univocal' and 'plurivocal,' and is both a 'realism' and an 'idealism.' If such terms are useful at all, then it is only to call attention to the particular sort of emphasis characteristic of a given philosophy in relation to others. They are, that is, purely relational terms within a certain limited type of signifying system and thus obscure as much (if not more) about any philosophies to which they are applied as they succeed in revealing. They should be used sparingly and only as very provisional ways of accessing the actual complexity of any philosophical view.

III. THE PRINCIPLE OF INTERREFLECTEDNESS

The basic conditions are asymmetrical with respect to one another and exist in different ways or modes; they also possess their own distinctive types of internal complexity. However, they also function together to constitute a single space or field, though one the internal contours of which can be shaped and occupied in different ways. The reason why they can, together, form a unitary field lies in the fact that the internal complexity of each is continually impinged upon and reflected in that of the others.

As actualities, the internal forces constituting each condition reach across the entire field all the way to the others. As a result, certain structural features of each condition are reflected in each of the others, resulting in a sort of reciprocity or 'interreflectedness' among the conditions. As a result of such relations among them, there are certain (though, as we will later see, partial) correspondences or homologies among the conditions that serve to unify the field of philosophy in determinate ways while leaving its contours open in others.

Although our later discussion will reveal considerably more internal complexity within each condition and hence more complex interrelations among them, we can illustrate this principle by considering a relatively simple set of general correspondences. We can begin with the fact that two well-recognized features of embodied human existence are space and time. To be an embodied human being involves, among many other things, being located at some determinate position within a greater array of other objects with their own locations and living or acting at some determinate moment (or series of moments), the present, within a broader continuum that includes past and future series. The embodiment (which includes consciousness) of human beings serves as an index with respect to which other things are regarded as, for example, 'closer' or 'further away' in space and 'earlier,' 'later,' or 'coexistent' in time. Although space and time are not opposed in the more logical way in which some other determinations might be (such as 'white' and 'black' or 'animate' and 'inanimate'), and they do interact in dynamic and important ways (more on this later), it is at least clear that space and time are different in crucial ways and constitute a type of difference that bars one from being fully reduced to the other. The difference between them, then, is neither 'purely logical' nor 'merely empirical' (as Kant so firmly insisted on both scores), but constitutes one of the actual conditions of embodied human existence.

This difference between space and time with respect to embodied existence is both reflected in and articulated by another important and irreducible (though again neither 'purely logical' nor 'merely empirical') difference within signification. As such poststructuralists as Derrida, Lyotard, and Foucault have most recently highlighted, signification occurs in both spoken and written modes. While the two can and do interact in important ways and stand in complex relations with one another, they are nonetheless different in crucial respects that prevent any final reduction of one to the other. Perhaps most important, the spoken mode of signification exists primarily as a temporal event, presupposing the temporal co-presence of the speaker and other hearers and unfolding within a determinate period of time. By contrast, the written mode of signification is primarily spatial, does not presuppose the temporal co-presence of the author and her readers, but permits (at least in principle) the relevant communication at any time that the written text is (usually spatially) present for a reader.

Leaving aside any asymmetries between the 'time/space' difference for embodied beings and the 'spoken/written' difference for significational actions or systems, the most important point to notice is that there are important ways in which each difference relates to and reflects the other. The difference between space and time fundamental to embodied human experience parallels and is reflected by the difference between written and spoken modes of signification. Viewed from the perspective of embodied being, there are two corresponding modes of signification precisely because there are two modalities governing any embodied experience. However, it is also true that we embodied beings are capable of distinguishing the spatial from the temporal aspects of our experience (at least in part) because this duality of modes occurs within signification itself. Certainly terms indicating the difference between spatial locations and temporal differentiations can occur within both spoken and written modes of signification, so it is not the case, for example, that the difference between spatial and temporal modes of embodied experience requires the development of systems of writing. But it does seem, through an admittedly more complex chain of connections, that any recognition and articulation of the differences and asymmetries between space and time require the existence of forms of signification sufficiently complex to assume both spoken and written forms. It is not so much a question of which form is 'prior'; rather it is the question of the potential convertibility of spoken into written form (and vice versa) providing a significational system rich enough to allow the explicit articulation of the differences between spatial and temporal experience for embodied beings.

These differences between the temporal and spatial experience of embodied beings and spoken and written forms of signification together influence, are reflected at, and in turn are affected by a parallel difference at the level of idealities. The most common way of conceiving and describing idealities in the Western philosophical tradition has been in terms of structure. Beginning with Plato, the sort of ideality that he calls *eidos* has commonly been thought of and translated as 'form.' Though Plato's own account is considerably more complex than just this, a recurrent feature of almost any account of *eidei* occurring in the dialogues is an emphasis on their formality in contrast to the materiality or content provided by the senses. From this point of view, a Platonic idea constitutes the underlying and essential structure of the multiple sensible and typically material things that 'participate' in or 'instantiate' the idea. To 'know' a chariot, for example, involves apprehending the essential structural features shared by all particular examples of chariots: that they have wheels, are drawn by draft animals, provide means for control by the charioteer, and so on. Although Aristotle seems to disagree with Plato on the separability or relative autonomy of such structures in relation to particular sensible things, he follows Plato in recognizing a crucial difference between the structure of a thing ('form') and that which serves to individuate the thing and constitutes it as a discrete sensible particular ('matter'). From there, this structural interpretation of idealities continues through the entire history of philosophy, from medieval 'essences,' through modern interpretations of mathematical and other 'abstract objects,' to Kantian categories, Husserlian 'ideas,' and well beyond.

However, already in Plato, there are suggestions of an alternative way of considering idealities. In such dialogues as the *Parmenides*, *Sophist*, and *Timaeus*, Plato entertains the thought that the ideas might also be considered either as parts of a broader *process* of thinking or the unfolding of a 'world-soul,' that is, that, like animate creatures or nature itself, they might have a dynamic life of their own. Aristotle, perhaps, appropriates this aspect of Platonic thought in the *Metaphysics* (among other ways) when he treats 'formal causes' in terms of *energeia* and *entelechy* as governing the dynamic movement from potentiality to actuality (as in processes of organic growth). This 'process-oriented' presentation of ideality, and its attendant contrast with 'structure-oriented' accounts, continues to reverberate through the philosophical tradition (to cite only a few instances) from Plotinus's doctrine of the emanation of ideas, through the medieval notion of universals as products of the divinity's thought-processes and self-revelation in nature, Spinoza's contrast between '*natura naturata*' and '*natura naturans*,' Kant's treatment of the relation between the 'transcendental unity of apperception' and the categorical structures to which it gives rise, Schelling's dynamic philosophy of nature, Hegel's dialectical logic and the system that it governs, and, later, the philosophical views of Bergson, Whitehead, and Deleuze.

Whatever we may hold about the details of this, it seems clear that two different and irreducible views or interpretations of ideality, which we can call the structural and processive, interact in multiple and complex ways throughout the history of philosophy and constitute an important part of its overall texture. From the perspective of embodied being, this difference corresponds, in important (though partial) ways to the embodied experiential difference between time and space. To regard idealities as structures is to view them principally in spatial terms, while to regard them as processes is to consider them principally within a temporal framework. Reciprocally, views that tend to emphasize the structural aspect of idealities will tend to underwrite explorations of embodied being that emphasize its spatial aspects, just as views that emphasize the processive aspect of idealities will do the same with respect to its temporal aspects.

A similar correspondence applies when idealities are considered from the standpoint of significational systems. The differences between written and spoken modes of signification correspond in important (though partial) ways to that between structural and processive views of idealities. To begin to see how this is so, let's take a familiar example. Some idea or thought about something occurs to me. At first, it is relatively vague and inchoate and, within the temporal flow of the 'internal monologue' of my thinking, I try various ways of expressing it and, perhaps, explore some of its implications or consequences. Eventually, however, I may come to transform some portions of my 'internal (basically spoken) monologue' into written form. In converting the temporal fluidity of my initial thought into writing, my initial idea comes to 'exist' in a spatial medium, which lends definition to its contours and renders it more specific and determinate. Writing, that is, serves to convert the original fluidity of my thought process into discrete structural elements—names, words, statements, sets of statements, etc.—whose relations among one another form further structures constituting a rudimentary 'logic' implicit in my initial idea. In turn, this elicits further thought regarding these relations, which may in turn require further written articulation in order to be made more determinate. The result is that, while my original idea arose within the temporal thought process of my internal (spoken) monologue, it only becomes more defined and determinate when it is converted into the more spatial form of writing and, in turn, remains 'alive' when its written formulation is further reflected upon.

However, even in this admittedly highly simplified account of a much more complex phenomenon, crucial differences between the processive and structural aspects of idealities remain—the 'conversion' of one aspect to the other is never complete, any more than spoken modes of signification can be completely converted into written modes or vice versa. To highlight the fact that an ideality emerges only within a broader process of thought necessarily suppresses its more determinate structural features, just as foregrounding its structural contours must necessarily arrest its origin and development within the temporal processes of thinking. In a sense, then, an ideality is always, and at the same time, *both* process and structure, but to focus upon its processive aspect tends to blur its contours and conceal its 'inner logic,' while to focus upon its structural aspect tends to obscure its origin and development within the ongoing life of thought.

This fundamental duality of process and structure within idealities, which reflects those of time and space for embodied being and speaking and writing for significational systems, has many and far-reaching implications for the field of philosophy as well as the specific historical philosophies that have occupied and territorialized it. For now, I'll only note that this explains, in part, why philosophy, as the German Idealists especially emphasized, must always aspire to assuming a 'systematic' (structural) form, even though there can be no single 'final form' that it can assume if it is to remain a living enterprise. Every philosophy, that is, possesses (implicitly or more explicitly) a 'systematic form,' its own 'internal logic,' but this form will always fail to fully capture its significance as a living process of thought. This is why, however hard they may have labored on a particular way of articulating an idea or position in writing, philosophers tend to return to and rework all or parts of what they've written. (This goes even for Hegel!) Even so, specific articulations can be sufficiently determinate at any given point to permit philosophers, when pressed, to defend a particular formulation of their thought in the face of critics whom they regard as 'having gotten it wrong.'

Put in the broadest terms, then, any philosophy involves idealities that must be regarded as 'structured processes.' However, because of the inherent duality of space and time within the condition of embodiment and speaking and writing within that of signification, the notion of a 'structured process' is itself unstable and dynamic. Especially where speaking predominates as the mode of signification, idealities (and ultimately entire philosophies) will appear more as unfolding and flexible processes and time (or, more broadly, history) will tend to serve as the entrée to questions about embodied existence. Where writing predominates as the significational mode, they will appear more as logical or systematic structures or matrices and spatiality (or, more broadly, a sort of 'philosophical geography') will tend to serve as the dominant theme in considering embodied existence.

IV. THE PRINCIPLE OF POSITIONALITY (THE STANDPOINT)

The term 'field' is a suggestive one for thinking about philosophy in a generic sense. To begin with, we often speak of philosophy, in a very straightforward and naïve way, as a specific 'field' of study, research, publication, academic organization, and so forth. In so doing, we assume that it is distinguishable from other such 'fields'—physics, chemistry, psychology, economics, history, and so on. But this implies that each field has its own intrinsic and determinate contours and limits. In the case of philosophy, we've argued that these contours and limits are constituted by three basic actual conditions—embodied being, significational systems, and idealities—and the complex relations among them. In this more fundamental sense, the 'field' of philosophy can initially be regarded as a sort of 'space' or 'territory' bounded by these conditions and their relations. However, at a still more basic level, we must recognize that each condition is itself 'internally dynamic' and stands in further dynamic relations with the other conditions. It is, so to speak, ultimately a 'field of forces,' a 'force field,' the internal motion or activity of which lays out, constitutes, and territorializes the more abstract idea of a 'space' or 'plane.' The term 'field' is thus a rich one that unites the ideas of philosophy as a specific discipline, a region of human thought and activity, and a complexly interrelated set of dynamic forces.

This, of course, only serves to characterize philosophy generically, which is to say that it is not adequate to account for or describe any particular, actual philosophical view or (as we often say) 'position.' In fact, there can be no such thing, no actuality, that might count as a 'generic philosophy,' some master account of philosophy that could include all particular actual philosophies within it (as, arguably, Hegel attempted to provide). Rather, common language is itself quite accurate in speaking of philosophy in terms of an array or multiplicity of various 'positions.' Within the generic (one might even be tempted to say 'virtual') 'field' of philosophy, every actual philosophy constitutes a particular positional point or, perhaps, region within the field.

Actual philosophies, then, are not 'particulars,' in the sense of 'instantiations' of some 'generic' or 'universal' idea of philosophy; rather, they are 'singularities.' By this, I mean to suggest several things.

First, there is no single, overarching, definitive, or '*a priori*' idea or concept of philosophy of which various actual philosophies would be particular instances or examples. Rather, every actual philosophy, in a sense, generates *and* instantiates its own 'idea' of what philosophy is. It may, and often does, go on to assert its own idea of philosophy as normative for anything else that might qualify as philosophy, but this is a sort of 'extra-philosophical' claim not part of its own actual content. Likewise, other philosophies may take a certain previous view of philosophy as normative for itself, as all philosophical 'neo-movements' do—Neo-Platonism, Neo-Cartesianism, Neo-Kantianism, etc.—but, again, such an assumption is, in a sense, pre- or extra-philosophical. Rather, every actual philosophy is a unique or 'singular' way of interpreting, combining, and existing among the basic conditions and negotiating their interrelations, a unique point or position, so to speak, in the field opened by the dynamic interplay of the basic conditions themselves.

Second, this means that there can be no such thing as a 'view from nowhere,' a notion that Thomas Nagel develops in a book by the same name. Every actual philosophy is situated within and adopts a specific viewpoint regarding the basic actual conditions, which, because they are actual or real, cannot be eliminated or reduced by any further argument, method, or procedure. True, actual philosophies can claim to ignore, dispute the relevance of, or 'bracket' one or more of the basic conditions, but, if such a position remains within the field of philosophy, this will, at best, be more of a deferment or repression than an elimination, reduction, or foreclosure. Of course, one or more of the conditions *can* be eliminated or reduced, but then the philosophical position becomes transferred into some other field (religion, science, or art, for example) defined by a different set or configuration of conditions; it will no longer be philosophy, however much it may be relevant to it in various respects.

Third, we should not take the claim that every actual philosophy is a singularity to imply either that it is impossible for philosophies to be related to one another in complex ways or that we cannot productively compare them or group them together. We should recall that the conditions are themselves internally complex as are the ways in which they interreflect one another. This means that the 'nodes' at which these forces cross (i.e. specific actual philosophies) will themselves be internally complex. Though I've suggested that every actual philosophy is a singularity, this should not be taken to imply that it is 'point-like' in the sense of bare simplicity or lacking in parts or further determination. Rather, every actual philosophy is a specific and qualitatively unique combination of forces which also run through and intersect at other positions, each relatively close to or distant from others. We may, for various purposes, choose to view relatively close positions as forming 'movements' or 'isms,' or we may contrast particular philosophies or groups of them with others, but there are dangers inherent in both procedures. To regard groups of philosophies under some general rubric like 'Platonism' or 'Kantianism' may obscure important differences among them, just as contrasting different philosophies or 'movements' may blur important similarities. At the most fundamental level, however, actual philosophies are most significant for the unique though always complex position that they assume with respect to the basic conditions. How they are related to or differ from others, at least in this respect, is a secondary matter, however much such comparisons or contrasts may help us understand a singular position's unique force and effectivity.

The 'Principle of Positionality' thus implies that every actual philosophy represents the unique though complex manner in which an embodied and finite human being articulates (signifies) its singular position in relation to various sorts of idealities. Another way of expressing this is to say that every actual philosophy constitutes a singular 'standpoint' with respect to finite embodiment, signification, and ideality. The notion of a 'standpoint' with respect to philosophy is one that has a long history in the tradition. While the term first appeared most conspicuously in the philosophies of Spinoza and Leibniz, the problem to which it refers can be traced at least as far back as Plato. Spinoza distinguished between the 'finite standpoint' of human beings and an 'infinite' or 'divine standpoint,' '*sub specie aeternitatis*,' as he put it. Leibniz also invoked a fundamental difference between the 'finite standpoint,' for which most truths were contingent 'truths of fact,' and the 'infinite' or 'divine standpoint,' for which all true statements, underwritten by the 'Principle of Sufficient Reason,' were necessary 'truths of reason.' Especially from Leibniz, the notion of 'standpoint,' under important revisions, entered the Kantian vocabulary, indicating several differences including that between the 'transcendental' and the 'empirical,' the 'phenomenal' and 'noumenal,' and the 'theoretical' and 'practical' standpoints. In fact, the notion of standpoint was so crucial to Kant's Critical Philosophy that it issued in an extensive debate among his immediate followers and critics under the title of '*Standpunktsphilosophie*.' The issues involved in this debate were subsequently taken up by the German Idealists, and continued into the work of, among others, Husserl, Heidegger, Bergson, and, today, certain strands in feminist philosophy and the philosophy of the social sciences.

The basic question posed by the notion of 'standpoint,' put in the terms we've been employing, concerns how it is possible to access or know transindividual or universal 'truths' (or other such idealities) from the finite perspective of embodied human being. With Spinoza and Leibniz, this was, at bottom, a metaphysical question, posed in terms of the relation between an infinite being and finite beings grounded in it. Since they regarded the infinite being (God) as both logically demonstrable and ontologically prior to finite beings, the question turned upon how the 'truths' known by the divinity and instantiated in its creation were accessible from the standpoint of finite beings. In a sense, then, they proceeded 'top down': given the totality of the 'divine standpoint' as ontological ground, they defined 'finite standpoints' as its various delimitations. In the end, 'finite standpoints' were understood in terms of the limitations of their access to the 'infinite standpoint, '*sub specie aeternitatis*,' that is, God's own standpoint.

Kant dramatically altered these contours by three interrelated claims. First, he insisted that all knowledge was strictly limited to 'possible objects of experience,' that which could appear in space and time. Second, he argued that space and time were themselves 'pure forms of intuition' rooted in the basic constitution of human consciousness and had no meaning beyond this sphere. Finally, he attempted to show that there could be no logically sound proof for the existence of a divine being. This last undermined any ontological idea of a 'divine standpoint,' fundamental for such thinkers as Spinoza and Leibniz, and implied that the only philosophically relevant standpoint could be the finite one of spatio-temporally existing human beings. Of course, finite beings could conceive, in a general way ('speculatively'), of a divine or infinite standpoint, but this could provide no ontological ground for addressing questions of truth or human knowledge. The result was what has often been called Kant's 'finitism.' This transformed the question of standpoint from a metaphysical to an epistemological issue. From the perspective of Kant's Critical Philosophy, the primary question became one, not of the 'ultimate nature of reality' ('*sub specie aeternitatis*'), that is, metaphysics, but of the fundamental conditions of human knowledge, that is, epistemology. Put simply, Kant transformed the question of what is into that of what can be known. For us actual embodied human beings, then, there was, in the broadest sense, only one philosophically relevant standpoint, that bounded by the spatio-temporal conditions of our own finite existence.

However, within the contours of finite human existence, Kant then reintroduced the notion of standpoint within his finitist philosophy to distinguish between an 'empirical standpoint,' which was concerned with the contingent 'facts' of experience, and a 'transcendental standpoint,' from which the necessary structures underlying all possible experience could be mapped and clarified. Further, he sometimes utilized the notion of standpoint to distinguish between what he regarded as the two divisions of philosophy, the 'theoretical' (concerned with the principles underlying human knowledge) and the 'practical' (dealing with the normative principles governing human action). As I mentioned above, this 'proliferation of standpoints' soon led to a lengthy and complicated discussion of the whole idea of 'standpoint' among his immediate followers, including Reinhold, Fichte, and the later German Idealists.

This phase of the discussion about standpoints finally culminated in Hegel. Often specifically referring to the various ideas of 'standpoint' occurring in Kant, Hegel, beginning with the Jena *Phenomenology* and continuing in his later system, attempted a final resolution of the entire issue by a dual maneuver, a 'both-and' or 'have your cake and eat it too' sort of approach. On the one hand, in the Jena *Phenomenology*, he insisted upon the ubiquity of the question of a philosophical standpoint. Employing a sort of 'progressive finitist' procedure from 'the ground up,' Hegel attempted to show that every finite philosophical claim or stance with regard, for example, to knowledge, ethics, politics, art, religion, and even philosophy represented a particular 'standpoint' from which all others were viewed. So, in one sense, Hegel proliferated and complicated the notion of standpoint well beyond anything his predecessors might have imagined. Every aspect of human experience or thought implied and must be articulated from its own distinctive standpoint. However, Hegel, in the same work, also insisted that this multiplicity of standpoints was ordered in a hierarchical manner, which he explicated according to an underlying schema (later called 'dialectic') which presented them as 'moments' of a single developmental process. On this schema, earlier standpoints were 'more abstract' (in the sense of less internally complex) than later ones, while later standpoints were 'more concrete' by virtue of including the structural features ('concepts' or 'determinations') of earlier standpoints within themselves. In this sense, every standpoint (except the first, 'Sense Certainty') was, in effect, a 'standpoint of standpoints,' that is, a standpoint from which all preceding standpoints could be viewed 'in themselves' as well as in their ordered relations with one another.

For reasons that we won't explore here, Hegel concluded the *Phenomenology* with the claim that this process must ultimately arrive at a final, 'absolute standpoint,' one which 'included' all others within it and could fully survey them in their relations with one another. The 'content' of the standpoint of 'absolute knowing' or 'the absolute Concept' was thus all other standpoints and its 'form' was the underlying structure of their relations among themselves. Hegel identified this 'absolute standpoint' with that of philosophy itself. We might say, then, that Hegel articulated an idea of the 'standpoint of philosophy' that was a 'view from everywhere.' From this panoptic perspective, all (and it was still a great deal!) that remained to be done was to articulate the conceptual structure operating within the various lesser standpoints though not yet explicitly thematized by them. This, in fact, would be the task of his philosophical system, beginning with the basic concepts of logic, moving to their 'objectification' in nature, and concluding with their reappropriation in the human and cultural realm of 'spirit' (*Geist*).

Where, then, did Hegel leave the original question about 'standpoint'? Put simply, Hegel, while accepting Kant's critique of the transcendent standpoint of what Hegel himself (along with Kant) sometimes called the 'old metaphysics,' attempted to show that all finite standpoints, when thought through to their end, terminated in a single 'absolute standpoint' that he identified with that of philosophy itself. That is, while he denied the sort of immediate and direct access to a 'transcendent standpoint' in relation to which finite standpoints (by 'subtraction,' to borrow a term of Badiou's) could be specified ('top down,' as it were), he also held that such a standpoint was, in fact, the necessary result of the ordered development ('bottom up') of finite standpoints (by 'synthetic addition') in their complete unfolding. Like the 'old metaphysics,' Hegel's 'new metaphysics' (employing Kant's own phrase) required the notion of an 'absolute standpoint' as the basis of philosophy. The crucial difference was that, for Hegel, this standpoint was (in principle, at least) accessible, with sufficient 'conceptual labor,' from within any given finite standpoint. Put in another way, Hegel attempted to show that Kant's 'finitist standpoint,' sufficiently broadened and developed, must ultimately arrive at a single and synoptic 'absolute standpoint,' only from which singular position philosophy itself could then be developed.

Rather than pursue some of the many subsequent criticisms of Hegel's claim to have constructed an 'absolute standpoint,' almost exclusively in favor of some finitist but 'trans-Kantian' view, let's return instead to our 'Principle of Positionality' in relation to other views of a 'philosophical standpoint.' At one extreme is a view that holds that the proper standpoint for philosophy requires that finite embodied beings be capable of suspending or transcending their finite limitations and occupying a position which is literally 'nowhere,' hence not a 'position' at all. At the other extreme is a view that maintains that the proper standpoint of philosophy can only be the ordered totality of all other standpoints, that it is a 'view from everywhere,' and hence, again, nowhere in particular. In between these two views stands (among many others) the finitist view of Kant, who holds that the proper standpoint of philosophy is always a determinate 'somewhere' defined by the limitations imposed by our spatial and temporal being.

In one sense, the 'Principle of Positionality' implies the rejection of the two extremes and agrees with Kant (though minimally) that any philosophical standpoint must be 'somewhere.' But it departs from Kant in maintaining that multiple positions are possible, that within the field of philosophy there are 'many somewheres,' each a specific and singular position. Kant's own Critical Philosophy is one such position or standpoint, but, as we have seen in our earlier discussion, it raises and then forecloses the problem of the '*analytic a posteriori*' that, when further developed, opens directly upon the more fundamental actual conditions determining the field of philosophy itself and allowing for other and different philosophical standpoints.

Having said this, it's now necessary to amend an earlier reference to Kant's position as 'finitist.' Although it's acceptable to use such a term with respect to Kant's standpoint in relation to others that are 'non-finitist,' for example, those of Spinoza, Leibniz, Hegel, and perhaps Nagel's 'view from nowhere,' within a context that insists on there being actual conditions for any philosophy, this term is misleading. On the present view, every philosophy (regardless of whether one characterizes it as 'finitist' or 'infinitist' with respect to standpoint) must be both and more. That is, as philosophy, it is both 'finitist' as produced by an embodied and limited being, 'infinitist' (or, perhaps better, 'transfinitist') in that it necessarily involves idealities, and 'more' in that it is articulated in intersubjectively functioning significational systems that are neither 'transfinite' enough to themselves constitute idealities nor 'idiosyncratic' enough to be regarded as merely finite things or productions.

To summarize, then, every philosophy is a singular position within a field constituted and bounded by the actual conditions; this position constitutes its standpoint, of which there are many possible, both realized and unrealized. Each such standpoint implies and adopts a particular perspective on the three conditions and necessarily locates itself with respect to them, and this specific position constitutes its singularity and uniqueness. It is, of course, possible for an individual to 'adopt the standpoint' of a different position, where s/he may choose to remain or not. But here we are speaking of philosophies as singularities within a field, of which embodied beings are merely an element. But within the field itself, there is never a 'nowhere' or an 'everywhere' available from which all other positions can be judged or evaluated, only 'another somewhere,' a different position. Hegel's 'everywhere,' for instance, is, in the end, actually a 'somewhere' that he himself named 'Absolute Idealism' in contrast to other idealist positions and today we do not hesitate to refer to 'Hegelianism' as a specific philosophical position. In the case of Hegel, his position may be heavily 'skewed' towards ideality, explicitly embracing certain elements of signification, and, for the most part, repressing issues of embodied being—but this means that it is still 'somewhere' within the field of philosophy, if quite near to some of its limits.

As a 'singularity,' every philosophy is therefore, in a sense, 'finitist' with respect to the field of philosophy itself and cannot be otherwise. When some recent thinkers, like Badiou and Meillassoux, rail against 'philosophical finitism,' they have other 'intraphilosophical' issues in mind, usually pertaining to certain features of Kant's philosophy and, more broadly, the tendency to focus on consciousness, 'subjectivity,' or 'correlationism' within modern philosophy in general. But on the issue of 'finitism' with respect to the standpoint of any given philosophy itself, viewed 'generically' (as Badiou might say), all, including their own, must, in a more fundamental sense, be 'finitist.' Or, we could say, alternatively, that 'finitism' with regard to philosophy is a mute point, since there are 'finitist' and 'transfinitist' aspects of every standpoint, viewed as positions within the field defined by the actual conditions of philosophy.

DIAGRAM 2: The Field of Philosophy and its Excesses

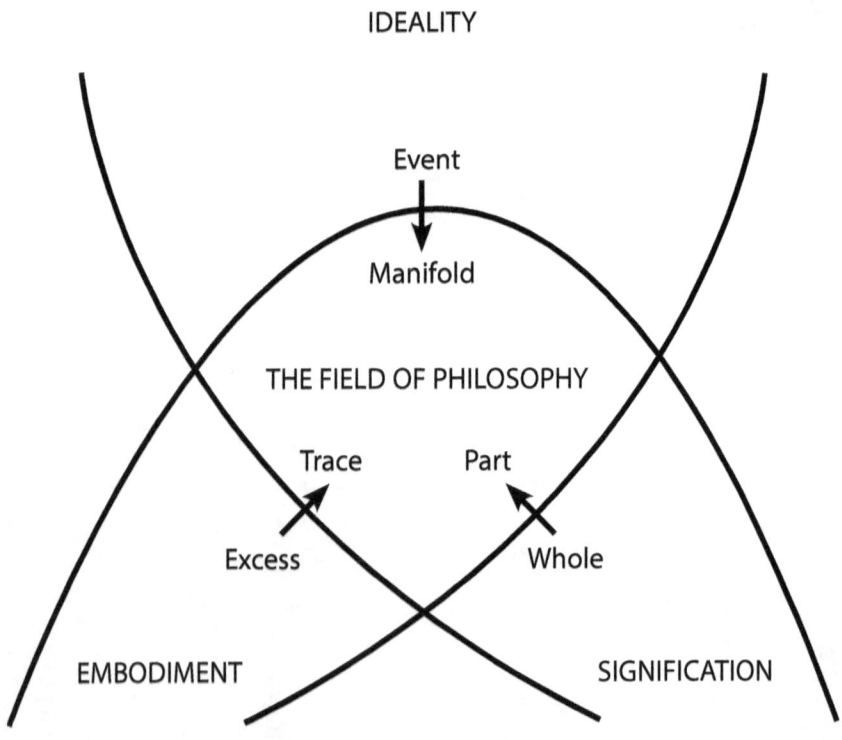

6

Limits, Excesses, and Consequences

It is crucial to realize that the three basic conditions of philosophy are 'real' or 'actual,' that they exist prior to and independently of any specific philosophical position. Neither embodied existence and its physical conditions, intersubjective systems of signification, nor idealities (at least as culturally and historically efficacious) are themselves products or creations of philosophy. Rather, any philosophical view or position is a singular way of interpreting, combining, relating, and situating itself among and with respect to the conditions. Put differently, in constituting the field of philosophy, each of the basic conditions functions like a force, each exerting its characteristic influence across the field. Every philosophical position, then, arises as a singular place of crossing, 'node,' or mode of interaction among these forces. The 'positivity' of a philosophy, its own singular force and significance, consists in the unique ways that it clarifies and illuminates the basic conditions and their relations from its own singular standpoint. In this sense, every philosophy is 'complete' in itself, an entire and integral viewpoint upon the basic conditions.

However, because the conditions are actual and, in an important sense, prior to any specific philosophical position, they also necessarily exist beyond and exceed any specific philosophical standpoint or characterization of it. Further, since each of the conditions is both irreducible to the others and possesses its own characteristic 'mode of being' or force, the ways in which each exceeds any specific philosophical interpretation or standpoint will also differ from those of the others. This means that every philosophical position is limited in (at least) three different and distinctive ways or, alternatively, that there will always be (at least) three 'remainders' or 'supplements' for any position. The task of this chapter will be to consider how each basic condition necessarily exceeds any specific philosophical attempt to characterize or account for it and then to explore some of the consequences of the excessiveness of the conditions as limitations upon any specific philosophical standpoint. (See Diagram 2)

I. EMBODIMENT

As human beings, we are all necessarily embodied. As philosophers (as well as biologists, psychologists, and, now, 'cognitive scientists') have stressed over the last two hundred years, we are, first and foremost, physical beings. In fact, it is fair to say that the repudiation of the Cartesian dualism of mind and body, perhaps the last serious philosophical attempt to distinguish and draw a firm line between the mental and physical aspects of our existence, between 'mind' or 'consciousness' and 'matter' or 'physicality,' is one of the few points upon which most modern thinkers agree, however much their views of the matter may otherwise vary. Certainly Descartes called attention to a fundamental philosophical issue to which there have been many responses (and will probably be many more), but it seems clear that, with the exception of certain religious or 'spiritualist' perspectives, there remains no serious thinker willing to defend the notion of disembodied consciousness or thought. This is as true for 'reductive materialists' as it is for such 'consciousness centered' approaches as phenomenology and psychoanalysis.

If we are embodied beings, this implies that we are also limited and finite. As physical beings, we necessarily exist in any moment at a specific place, at a determinate time, and with limited capacities to interact with our environment, including other embodied beings within it. Further, in a more extended sense, the totality of our lives is delimited by the physical processes of birth, aging, and death, all of which are themselves dependent upon and influenced by an ensemble of natural forces (proximately our immediate environment, ultimately 'the universe' itself). And were we to speak of 'consciousness' as being an 'emergent property' of our embodied state, we would also have to say that it too is limited in the things and situations of which it can become aware, the experiences that it can undergo, the objects that it both actually knows and is capable of knowing, the intentional acts that it is capable of performing, even the thoughts that it is capable of thinking.

To say that our embodied condition imposes such limits upon us, however, cannot be the whole story. For, as Kant's successors (most notably Schelling and Hegel) clearly and almost immediately responded to his own attempts to assay the limits of human knowledge and experience, the very idea of 'limit' implies both a here, 'this side of the limit,' and a beyond, that which both exceeds the limit and yet is presupposed by it. In the German Idealist tradition, this could be dealt with by claiming that 'pure Reason,' which they regarded as a 'natural human capacity,' provides us with the idea of a totality which, though 'unknowable' by finite beings, constitutes the basis for claiming that what we *can* know from our finite perspective is limited. However, if we leave the sphere of idealist discourse, which tends to privilege consciousness over actual embodied being, then a different sort of account is necessary.

However, we will see that, transposed out of the idealist idiom, there is still something important and useful to learn from the structure of this discussion among Kant and his idealist successors. It is that the actual, finite condition of embodiment already registers within itself a multiplicity, both quantitative and qualitative, of 'excesses' which, while imposing their various sorts of limitation upon it, remain necessarily opaque to it and beyond its grasp. Put in other terms, we could say that that which lies beyond the limits of our embodied being nonetheless remains in the form of never fully comprehensible or articulable 'traces' within embodied being itself. However, such 'traces' are not 'pre-given' to thought (as Reason was for the Idealists) but reveal themselves (though only always partially) within the concrete activities and discourse of embodied beings.

Another lesson, too, can be learned from the idealists. Short of introducing a ready-made, 'apriorist' distinction between Reason and Understanding (or, more generally, finite experience), we can at least point to a crucial difference between thinking, knowing, or saying *that* something is the case and specifically describing or knowing it 'in itself,' in its actual detail. We can, that is, both be aware or even know (in an appropriate sense of this term) that we are limited and that this implies an excess beyond the limit, without at the same time claiming to be able to describe or explain this excess in any complete or detailed manner. For instance, I know *that* there are many other solar systems or galaxies beyond the one in which we live, but I neither know their exact number, exactly where they are located with respect to our own, or what it would be like to inhabit them (and will never be able to). To borrow a phrase that recently received some press not long ago (though hopefully employ it in a more philosophically sophisticated way), we can say that it does make sense to distinguish between 'knowns' and 'known unknowns,' between that which we do or are able to know and that which we know that we cannot know. Somewhat analogous to the way in which Kant regarded one meaning of 'metaphysics' as a 'natural human desire,' I ultimately want to claim that these 'traces' within embodied being, these access points to 'known unknowns,' are one of the perennial sources of philosophy itself. Put in the strongest terms, were we not *finite* embodied beings but also bearing traces of finitude's excesses, there would be no philosophy. Alternatively, we could say that it is our very finite but 'trace-bearing' condition that leads us toward discourse with other embodied beings under the aegis of trans-embodied idealities—it is the very seat of what Plato called the 'wonder' that underlies all philosophy.

Although there is clearly much more to be said on this topic, I will here highlight, in this section, four ways especially important with respect to philosophy in which the 'embodiment-excess-trace' structure operates:
1. Conscious cognition and the unconscious
2. Physical 'life processes'
3. Nature or 'the universe'
4. Signification and ideality

1. Conscious Cognition and the Unconscious

Perhaps the simplest and most straightforward illustration of this idea is that of a physical scar. A scar, from, say, abdominal surgery, is a physical trace upon my body of something that happened to me at some earlier point in time. I know that I have a scar and, in general, that it resulted from a surgical procedure. But since I was anaesthetized and unconscious during this procedure, I was neither aware at the time of exactly how it came to be nor of most of the exact processes of the surgery itself. I know that certain events occurred in the operating room that day, but I cannot describe those events in any detail (much less all the factors that went into the surgeon's training in the skills for performing such an operation, and so on). My scar is, therefore, a physical trace of an excess that remains, in principle, unavailable to my own conscious cognition and knowledge.

To broaden this even more, evidence has often been cited that most events that happen to our bodies are registered by them and leave their traces in our physical musculature, internal organs, and nervous system (of which the brain is, of course, a part). Well-known examples are cases of Posttraumatic Stress Syndrome, early childhood abuse, back pains due to environmental stress, and so on. All of these can be regarded as physical traces of processes that exceed the sufferer's immediate awareness, ability to remember, or capacity to fully explain. We know *that* we're having pain, for instance, but we don't (and can't) know all the causal factors involved.

More directly relevant to typical philosophical concerns, the case of perceiving a physical object is also already involved with the same structure we have been discussing. (Much of what follows here will already be familiar to any reader of Merleau-Ponty's *Phenomenology of Perception*.) As an embodied being, I perceive an object, say, the bookshelf next to the desk at which I am writing, as another object spatially distinct from my body. As I look at it, I view it from a specific perspective which, in this case, only includes two of its sides. However, I know both that this object has other sides (that against the wall and the bottom and top surfaces) and that, if I set it away from the wall and move around it, I will be able to obtain views of other of its sides as my perspective upon it alters. However, from *any* perspective, I will always be able to say, "This is my bookcase," never (at least under ordinary circumstances) that any single perspective upon it is identical with 'my bookcase.' Ultimately, there are an unlimited number of perspectives upon my bookcase, different angles from which I can view it, different distances I can stand away from it, and so on. The point is that, as an embodied being, I can only perceive any physical object from a single perspective at a time, although it remains the same object from whatever perspective I view it. Even when I have walked completely around an object and viewed it from multiple points of view, I know that I have not exhausted the possible perspectives upon it. True, I will have joined or synthesized the various perspectives that I've experienced and can refer to this synthesis as 'my bookcase,' but this requires neither that I claim to have exhausted the possible perspectives upon it nor that I identify the bookcase itself with any single perspective. Rather, in relation to the spatially located perspective of my body, I can necessarily have only a single perspective at any given time (and perhaps retain others in memory), though I also realize that an unlimited number of others are possible that I neither have nor will ever adopt.

We can say, then, that any physical object necessarily exceeds both any immediate perception of it and any multiplicity of perspectives that may have been adopted upon it. At the same time, it is equally clear that there is something, the object itself, that is the fixed referent of all these and other possible perspectives. In a sense, then, this 'object in itself' functions as a sort of 'trace,' registered in my physical interactions with it, yet never exhausted by them. There will, that is, always be a 'perceptual remainder,' perspectives or interactions with the object that exceed anything that I have or can experience.

The same, of course, can be said of my relations with my own body, regarded as a physical object. Although I know that my eyes, for example, are the organs that allow me to see other objects (or even other parts of my body), I never see my own eyes in the process of viewing another object and can only see them at all when some external device, such as a mirror or photograph, converts them into another physical object (and then only from a very limited set of perspectives). Even my own eyes, then, function here as liminal traces and exceed any set of possible perspectives upon them.

Beginning in the later 19th century, this basic 'trace-excess' structure became dramatically expanded and generalized to include consciousness itself under what has been called 'the hermeneutics of suspicion,' the most frequently cited representatives of which were Marx, Nietzsche, and especially Freud. At the heart of this critical enterprise was the notion of 'false consciousness,' the idea that conscious cognition itself is in principle incapable of being aware of many of the actual forces that formed and influenced it. Psychoanalysis, in particular, came to express this in terms of 'the unconscious,' formed initially by the 'primary repression' which first gave rise to a sense of a discrete 'conscious self' capable of distinguishing itself from other objects and a broader 'world' beyond itself. Like perception, such accounts employ the same structure of 'trace' and 'excess.' Consciousness itself, that is, is a 'trace' of unconscious processes and structures that exceed all its powers to gain awareness of its own intentions or the underlying forces by which it developed or functions. This need not be taken to imply, as some have, that the philosophical injunction to 'know thyself' is a pointless enterprise, but should rather be taken as a warning against the possibility that this can ever be fully accomplished.

The result, then, is that, whether we adopt a 'realist' perspective and examine our perception of physical objects or a more 'idealist' or 'psychic' one and consider the broader relation between consciousness and the unconscious, we find that our own individual embodied existence necessarily involves excesses that we are in principle incapable of cognizing in detail even though their traces within us certify *that* there are, in fact, such excesses.

2. 'Life processes'

From a yet broader perspective, which equally highlights the issue of our temporal being, we also know that we underwent the process of birth, though we remain ever unconscious of its details. We must have had parents, though (as many who were adopted discover later in life) we cannot be absolutely certain who they were. We also know that we will one day die, though, as has often been pointed out, we will not actually experience our own death. Within the life that we live in between, both our birth and our death function as traces of excesses in principle beyond our immediate cognition. Heidegger, especially in *Being and Time*, explored our relations to the excesses of birth and death under the terms 'thrownness,' to indicate the excess (among others) of conditions determining our lives at birth, and 'projection,' to indicate the excess (again among others) of possibilities limited by the death that 'in itself' I cannot experience. My sense of the limitation of my possibilities resulting from being born as an embodied being and of the ultimate finality that death represents for all my 'life projects' are thus inescapable traces within my life as an embodied being of excesses that temporally have preceded and will succeed the conditions under which my 'present' life is lived.

We can, however, go even further. Within our lives, we each experience the physical processes of aging. Part of our present condition is always determined by where we are located within the 'life process,' the temporal unfolding of our lives themselves. If we get so far, we gradually discover that things we could once do easily require more effort and eventually become impossible altogether. In a more psychological vein, we also become aware that possibilities that, at an earlier time, seemed open to us are now foreclosed (the result often being the well remarked 'mid-life crises' which often take such physical forms as change of physical location or engagement in sexual activities). In either case, we sense that some change has occurred, something has registered as a 'trace,' the reasons for which exceed our powers of direct cognition, memory, or articulation.

One important but less discussed aspect of this, which Heidegger explored only briefly in his discussion of 'mood' (*Stimmung*), concerns what we might, somewhat less subjectively, call (any determinate word for this lacking) the different 'atmospheres,' 'auras,' or 'colorations' of our physical experiences from one time to another. (Philosophers have generally taken little note of this, though authors such as Proust have made it a principal focus of their work.) For example, most of us can remember a number of 'Christmases past,' where each involves many of the same practices and rituals. However, although the 'facts' (where we celebrated, what gifts we gave or received, and so on) escape memory, we tend to remember and distinguish them (when we can) on the basis of a sort of mostly inexpressible quality, a certain physical and emotional atmosphere that remains with us as a trace. This is something less than an articulable meaning but more than some mere recitation of facts of a given season; it is something that remains as a trace, a sort of physical 'feeling' that is not quite the same as merely my 'mood' at the time. Such, then, is a trace formed by factors that exceed both my ability to consciously experience and my capacity to articulate the factors involved. It is registered, rather, as a certain subtle condition of embodied experience in relation to a 'world' beyond me. It would not be too much of a leap, in fact, to claim that this sort of trace ultimately 'colors' all our experience, modulates our more subjective 'moods,' and plays an important role in how we perceive the physical process of aging at any particular time.

3. Nature and 'The Universe'

As embodied beings, our only access to 'nature' or 'the universe' is necessarily from this condition. Certainly we have dramatically expanded the limits imposed by our physical sense organs through the invention of various prosthetic devices (microscopes, telescopes, spectrographs, audio-amplification, and so forth), and have enhanced our abilities to obtain, assemble, and analyze data through digital means. One might also point to the collaborative nature of science and other ways of knowing as enhancing the cognitive abilities of individuals. But, in the end, all of this must be appropriated by embodied human beings and become meaningful and applicable for them. In this sense, although the limits of our knowledge of nature and abilities to control and alter it are not fixed and may continue to expand indefinitely, they are nonetheless always conditioned by the fact that they expand due to the efforts of embodied beings and must ultimately be appropriated under this condition. In this sense, even if the limits are not fixed or completely determinable '*a priori*' (as Kant would have it), it remains the case that embodied human existence will remain as a sort of final index point or terminus, a sort of 'open limit,' for our abilities to know and operate on nature. Thus, at any given point in time, the embodied condition of our existence will itself constitute a general limit in relation to that which always exceeds it, which we often refer to as 'the universe.'

On the other hand, we also know that our own bodily existence, both individually and as a species, is a product of processes and forces beyond ourselves, both in temporal terms of our evolutionary emergence and in more atemporal terms of the environmental conditions that support human life. Our bodies themselves are, then, traces of excesses that stretch back in terrestrial and cosmic time and extend through the series of terrestrial and cosmic environments that make life possible. As the saying popular in the 60s has it, we are ultimately made up of 'stardust' which comes from an 'excessive elsewhere' and remains as a trace in our own bodily being.

Some recent philosophers (especially Quentin Meillassoux and the so-called 'Speculative Realists') have especially insisted against any Kantian or more generally 'idealist' or 'subjectivist' approach that we know *that* our existence as embodied beings depends upon a number of factors both for its physical emergence and continuation without ever being able to comprehend the full range of these conditions or any logical (or even physical) necessity for this being the case.

Meillassoux refers to one dimension of this as the problem of 'ancestrality,' the idea that we know from the natural sciences that human consciousness (not to mention embodied human being) is a relatively recent 'evolutionary event' within an 'objective' time and space exceeding that which takes human consciousness as its indexical reference point. This idea is aimed directly at Kant (and, for these authors, most of modern philosophy beginning with Descartes and following Kant), whose operative assumption was that all philosophy (and hence all philosophical views of space and time) begin from and with human consciousness. The objection, then, is that any such 'subjectivist' or 'transcendental' view both conflicts with the findings of modern science (cosmology, paleontology, biological evolution, etc.) and is, on its own terms, logically inconsistent.

Though one could imagine cogent responses within a Kantian framework to Meillassoux's quite detailed arguments in *After Finitude*, I think that the approach adopted in the present work beginning from the problem of the 'analytic *a posteriori*' arrives at much the same place, with the additional benefit of providing Kant with a more positive philosophical role in this discussion than as a mere foil for an opposed view. Kant was not philosophically 'wrong' as a mere empirical matter, nor was he merely confused in the manner in which he employed the terms 'contingency' and 'necessity,' both of which Meillassoux seems to suggest. Rather, despite all 'speculative realist' critiques of Kant, his Critical Philosophy has a certain integrity within the limits that it functioned (as I've already tried to suggest) and it is as important to acknowledge where and how Kant was right as much as it is to criticize him.

To broaden the discussion in a way that might accomplish this, we can say that Meillassoux and 'speculative realism' object to a particular way of interpreting the so-called 'subjective-objective' distinction. For Kant (and, if the 'speculative realists' are right, much of the modern philosophical tradition), the agenda of philosophy has been set by both accepting the subject-object distinction as an unsurpassable framework for philosophical thought and, at the same time, claiming that the only human access to this issue must be through the subjective side of this dichotomy. Ultimately, they believe that modern philosophy (in contrast to the natural sciences) has reduced the objective to the subjective, resulting (among other things) in the well-remarked 'dangerous division' between modern philosophy and the natural sciences. For their part, through problems such as that of 'ancestrality,' they seek to redress this imbalance by, in effect, reducing the subjective to the objective. Having done this, they then claim that such important philosophical notions as necessity and contingency must be rethought outside of any 'subjectivist,' 'transcendental,' or (to use their preferred term) 'correlationist' framework (the subtitle of Meillassoux's work is *'An Essay on the Necessity of Contingency'*).

Surprisingly, however, while Meillassoux wants (with the present view) to insist on the contingency of the actual existence of philosophy as well as to undermine any notion of necessity operating within philosophy (where we part ways), he has little to say about what we've been calling the actual conditions of philosophy and employs arguments against his opponents in ways that seem to presume, contrary to other claims that he makes, that logical necessity obtains in full force. While he would probably reject our counting signification and ideality as additional conditions, it is especially surprising that he has little or nothing to say at least about embodiment, which I take to be the real crux of this discussion.

Let's then return to the subject-object issue from the point of view of embodiment. As Schelling claimed even before Kant's death in 1804, human being is, along with language and artworks, precisely a 'subject-object.' That is, we are, at once, objects in a world of other objects as well as subjects conscious of other objects and of ourselves as conscious embodied beings. On a view like Schelling's, no consistent philosophy can any more reduce consciousness to objective physical processes than it can eliminate all reference to our physical basis through an account based on consciousness. Rather, from the point of view of objectivity, human consciousness will always appear as an excess, something 'supra-physical,' while from the point of view of subjectivity, physical being will always remain as an inassimilable excess. The point that I wish to stress, however, is that, if we begin with the idea of embodied existence (as Schelling seems not to have done, at least explicitly), we realize that we are ultimately incapable of consistently adopting either a 'purely objective' or a 'purely subjective' standpoint. To do the former would nullify the idea of adopting any conscious position at all, while to do the latter would collide with the very sorts of problems that Meillassoux et. al. attribute to Kant and much of modern philosophy.

Schelling offered a suggestive approach for regarding such matters. He proposed that the relation of 'Nature' (the 'objective' and 'trans-human') and 'Spirit' (the realm of human consciousness and activity) stands in a sort of dynamic, circular or 'mutually implicate' relation. On the one hand, natural processes developmentally proceed to the production of human consciousness or Spirit; on the other, Nature is completed by consciousness or Spirit in the forms of knowledge and human activity. Nature, that is, produces the physical basis that makes consciousness or Spirit possible and consciousness or Spirit completes and mirrors this process by knowing and acting upon its natural basis. In his so-called 'Philosophy of Identity,' Schelling went on to claim that Nature and Spirit were thus 'both different and the same': different as two separate 'realms' or sets of processes and the same both as part of a single 'cosmic process' and as mirroring one another in their basic structures.

If, as I've suggested, we begin (as we must) with embodied being, a somewhat different but, in important ways, parallel account is required. Unlike Schelling, who remained committed to an idealist position with respect to the totality formed by these processes mentioned above, we must say that, employing Schelling's terms, both Nature and Spirit represent excesses from the point of view of embodied being. 'Speculative Realism' is right in emphasizing the underlying 'contingency' of Nature and its excessiveness with respect to human experience and knowledge. However, it must equally be emphasized that, for embodied being, consciousness or Spirit is equally excessive, since there is no 'position,' philosophically or otherwise, from which all remainders (the Freudian unconscious or otherwise) can be eliminated. This is, of course, just as true of 'Speculative Realism' as any other philosophical position. While we can agree with Schelling that, in many ways within embodied being itself, Nature and Spirit co-implicate and reciprocally influence each other, this occurs as an interaction of traces of both within embodied being, never in the form of a 'totality' of either Nature or Spirit themselves or of some idealist unity of them.

To put this straightforwardly, as embodied beings, we are produced and maintained in our existence by natural forces that necessarily exceed the finite limitations of our condition. We are, to a great extent through science, capable of knowing *that* this is the case without being able to know or fully articulate *how* it is the case in terms of some physical or logical necessity (which thinkers like Meillassoux register by insisting on the contingency of nature). But it is equally true that any philosophical shift to the conscious aspect of embodied being, such as suggested in Kant's 'Copernican Revolution,' will confront excesses of its own, both with respect to Nature and with respect to the limitations upon its own capacity for 'self-knowledge.' Because we are embodied beings, neither natural sciences nor analyses of the structure of consciousness can provide us with firm philosophical foundations. Rather, we, as philosophers who are embodied beings, always operate with and among traces of nature and conscious experience that both point beyond themselves to the excesses which are their sources and, at the same time, mark out limits, if partially negotiable ones, for knowledge, experience, and activity.

4. Signification and Ideality

I suggested earlier that a 'Principle of Interreflectedness' obtains among the basic conditions. It now makes sense to state a sort of 'informal corollary' of this: that significational systems and idealities can, *from the perspective of embodied being*, also be regarded as traces of realms which exceed embodied being itself. I've deliberately phrased this in an informal and qualified way because we'll later see that, when we shift our focus to the conditions of signification and ideality, a relational structure different than the 'trace-excess' that we've so far been employing will be required. At this point, I merely want to note that signification and ideality, taken generically as conditions, are already reflected in embodied being itself. Since this will be merely anticipatory for the fuller discussions that will follow, we can be brief.

Perhaps the simplest access to this is merely to note, employing a turn of phrase that has become current among cognitive scientists and psycholinguists, that embodied beings (or at least that limited aspect of embodied beings called 'brains') seem to be 'hard-wired' for language. That is, the capacity for linguistic (or, more broadly, significational) expression and comprehension seems to be an 'inborn' human capacity based, at least in part, upon the physical and chemical structures of our nervous systems and brains. In Stephen Pinker's phrase, human beings possess a 'language instinct,' a sort of natural potency resident from birth in our very embodied condition.

However, because this 'language instinct' can be realized in an unlimited variety of ways—including gesture, signing and sign recognition, speaking, and writing—and each of these can, in turn, assume many different concrete forms, we can regard them generically as excesses with respect to the basic 'instinct' itself. The main point is that signification is not merely an adventitious feature of embodied human being but is a necessary, even defining element of what it means to be a human being. As Aristotle asserted, embodied human being can be defined as 'ζῶον ἔχον λόγον,' the animal having language, discourse, or, more broadly, signification. Although no specific form of signification can be 'deduced' from our 'language instinct,' and any form will be excessive with respect to the bare instinct itself, the fact remains that there will always be an embodied, physiological element of any significational system or complex, hence an intimate and ineliminable relation between our embodied condition and any possible form of signification.

Likewise, from the perspective of embodied being, ideality also (and in ways that become complexly intertwined with signification) can be viewed in terms of the 'trace-excess' structure that we've been employing. Besides the 'language instinct,' we, as embodied beings, possess 'instincts' or 'potencies' that direct us toward objects and activities necessary for our physical survival and maintenance. In the most basic sense, this takes the form of primal, and often unconscious, desires. Lacan, among others, has described desire in terms of a 'lack' seeking fulfillment by something that is other than, hence excessive in relation to, the embodied organism itself. Viewed in this way, 'desire as lack' is itself the trace, within embodied being, of an excess that would fulfill or satisfy it. From this perspective, we can think of ideality, generically viewed, as any object, condition, or cognition (which would include imagination or 'fantasy') that would serve to fill the lack implicit in desire.

Of course, as Lacan also emphasized, there is always a 'short-circuit' between desire and its 'objects,' since there is, for finite embodied being, no final or complete state (other than biological death) that could completely fill the lack of desire. Desire-as-lack, that is, continually reproduces itself as it experiences what can only be partial fulfillments. As primal 'desire as lack' continually morphs and expands, it is, according to Lacan, transected by signification (what Lacan calls the 'Symbolic Order'), which directs it along its own intersubjectively prepared channels. One outcome of this is the sort of idealities, 'universals' or formal structures, which have traditionally been regarded as the foci or 'nodal points' of philosophy. This connection between embodied desire as lack and the idealities of philosophy has, of course, been long been familiar since Plato's 'erotic dialogues,' especially the *Symposium* and the *Phaedrus*. But it is a point worth restating in the face of the tendency of so many philosophical views to focus only on ideality to the exclusion of its roots in embodied desires. Philosophy, that is, always remains driven by embodied desires-as-lacks, whether it chooses to explicitly acknowledge this or not. Put in other terms, philosophy always emerges and develops in the gap between the traces of embodied desire-as-lack and the excesses of whatever it may take to be that which might remedy this lack.

II. SIGNIFICATION

We suggested earlier that the actual conditions of philosophy are 'asymmetrical' with respect to one another. That is, though equally actual or 'real' and hence excessive, they 'exist' in different ways or modes and are structured in different ways. While the 'trace-excess' structure is dominant for and from the perspective of embodied being, significational complexes require a different sort of account. We can express this in terms of a specific form of the 'whole-part' relation.

Paralleling our introduction of the 'trace-excess' relation for embodied being in terms of a scar, we can initially think, somewhat fancifully I admit, of signification in terms of a large tattoo that covers our torso front and back. Whereas the scar is an inchoate, chance remainder or trace of an excess, some physical trauma that has left a formless, random, and limited mark upon us, a tattoo is a visual structure of parts interrelated in a way so as to constitute a whole unitary pattern. The scar is 'meaningful' only as an indexical sign (to borrow a term from Peirce) of some excess whose occurrence it merely registers but fails to explain; the tattoo, however, is 'meaningful' in a different sense that involves the relational organization of its various parts or areas within a whole structure.

In the most fundamental sense, a tattoo is also excessive (and I don't mean as an 'extreme fashion statement,' though this may also be true) in a different way than a scar: it is excessive in the sense that the whole tattoo always exceeds any of its parts, and yet it exists as a determinate whole. Although neither the person tattooed (over the torso front and back, remember) nor other observers will actually be able to view the whole tattoo all at once as a unitary structure (from any given perspective, that is), we nonetheless know *that* it forms a whole based upon of the continuous relations among the parts that we can see from various perspectives.

Further, if the tattoo depicts words or representational elements as some of its parts, it will be excessive in yet further senses. The representational parts of the tattoo will also function as 'signifiers' linked to other 'signifieds,' forming 'signs' related to yet other 'signs' beyond their juxtapositions within the overall tattoo itself (think of the typical heart with 'mother' across it or the US Marine Corps emblem, perhaps along lines analyzed by Roland Barthes in his *Mythologies*).

We might also consider the fact that the tattoo (or parts of it) was likely first rendered diagrammatically in two dimensions to serve as a guide for the 'tattoo artist' (herself drawing upon existing signs and representational conventions), something entirely lacking in the case of scars. And even more, we can observe that the form of the tattoo must both accommodate itself to the contours of the body on which it is inscribed and, following the tensile properties of the skin, slightly alter its shapes with the body's natural movements, something much less the case for scars, which tend to have an insistence of their own.

We can leave off considering the tattoo as metaphor here since, like all metaphors, it has its advantages and its limits. But it does serve to introduce (by way of contrast with scars) some of the distinctive ways in which the structure of signification differs from that of embodiment with respect to its excessive character. I'll first enumerate some of these characteristics especially relevant for philosophy and then discuss them in more detail in the rest of this section.

1. Significational systems, generically considered, are 'virtually relational.'
2. The primary structure of their internal relations is that of 'whole-part.'
3. A significational whole is always excessive with respect to its parts.
4. Significational parts are always, in a certain sense, excessive with respect to the wholes to which they belong.
5. The 'virtual relations' of significational systems become actual in concrete usage or employment.

The conclusion toward which we'll be working our way is that, while a significational system (and, in particular, language) is an actual condition for philosophy, that is, is presupposed by philosophy for and by its very concrete existence, any significational system in which philosophy is articulated is excessive with respect to any possible philosophical position. Put in a less complicated way, we can say that there can be no language which can serve as a neutral, innocent, or fully transparent 'vehicle' for philosophical expression. Or, even more simply, any philosophical discourse necessarily says both less and more than it intends.

1. Significational Systems and 'Virtual Relationality'

If we consider significational systems generically, we must first acknowledge (with semiology and structural linguistics) that they are relational structures. This means that there can ultimately be no such thing as a 'simple' or 'discreet' sign. Rather, to be a sign is to be related to other signs in some recognizably regular way. The structuralists even went so far as to maintain that every sign is itself a relation between a 'signifier' and a 'signified,' both of which, in turn, are related to other signs, themselves also relations.

They further maintained (misleadingly, I think) that this implied a fairly firm methodological distinction between *'parole'* and *'langue,'* roughly, language as actually spoken or written and language as the totality of these relations among signs. Against the prevailing linguistic approaches of their day, they wished to focus almost exclusively upon *langue*, which they proceeded to treat as a totality existing almost as a 'thing in itself.' While I want to agree with the structural linguists and semiologists that it is possible (and in some ways useful) to distinguish the structural relations among signs from the instances of their occurrence in actual discourse, it is important that the crucial link between the two not be theoretically severed. I try to indicate this by saying that signifying systems can be viewed generically and that to do so means that the relations in question be regarded as 'virtual' (that is, as not actual until employed in concrete discourse). To bring Wittgenstein into the discussion as another interlocutor, I want to say, reformulating his view just a bit, that, while the meaning of a sign consists in its use in concrete contexts, its selection for actual use in a given context is largely determined by its 'virtual relations' with other signs, which can be (at least partially) analyzed apart from, though never completely independently of, their actual usage. (Indeed, any fleshing out of Wittgenstein's notion of a 'language game' seems to require just this.)

Another question that often arises is whether 'reference' plays any necessary role in an account of significational systems, whether they should be regarded as self-contained totalities of completely 'arbitrary' signs or as 'connected with reality' at various points. On this score, I'm inclined to say that, purely from the perspective of a generic account, this isn't really an issue. It *is* an issue from a different perspective, that of embodied human beings employing signs within actual contexts (a 'world,' if you will) where signs are used to express oneself to other embodied beings. From such a perspective, it is clear that signs often do refer to a world beyond that of a significational system and that their use is far from 'arbitrary.' But it is possible (though this will never constitute an entire 'philosophy of language') to consider significational systems as determinate sets of virtual relations,' and for this it will make no difference whether some of their constituents refer to objects beyond the system or not. If anything, this problem merely marks an important limitation of any philosophy that bases itself solely on the analysis of language or signification, which, in the end, is another version of the sort of 'idealism' that we have already questioned on other grounds. On such views, *langue* viewed independently of *parole* is no more 'idealist' a position than others, presented as more modest, that continue to proceed as if all serious philosophical issues can ultimately be reduced to questions about language. Language, that is, is certainly one but can never be the only condition of philosophy.

2. Significational Systems and the 'Whole-Part' Relation.

The structuralists tended both to affirm *langue* 'synchronically' as a 'closed totality' of signs and their relations and to proceed to 'map' various areas of the totality in more or less discrete detail. Though there is no reason to accept their notion of significational systems as being 'closed' (it was more an article of faith than anything actually argued by them anyway), their emphasis upon the importance of viewing significational systems as 'wholes' remains important. However, they tended to treat the relation of significational parts to their wholes by proceeding as if, once the whole was methodologically secured, enough analyses of the parts would eventually amount to a full account of the whole. This, of course, could never in fact succeed, as their poststructuralist critics, beginning as early as Barthes and Bataille, would clearly indicate. In fact, we could summarize this element of poststructuralist critique as maintaining that the sort of whole that significational systems represent must be excessive with respect to any and all of its parts (and, in some specific ways, vice versa). Still, poststructuralist critique itself then tended to reject the 'whole-' side of the 'whole-part' distinction altogether, focusing rather upon the many ways in which the former parts, now viewed as particular texts or parts of texts, were always and necessarily excessive.

It was in a different though, in part, contemporaneous tradition that the 'whole-part' issue with respect to significational systems was explored in ways that may prove more helpful for us. As early as Schleiermacher in the first decades of the 19th century, and reworked by such thinkers as Dilthey, Heidegger, and Gadamer, the notion of a 'hermeneutic circle' was seen as fundamental for any account of human language and signification (and ultimately for understanding and cognition). It was first applied to written texts and called attention to the seeming paradox that, on the one hand, the meaning of a given text depends upon the meaning of its parts (words, sentences, paragraphs, etc.) while, on the other, the parts themselves are meaningful only within the whole of the text which they constitute. Put a different way, we can only come to understand a text by serially reading through its parts, but we can only understand the significance of its parts by understanding the whole text. Human understanding itself (and, we might add, cognition in general) thus has a 'circular' structure, since every whole is a meaningful unity of its parts while being a part implies a whole of which it is a part. Or, there can be no parts that are not parts of a whole and there can be no wholes which do not have parts as their constituents.

The basic idea, then, shared by both the structuralist and hermeneutic traditions, is that any account of significational complexes must involve a specific form of the 'whole-part' relation. Even in Wittgenstein's idiom, particular instances of 'language in use' are ultimately meaningful only within the larger whole of a 'language game' and its rules. This widely shared insight opens immediately upon the question as to how further to understand this 'whole-part' relation with respect to actual examples of discourse.

3. The Excess of Significational Wholes in Relation to Their Parts

That significational wholes are excessive with respect to their parts, in other words, that any language is excessive with respect to any actual instance of discourse that can be generated in that language, follows directly. To produce meaningful sign-combinations within a given significational structure or to make statements within a given language is to realize or make actual a specific possibility implicit in the virtual relations that make up a significational system or language. This means that no actual statement or set of statements employing a given system or language can exhaust the possibilities inherent in that system or language. This, by the way, is just as true for very complex sets of statements such as those constituting a 'philosophical position' as it is for very simple statements. Every such 'actual complex' still falls short of the 'whole' of possible statements that can be generated within that language, which means that the 'whole' must remain 'virtual' with respect to any actualization of its 'parts.'

One might object that, in the case of very simple and limited significational systems with only a finite and denumerable number of elements, we can, in fact, exhaust the possibilities of that system by listing all the actual combinations that can be generated from it. (One thinks here of Leibniz's unrealized project of a '*mathesis universalis*' as well as its later progeny, certain types of modern symbolic logic.) But even in such cases, which fall well short of the complexity of natural languages, the whole still exceeds any enumeration or listing of its parts. This is because the whole consists not only of parts or basic elements (lexemes, morphemes, words, etc.) but also of 'virtual relations' or 'rules of formation' among them which, though they may govern the formation of actual instances, are not themselves expressed within the enumeration of the actual instances. (This point was developed formally by such thinkers as Russell in terms of 'set-theoretic paradoxes,' which he early on attempted to resolve by a theory of 'levels of types'—which amounted to another sort of admission of the excessiveness of the relation of wholes to their parts.) We can conclude, then, that every whole is excessive in relation to any merely 'additive' enumeration of its parts: anything regarded as a whole will always be more than any mere enumeration or addition of its parts, since it will involve virtual relations among the parts which are not included within any actual occurrence of the parts themselves.

It is also worth adding that, beyond this crucial difference between 'wholes consisting of parts' and 'parts enumerated additively or serially,' there can, in fact, be no complete enumeration of actual parts, that is, actual statements, which can be formed within any natural language. Though rather technical arguments might be provided for this point, it's sufficient for present purposes to point out that to maintain this would be to claim, in effect, that no genuine creativity, hence no poetry or novel philosophical positions for instance, are possible within natural languages; at most, they would be mere rearrangements of parts already in principle available. We can summarize this section, then, by saying that every whole is excessive in relation to its parts, and this is especially true for natural languages where no complete enumeration of parts seems possible.

4. The Excess of Significational Parts in Relation to Their Wholes

From the perspective of structural linguistics, which defines, '*a priori*' as it were, the parts or elementary constituents of signifying systems solely in terms of their 'differential relations' within the system itself, the claim that the parts are excessive with respect to the whole of the system itself would be ruled out. However, we saw above that there is a crucial difference between any actual enumeration of the parts of a whole and the whole itself. Against the structuralists (and with their hermeneutic and poststructuralist critics and, I suspect, such 'ordinary language' approaches that of Wittgenstein), I want to claim that the parts of significational systems (especially natural languages) are also excessive with respect to their wholes, the system of which they are constituent parts.

One way of considering this is to say that every actual employment of a sign or use of a word or sentence can be interpreted in (at least) two ways. Understood as 'part of a whole,' as a particular instantiation of a set of possibilities (i.e. virtual relations) determined by the whole of a system or language, it can be said to have a 'conventional' (or perhaps 'denotative') meaning as the actualization of a possibility included within the virtual relations constituting the whole itself. However, any actual employment of a sign, word, or statement also has its own insistence, beyond the conventional meaning assigned to it by the virtual relations constituting the whole. This singular excess of the parts of any significational whole has been registered in various ways. Some have characterized it in terms of 'connotation' as opposed to 'denotation,' the idea being that different 'addressees' will associate with a given sign or word other meanings (for example, those derived from another significational system, such as another natural language) beyond that 'conventionally' assigned to it within its own system or language. The hermeneutic tradition prefers to speak in terms of a 'horizon of meaning,' which includes but exceeds any conventions governing the meaning of a discreet sign, word, or statement within a given system or language. And poststructuralists sometimes speak of the 'sliding of signifiers' to indicate (among other things) that, even within the conventions of a given system, the meaning of a specific signifier will vary in its occurrence within a discourse or text beyond the place it is assigned by the virtual relations defining any particular system or language.

The fact, then, as every poet knows, is that signs and words possess a certain 'weight' of their own, a kind of singularity of meaning, that exceeds their conventional meaning as 'parts of a whole,' as elements assigned a particular place within a broader significational system or language. Another way to put this is to say that, beyond the 'particular,' conventional place assigned to them within a system or language, signs or words have a certain insistence or 'singularity' that exceeds the place assigned to them by the virtual relations that constitute their whole.

5. *The Actuality of Signification*

I have, all along, described signification as an actual condition of philosophy. While I've granted the utility of the structuralist account of signification as a starting-point for discussion, especially as a way to present the excessiveness of signification even on their own assumptions, it remains important to say that, most fundamentally, signification is something that embodied beings *do* and that, in the primary sense, any access to signification is through the productions of embodied beings. Like the problem of the 'analytic *a posteriori*' in Kant, the issue of the excessiveness of wholes in relation to their parts (and vice versa) with respect to significational systems exposes and transgresses the implicit 'idealism' of most modern treatments of signification and language. The point is not that structuralist accounts of signification lack a certain 'necessity' with respect to their own viewpoint, but that their entire approach encounters determinate limits with respect to the 'actuality' with which they deal.

Although we can regard any actual instance of signification, any linguistic statement, as a instantiation of a virtual relation constituting a signifying system or language, we also know both that the system itself exceeds any of its instances and that any instance, as a singularity, exceeds any place assigned it by the system. However, if we take seriously the singularity of any sign, statement, or text, the fact that it is a production of an embodied being expressing itself to other embodied beings, then we must say that, while there is a threshold of meaning governed by the system which it deploys, this is always exceeded both by the significational system itself as well as by meanings that exceed the system when considered in their own singular occurrences.

Every actual act of signification, then, whether it be a sign, word, statement, or philosophical position, is (at least) 'doubly exceeded.' On the one hand, it is exceeded by the signifying system of which it is a part. But, as a singularity, it is also excessive with respect to any place assigned it within the whole of a system. Every spoken or written word, sentence, poem, novel, or, for that matter, philosophical text is both a part of some 'virtual whole' that exceeds it and is, at the same time, a singular event that exceeds any such whole or set of virtual relations comprising some significational system.

The fundamental point, however, is that signification, as an actuality, exists, in its primary sense, as a concrete production of embodied beings for other embodied beings. This is determined by another actuality, a 'signifying system,' but one which both exceeds it and which, in turn, it, as a singularity, exceeds in a different way. Both a view which reduces its actuality and singularity to the whole of virtual relations of a system (structuralism) as well as one which 'deconstructs' its singularity into the 'intertextuality' of other systems (poststructuralism) are, in the end, 'idealisms' which fail to take seriously the actuality of signification itself.

III. IDEALITY

Our theme in this chapter has been the excessiveness of the conditions of philosophy with respect to the enterprise of philosophy itself. To say that embodiment and signification, as actual conditions, involve excesses seems fair enough. But to say the same of idealities will meet with resistance. On the one hand, if idealities are regarded either as 'concepts' produced by the 'subjective thought' of embodied beings or as 'epiphenomenal excrescences' of significational systems, then they cannot really exceed either of these. Rather, they are, so to speak, already included either in embodied being (as 'subjective concepts') or in significational complexes (as 'meanings' of its constituents). On the other hand, if they are regarded as a fully autonomous 'mode of being' (like certain accounts of Plato's 'Theory of Forms'), then they will be excessive for but ultimately inaccessible to finite embodied being or signification (as Plato himself argues in the *Parmenides*.) Thus, in order to claim that idealities are excessive with respect to the other conditions but are nonetheless accessible to them, an account is required which avoids reducing idealities either to 'subjective concepts' or the 'meanings' of the terms of significational systems while elucidating their connections with them.

Note that, in order to accomplish this, a different sort of relation will be needed than the 'trace-excess' structure for embodied being or the 'whole-part' relation for significational systems. I suggest (with credit especially to Heidegger and Badiou) that the structure of the excessiveness of idealities with respect to the other conditions is that of 'event-manifold.'

To explain this, we must recall our earlier discussion of the relations among the basic conditions. We claimed that ideality presupposes both embodied being and the capacity of embodied beings to signify; if there were no embodied human beings or if there were but they failed to develop and employ significational systems, there would be no idealities. Idealities, that is, are not part of 'ancestral nature' or somehow innately resident in the constitution of embodied beings. Neither are they native features of significational systems (such as 'meanings') or the 'virtual relations' regarded as constituting them when viewed independently of their actual employment by embodied beings. But, they *do* emerge, and necessarily so, as an autonomous and ineliminable condition, given embodied beings actually engaged in intersubjective activities of signification.

To take a simple (but, given the importance of mathematics for a great deal of the philosophical tradition, crucially important) example of an ideality, consider a number, say '7.' On the one hand, the ideality '7' is not some 'given' or 'fundamental property' of nature itself. At most, we can characterize nature as bare multiplicity. Nature itself does not, so to speak, prepackage its unlimitedly multiple elements in 'sevens' or any other determinate number. Rather, as the early Greeks were well aware, any number represents a sort of limitation upon that which is '*apeiron*,' unlimited or merely multiple. Kant was, therefore, correct in claiming that number (or 'determinate quantity,' as Hegel further clarifies in the *Science of Logic*) depends upon the synthetic capacity of human consciousness (which Kant called a 'pure form of intuition'). On the other hand, a point which Kant's transcendental idealist assumptions obscured for him, mere number or 'determinate quantity' does not yet constitute arithmetic, since arithmetic is a significational system involving various kinds of 'trans-numerical virtual relations' (additional, subtraction, multiplication, division, etc.) among its elements (numbers). That arithmetic exists at all, then, is dependent both upon the contingent existence of embodied conscious beings and the contingent 'fact' that they are capable of elaborating and employing significational systems. However, once these two conditions obtain, then the 'necessity' of such things as arithmetical statements or propositions follows. To return to the number '7,' as an ideality it is at once a product of embodied conscious being and stands in necessary relations with other numbers, governed by the virtual relations constituting the significational system of arithmetic itself. The main point is that the number '7' is neither only an arbitrary product of human consciousness nor a merely a neutral 'placeholder' within a 'virtual' arithmetical system. Rather, '7' is an ideality that involves both the capacity for finite determination possessed by embodied beings *and* the virtual relations that constitute the significational system of arithmetic.

This becomes even clearer if we take Kant's own famous and more complex example of a necessary arithmetical statement, '7 + 5 = 12.' While Kant treated this as a 'synthetic *a priori* judgment' whose necessity was based upon the 'countability' of units implicit in the 'pure form of intuition' of time, Kant failed to note that the arithmetic 'operators' (here '+' and '=') were of a different order than the numbers with which they occur. While numbers are produced by consciousness (or the conscious aspect of embodied beings, as we'd prefer to say), the operators are, rather, features of arithmetic regarded as a significational system. As such, they are part of the virtual relations that make up that system and it is only when the two (certain productions of conscious embodied being and the significational system of arithmetic) come together that we can say of any actual statement, such as '7 + 5 = 12,' that it is 'logically necessary.' In a sense, then, we can say that while embodied being provides the 'material' for actual necessary statements, the 'virtual relations' of the signifying system provides its 'form.'

This suffices to show how the present account of ideality squares with our earlier discussion of the basic conditions. But how is ideality to be understood as excessive to both embodied being and signification in terms of an 'event-manifold' schema? From the most simple case of an 'ideality' (like the number '7'), through objects of desire, to such complex idealities as 'justice,' we will say that every ideality constitutes an 'event' of human consciousness, thought, or understanding as engaged with a significational system.

The key notion of 'event,' however, requires some initial explanation, since it has, in recent times, been employed in a number of diverse and sometimes quite complex ways. At one extreme, 'event' has served as a sort of ubiquitous though usually undefined and almost primitive term in the natural sciences, especially post-Newtonian physics, to indicate any 'objective complex' upon which scientific theory can be brought to bear. In fact, the 'relativity revolution' in physics signaled a shift from thinking and speaking in terms of 'material objects' to the idiom of 'physical events.' In this sense, any physical process whatever can be regarded as an 'event' and the world or universe, according to physics, is itself a sort of ensemble of a virtually infinite set of interconnected 'events.' At the other extreme, certain recent philosophers such as Heidegger and Badiou have deployed the term 'event' in a much more restricted though intensive sense to indicate something like a rare singular occurrence that functions as the origin, impetus, and creative source for the subsequent unfolding of deeply significant and portentous trajectories of intellectual, cultural, or historical processes. Heidegger, for instance, regards the modern 'enframing' of nature (or Being) as an 'event' that delivers Being over to global technological exploitation, while Badiou cites, as important examples, the 'Christ-event' as interpreted by St. Paul, the French Revolution, the Bolshevik Revolution, and May '68. In between these extremes, the ordinary usage of the term can range from occasions of only individual or limited significance (breaking my ankle or wrecking my car), through 'mid-range' cultural happenings (sports or cultural 'events'), to large-scale cultural or historical occurrences (the US Presidential Election of 2008 or 9/11).

For our discussion, the focus will be upon formulating a sense of 'event' relevant for philosophy and its activities, especially with respect to the condition of ideality. It's initially clear that, in this context, the term 'event' will be of little help if we use it to mean (on the analogy of modern physics) just anything that is included under the rubric of philosophy—we don't want to say that all philosophical or intellectual activities, texts, or positions are 'events.' On the other hand, its meaning will be too restrictive (probably verging upon opaque) if we reserve it for indicating something like entire philosophical positions, traditions of philosophy (Platonism, Kantianism,

Poststructuralism), or epochs of philosophical thought (ancient philosophy, modernity, postmodernity, etc.) Rather, we want to say that a 'philosophical event' is something like a fundamental philosophical insight or moment of thought or understanding on the part of an embodied human being that is expressible in discourse.

As Badiou points out, one crucial feature of the constitution of an event is that it receives a name, a process that, posterior to the event, signifies that 'an event has occurred' and serves to preserve the originary force and meaning of the event in the midst of the various trajectories that flow from it. I propose that, with respect to philosophy and its condition of ideality, what we generally call concepts or ideas are, in fact, the relevant events. To see how this is so, consider, first, that a concept or idea is, on the one hand, a product of cognitive processes (often, though not exclusively, what we call 'thinking') of a conscious embodied being. We fairly regard concepts or ideas as occurring within or emerging from our thought-processes. However, we also realize that this thought-process will remain vague, indeterminate, and in flux until we have employed some sign (usually a word) to arrest it at a particular point and fix it in a form in which it can be expressed to others and to which we can return in our own thinking. A 'named concept' or 'idea,' then, is no longer merely a passing moment or vague intuition that rises up and then recedes as our thought-process moves on; as named, it becomes '*the* concept or idea that I had,' can have again, and can express to others. However, in giving it a name, I must deploy the resources already available in some significational system. Even if, as Kant often did, I invent a new word or use a familiar one in a novel way, its meaningful use will end up reinscribing it within some intersubjectively intelligible significational complex. This implies both that, for embodied being, an event of thinking or understanding, once named, can no longer be regarded as entirely dependent upon my own subjective thought-processes (even for me who 'originated' it) but also that the 'thought-event' that has received a name is more and other than any 'name' that it bears. Such a subjectively-derived but significationally fixed event is an ideality which, in the field of philosophy, we generically call a 'concept' or 'idea.'

My claim, thus far, is that idealities (the events which are 'named concepts' or 'ideas' in philosophy), while dependent for their origination on the cognitive activities of embodied beings and for their fixation on significational systems, nonetheless, once constituted, are thenceforth an irreducible and autonomous condition of philosophy. To emphasize the autonomy of idealities is immediately to suggest that they have 'lives of their own' in some ways separate from but always related to the ongoing lives of embodied beings and the intersubjective functioning of significational systems. To bring this quality into further focus, I will introduce the term 'manifold,' employed in a specific way. Clearly poaching a term most familiar from

Kant where it indicates 'that which stands under the unity of consciousness' in the 'Transcendental Deduction,' I will say that a 'manifold,' in its generic sense, is the open, as yet indeterminate, though gradually determinable set of trajectories that issue from the 'event-origination' of an ideality.

One typical way of putting this is to say that every concept or idea has 'logical consequences' that follow from it. However, as Hegel pointed out, considering these dynamic trajectories solely in terms of relations familiar from formal logic obscures and forecloses two of their most important features. First, it obscures the fact that the 'unfolding of logical consequences' is itself a dynamic process of thinking, which becomes absorbed without remainder into the static forms of logic. Second, it fails to capture the fact that following the trajectory of an idea or concept gives rise to other 'events of understanding,' other idealities (concepts or ideas); that the process of thinking the ideality-event is productive of other ideality-events with their own trajectories. In other words, idealities generate further thought-processes that unfold not only that which is already implicit in the ideality (to which formal logic is limited) but originate other idealities that stand in relations to the original ideality more complex than that permitted by the linearity of logical deduction. As Hegel would insist, there are productive and systematic connections among idealities that cannot be captured within the limitations of formal logic. It is these features—processive, productive, and systematic—that I wish to preserve in speaking of the 'manifold,' literally, the 'multiple (un)folding,' of idealities.

This has been a lengthy introduction to our original question of how idealities are excessive with respect to embodied being and signification. It was necessary, however, due to the need to introduce the notions of ideality, event, and manifold which are likely less familiar than some of the terms used within our discussions of embodied being and significational systems. Now we should be in a position to more directly address the question of excess with respect to idealities. In some ways, in explaining these terms, we've already glimpsed some lines of response to this, so what follows can be a bit briefer than otherwise. However, we will need to connect this latest discussion with some earlier themes. The main points I wish to emphasize are:

1. Desire-as-lack is a defining feature of conscious embodied being and philosophical thought is desire seeking full conscious articulation.
2. Idealities originate as 'thought-events' that occur at the intersection of embodied desire and signification.
3. Concepts or ideas in themselves necessarily exceed both embodied desire and signification.
4. As generating 'manifolds,' concepts or ideas also necessarily exceed themselves.

1. Thought as Articulated Desire

Although we tend, along with a good deal of the philosophical tradition, to regard desire as some 'lower,' maybe physiological process, and thought as a 'higher faculty,' if we regard embodied human being as a single condition of any cognition whatever, then any firm distinction between desire and thought becomes untenable. Thinking, that is, is just as much something that embodied human beings do as desiring, feeling, imagining, and so forth. Any other conclusion will return us to an idealism that we've already found reason to reject.

We've already seen that desire is structured as a 'lack' seeking fulfillment by some excess beyond embodied being itself. But this is as true of thinking as any other cognitive process. We might say, then, that thinking is a sort of desire that seeks fulfillment in understanding. But understanding is an event of our conscious life that, when it receives a name drawn from a significational system, becomes an ideality (in philosophy, a concept or idea). So, philosophical concepts or ideas (or, generically, idealities) must be regarded as a distinctive type of actuality that serves to partially satisfy a particular sort of desire, the desire for understanding or knowledge.

However, on the one hand, as with all desire-as-lack, philosophical desire also proliferates, it continually reproduces itself as further lack beyond any given ideality, forcing it to 'think further.' This process, in turn, again connects it, at other points, with signification, producing other idealities. From the perspective of embodied being engaged in philosophy, then, while we can posit *that* the desire of thinking would involve a complete and lucid self-articulation, this 'virtual totality' will always be excessive with respect to thought's own desire-as-lack which can only proceed within the limits of its own temporal and embodied being. The result is that the condition of ideality with respect to embodied being is always excessive in relation to the finite condition from which desire originates.

2. The Intersection of Embodied Desire and Signification

Consider the following admittedly rather simplistic and schematic account that may help to clarity some features of what I'm trying to express here. As a manifestation of embodied desire, actual thinking (unlike most theoretical accounts of it) is a restless and unstable temporal process, a running through of vague and mostly inchoate 'ideas' mixed together with fragments of words and other signs, often punctuated by such things as perceptions from the immediate environment, memory traces, feelings, fantasies, and so forth. It's the sort of thing elicited, perhaps, when the legendary philosophy professor, on the first day of class, enters the classroom, writes "THINK!" on the board, and then leaves for the day. It is a sort of psychic agitation lacking any real form other than a generic desire for some sort of understanding or clarity.

At some point, however, this process is temporarily arrested at a point where it is intersected by a significational system. At such a point, a sign (usually, in philosophy, a word or phrase) intervenes, introducing a determinate point within the process, an element of structure in relation to which subsequent thinking becomes oriented and organized. It is such a point of intersection between the thinking process and part of a structured significational system or language that we've called an 'event,' more specifically, an 'event of understanding.' This event is marked by its associated sign, which serves as a 'name' for it, and this 'named event' is what we have called an 'ideality'—in philosophy, a concept or idea. Once such an ideality arises, it then serves to focus and redirect the thought process along lines in part laid out by the virtual relations that make up the signifying structure with which it has engaged. It thus generates further thought-processes, which intersect the significational system at other points, producing further 'events of understanding' with their own 'marker-name-concepts,' that is, further idealities.

I don't want to rest too much on such a rather (both logically and phenomenologically) unsophisticated account, but it does serve to make clearer a point I want to emphasize. It is that the events that we call idealities are always intersections of processes and structures. They are like 'nodal points' (or, to borrow a metaphorical phrase from Lacan, 'quilting points') where the process of thinking is joined to a part of a significational structure, where the chaotic process of thought becomes fixed and articulable by virtue of the structure inherent in a significational system or language. What is crucial to realize, however, is that philosophical concepts or ideas involve always and necessarily both process and structure. If, as has been typical of a great deal of the philosophical tradition, we regard concepts solely as logical structures, then we reduce them to empty and meaningless 'placeholders' (like the 'p's and 'q's of formal logic, which are not any determinate concept or idea or statement expressing them whatsoever). In doing so, they become severed from the desiring and thinking life of embodied beings, leaving us either unable to account for their origins or committing us to some problematic form of idealism. On the other hand, if we regard them merely as passing moments of subjective processes (perhaps like Hume) or as evanescent phases within some broader process (such as Nietzsche's 'Will to Power'), then we will have undermined the possibility of any understanding whatever (something that seems self-contradictory on its face). If for nothing else, we have Hegel to thank, especially in his critique of the Kantian categories, for forcefully making the point that idealities ('concepts' as he would say) are structures whose true nature is processive. More broadly, this means, as I think Hegel would also agree, that philosophy itself can never be identified either solely with the results of thinking (some lifeless array of logically related concepts) or solely with the mere activity of thinking ('a rummaging about in the grab bag of words and concepts,' as Kant once said). Rather, it is an activity engaged in by living, desiring embodied beings which issues in concepts or ideas possessing sufficient structure to be articulable and intersubjectively communicable.

3. The Excessiveness of Idealities

While I've gone to some lengths to emphasize the dependence of idealities on the thought-processes of conscious embodied beings as structured by significational systems, I now want to stress that idealities, once arisen, are, in important ways, autonomous of or excessive with respect to the conditions out of the intersection of which they originate.

First of all, there can be no such thing as a 'merely subjective concept or idea.' As we've seen, the event giving rise to idealities only occurs at a point of intersection between a part of a significational system and the thought-process of an embodied being. But significational systems (or language) are never 'merely subjective' (here we can recall Wittgenstein's arguments against the possibility of a 'private language'). So any ideality, in its significational aspect, will necessarily be excessive with respect to embodied being and its desiring and thinking processes. Put in other terms, this means that idealities, even though they arise in the course of my own thinking, remain always partly beyond my (or anyone else's) control inasmuch as they are expressed in signs or language. While language is a necessary condition for there being idealities, it imposes upon them part of its own structure which can, at the same time, resist thought's own intentions. This is why philosophers often restate or reformulate their views in various ways. It is not necessarily that they have altered their views or introduced new idealities, but they must often work against the resistances posed by the very 'medium' of their expression. (Think, for example, of Plato's numerous presentations of the so-called 'Theory of Ideas' or Kant's famous reformulation of the 'Transcendental Deduction.')

However, if idealities exceed any merely subjective thought processes or 'intentions' that may accompany them due to the native features of the significational system in which they are articulated, it by no means follows that idealities are mere 'meanings' of elements of a pre-given system or language. Just as idealities exceed any 'subjective' thought-process of an embodied being, they also exceed any specific determinations or virtual relations constituting the sign-system or language in which they are expressed. The 'thought-event' which founds idealities is creative in the sense that, although it necessarily involves the deployment of a sign or word, this 'deployment in the service of an event' partially detaches the sign or word from its place within a significational system, isolates it (so to speak), and accords it a significance beyond its native place within the significational system. A concept or idea, that is, is not just a word that retains its ordinary meaning within natural language; rather, the word itself becomes, at the same time, a marker of the fact that a 'thought-event' has occurred, that an embodied being has understood something not already contained in the language itself. Wittgenstein, then, was right to call attention to the fact that philosophical thought must borrow from the resources of 'ordinary language' to articulate itself, but wrong in thinking that, when this occurs, 'language has gone on a holiday' and no longer functions productively (philosophical language thus 'idles,' he says, like an engine that is running but not in gear). Rather, we can follow Heidegger far enough to say that language becomes 'appropriated' (*ereignetet*) for a different purpose, that of marking an event of understanding of an embodied being (and other such beings who, in turn, appropriate it).

To summarize, an ideality is neither merely a 'subjective notion' nor a mere 'meaning' of an element of a significational system. Rather, as a 'marker' of an event of understanding, it exceeds both. In so doing, we can say that it exerts its own distinctive force along two 'vectors.' With respect to embodied beings, it provides a point around which what was previously a vague and chaotic thought-process can be organized; with respective to the significational system from which it borrows, it possesses the potential for altering that system by injecting into it new dimensions of meaning opened by the event of understanding.

4. Idealities as Exceeding Themselves

As we've already seen, idealities, once constituted as partially autonomous of subjective thought and significational systems (considered 'in themselves,' so to speak), initiate trajectories ('lines of flight,' as Deleuze would say) of their own. A concept or idea, that is, serves as a point of departure for further thought-processes whose destinations will be other idealities, other events of understanding that will, in the same way as before, require signs or names either borrowed from a significational system or 'invented' in such a way as to permit its functioning within the virtual relations of a significational system. We have called the result of this following of trajectories issuing from an ideality its 'manifold.'

An appropriate generic characterization of the relation between an ideality and its manifold (or of a concept or idea and its 'unfolding') must, on the basis of what we've established, avoid two extremes familiar from the philosophical tradition. On the one hand, we can't adequately describe this relation in terms of some formal logical analysis of what is already 'contained' in the concept or idea (as Leibniz, followed in part by Kant, proposed) because it is only in the subsequent trajectories initiated by the event upon which it is founded that the concept or idea comes to have determinate content.

The 'content' of an ideality, that is, is not somehow 'given' with the ideality but requires further events of understanding, further thought-processes and their engagement with other elements of language, in order to become determinate. (We can, for example, understand the number '7' or the concept of 'mammal' without immediately knowing all the numbers, including fractionals, whose sum equals 7 or all the species of animals included within the concept 'mammal'). On the other hand, not just any subsequent process of thought that more or less randomly poaches a word to name a 'new event' can suffice because this would not lead to any further determination of the original ideality and would return us to 'square one.' We would continually be *merely* starting over and would fail to preserve and 'remain committed to' the original event of understanding.

We must, then, say that a 'manifold' relates to its ideality as a sort of 'determinate excess.' A manifold (as Kant suggested in a different register) possesses a sort of unity, conferred upon it by the ideality from which it originates. However, unity itself (as Kant also realized) is a sort of force exerted over a multiplicity of elements. With respect to the sort of unity conferred by an ideality upon its manifold, this force is not so strong as that implied by 'conceptual inclusion' capable of analysis under the rubric of 'logical necessity,' nor so weak as to be dissipated and lost among a mere collection of other idealities or, worse, empty words. Rather, the sort of unity conferred by an ideality on its manifold (and reflected back into it as its manifold 'unfolds') is more analogous to that of a process of natural development where new events, giving rise to new forms (idealities), emerge, while maintaining the continuity of its connection with its origin. Understood in this way, we can say that the manifold is an 'unfolding' of an ideality that, in its 'unfolding,' exceeds it. When thinking, that is, is oriented by and with respect to an ideality, it is at once anchored by that ideality and follows a trajectory that leads beyond it and exceeds it. Viewed from the perspective of the original ideality, we can say that other idealities along a certain trajectory serve as further determinations of it; viewed from the perspective of these further idealities, new events of understanding, not 'contained' in the origin, have arisen and initiate new trajectories of their own. It is thus the nature of idealities to 'exceed themselves,' in the sense that they produce manifolds that receive their unity from them while, at the same time, are exceeded by their manifolds in the process of their unfolding.

IV. THE TRAGI-COMEDY OF PHILOSOPHY

Freud once famously remarked that while, according to Holy Scripture, a man cannot serve two masters, he is, in fact, in the tragic situation of having to serve three: the id, the superego, and the 'Reality Principle.' Something parallel could be said of philosophy. While Kant thought that Reason had just two fundamental limits, intuition and concept, it turns out that there are three—embodiment, signification, and ideality—*and* that each of them are excessive in more complex ways than Kant ever envisioned with respect to the limits that he attempted to establish.

Realizing the scope and complexity of the actual conditions of philosophy and the extent of the excesses that they imply might well induce vertigo and ultimately despair. How could something, a tiny part of a universe beyond its own comprehension, not even fully aware of its own bodily processes or its immediate environment; that must try to express itself with often clumsy means that continually defy its best efforts; that, even when it does manage to establish some tentative reference point, often finds it slipping away or morphing into something else—How could such a being ever presume to struggle through this all and pursue something like philosophy? And wouldn't the thought that this is even possible represent an ultimate act of *hubris*, of the pride which, to the Greeks, was the fatal flaw of the tragic hero, leading him inevitably to his fate? Nietzsche, against the grain of an entire historical tradition, grabbed us by the neck, shook us, and made us watch while he staged the tragic spectacle before our eyes. Nietzsche is important to all later philosophers because he deeply felt and sang, by heart, the songs of the suffering body, the deceitful sign, and the ephemeral idea: the song of the tragedy of philosophy.

But, like many great performers, Nietzsche's repertoire was limited. There are other songs, as well, unfamiliar to him. Nietzsche was wrong on at least one important point: philosophy did not eventually dissipate itself in the rhetorical flourish of Euripides and the cynical dramaturgy of Aristophanes. Nor did it ransom its original tragic sense for the cheap optimism of the Christian 'Divine Comedy.' Philosophy, confronted by the excesses of the actual conditions of its existence, has always born its tragic sense within itself, though it has sometimes needed a skeptic or 'critical philosopher' to remind it of this. But the songs Nietzsche didn't know were those of the philosophers who, despite the forces of excess arrayed against them, continued to find ways to bring their lives, words, and ideas into a fragile configuration that, at least for its time, might inhabit a point of their crossing and produce some harmony among them. And this was as true for medieval Christian, modern rationalist and empiricist, Kantian, and whatever 'philosophy' might come after. To poach a phrase from Dr. Johnson, like a dog walking on its hind legs, it's not that they do it very well, it's that they do it at all. And that's the comedic aspect of philosophy and what makes philosophy, in the end, tragi-comic (and not *either* tragic *or* comic but never both, as Nietzsche had it): that philosophy exists at all, that serious and talented thinkers still pursue it, and that it continues to develop as a set of practices, texts, and ideas—against the overwhelming odds. This, in itself, is comedic.

As I suggested earlier, there is no necessary or philosophical reason why we embodied beings are here or are the way we are. Neither is there any necessary reason why, once here, we developed the ability to signify to others. But once these two conditions obtained, ideas or concepts did emerge, we could begin to articulate why this happened, and, in so doing, we retrospectively but necessarily reflected on the other conditions—and with that philosophy (had already) commenced.

And so the seeming paradox of claiming that philosophy is 'tragi-comic.' It is tragic when considered in relation to the forces arrayed against it, almost doomed to oblivion it would seem, but comic in the fact of its persistence and its ability to regenerate itself, across epochs and cultures, in the face of these forces. Nietzsche seemed to think that the only effective response would be to master the excesses through some supra-philosophical act of will. He didn't understand that merely to persist among them, and persist enough to regenerate, was itself a victory—a tragi-comic victory that Nietzsche never envisioned.

DIAGRAM 3: The Conditions as 'Forces' with their own Trajectories (The 'Implosions' of Philosophy)

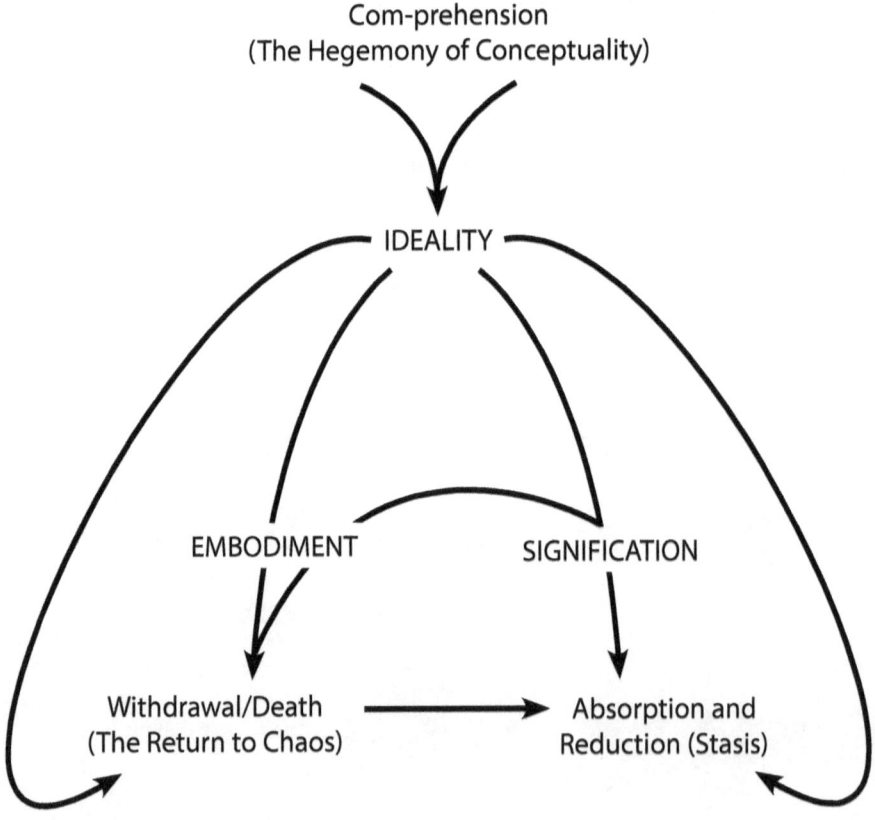

7

Trajectories of the Conditions: Withdrawal, Reduction, Com-Prehension

I've insisted all along that the conditions of philosophy are actual, that they are not merely subjective constructions or mere features of some particular philosophical view but are 'real' (not just 'transcendental') grounds for the possibility of there being such an enterprise as philosophy, whether regarded as a kind of activity, body of texts, or overall viewpoint or position. As actual conditions, they constitute the field that is occupied by any particular philosophical position. Every philosophical position, then, represents a specific way in which these conditions are brought together and within which they interact. Because they are, in a sense, anterior to any philosophical position, each must necessarily exceed any philosophical position itself. In the last chapter, we focused upon the specific and characteristic ways in which each actual condition must exceed any philosophical attempt to accommodate it. In this sense, particular philosophical positions can be regarded as 'remainders,' what is left when the 'excesses' are subtracted.

However, if we regard every actual philosophical position as such a remainder, a space carved out within the broader interplay of excessive forces, we must still remind ourselves that those forces continue to exert their distinct types of influence upon the remainders themselves. In this chapter, I will offer generic characterizations of how each condition, understood as excessive to the field, affects positions within the field. We might say that, while in the last chapter we adopted a generic perspective *within* the field and asked how the conditions exceeded it, we'll now, in a sense, adopt the perspective of the conditions themselves and describe, again in a generic way, how their specific forms of excess exert forces upon the field and any position within it.

Put another way, part of the task of every philosophy consists in accommodating and somehow holding together three different forces acting upon it. However, each condition exerts its force in a distinctive way, posing its own distinctive problem for any specific philosophy. Further, it can happen that one of the forces comes to overpower and threaten to detach itself from the others within a given philosophy. Such cases will prove particularly helpful in further understanding how the conditions also serve as limits of philosophy which, when breach of a limit threatens, tend to deflect the trajectory back into the field of philosophy. (See Diagram 3)

I. EMBODIMENT AND 'WITHDRAWAL,' OR PHILOSOPHY AND DEATH

We saw in the last two chapters that the condition of embodied spatiotemporal being constitutes the basis for both the realization that we are limited and 'incomplete' beings as well as the dynamic impetus to respond to this situation. Put another way, the condition of embodied being is 'desire-as-lack' and it is this 'desire-as-lack' that is the root of any human enterprise, perhaps paradigmatically that of philosophy. The *possibility* of philosophy does not consist in the fact that we *already*, simply by being human, share in something 'divine' (Plato) or are 'rational beings' (Aristotle) or possess a 'faculty of Reason' (Kant); nor must philosophy be judged *impossible* because we are hopelessly finite or merely products of instinctual urges (as some more recent thinkers have concluded). Rather, it is our sense of our own finitude, our own limitations, our 'lack' that opens the space in which the desire that ultimately leads toward philosophy can operate. The finitude of embodied being, then, is not a barrier to or negation of philosophy but its very condition. We engage in philosophy not in spite of or in addition to the fact that we are finite, but *because of* it. (We might add here that the same, up to this point, might be said of religion.)

However, desire-as-lack, operating philosophically, is Janus-faced. On the one hand, it impels us toward creative acts of understanding that issue in something excessive with respect to our finite being, toward the 'named events' that are idealities. On the other hand, these same impulses leave something in their wake, the 'dead weight' of embodiment itself. Despite all the efforts of philosophical desire to supply its lack, to 'fill the hole' that constitutes it, we remain limited, finite beings who will eventually cease to be; our philosophical efforts serve, at the same time, to remind us of this.

Freud (in a way that he himself admitted was both speculative and clumsy) posited, at the end of *Civilization and its Discontents,* two fundamental 'drives' or 'instincts': '*Eros*,' or the 'life instinct,' which he described as the desire to incorporate into ourselves that which is excessive to us; and '*Thanatos*,' or the 'death instinct,' the desire to return to an unconscious, inorganic state, to withdraw from engagement with excesses and, in effect, close the 'hole' or 'lack' constituting desire itself. Both of these drives or instincts represent ways of attempting to resolve the problem posed by desire-as-lack. More specifically, philosophical *eros* impels us toward idealities and their proliferation in manifolds. This, however, can only be a partial or momentary resolution, since ideality and signification always remain excessive despite all efforts. Philosophical *thanatos*, however, *is*, in fact, a 'final solution,' an '*Endlösung*' (and I use this term very deliberately with all its terrible weight). To despair of and cease thinking and trying to understand, to give oneself over to the 'pure finitude without excess' of embodied being, to return to a pre- or inorganic state, ultimately to die—this remains a temptation, a counter-force operating against the trajectory of all philosophical *eros*. And it *is* a vector to be taken seriously precisely because it offers the sort of finality at which philosophical *eros* aims but can never accomplish on its own.

Plato confronts this issue directly (if perhaps in the mode of provocative irony) when he has Socrates, in the *Phaedo*, assert that philosophy is a sort of 'training' or 'technique' for dying. His argument, briefly put, runs as follows. Death is the separation of the soul from the body. Philosophy is the *eros* or desire of the soul for that which is excessive in relation to the body (the Forms or Ideas), but it is prevented from satisfying its desire by its very embodied condition. In order to satisfy this desire, the philosopher must practice the 'art' of separating the soul from the body. Full satisfaction can be accomplished, however, only when the soul is completely separated from the body in death. Therefore, the philosopher should welcome death as the culmination of what his practice had been anticipating all along. Of course, as most novice readers of Plato can readily see (and as Socrates' young interlocutors seemed to grasp), this account, taken as an argument, is flawed for several reasons. Nonetheless, it makes a serious point, and one that goes well beyond Freud's simple positing of two opposed drives. Philosophical *eros* is at once rooted in our embodied condition, is directed toward that which exceeds it, and finally terminates with the dissolution of the body. The problem, of course, is that the 'final solution' of the problem of philosophical desire is the 'dissolution' of desire and the possibility of philosophy itself. As we would say, it is the complete withdrawal of the condition of embodiment from both ideality and the world of human discourse.

This temptation of a final solution to the problem of philosophical desire-as-lack is, then, the distinctive force that the condition of embodiment exerts upon the field of philosophy and any position within it. It is our embodied condition that both, in its limitation and finitude, opens the space for philosophical desire-as-lack at the same time as it offers the only final solution in the form of its own complete withdrawal from the other conditions. Every philosophy, then, is a particular form of resistance to the force of withdrawal of our embodied condition from its engagement with other conditions. In this sense, *pace* Nietzsche, every philosophy is necessarily 'life-affirming,' whatever more particular assertions it might make—including even Schopenhauer's defense of suicide and E. von Hartmann's view that suicide is a 'moral imperative.' Were they actually to commit suicide, it would not be as philosophers or as a consequence of their philosophies; it would be as embodied beings succumbing to the force of withdrawal exerted by the condition of embodiment itself. One can 'choose' death over life, but not on philosophical grounds, as the protagonist of John Barthes' *The Floating Opera* discovered.

Still, short of such extremes, philosophical views that become fixated upon or obsessed by the condition of embodiment will typically share two features. First, they will tend to attack ideality on the grounds that any sort of 'ideas' or 'ideals' are 'betrayals of the body.' Often a favorite rallying cry will be 'anti-Platonism.' Second, available significational systems and language will tend to seem inadequate for expressing the body's excessive desires and the intensities of its physical experiences, so significational systems will be pushed to their limits and language tortured in order to express these excesses and intensities. Both aggressive anti-Platonism and extreme linguistic experimentation are hallmarks of such thinkers as Nietzsche, Breton, Bataille, and Blanchot, who all seem to believe that 'being true to the earth and the body' entails rejecting both ideality and any established form of signification. At its most extreme, such views that may have begun as philosophical positions morph into a sort of literary experimentation that hovers on the border between philosophy and literary art if it does not withdraw from the field of philosophy entirely. In moving from the body to the 'earth' and ultimately to 'anterior nature' itself, they enact a sort of symbolic 'philosophical suicide.' Nonetheless, they remain important for the field of philosophy by revealing, in dramatic ways, the insistence and excessiveness of embodiment as an actual condition of philosophy.

A further lesson can be learned by briefly noting the trajectory of some responses to this detachment of and withdrawal into the condition of embodiment. To take the case of Merleau-Ponty as an example, few philosophers have more emphasized or more extensively explored embodiment as a fundamental condition of philosophy. Yet, in the face of the detachment and withdrawal into embodiment of some of the figures we've mentioned, Merleau-Ponty equally insisted that signification and the intersubjectivity that it implies were, even on phenomenological grounds, essential potencies of the 'lived body.' Further, on the basis of his phenomenological account of embodied signification, he also reintroduced the notion of 'sense' as excessive to any significational system. In other words, his philosophy reconnected the conditions of signification and ideality with that of embodiment. In such a case, then, we see that the field of philosophy proves resilient in reconstituting itself in the face of the tendency to withdraw and dissipate itself within the excesses of embodiment.

II. SIGNIFICATION, ABSORPTION, AND REDUCTION

The force exerted by the condition of signification is qualitatively different than the dynamic process of withdrawal characteristic of the condition of embodiment. Whereas withdrawing into embodiment and its physical bases ultimately tends toward a sort of dynamic, bacchanalian dissolution of philosophy into the 'eternal' play or chaos of natural forces anterior, posterior, and transverse to finite embodied being, signaling the 'death' of singular embodied beings, the force of signification arrests the dynamic of desire by reducing it to the static structural features of its own virtual relations. At its extreme, it produces a sort of 'philosophical death by other means.'

The force exerted upon philosophy by the condition of signification, whose own existence is contingent because dependent upon the contingent existence of embodied being, functions as a process of reduction and absorption. Signification, that is, detaches itself from its relation to embodiment by reducing embodied being to a sort of hollow or neutral 'circuit' through which its own virtual relations pass. At the same time, it detaches itself from idealities by reducing them to mere 'functions' (e.g. 'meanings') of significational units or their relations. This, too, represents a sort of 'symbolic death' of philosophy, but now in the form of a 'stasis,' a structural whole to which nothing else, neither living embodied being nor events of understanding, is excessive. It is not the 'bacchanalian revel' of withdrawal and dissolution into chaos but the 'transparent and simple repose' of structural stasis (two metaphors that Hegel tried to think together from a different perspective, though without complete success, as we will later see). Within modern philosophy, this tendency to reduce embodiment and ideality to signification has taken three main forms, all of which give rise to counter-movements back into the field of philosophy (as we've already seen in the case of the withdrawal into embodiment).

1. Structuralism

Structuralism is the most familiar form produced by the forces of reduction and absorption within what's sometimes called the Continental philosophical tradition. Though there are numerous variants of structuralism, all seem to agree on one point: that the 'subject,' which had been a central assumption of modern philosophy since its inception, is an effect of the structures governing significational systems. Although structuralism emerged a bit later, it continued the general theme first announced by the great practitioners of the 'hermeneutics of suspicion'—especially Marx and Freud—who held that the subject or consciousness was in large part excessive and opaque to itself, that its desires and, indeed, very worldview was the product, respectively, of political ideology or the psychoanalytic unconscious. Still, both Marx and Freud maintained that there *are* subjects; they simply could not be the sort of things that can ever be capable of effectively pursuing the Socratic injunction of 'knowing themselves,' i.e. of engaging in philosophy. Structuralism, then, took the next step of, in effect, erasing the notion of a subject entirely by reducing it to a mere function of the operation of signifying systems. This more radical insight was, in turn, incorporated in various ways by such 'neo-structuralist' thinkers still committed to either a Marxist (e.g. Althusser) or psychoanalytic (e.g. Lacan) agenda, a stance that their critics have often called 'anti-humanist'—a label that they usually readily accepted.

This 'anti-humanist' tendency might further be seen as 'anti-philosophical.' In our terms, we can say that they attempted to absorb the modern idealized form of the actual condition of embodiment, the 'subject,' into significational systems by reducing its desires and the idealities emerging from them to mere functions of signification—to the 'values' of signs and the virtual relations obtaining among them.

Although poststructuralist thinkers have often been interpreted as further radicalizing the basic anti-humanist and anti-philosophical trajectory of structuralism, this requires some important qualifications. On the one hand, relying heavily on certain aspects of the thought of Nietzsche (and their development by Heidegger), they have, in fact, offered trenchant critiques of the structuralist account of signification. For example, both Derrida and Foucault, though employing different strategies, have suggested that significational systems cannot be regarded as self-enclosed totalities but, in fact, involve important elements of excess—*'differánce,'* the 'sliding of signifiers,' metaphor, intertextuality, political power, historical context, etc.—that serve to render them much more chaotic than the structuralist account of significational systems assumed. Such critiques did not aim to reinstate any concept of a 'subject,' of course, but they did restore important elements of excess to the condition of signification. On the other hand, again led by other aspects of the thought of Nietzsche and Heidegger, the poststructuralists at least partly reconnected signification with embodiment in highlighting the body as the fundamental locus or reference point upon which the force of signification, in the form of political power, exerted itself (something especially clear in the case of Foucault).

Viewed in this way, we can say that poststructuralism did represent a movement back into the field of philosophy from the limit to which it been brought by structuralism (which, tellingly, usually presented itself not as philosophy but as a new movement in the 'social sciences'). It remained for other now widely discussed thinkers, such as Deleuze and Badiou (whom I would regard as 'post-postructuralist'), to return fully to the field of philosophy. Not only have both explicitly defended philosophy as an autonomous enterprise but, predictably for us, they have done so by emphasizing the importance of idealities and the events from which they spring (cf. Deleuze and Guattari's *What is Philosophy?* and Badiou's *Being and Event.*) If structuralism was 'anti-philosophical' in reducing embodiment and ideality to the operation of significational systems, and poststructuralism was 'liminally philosophical' in 'deconstructing' the assumed signifying structures assumed by structuralism and linking them to embodiment, then this 'third wave' of thinkers can be said to have explicitly returned to the field of philosophy by bringing ideality back into relation to the conditions of embodiment and signification. Such a development is instructive for us because it illustrates how the actual conditions of philosophy tend to reassert their forces and, in a sense, reconstitute and rebalance philosophy's field in the face of movements to and beyond its limits.

2. Logicism

Although rooted in the philosophical tradition running from Aristotle, through Leibniz and Hume, to Kant and Frege, what I will generically call 'logicism' represents another form, recently most typical of Anglophone philosophy, that, at least implicitly though sometimes explicitly, reduces embodiment and ideality (and ultimately philosophy) to functions of a signifying system. However, unlike the structuralists, who usually acknowledged a multiplicity of significational systems, each with its own distinctive structural features, logicists tend toward the view that there is some single, fundamental structure, i.e. logic, underlying all experience, thought, and their expression. Although they differ considerably about how to describe this structure or the sort of formal apparatus in which to present it, they agree that there is such a structure and that correctly describing or presenting it can be pursued independently of the conditions of embodiment and ideality. In its most extreme forms, such as 'logical positivism' (or, as it is sometimes called, 'logical empiricism'), logicism explicitly aims to 'reduce' idealities to the meanings of words, natural languages to logical calculi, philosophical statements to 'meaningless expressions,' and the field of philosophy itself to that of the natural sciences. In one sense, such a logicist program is more radical than that of structuralism, since it has as its aim the wholesale elimination of philosophy in favor of mathematics and the natural sciences, something that structuralism, which presented itself as an alternative to philosophy, never explicitly attempted. In another sense, it is less radical in that it arises out of and in response to traditional philosophical problems and (problematically or even paradoxically, as has often been pointed out) utilizes decidedly philosophical arguments to undermine philosophy.

Logicism has never explicitly presented itself as 'anti-humanist,' but, considered from the perspective of its results for philosophy, its differences from such a view are slight (if there are any at all). Logical Positivism (or Logical Empiricism) represents the most extreme case of what I've generically called 'logicism.' Most expositions begin by dividing all 'meaningful' statements into necessary and contingent and asserting that all necessary statements are logical tautologies and all contingent statements are empirical, that is, based upon sensory experience. Already, there are three related processes of reduction at work here. First, such a view involves a specific decision about the 'meaning of meaning': from the beginning, 'meaning' is regarded strictly as a function of 'statements,' but to further underline the logical structure lying at the heart of 'meaning,' the logical positivists usually preferred to speak of 'propositions' to make clear that 'meaning,' as they wish to employ the term, is not confused with the more usual looser sense of the 'meaning' of actual statements formulated in natural languages. Second, the definition of 'necessary propositions' as logical identity statements or tautologies reduces necessity to a function of logical relations among terms, which are often set forth in formal logical calculi. Any other sense of necessity (such as employed by Kant or that we have sometimes employed) becomes absorbed into functions expressible either in a formal calculus or not at all. In particular, idealities are reduced to mere placeholders in a logically necessary structure governed by formal identity. Third, in claiming that all contingent propositions are empirical or based upon and ultimately traceable to sensory experience, the rich texture of lived embodied experience is reduced to what some logical positivists (e.g. the early Russell, Wittgenstein, and Carnap) called 'atomic statements' (or 'propositions') expressing a pure registering of physical phenomena ('this, here, now') upon equally physical sensory organs. Embodied experience is thereby translated into contingent empirical propositions, which can then serve as 'substitution instances' for the 'p's and 'q's representing statements or propositions within a formal calculus.

The main upshot of this original philosophical decision about the 'meaning of meaning' is that, unless a statement expresses a formal logical structure or can function as a 'substitution instance' of a 'variable' within that structure, it is 'meaningless.' This immediately implies that virtually all distinctively philosophical statements, and most statements that make up our daily social intercourse, are meaningless. That is, the three reductions mentioned above converge in a general reduction of lived embodied experience, intersubjective significational interaction, and the events of understanding that found idealities to the pure structural features of formal logic. Joined with a 'theory of verification' (that all 'empirical statements' must be grounded in elementary sensory experience) and an analysis of science based upon purely logical operations (to which they attempted to reduce mathematics) applied to such 'empirical statements,' they proposed the ultimate reduction of philosophy to natural science. If, as they thought, philosophy had, in the modern period, managed to discredit religion as the superstition of the 'childhood of the human species,' then they saw as their task the discrediting of philosophy as the characteristic superstition of its 'adolescence.'

We need not review the specific philosophical arguments deployed, often by figures otherwise sympathetic to their program and sometimes later on even by themselves, against some of these tenets. Rather, it is more instructive to note the general trajectory of thought that followed in the wake of the logical empiricists. In a broad sense, a movement occurred parallel to that which followed structuralism: gradually (and often grudgingly) the forces of the other actual conditions that they had attempted to reduce and absorb into a very limited sort of significational system asserted their forces, again reconstituting the field of philosophy. Wittgenstein, himself originally espousing a form of logical empiricism in his *Tractatus*, gradually came to reject the narrow and reductionist sense of meaning insisted upon by the logical positivists in favor of a view of meaning as 'use' in ordinary contexts of human life, which he presented as 'language games' defining and defined by 'forms of life.' His was a gesture that, if it did not reinstate the force of idealities and remained committed to the view that philosophical statements were meaningless, nonetheless began to reconnect with the condition of embodiment (although still emphasizing signification in the form of 'ordinary language'). Certain elements of Wittgenstein's later thought spawned further movements toward embodied experience, a notable example of which was the attempt to see in 'speech acts' and the rules governing them (as opposed to formal logical structures) the primary access to understanding signification. If this was not exactly a reinstatement of ideality, it did serve to emphasize the importance of events of discourse connected with actually existing embodied beings. From another direction, such philosophers as Quine opposed the extreme reductionism of logical empiricism by multiple strategies, including a trenchant critique of the main 'dogmas of (logical) empiricism'; the suggestion that there can be no single significational system (i.e. formal logic) that can be shown to underlie all other such systems; a guarded return to idealities in that every logical calculus implies 'ontological commitments'; and a generally pragmatist outlook that, to some degree, acknowledges the importance of the lived situation of embodied beings. This trajectory, by which the field of philosophy was reconstituted from its positivist reduction to signification by the counter-forces exerted by embodiment and ideality, has developed in recent times into full-blown 'metaphysical' discussions involving 'possible worlds' (S. Kripke, D. Lewis, and R. Stahlnaker) and returns to traditional philosophical problems posed by such historical figures as Plato, Aristotle, Hume, and Kant (H. Putnam, for instance). The important point, then, is that, while logicism has remained an important undercurrent and often 'default position' of Anglophone philosophy, its reductive force has been considerably weakened as the forces of other conditions have reasserted themselves.

3. Cognitive Science and 'Eliminative Materialism'

The most recent manifestation of the reductionist force operating over the field of philosophy is that stemming from what's often called 'Cognitive Science.' It is a discipline, or perhaps more accurately research project, that has emerged from the confluence of such areas as computer science, neurophysiology, psychology, linguistics, and certain elements of (mainly positivist-leaning) philosophy. As the name implies, it has usually situated itself among the sciences, often at the interface of the natural and behavioral sciences. At the heart of its research program is the conviction that all human activity, including physical action, language, and thought, can be explained by neural and associated biochemical processes occurring in the brain.

While sympathetic philosophical observers and participants remain somewhat divided about how to explain cognitive science's relation to and implications for traditional philosophical issues, especially the 'mind-body' problem as posed by Descartes, a liminally philosophical view has emerged which two of its advocates, Paul and Patricia Churchland, have named 'eliminative materialism.' This view, which claims that all reference to 'mental events,' which taken together constitute what its advocates call 'folk psychology,' should, can, and will eventually be eliminated in favor of materialist accounts of brain functions. Its advocates generally prefer not to speak in terms of 'reduction,' since, on their view, this seems to grant too much to the 'mentalism' of 'folk psychology.' It is not that cognitive science should be pursuing some 'mapping' between mental events and material brain states; rather, it should aim (with the assistance, perhaps, of philosophers) to discredit and entirely eliminate any discourse about or reference to what we generally take to constitute subjective, lived experience—things like desires, feelings, intentions, thoughts, and so forth.

Though this point may make some sense in terms of the way cognitive science views and pursues its research program, philosophically speaking, we can fairly say that 'eliminative materialism' is, in fact, a radical form of reduction. The sort of reduction proposed by eliminative materialism has several aspects. It begins by reducing the condition of embodiment, together with its lived experiences, to the material processes occurring in one of the body's physical organs, the brain. It also reduces the thought and understanding (important parts of the discredited 'folk psychology') involved with ideality to brain processes or events, and reduces signification even further to events that occur in specific parts of the brain.

On the face of it, it would appear that eliminative materialism, contrary to what we've said before, should be regarded more as a withdrawal into a limited aspect of embodiment rather than a reduction to the condition of signification characteristic of structuralism and logicism. Ultimately, however, I think that this is mistaken and that eliminative materialism should, in fact, be regarded as the most recent form of exactly this reduction to signification. Briefly put, eliminative materialism can be stated as a philosophical position only under the actual conditions forming the field for any philosophical view. It requires embodied beings capable of being aware that their bodies involve distinguishable parts (one of which is a brain, though we perhaps have no direct 'phenomenological' knowledge of this). Rather, the functioning of my brain is one of the excesses involved in my embodied being; I can know *that* I have a brain, but can never understand, at any given time, the details of its functioning in any act that I perform involving it. Further, the word 'brain' is itself a signifier whose meaning consists, at least in part, in its place within a system of signification (to begin with, the differential system of terms by which I am able to distinguish and refer to parts of my body). Finally, if eliminative materialism is a distinctive philosophical position, it will have arisen from events of understanding and their development in manifolds excessive to them.

Eliminative materialism, then, taken as a philosophical view, is ultimately another sort of reduction to signification. In this case, the form of signification involves, as its basic terms, 'brain states' and 'locations.' Were cognitive science to succeed in its aim, the underlying 'logic' relating these would be formulated in terms of neural (and ultimately, perhaps, biochemical) processes. Maybe human beings could ultimately learn to speak such a language (just like they can learn to manipulate logical symbols), but this would not in any sense 'eliminate' an embodied speaker who must desire to speak such a language, the excesses of significational systems (especially that we can never refer to our 'brain states' at the time that they occur), and the events of understanding upon which the articulation of such a project rests. While eliminative materialism might be taken as expressing the 'desiderata' of a scientific research program (somewhat like Laplace's deterministic extrapolations on Newtonian science), it is either a philosophical position (though one which must operate, inconsistently, within actual conditions that it expressly denies) or it is merely another 'reduction to signification' which again, at best, serves to reveal the limits and contours of the field of philosophy itself. In the end, it seems to be a decision in favor of a particular and very limited type of description and analysis rather than a philosophical position.

It is interesting that some of the more recent generation of 'cognitive scientists,' such as Alva Noë, have become highly critical of some of the basic assumptions and approaches of the field. Noë, in particular, has insisted upon the importance of focusing upon 'embodiment in a world' (citing, among others, Merleau-Ponty) rather than the brain and have begun exploring the implications of this for reevaluating the role of language and thought in shaping conscious experience. Once again, the forces of the actual conditions seem to be reconstituting the field of philosophy from the reductive limit that cognitive science had reached.

III. IDEALITY AND COM-PREHENSION

Like the other basic conditions of philosophy, ideality exerts its force on the field of philosophy and positions within it in a distinctive way. Unlike the withdrawal characteristic of embodiment or the reduction characteristic of signification, the force of ideality expresses itself as what I will call 'com-prehension.' The hyphen serves to indicate the difference between what I have in mind and the more limited sense of the non-hyphenated term, which might naturally be taken as a mere act or event of understanding. The term 'com-prehension' should be read, rather literally, as 'grasping together,' as indicating a sort of expansive embrace or inclusion.

There are, in fact, two well-known names for views that emphasize the com-prehensive character of ideality: they are metaphysics and ideology. (Here I'll only discuss the first; I'll take up the second in a later chapter when I deal with 'engaged philosophy.') Metaphysics seeks neither to withdraw from the other conditions nor reduce them to something other than themselves. Rather, while acknowledging the forces of the other conditions, it aims to com-prehend them, to view them as parts or aspects of idealities unfolding into their manifolds. Metaphysics never withdraws into embodied being or reduces all else to signification. Rather, it aims to embrace and include both embodied being and signification within the com-prehensive scope of ideality.

Aristotle, who is usually credited with coining the term, defined metaphysics as the 'science (or knowing) of being-qua-being.' The implication was that, since all things (including all aspects of embodiment and all forms of signification) *are*, then the knowledge of them, the science which begins with the ideality 'being,' will com-prehend them. For Aristotle, metaphysics is neither a withdrawal from the other conditions or a reduction of them. He accorded full insistence and integrity to biology, logic, and all the permutations that their interactions could produce. But metaphysics, based upon the ideality of 'being' and its unfolding into a manifold of other idealities, embraced and included them. Both the physical functioning and experience of embodied beings (biology, psychology, ethics, and politics) and the underlying structures of signification (logic, rhetoric, interpretation) were com-prehended—embraced, included, and ultimately derived from—'first philosophy,' the 'master science' of the ideality 'being,' that is, metaphysics.

However, contrary to many modern interpretations of metaphysics that identify it exclusively with the concern with the ideality 'being' (Heidegger and his followers in particular), metaphysics has, in fact, taken other idealities as the most com-prehensive; for instance, 'the Good' for Plato; 'God' for the neo-Platonists and Augustine; 'Nature' for Schelling and the Romantics; 'Spirit' for Hegel, and so on. The 'essence of metaphysics' is not, *pace* Heidegger, a particular ('ontic') interpretation of 'Being,' but a more general tendency to regard some ideality (whatever it might be) as com-prehending the other conditions of philosophy, including their excesses. Metaphysics, then, is not necessarily a specific interpretation of 'Being' (though that may be one version of it) but a way of regarding and unfolding any ideality in a way that claims to com-prehend, to embrace and include, the many manifestations of the other conditions within itself.

It is important to see that the first modern critique of metaphysics, that of Hume, specifically asserted the force and its excessiveness of embodied being against the tendency of metaphysics to com-prehend it. The most serious part of Hume's critique of metaphysics was not his more localized critique of causality, as it is often presented, but his insistence that all that we experience and claim to know begins with 'impressions,' that is, the temporally fluctuating features of embodied existence as experienced. Hume's critique of metaphysics asserted the insistence and excesses of embodied experience against any ideality that might be asserted as com-prehending this excess.

Kant's Critical Philosophy, the second major modern critique of metaphysics, radicalized Hume's mere invocation of the excessiveness of embodied experience. On the one hand, it attempted to define the conditions of embodiment itself in terms of space, time, and object, and affirmed these as the fundamental matrix of embodied experience (hence further specifying the 'conditions' that were required to bolster Hume's critique). On the other, it asserted the force of signification, in the (limited) form of formal logic, in claiming that the 'discourse of metaphysics' was inevitably 'paralogistic,' 'antinomic,' and self-contradictory. Ultimately, then, Kant's critique of metaphysics asserted, within the limits of his idealist stance, both the forces of the condition of embodiment and of signification against the com-prehensive force of ideality. Though himself profoundly critical of the limitations of Kant's idealist stance, Nietzsche continued in this trajectory of asserting the excesses of embodiment and signification in the face of the com-prehensive pretensions of metaphysical ideality, though he himself succumbed, in part, to the temptations of ideality by positing the 'Will to Power' as the ultimate 'com-prehensive' concept or idea.

Especially with Heidegger, the critique of metaphysics entered a (problematic) third phase, that appears to continue unabated today in certain quarters. Heidegger (among other things) radicalized the former critiques of metaphysics in three important respects.

First, through the deployment of the notion of 'ontological difference,' the fundamental distinction between Being itself and its particular manifestations as 'beings,' he came to view the 'essence of metaphysics' as a 'forgetting' and 'erasure' of the 'ontological difference.' On his view, metaphysics, from Plato on, came to view the 'question of Being,' the '*Seinsfrage*,' wholly in terms of beings and their various 'kinds.' Metaphysics, on Heidegger's interpretation, remained founded upon a single ideality, that of Being, but understood Being only in terms of various 'kinds' of being (Forms, substance, 'the One,' 'God,' consciousness, experience, nature, Spirit, Will, etc.). Given such a move, Heidegger then proposed the project of a 'destructive recovery of the history of metaphysics' that would reopen and reinstate the difference between Being and beings and allow philosophy once again to 'authentically' raise the original question of Being that the history of metaphysics had 'covered over' and obscured. Heidegger's radical critique of metaphysics, then, was not primarily a reassertion of the condition of embodiment or that of signification against the com-prehensiveness of ideality but, rather, an indictment of the way in which philosophy, in the form of metaphysics, had developed what he asserted as philosophy's own primary ideality, that is, Being.

Second, Heidegger further radicalized this indictment of metaphysics by claiming that the entire enterprise of philosophy was, at root, metaphysical. Unlike earlier critiques of metaphysics, which viewed it as a particular kind or discipline of philosophical endeavor and maintained that not all philosophy need be metaphysical, Heidegger proposed that all philosophy was rooted in metaphysics and that all metaphysics involved the privileging of a certain ideality, 'Being,' under a universal and, for him, fatal misinterpretation. In a way similar to the thanatonic withdrawal into embodiment and the reduction-without-remainder to signification, Heidegger's critique of metaphysics, that also began in the field of philosophy and utilized its resources, brought philosophy to another of its limiting conditions, in this case, ideality. The erasure of the ideality (recall Heidegger's famous 'crossing out' of Being) on which metaphysics was anchored would also signal the 'end of philosophy' (the title, in fact, of one of his lectures) conceived as rooted in metaphysics.

Third, Heidegger further insisted that this 'destruction of metaphysics,' that also heralded the 'end of philosophy,' must be accompanied by a 'recovery.' Freed from the misunderstanding of Being as one or multiple types of beings, we would now be in a position to 'recover' the 'authentic meaning of Being' and of the sense of the original question about it. However, this 'recovery' would now take the form, not of philosophy as practiced in the tradition, but of 'thinking.' Such an 'ontological' (as opposed to 'ontic') thinking would then return to the conditions of embodied being and signification in a way freed from the fatal misunderstanding that had formerly plagued 'philosophy-as-metaphysics.' Under the force of such thinking, the condition of embodied human being became '*Dasein*,' a radically finite 'being there,' as explicated primarily in *Being and Time*, where the emphasis was upon the 'temporal' and 'historical' sense of the 'there.' The condition of signification would likewise become understood as '*Sprachlichkeit*,' a mode of 'belongingness to Being' in which Being 'be-speaks' itself in and through the 'authentic words' that make up this new relation of '*Dasein*' to language.

But can we not discern in the 'turnings' of Heidegger's 'thought' something familiar, something even 'metaphysical' in our own sense of the term? Heidegger's own response to his radical 'destruction' of the history of philosophy as metaphysics, that is, his 'recovery' of this history, led him to reinstate the conditions of philosophy. Being remains an excessive ideality that com-prehends both embodied being (in the form of '*Dasein*') and signification (in the form of '*Sprachlichkeit*'), while insisting on the excessiveness of both as 'belonging to Being.' If we remember that the actual 'essence of metaphysics' lies not in the particular ideality taken as fundamental but in the force of com-prehension that the fundamental ideality, whatever it might be, exerts upon embodiment and signification (a point made especially clear by Levinas), then we must say that Heidegger's own thinking represents an 'ultimate metaphysics,' another sort of 'final solution' to the problem of philosophical desire and its articulation like those of withdrawal and reduction. In this sense, Heidegger can, despite his own intentions, be read as reconstituting the field of philosophy, and many latter-day Heideggerians have, in fact, interpreted him in exactly this way.

However, there are two other trajectories out of Heidegger's radical critique of metaphysics that have emerged. The first is religious and tends to view Heidegger's insistence on the 'ontological difference' and its associated 'recovery' of the 'question of Being' as a new foundation for theological reflection and a path by which the nature and human significance of religion and religious language might be reinterpreted. This religious or theological path out of Heidegger tended either to equate Heidegger's Being with the 'God' of Christianity (as in Bultmann and some Catholic theologians such as Rahner) or viewed Heidegger's thought about Being (sometimes aided by certain poststructuralist textual strategies) as an opening to reconsider the entire 'history of onto-theo-logic,' an attempt, that is, to effect a 'destructive recovery' of theology in a way paralleling Heidegger's own 'destructive recovery' of the history of metaphysics. (J.-L. Marion, on the Continent, and Mark Taylor and John Caputo, in the U.S., are major representatives of this latter approach.) Here, I am not concerned with whether this religio-theological trajectory out of Heidegger represents some fair or accurate extrapolation of Heidegger's own thought about Christianity, religion, or theology; rather, I want only to call attention to the fact that it is a trajectory, made possible by Heidegger, that ultimately abandons the field of philosophy in favor of some other 'field' (a new type of theology, perhaps, or, in some cases, a sort of mysticism) by a gesture that both detaches an ideality ('God' or 'Being') from the other conditions and, at the same time, emphasizes its com-prehension of all else even in its detachment. While I realize that most of these thinkers would likely disagree with my characterization, probably by claiming, among other things, that 'Being' or 'God' is both 'transcendent' and 'immanent,' I would reply that, from the point of view of the actual conditions of philosophy as I've described them, philosophy itself can *only* be regarded as 'purely immanent' and *any* suggestion of transcendence in the sense that theology or religion intends must necessarily transgress the limits of the field of philosophy and occupy another, different 'field.'

The second trajectory is the ideological. Some interpreters of Heidegger (such as Victor Farias, Hermann Ott, and, most recently, Emmanuel Faye) have argued that this trajectory was already present in Heidegger's own thought. Faye, in particular, has proposed that most of Heidegger's basic 'philosophical' terms served as only thinly veiled and mystified (if even that) 'code words' for, at the time, well-known elements of National Socialist ideology. (In point of fact, Faye's indictment of Heidegger is much broader than this, but this is sufficient for my present purposes.) Here is not the place to attempt to confront what has become called the 'Heidegger controversy' as posed by some of the figures just mentioned. Rather, at this point, I want merely to observe that, when an ideality (such as 'Being') becomes emphasized at the expense of the other conditions, there remains always the possibility of the reinterpretation and consequent political manipulation and dominance of embodied being and signification derived from the com-prehensive force of a 'master ideality.' To use terms that may be more familiar, any philosophical approach that, disregarding the actual limiting conditions of philosophy, permits the other conditions to be com-prehended under a single totalizing idea or concept harbors the possibility, intended or not by the philosopher, of ideological deployment. Under the sway of such an ideological deployment, there remains a permanent possibility that embodied human being will be devalued and converted into mere 'material' for the 'historical realization' of political aims and that signification will become hijacked and distorted by political propaganda and the control of the means of its dissemination.

It is worth noting that the three trajectories issuing from setting loose the com-prehensive force of ideality are not unique to the case of Heidegger. It seems, in fact, to be the case that this set of results follows from any philosophical position that comes to privilege ideality at the expense of human embodiment and signification. Two familiar examples are provided by Plato and Hegel. Having presented 'the Good' in the *Republic* as the 'supreme Idea,' as the 'intelligibility of all Forms,' Plato (and others who have followed this 'philosophical trajectory') remained within the field of philosophy by continuing critically to examine the consequences of such a view (e.g., in the *Republic* itself as well as in other 'later' dialogues). However, a 'religious trajectory' also issued from Plato (and neo-Platonism), ultimately coming to serve, in Augustine, as the basis for a different 'field,' Christian theology. Finally, Plato himself (and perhaps some others inspired by him in later times) seems to have pursued an 'ideological trajectory' in drawing the political consequences of his philosophical thought and actually attempting to apply them in an actual *polis*. (It was not so long ago that some thinkers like Karl Popper saw in Plato the 'original totalitarian ideologist.') A similar set of trajectories issued from the thought of Hegel, who proposed a 'system' designed to com-prehend human experience, logic, nature, and culture under the ideality of 'Spirit' or 'the Absolute Concept.' Three main trajectories followed in the wake of Hegel: a (so to speak) 'orthodox' Hegelian school, which, remaining within the field of philosophy, sought to critically explore the structure, consequences, and limitations of Hegel's thought; the 'Hegelian Right,' which appropriated Hegel's thought to reconsider religious and theological issues; and the 'Hegelian Left' (or 'Young Hegelians'), who both read Hegel as himself an 'ideologist' of the bourgeoisie state and borrowed elements of his thought for their own ideological ends. In all such cases, the main point to be learned for our discussion is that when the comprehensive force of ideality exerts itself at the expense of embodied human being and signification, philosophy encounters one of its limits. At such a point, thought can either reconstitute the field of philosophy by, in some way, reinstating the other conditions; it can exit the field in favor of that of theology, religion, or mysticism; or it can turn its force upon the other conditions, assuming the form of a totalizing and hegemonic ideology.

IV. IN SUMMARY

As I've already argued, it's important to understand that the three conditions are asymmetrical with respect to one another in their order of dependence, their respective internal structures and processes, and the forms in which their forces act upon the field of philosophy. The over-emphasis or dissociation of any one condition from the others represents a catastrophe for the field of philosophy, but the type of catastrophe and the options left open differ from one condition to another. In the case of the withdrawal into embodiment, the catastrophe is more particular, individual, and subjective. It terminates in physical dissolution and ultimately physical death and admits only a single alternative, a choice between death and philosophy itself as a living activity. Reduction to signification is also a catastrophe, for it signals the symbolic death of philosophical meaning. But it does offer an additional alternative, since its trajectory can transgress the limits of philosophy in the direction of another field, the sciences. It does not necessarily lead (in any direct way, at least) to the death of the individual, but it does threaten, generically, the 'death of the human.' Finally, the com-prehensive force of ideality, while not intrinsically 'death-driven' and even, in its way, erotic and 'life-affirming,' offers further alternatives. To choose to continue philosophical thought in the face of the totality is to choose, in its way, continued life and humanity. To follow the religious or mystical trajectory is, perhaps, in some sense akin to Pascal's 'wager.' With 'luck,' it may constitute a living solution to the problem of 'desire-as-lack'; or, it may come to constitute a field other than philosophy, with problematic dynamics of its own; or, it may just as well be, as Kierkegaard suggests, a leap into the abyss. Finally, following the trajectory of ideology involves, perhaps, the highest stakes. It is not directly the death of philosophy, since philosophy continues into ideology in a sort of attenuated and ossified form, from which it may even, at times, be capable of liberating itself. But, carried through to its conclusion, the path of ideology can either terminate in a universal liberation of embodied being and signification or in the horrific suffering of embodied being and the total perversion of all sense and human significance—in death camps, gulags, and military prisons. That it has so rarely eventuated in the former and so often in the latter should amply warn us of the dangers inherent in the force of com-prehension, at the same time as further convincing us of the powerful efficacy and robust actuality of the condition of ideality.

DIAGRAM 4: The Interreflections of the Conditions (Chapters 8-10)

(3) Philosophy as **Body of Ideas** or **'Doctrine'**:
The Actual Condition of **Ideality**

    Event – Singularity
    Structure – Universality
    Process – Particularity

(1) Philosophy as **Activity**:  (2) Philosophy as **Text**:
The Actual Condition of   The Actual Condition of
Embodied Being: **Signification:**

    Eidetic Construction   Speculative Sentences
    Reflection   Logical propositions
    Analysis   Expressive Enunciations

8

Philosophy as Activity and Its Components

INTRODUCTION: THE GENERIC ARCHITECTURE OF PHILOSOPHY

The last chapter explored the results that ensue when, within a philosophical view, one of the basic conditions comes to dominate the others or, in the most extreme cases, either attempts to ignore the others or deals with them in some reductive way. Viewed from this perspective, we might say that each condition is capable of exerting its own sort of force over the field of philosophy that can subvert and, in the most extreme cases, collapse the enterprise into a sort of ever-narrowing vortex where it becomes no longer recognizable as philosophy. However, I earlier suggested, as a sort of general principle, that, so long as this does not occur, that is, when the three conditions remain in some sort of balance or equilibrium, the forces distinctive of each will be registered in the others. That is, something of the internal structure of each condition will be reflected in that of the others. It is this mutual interreflectedness of the conditions that constitutes the unity of the field of philosophy and, at its most generic level, a 'basic architecture' of philosophy. Viewing the field of philosophy in this way, then, allows us to map the most general determinations or distinctions that tend to recur within individual philosophies and across their historical interconnections.

Recall that, at the beginning, I noted that philosophy has (at least) three meanings and concrete manifestations: it can mean or appear as a type of activity; a discourse, text, or group of them; or a general idea, 'doctrine,' or set of related views (though, of course, in any concrete example, philosophy involves all three). I further argued that this is so because these various manifestations of philosophy directly result from and correspond to what I've been calling the actual conditions of philosophy. To say that philosophy is a sort of activity assumes that there are embodied beings capable of performing such an activity. To regard philosophy as a discourse, text, or set of these is to presuppose that there are significational systems (usually a suitable language) in which philosophical activity can be expressed and communicated to other embodied beings. And to consider philosophy as a body of ideas, views, or even some nameable 'position,' such as 'Platonism' or 'realism,' assumes that there is something excessive and irreducible to either embodied being or the significational systems that it deploys—what I have called 'idealities'—that are generated in the process of philosophical activity articulating itself in some significational system.

In presenting such an admittedly abstract schema, we've, so far, connected these three meanings or manifestations of philosophy, and their corresponding conditions, through a sort of 'genetic' account. It could be described by saying that embodied beings and their activities are necessary conditions for there being significational systems, and particular types of deployment of significational systems on the part of embodied beings constitute a necessary condition for there being 'philosophical idealities.' But beyond such a genetic account, the question now arises about the affinities among the basic conditions that allow them to come together in the sort of singularities that can be identified as specific instances of philosophy (or, in terms we've also used, identifiable positions or regions within the field formed by the three conditions). This broad question can be approached in terms of three sub-questions.

1. What sort of activities must embodied beings be capable of performing in order to engage with the other conditions in such a way that can issue in something recognizable as philosophy? Put another way, are there any fundamental practices (and, if so, what would they be) that, operating together, can eventuate in an instance of philosophy? Or, once again, how is it possible for embodied being to serve as a nexus for connecting transfinite idealities with the expression of its own finite activities?

2. Are there distinguishable functions or aspects of signifying systems that, on the one hand, allow them to be deployed for philosophical purposes by embodied beings and, on the other, connect with the idealities generated by such deployment? What, that is, permits significational systems to serve both as vehicles expressive of the activities of finite embodied beings and as ways of access to transfinite idealities?

3. How are we to characterize idealities in a way that permits access to

them on the part of embodied beings, clarifies how they are capable of being articulated within significational systems, and yet acknowledges their excessiveness to both embodied being and any particular significational system? In other words, what features must idealities have such that embodied beings can both grasp and 'think' them and communicate such activities to other embodied beings, even as they remain excessive to both?

I will suggest that the functions that each of these questions require us to distinguish and recognize not only provide, taken together, a sort of overall architectural framework or schematic for any more specific philosophical position, but that their ubiquity and insistence is confirmed, though admittedly formulated in quite varied ways and with varying emphases, by actual positions within the history of philosophy.

Schematically, each of the manifestations of philosophy (activities, texts, idealities) involve three elements, two that connect, respectively, with the other two manifestations and their underlying conditions and one, mediating between this pair, that is distinctive for that manifestation and its associated condition. (See diagram 4) As I will explain in what follows, there are three basic activities of philosophy: analysis, reflection, and construction. There are three basic forms of philosophical signification: expressive enunciations, logical propositions, and speculative sentences. And there are three basic modes of idealities: singular events, universal structures, and particular processes. I should note that, in each case, the 'middle term' is the dominant one for each manifestation of philosophy and its corresponding actual condition and serves a connecting or mediating role with respect to the other two.

That said, one important caveat is needed at this point. Given our earlier acknowledgment of the relative autonomy and irreducibility of the actual conditions, this schematic should not be regarded either as some 'table of categories' (like Kant's) or as some 'system of concepts' (like Hegel's). Rather, it constitutes, at most, an intrinsically open framework or matrix of possibilities that delineates the 'space' or 'field' of philosophy. The thesis upon which we earlier insisted, that the actual conditions of philosophy are always and necessarily excessive with respect to any singular point or position within the field of philosophy, or, for that matter, of any more generic account of philosophy, will remain in full force.

The present chapter will focus upon the first set of questions posed above concerning philosophy regarded as an activity engaged in by embodied beings; the following two chapters will deal, respectively, with philosophy regarded as texts expressed in significational systems and as views or positions constituted by specific configurations of idealities. (For this and the following two Chapters, refer to Diagram 4)

I. THE FUNDAMENTAL PHILOSOPHICAL ACTIVITIES OF EMBODIED BEINGS

In the tradition of philosophy, what I will call 'reflection' has occupied a pivotal place among the various activities in which philosophers have engaged and sometimes attempted to describe. The very beginning of this tradition has often been traced to the injunction found in the Platonic dialogues to "know thyself" and the closely associated claim that "the unexamined life is not worth living." A major foundational document of the Middle Ages was Augustine's own autobiographical self-examination, *The Confessions*. At the beginning of the modern period of philosophy stands Descartes' *Meditations on First Philosophy*, a work that seeks to ground all human certainty and knowledge on a self-reflexive act of consciousness expressed in the form of the statement, "*Cogito ergo sum*." The empiricist thinkers of the 17th and 18th centuries consistently placed major emphasis upon a painstaking reflective observation and analysis of the contents of our mental activities. Kant, responding to both, sought to ground philosophy itself in a reflective procedure that he called 'transcendental,' and his idealist followers, especially Hegel, came to characterize Kant's entire philosophical viewpoint as a 'philosophy of reflection.' With certain reservations about the limitations of Kant's own transcendental approach, his idealist progeny nonetheless adopted the basic trajectory of his thought, expanding it to serve as the privileged universal framework for constructing philosophical 'systems.' Though suspicious of the sort of 'metaphysical expansion' proposed by the German Idealists, versions of Kant's interpretation of philosophical reflection in terms of a transcendental method continued to occupy a central place in both the phenomenological, hermeneutic, and existential movements as well as, in the form of long-running discussions about 'transcendental arguments,' in the reflections of such more empiricist-minded philosophers as Peter Strawson and other Anglophone thinkers.

From the perspective of the individual engaged in philosophy, of embodied being, then, there is a primacy that must be granted to the activity of reflection. Given all the quite varying evocations of reflection as the paradigmatic philosophical activity, we must first ask what these might have in common? Is it possible to give some generic account or description of the activity of reflection? Second, we'll need to consider how philosophical reflection somehow emerges as one among the broader set of activities of embodied being. We must ask, that is, about whether or not philosophical reflection is somehow continuous or isomorphic with other embodied activities? This will lead us to the third question of how the other actual conditions find expression in philosophical activities that are involved with or related to reflection?

1. Reflection as the Primary Philosophical Activity of Embodied Being

In the tradition, we can distinguish three major versions of reflection viewed as a philosophical activity. The first stems from Plato and emphasizes reflection as the unique activity involved in 'knowing oneself' or 'examining one's life,' a sort of 'theoretical practice' that results in changes in one's concrete activities and, ultimately, way of living. Reflection from a Platonic perspective, that is, is a special sort mental or intellectual activity of the soul that progressively alters and may ultimately transform the soul's (or mind's) own fundamental constitution, leading it to alter its further practical activities or behaviors. Admittedly, there is no exact Greek equivalent for 'reflection,' but I think the phrase 'theoretical practice' captures something of the dual emphases that 'knowing oneself' or 'examining one's life' is a sort of *intellectual* activity and that this ultimately issues in alterations in other life activities that are not specifically theoretical (perhaps most importantly, reconfigurations of priority among desires).

The second is the empiricist account of reflection, wherein the mind, at various more or less sporadic 'philosophical moments,' examines its own 'contents' (its 'ideas,' as Locke terms any mental content). For the most part, its more modest aim is not so much some reconfiguration of desire or large-scale life reorientation, but an enhanced theoretical clarity about mental functioning. Although indispensable for empiricist philosophy, reflection is not, on the empiricist account, a sort of activity that many or even most embodied beings need to or, in fact, do engage in, nor is it one that receives much further clarification in empiricist philosophy.

Finally, there is the transcendental idealist account of reflection (referring to that of Kant and his successors, including, among others the phenomenological tradition). Although its aim is more modest in scope than that of Plato's life-altering version, reflection *is* viewed as the central and unique activity of human consciousness (the idealized version of what we have been calling 'embodied being'). On this view (as first suggested by Kant, made explicit by Fichte, and significantly expanded by Hegel), reflection has a determinate structure (something largely unspecified in the first two versions) with several defining features. First, any specific conscious or mental 'content' is always attended by the possibility of reflecting upon it. (Kant puts this generically in terms of the 'I think' that accompanies any representation; Fichte identifies the capacity for reflection with the intrinsic freedom that he attributes to consciousness itself.) Second, reflection is productive, in that its very performance constitutes a transformation from the initial state of 'mere consciousness' to a new state of 'self-consciousness.' Put broadly, it is in the activity of reflecting that a 'self' is created. Third, this newly produced state of self-consciousness is interpreted transcendentally, that is, it is understood to constitute or function within a different 'ideal' order than that of the 'real' spatio-temporal nexus defining mere consciousness. However, since self-consciousness is possible *only* as a reflection upon consciousness, the transcendental idealist view maintains that the new state or position of self-consciousness includes or contains within itself the consciousness defining its starting-point. In its furthest expansion, Hegel adds that the process of reflection is, so to speak, recursive, that any self-conscious state can, in turn, serve as the object or starting-point of another act of reflection, which, on his own view, terminates in a completed reflective process that he variously calls 'Absolute Spirit,' 'the Concept,' or just 'the Absolute.'

It is against this background that any account of the structure of reflection as the central philosophical activity of embodied beings must be framed. I suggest that an account of reflection that acknowledges the actuality, irreducibility, and excessiveness of the three conditions upon which we've been insisting must both preserve important insights from each of the three accounts outlined above while departing from each of them in significant ways. One key to such an account will lie in showing that, in its basic structure, the activity of reflection is isomorphic with other affective activities or processes of embodied beings while insisting upon its uniqueness and irreducibility to them. Put another way, while the activity of philosophical reflection is continuous with other life processes or activities, indeed is embedded within and occurs within their midst, it nonetheless plays a unique role within the experience and life of embodied beings. Or, again, while philosophical reflection is nothing extraordinary or occult, while it is a natural part of our embodied life and must always take its place within the excesses to which embodied existence is subject, it nonetheless possesses a distinctive and irreducible character of its own.

As a preliminary response to the three views of the activity of reflection offered by the tradition, we might say that the Platonic and empiricist versions tend to view it as something primitive and undifferentiated, even perhaps mysterious or at least not further analyzable, while the transcendental version offers an account that is, perhaps, extravagant in its assumptions and ramifications. By contrast, I will claim that philosophical reflection is, on the one hand, an activity that, like many other activities of embodied beings, involves other components (think of the various 'sub-activities' involved in riding a bicycle or playing a guitar), but, on the other, is not some 'master activity' that requires the deployment of all our capacities.

I suggest, then, as a first pass, that the basic components of reflection are memory, desire, and construction (the latter in a quite specific sense that I'll explain shortly). To begin with, any act of reflection, philosophical or otherwise, is upon or about something; though we sometimes say things like, "I'm in a reflective mood today," this is an empty claim unless, when asked, we can supply some answer to the question, "What are you reflecting or thinking about"? In general, the answer will necessarily invoke some aspect of my past experience that becomes present for me through the operation of memory. This is true whether the remembered 'object' of reflection is some concrete perception, event, or even an abstract idea with which I've previously become acquainted. Of course, remembering is itself a mental act, so memory always functions as one of the 'act-components' of reflection. This point is important since it rules out the possibility of understanding reflection as either some independent mental capacity or purely formal structure, a view that sometimes seems to be implied in ordinary discourse and even, on occasion, in the philosophical tradition.

The philosophical act of reflection, however, cannot be simply identified with the act of remembering, since it also involves adopting a distinctive attitude or stance toward what is otherwise merely remembered. To reflect upon some content provided by an act of remembering is to actively engage with it by opening a broader field of other possibilities—other experiences, memories, or ideas—to which it may be linked or within which it can be situated. This virtual field of possibilities opened by the reflective engagement with something remembered is, with respect to the actual 'memory-content' itself, a present 'lack' of further determinate content that will only be filled in (and this only partially) by further acts of reflection. This experience of lack attending the reflective consideration of something remembered, together with the impetus to remedy it, is a form or aspect of the sort of intellectual desire (Plato might call it 'philosophical *eros*') that we earlier described. As such, desire constitutes an irreducible aspect of philosophical reflection that seems mostly absent within and even opposed to modern idealist accounts of reflection, whether in the form of Kant's opposition between reason and desire, Hegel's locating the dynamism of reflection in the 'impersonal' movement of concepts themselves, or Husserl's quest for a 'phenomenological method' purged of all 'prejudices' (including desires) of the 'natural attitude.' It is not, of course, that their own projects weren't driven by a type of desire, only that they accorded no crucial place to it in their stated views of philosophy.

Finally, however, the distinctively philosophical aspect of a reflective act isn't fully described so long as we leave reflection merely as an act of remembering opening a field of possibilities that provoke an act of desire. Many such memorial acts unleash a complex of desires without ever becoming distinctly philosophical (as Proust's great opus explores in minute detail). Rather, another factor must intervene and I will (for lack of a better phrase and at the risk of possible misunderstanding) call this 'eidetic construction.' In the sense intended here, 'construction' indicates a distinctive act by which the open field of possibilities or meanings constituting the field of philosophical desire becomes populated by idealities that serve as more determinate objects of that desire.

The third aspect of philosophical reflection, then, is that it is productive, and in this our account agrees with the modern idealist tradition, which also held that every act of reflection produces a new 'object' for further reflection. It differs from this, however, in two important respects. First, while it is no doubt possible to take an earlier act of reflection as an 'ideal object' of further reflection, this by no means exhausts the field of idealities as possible ways of determining the objects of philosophical desire. Philosophical reflection, that is, need not assume that its only possible productions are exclusively further reflective acts, an assumption forced upon modern idealists by their own position. Second, because these idealities are objects of *desire*, and, as we have already seen, because desire ultimately occurs within a context defined by ineliminable excesses, no such product (or complex of products) of eidetic construction will ultimately serve to completely fulfill or satisfy philosophical desire. With respect to philosophical desire, such products can never, of themselves, exhaust the field of desire's essential lack and will always remain open to other possible lines of development. That is, no ideality, complex, or even systematic organization of them will serve to arrest the philosophical desire operative within the act of philosophical reflection.

One final remark is required regarding the phrase 'eidetic construction.' I employ this phrase both to link it to certain aspects of the modern idealist tradition as well as to indicate an important difference. Among other philosophers, some of the modern Idealists (especially Kant, Fichte, and Schelling) employed the phrase 'intellectual intuition' to indicate a (in some cases, though not all, merely hypothetical) type of knowledge of or access to 'ultimate truth' unmediated by the finite and limiting conditions of embodied being. In particular, were there such a faculty, it would be one that operated independently of sensory perception, memory, or, in particular, any sort of reflection. As a direct and hence unreflective knowledge or insight, 'intellectual intuition' introduces an untraverseable gap between itself and reflection as an activity of embodied and finite beings. As Kant, the later Fichte, and Schelling all insisted, reflection can never attain 'intellectual intuition' by its own devices and, indeed, serves only to distance reflection from it by interposing increasingly complex conceptual determinations that obscure it further. By contrast, by employing the phrase 'eidetic construction' as an aspect of reflection itself, I want, on the one hand, to deny that there can be any philosophically relevant form of (non-reflective) 'intellectual intuition' while, at the same time, acknowledging that an essential aspect of reflection involves the production of idealities that are not reducible merely to the activity of reflection itself. To take the principal ideality of the idealists, 'the Absolute,' I would assert that it can only be a product of eidetic construction operating as a component of reflection itself, not something that grounds some other non-reflective philosophical activity. The principal philosophical activity of embodied beings, that is, is completely limited to reflection and possesses no other 'philosophical faculty' that is not involved with reflection.

This becomes especially clear when we consider the structure of reflection in relation to that of other activities of embodied being. In the idealist tradition, reflection was understood generically as an activity of consciousness becoming self-conscious. However, I want to suggest that, looked at from a different perspective, the underlying structure of reflection can be seen, when extracted from the idiom of idealism, also to govern the physiological activities of embodiment itself. That is, reflection, regarded as a generic structure, is not exclusive to consciousness as conceived by idealism but is already present as an operative structure in embodied existence. This means that there is much more of a continuity between the physiological and the mental or conscious aspects of embodied being, between life and philosophical reflection, than idealism was capable of acknowledging.

To accomplish this, however, we will need briefly to reconsider in a bit more detail the idealist account of the structure of reflection. The idealist account proposes that the activity of reflection involves a movement from a 'state' of representation (in Kant) or consciousness (in Fichte, Hegel, and, under a different interpretation, Husserl) to a further 'state' of 'reflective consciousness' or 'self-consciousness.' Given any state of consciousness, that is, it is always possible to perform an act of reflection upon it, thus generating a new state that both includes the first as its object and provides a new standpoint from which to analyze or articulate the original state. So understood, the activity of reflection is always a matter of 'auto-affection,' in that the act of reflection occurs exclusively in the interval between two states of consciousness. Put in other terms, for the idealist, excess is involved in reflection only in a weak sense: consciousness is excessive solely in relation to itself. Idealist reflection, then, is always a matter exclusively internal to consciousness; as Kant first proposed, later seconded by Fichte, Hegel, and Husserl, 'we need not go far afield,' for all that is involved is 'contained in my own self,' as Kant puts it in the first Preface to the *Critique of Pure Reason*.

Embodiment, however, is never monadic, self-contained, or exclusively a matter of auto-affection. To be embodied is already to exist within a spatial, temporal, and material environment (or, perhaps better, set of environments) constituted by other physically embodied beings (some conscious, some not). Quite apart from any more rarified notion of consciousness, an embodied being with a sufficiently complex physiological constitution is *affected by other* embodied beings in its environment(s). In this sense, to 'be affected' means that its present state at any given point is altered in specific ways, thus producing a new state of its embodied condition. In some cases, this new state will serve as the basis for a specific response, an action, on the part of the embodied being (though, since the environment is always excessive with respect to embodied being, everywhere and continually affecting it, not all of the 'state transformations' will do so). An action directed toward that which has affected it will then both alter the state of another being and, in turn, alter its own state. This is, of course, a fairly unsophisticated account, but the point I want to make is that the basic structure of this process—from a pre-affected state to another which includes the first within its trajectory of unfolding but elicits activity which alters part of its pre-affective environmental context—is structurally different than that proposed by the idealist account of reflection. Specifically, whereas the act of reflection, on the idealist account, immediately generates the new state and thus occurs in the interval *between* one state of consciousness and another, from the perspective of embodiment, an act (including reflective awareness) occurs only after the two states of embodied being have been produced. It does not generate the second state but responds to or registers the fact that a 'state transformation' has occurred. We might say that, instead of the sequence 'state 1—reflective act—state 2' (the idealist account), a different sequence governs embodied reflection: 'state 1—state 2—reflective act of comprehending the alteration that has occurred.'

I suggest now that reflection, as a conscious activity of an embodied being, must be understood according to a similar structure. That is, philosophical reflection is not an activity that, in the first instance, generates its own new state or standpoint but, rather, attempts to comprehend and articulate the manner in which the excesses operating upon embodied being have already effected (and continue to effect) a 'state transformation' in embodied being itself. Put schematically, its structure is isomorphic with that of physiological affect and emerges as a reflective understanding of a process that has already occurred. At the level of embodied being, then, though reflection remains an act (analogous to physiological responses to the environment or 'life-world' of the embodied being), it is an act that does not, of itself, produce the change of state but attempts to understand and comprehend a change of state that has already occurred when an embodied being is affected by, interacts with, and responds to its environment. Reflection, then, is not, as the idealist account would have it, an act that, in the primary instance, produces new states by auto-affection, but one that seeks to understand and comprehend new states produced by that which is excessive to embodied being itself.

However, this is not the end of the story, and herein lies the truth of the idealist account. Just as, physiologically, this structure can lead to a physical act responding to the initial 'state change' that can reconfigure the operative complex and produce another set of 'state changes,' so the act of reflecting upon the change in the condition of embodiment also produces new configurations with their own possible trajectories. The act of reflection, that is, does not only register some change in the state of embodiment that has occurred, but itself becomes a factor in further transformations, though it does not produce them exclusively by its own mere occurrence. From the point of view of embodied being, there is an essential difference between merely registering a change in its condition and reflectively understanding or comprehending it: the former ('pure perception,' for example) merely awaits another affect; the latter intervenes as a factor, though one among and embedded within others, in the ongoing process.

Put in other, more generic terms, philosophical reflection emerges as a specific type of response to the excesses affecting embodied being. Previously, we've described this in terms of desire as the fundamental response on the part of embodied being to the excesses impinging upon it. As such, desire aims at a 'state-transformation' of embodied being in relation to its excesses that is actuated by reflection. Philosophical desire remains unsatisfied or always incompletely fulfilled because the excesses provoking it remain also excessive to reflection itself. Nonetheless, reflection does provide a provisional response to 'philosophical *eros*': provisional, in that something always remains excessive to reflection, but a response nonetheless, in that some gain is made with respect to identifying certain features of excessiveness and understanding the roles they play in relation to embodied being. Idealism is, then, to a certain extent right: philosophical reflection does, in fact, make a difference, it does produce a different state in the condition of embodied being; it does not leave this condition the same as before. But this new condition is as much subject to the affects of the excesses of embodied being as was its starting-point. Philosophical reflection, that is, does not progressively *eliminate* the excesses; rather, it opens the possibility of their reconfiguration from a new position with respect to them.

The act of philosophical reflection, then, never amounts to the total mastery or 'com-prehension' of that upon which it reflects. Although it is a form of response to the excesses inherent in embodied being, and although it does represent a recognition *that* there are excesses and *how* these excesses continue to affect embodied being and its activity of reflection, it results, not in an elimination of the excesses, but only in a reorientation of embodied being with respect to them. Philosophical reflection therefore neither eliminates the excesses nor masters them, but, at most, reorients the condition of embodied being toward them. In this sense, it is continuous with physiological acts with respect to the physical environment of embodied being.

2. Analysis as a Philosophical Activity

While I have argued that reflection has a certain primacy with respect to the philosophical activities of embodied beings, still it is not the only such activity. As we've seen, one of the component acts of reflection is memory, which serves as the point of commencement for reflection. Memory, however, is, as is often said, selective or, as we might put it, differential. To remember an experience, event, or even thought is to distinguish and isolate it, to cut it out or disentangle it from the forces of excess that play across the physical and mental life of embodied being. To borrow a metaphor from Husserl, the act of remembering is a sort of 'focusing,' where that which was previously submerged in the excesses involved in lived experience and thought comes to stand forth in the detail made possible by the 'higher magnification' of memory. Of course, it is possible *merely* to remember something, even savoring various features of it in detail. However, this becomes a philosophical act when, under the impetus of a certain form of desire, we come to explicitly identify, distinguish, and relate these features. In a sense, we could say that this process is itself a form of philosophical reflection. But, more properly, we should describe this process of identification, distinction, and relation as a mode of philosophical reflection limited to the content provided by memory. Analysis, the name commonly given to this sort of philosophical activity, is therefore a sort of partial or circumscribed sort of reflective activity directed toward the contents provided by memory as one aspect of the broader activity of philosophical reflection. It is a form of philosophical reflection, but one that foregrounds and focuses upon that aspect of reflection involved with memory.

This is one crucial point at which signification, especially language, impinges upon reflection. Many philosophers, including Plato, Aristotle, Locke, Hume, Hegel, Husserl, and Wittgenstein, have observed the intimate connection between memory and language. Hegel, for instance, insists, in the section on language and representation in the *Philosophy of Spirit*, that it is only when appropriate words are available that experiences, things, and ideas assume a form in which they can be effectively retained, reiterated, distinguished, and related to one another. Linguistic determinations, that is, first permit a more objective structuring and fixation of the contents of memory that would otherwise present us with a more or less inchoate and temporally fluctuating mass of Humean-like subjective impressions. While, perhaps like animals, various memory-traces can recur in the absence of language given appropriate stimuli, it is only through linguistic determinations that they can be reliably reidentified as 'the same.' Likewise, differentiation of memory-traces is possible only when (at least) two have been so identified, held in awareness simultaneously though linguistic reference, and seen to be different, not just ever-changing aspects of a single temporal flow. Finally, it is possible to establish relationships among linguistically differentiated memories, to consider in what aspects they may also be the same or related, only due to the capacity of language for forming sentences or judgments, which provide the bases for exactly such reflective activities. Language (or other forms of signification) thus intervenes in the memory-activities of embodied beings, providing determinate content for the activity of analysis. Analysis, in turn, constitutes an essential component of the broader activity of reflection, providing it with both basic structures and possible continuous trajectories.

However, while it is understandable why various philosophers have highlighted the analysis of linguistic statements as the most important (or, in some extreme cases, the only) genuine philosophical activity, such a characterization can only be regarded as, at best, a partial description of such activity. As we have seen, the content or 'analysand' of analytical activity must come from elsewhere—involving both embodied experience and existing significational systems—than mere analysis itself. Whatever the content of analysis is held to involve—whether empirical experiences, linguistic phenomena, or concepts (and, usually, it involves some combination of all three)—analysis of itself generates none of these but rather serves as a particular and limited way of treating them. It follows that analysis can never itself be some autonomous or self-standing activity but only finds its place within the broader activity of reflection, of which it is one element among others. More specifically, philosophical analysis (of language or any other assumed content), whether this is made explicit by a particular philosopher or not, is driven by a kind of desire (minimally, perhaps, for clarity or precision), and this in turn is usually linked with broader philosophical motivations involving critiquing or affirming some broader philosophical concept, view, or position. Further, even if analysis is directed proximately to something regarded as 'primitive' (Hume's 'impressions,' the Logical Positivist's 'atomic facts,' or 'ordinary language'), various concepts or other idealities are always already at play in the identification, differentiating, and relating—the framing, so to speak—of that which is to be analyzed.

These points, rather obvious to be sure, are nonetheless important to emphasize in light of modern controversies pitting 'analytic philosophy' against other philosophical approaches such as metaphysics, phenomenology, or, 'Continental philosophy.' Such a contrast will always be at least misleading if not downright spurious. For one thing, from Plato's quest for definitions and Aristotle's taxonomies (and their medieval developments), through the empiricist attempts to classify various types of experience or ideas, to Kant's 'analytics,' Hegel's logic, and Heidegger's 'analytic of *Dasein*,' virtually all philosophers have, as an essential part of their activity, practiced analysis. On the present view, then, there simply is no philosophical activity that does not include some element of analysis. On the other hand, philosophers who privilege the activity of analysis over other philosophical activities cannot seriously claim that the latter are entirely absent from their framing of that which is to be analyzed. We want to say, rather, that, on the one hand, all philosophy is, in some important sense, 'analytic' and that, on the other, any philosophy that proposes to be merely or mainly 'analytic' involves other activities as well, even if this is left implicit or unstated. At most, then, from the point of view of philosophy as a distinctive activity of embodied beings, such contrasts as that between 'analytic' and 'Continental' philosophy turn more on differences in emphasis or overall style rather than upon any fundamental difference between them with respect to the principal reflective activity of philosophy itself.

3. Eidetic Construction as a Philosophical Activity

If the activity of analysis, directed originally toward an embodied being's capacity for memory, provides a structured content for the primary philosophical activity of reflection, this broader activity never terminates with analysis. Rather, as we claimed earlier, reflection is an activity undertaken in response to a type of desire of embodied being in the face of the field of excesses in which it stands. While analysis provides a 'structured content' for the activity of reflection, it cannot, of itself, serve to present or register the fundamental excesses with which the lives of embodied beings are continually confronted. Rather, taken alone, analysis accomplishes a sort of reduction of complexity of embodied experience, offering to reflection a 'structured content' that it would otherwise lack. Without the results of the activity of analysis and its linguistic articulations, that is, the broader activity of reflection would amount to little more than a random or nomadic wandering among various elements of excessive experience or fragments of significational systems. But, however essential a role analysis plays in the broader activity of reflection, the philosophical desire that initiates the activity of reflection aims, in the first instance, not merely at the reduction of the excess of embodied experience but at ways of recognizing, understanding, and orienting itself with respect to these pervasive excesses. Put simply, we do not resolve fundamental issues involving the excesses encountered by embodied being merely by reducing them to the more manageable forms produced by analysis, but rather desire ways of locating and orienting embodied being among the excesses that continually play across it. In its broadest scope, then, philosophical *eros* and its reflective activities cannot remain satisfied with the results of analysis that, in effect, reduce the excesses of embodied being to its own limited forms; it can never accept as final any verdict that responds to the excesses that engender it simply by denying their claims upon us.

Reflection, as the fundamental philosophical activity, therefore must involve another element beyond that of analysis, an activity that commences with and builds upon the results of analysis. I have called this activity 'eidetic construction.' To begin with, we should not think of eidetic construction as something opposed to or independent of the activity of analysis. First, the results of analysis remain the indispensable basis for eidetic construction: were it not for the structured content produced by analysis, especially in the form of linguistic statements and complexes of them, reflection would be momentary, formless, and lacking in any directionality. Second, it is the very simplification and, hence, limitation imposed upon the excesses of lived experience by analysis that provokes the philosophical desire to confront these excesses operating beyond the limited results of analysis. Just as we claimed earlier that there would be no impetus to philosophical activity without our recognition of our own finitude in the face of the excessive conditions among which we exist, so there would be no further philosophical reflection without the essential limitations revealed to us by the activity of analysis. In encountering the limits of analysis, philosophical desire is, in a sense, recharged and redirected. (Recall, for instance, in Platonic dialogues like the *Republic*, how the 'dialectical ascent' to the 'Ideas' is launched by realizing the limitations of 'analytic' attempts to define a term or word.) What becomes clear to reflection is that more analysis will not, of itself, suffice.

What, then, remains beyond the limited results of analysis? We can describe this provisionally as the virtual, though initially undetermined, field of possibilities for reflection constituted by the excesses of embodied existence that were foreclosed by or escaped the structures imposed by analysis. At this point, however, I'll focus on the *activity* of construction as a crucial element of philosophical reflection, leaving to a later chapter a more explicit discussion of the eidetic results of this activity and their complexities. For now I'll just refer, in a very simplified way, to the results of eidetic construction generically as 'ideas,' following a good deal of both the ancient and modern philosophical traditions. Here I want only to sketch, in broad strokes, the philosophical role played by construction and the manner in which the broader activity of reflection serves to relate the activities of analysis and construction.

I have already highlighted the crucial role that significational systems, especially language, play in the activity of analysis. When limited to the activity of analysis, reflection tends to treat its content as more or less adequately expressed in words and their combinations and seeks to produce other linguistic expressions that either define or explain the linguistic expressions with which it begins. However, the three excesses upon which we've insisted inevitably exert their force on the activity of reflection, provoking the philosophical desire for ways of registering or mapping points where these excesses come together, thus establishing more concrete points in relation to which embodied being can orient itself. For now, we will say that 'ideas' are just these points or nodes of contact or connection, beyond the activity of analysis, among the fundamental excessive conditions defining the field of philosophy.

This means that every actual idea will involve three components. First, it will be connected with the lived experience of embodied being through its capacity for memory and analysis. All ideas, that is, no matter how abstract or remote they may seem, will be connected with, occupy a place within, and produce effects upon the configuration of embodied being itself. Second, they will at once draw upon elements of significational systems while registering the excessiveness of signification to any of its actualized instances. An idea, that is, arises when one (or some) of the inchoate possibilities making up the 'space' beyond analysis becomes actualized by association with a significational 'marker,' usually a word or phrase, which serves to 'name' the idea. However, such names are differential, in a sense deploying one element of a signifying system by excluding all others that might also have been deployed. It is important to notice, however, that, as opposed to the activity of analysis, which took its 'significational content' as functionally equivalent to the 'experienced content' of memory, the 'name' of an idea is never completely identical to the idea itself. Rather, and thirdly, the activity of naming or finding a word or expression for an idea only provides a 'marker' indicating a point of intersection among the trajectories and effects of other ideas, some already possessed of their own 'names,' others virtual but not yet constructed possibilities of the 'intellectual space' exceeding analysis. To summarize, then, every idea is a point of intersection among the ever unfolding excess of embodied being, the excessiveness of the significational system from which its 'name' is drawn, and the excessiveness of other ideas both actual as well as virtual, as yet unthought and unnamed.

With this admittedly somewhat schematic discussion of the results of eidetic construction, we're now in a position to say more about it as a reflective philosophical activity. Constructing an idea begins with the opening of the 'virtual space' of possibilities that lie beyond the limits of analysis. The structured contents of analysis both provide a determinate starting-point for further philosophical reflection and, at the same time, provoke philosophical desire by their very limitations. Sometimes an 'idea' is already available, familiar and named, and eidetic construction takes the form of just retracing the path by which the idea came to be constructed and named. However, in other cases, we sense, perhaps vaguely at first, that there is a possibility, a new conjunction of excesses, one that has not yet been actualized or named. The activity of reflection, driven by a special type of desire, then reveals itself at its most creative. In the midst of the excesses of embodied experience, drawing upon elements of already existent signifying systems, and aware of the virtual web mapped out by other already named ideas and the trajectories among them, reflection introduces a new 'node' within this network by actualizing what before was only one among an unlimited multiplicity of possibilities. In fixing upon this as yet unrealized possibility, naming it, and exploring its connections with other already actualized ideas, it constructs a new idea. And in the course of exploring the new connections and trajectories of this idea (which may, in turn, lead to further eidetic constructions), a new philosophical view or position, leading to a new orientation of embodied experience to that which is excessive to it, may arise.

II. PHILOSOPHY AS AN ACTIVITY: A REPRISE AND FURTHER CONSIDERATIONS

I'll conclude this discussion of philosophy as an activity with several more generic (and, in some cases, controversial) points that it implies.

1. I suggested earlier that, despite the fact that the tradition has viewed reflection as the primary philosophical activity, it failed to provide a satisfactory answer to the question of what is, in fact, involved in such an activity. On the one hand, Plato, who famously spoke of 'knowing oneself' or 'examining one's life,' a serious matter to be sure, seemed to leave the origin or any further determination of this activity shrouded in the mystery of such tropes as 'wonder' or the inexplicable 'turning around' of the denizens of the shadow-world of the Cave. The empiricists fared little better, simply counting reflection as one among other 'mental faculties,' while the rationalists tended to refer to some equally unexplained faculty of 'apperception.' In marked contrast, the German Idealists, led by Kant's 'Copernican turn,' made the structure of reflection their major focus, though their treatment of it was vitiated by their idealist assumptions, thereby rendering it disconnected from both embodied experience and, for the most part, the resources of significational systems that both limit and exceed it. By viewing the structure of philosophical reflection as continuous or isomorphic with embodied experience, I attempted to show that the activity of reflection is nothing itself mysterious, autonomous and self-contained, or in any way disconnected from the life of embodied beings, that it is, in fact, a natural and even necessary activity of embodied signifying beings. At the same time, I have insisted that it is, nonetheless, a distinctive activity, with a sort of structure of its own, irreducible to other human activities.

2. The account I've offered departs from both the Platonic and modern idealist versions on a point worth further emphasis. Both traditions seem to regard the activity of reflection as somehow hegemonic with respect to its 'content,' that is, whatever it is upon which reflection is directed. The famous Platonic dictum, "Knowledge is virtue," that reflectively knowing what is true, and only this, can provide the basis for a virtuous life, seems distantly echoed in the modern idealist claim that philosophical reflection produces a new stance in which that which has been reflected upon becomes absorbed and mastered without remainder ('*ist aufgehoben*,' as Hegel says). The present account, by contrast, emphasizes that the activity of reflection not only occurs within a field constituted by excesses, but that, however thoroughly undertaken, the basic conditions remain always excessive to reflection. While it may be that the activity of philosophical reflection has an important, even necessary, role to play within the lives of embodied beings, it can never, taken alone, constitute some final satisfaction for human desire. Philosophical reflection can serve embodied being in many ways, especially

in assisting embodied being in orienting itself with respect to the excesses to which it is subject, but it is never capable of mastering or eliminating them. Like Kant urged, the activity of philosophy requires a certain humility about its aims and ends; but he stopped short of realizing the true fragility, and thereby also the nobility, of the activity of reflection.

3. Paralleling these points, the role of the activity of analysis within the broader activity of philosophical reflection has likewise been both under- and overrated. Analysis can never be the sole activity of philosophy, as some, especially modern, thinkers sometimes seem to hold, but neither is it either dispensable or a mere preparatory exercise for 'genuine philosophical reflection,' as some more metaphysically inclined thinkers would have it. Rather, it is an essential and indispensable 'sub-activity' of any activity of philosophical reflection and deserves to be accorded its rightful place within reflection without thereby limiting reflection exclusively to its analytic activities.

4. For many, the activity of eidetic construction will likely present the most problems. I will return to this in greater detail later, but two issues are worth mentioning at this point.

First, both a Platonist as well as a Kantian might claim that the very notion of 'eidetic construction' harbors a contradiction. Either of them (though on different grounds, to be sure) might claim that something like 'ideas' (in some strict sense) or fundamental concepts like 'categories' are just not the sort of things that can be constructed. They would, perhaps, grant that some 'lower order ideas' (Kant would call them 'empirical') may be constructed, but they would hold that, in the strict sense, genuine 'ideas' or 'categories' must be regarded as the bases of any further construction and hence must themselves be 'objective' with respect to the activity of construction and hence be themselves 'unconstructed.' On the view I'm proposing, however, such assertions ultimately disregard the fact that philosophy is, in its most basic form, the reflective activity of finite embodied beings and that whatever 'ideas' or 'categories' that may be claimed as fundamental must first be identified through the analysis of lived experience and then constructed as different from or 'transcendent' to the analyzed content of this ongoing life-process. That is, the activity of reflection provides us no other platform outside of embodied experience itself from which such a distinction could be made. Further, such claims also disregard or suppress the fact that even the most fundamental ideas or categories can be articulated only drawing upon the resources of significational systems already functioning as human discourse prior to their deployment for naming and elaboration in distinctively philosophical activity. Because philosophy begins in the finitude of embodiment and must deploy significational systems in its activities, there can be no 'unconstructed ideas,' but, at most, on some views of the matter, orders of hierarchy among ideas that are, nonetheless without exception, constructed.

However, this seems to open the door to the opposite charge of relativism. If all ideas are constructed, then, as various empiricist- or skeptical-minded thinkers might claim, all ideas are, by the same token, arbitrary and contingent. Now there is a sense in which this can be granted: every idea does, in fact, originate within the excessiveness of lived experience; it presupposes an analytically structured content from which to proceed, which itself involves an activity of selection and simplification; and there is never some single or privileged significational system within which it is articulated. However, this charge misses several other important elements of the constructivist view I've sketched. First, as I've already argued, the actual conditions which constitute the field of possibilities for constructing ideas are not themselves arbitrary: they are not themselves 'constructed ideas' but actualities that together constitute the field in which any philosophical construction can occur. Second, whatever significational system is deployed in the activity of construction imposes its own structures upon what can be identified and articulated within it. Finally, an idea, once constructed, takes its place within a field or network of other ideas and comes to, so to speak, live a life of its own independently of the activities by which it was constructed. As I've said earlier, although it is entirely contingent that there are embodied beings and that these beings developed significational systems within which to communicate, the ideas constructed when these two conditions obtain can stand in non-arbitrary (and to this degree 'necessary') relations among themselves.

To invoke Kant once more, one of his principal philosophical insights was that, although what we call the 'world' is constructed by the synthetic activities of human consciousness, it is not some arbitrary concoction or fantasy of the mind but possesses a determinate and necessary structure fully adequate to grounding objective, intersubjectively verifiable knowledge claims. Rearticulated beyond the philosophical limits that Kant's idealist assumptions imposed upon him, we will say more broadly of ideas that, although they are, without exception, constructions of the reflective activities of embodied beings, they are not, once named and elaborated, arbitrary but stand in definite relations to other ideas due, in part (but only in part) to the already existing structures resident in the significational systems in which they are expressed. How these significational systems, out of which arise the texts that, after activity, constitute the 'second meaning' of philosophy, serve to link embodied being with ideas while, at the same time, exceeding and, at points, destabilizing these connections will be the topic of the next chapter.

9

Philosophy as Texts and Their Elements

I. PHILOSOPHY, EMBODIED BEING, AND TEXT

Philosophy is, in its most basic sense, a reflective activity of embodied beings, a special sort of activity in which embodied beings engage. Although signification enters into this activity at (at least) two crucial points—in the reflective 'subactivities' of analysis and eidetic construction—it is certainly possible to 'do philosophy' in a sort of limited way without actually creating those results of philosophical reflection that are called 'texts.' The converse, however, is not an option: even if we regard philosophy as the set of texts in which it is expressed or articulated, we will be able to identify them as distinctively philosophical only if we presuppose that they are the results of the activity of philosophical reflection. In fact, we can be more specific: eidetic construction, in particular, requires that a signifying system such as language be capable of operating in a different and distinctive register than mere communication, that it also be capable of 'naming' ideas and articulating their relations at the same time as maintaining the distinction between the significational elements that it deploys and the ideas that they serve to articulate. Ideas and their relations, that is, must be excessive to any concrete instance of their signification or articulation and, conversely, signification must remain, in a different way, excessive to any ideas or relations expressed or articulated within it.

Put in terms of the texts that are usually called 'philosophical,' while no text or body of texts can ever serve as the *final* expression or articulation of a particular idea or complex of ideas, it is likewise true that the significational system(s) deployed to express or articulate an idea, system of ideas, or general philosophical position contains further possibilities for expression not included or com-prehended within the texts themselves. The very fact that, in the history of philosophy, most philosophers have made multiple attempts to articulate their views affirms both points. That almost all felt it necessary to approach their ideas within a variety of different texts implies that what they were aiming to express exceeded any and all of the various texts within which they attempted to express them. And that they could rearticulate their ideas or views in different forms suggests that the resources of their signifying system(s) exceeded (though in a different way) that which they were attempting to articulate. (This 'double excess,' of course, parallels that which we earlier encountered in our discussion of the reflective limits of analysis.)

All this suggests three basic questions about philosophy regarded as text that we must consider. Again, our guiding theme will be how embodied being and ideality are reflected and related within the sphere of signification.

1. How do the reflective activities of embodied beings come to be expressed and articulated through such significational means as spoken discourses or inscribed texts? Are there identifiable marks or traces of their embodied origins that remain in philosophical texts, even, perhaps, the most 'abstract'? And how do philosophical texts both detach themselves from and nonetheless remain connected to the lived experience of embodied beings?

2. Is there some particular form or structure among the possibilities of significational systems that is primary for philosophy? Put in a different way, is there some underlying or primary significational form that allows us to regard a text as distinctively philosophical rather than of some other kind? And if so, how does it manage to reflect within itself and hold together both its origins in embodied being and the ideas that it expresses?

3. How are philosophical texts capable of articulating and rearticulating ideas which are both excessive to them and which they, at the same time, exceed in their own way? Can we identify some particular aspect or dimension of significational systems that can account for this?

To begin to respond to these questions, we must first draw a distinction between communication and signification, without placing them in mere opposition. The sort of distinction I will employ turns on the fact that embodied beings, including many non-human embodied beings, are capable of communicating without thereby signifying, although the converse does not hold. This is to say that all signification is a form of communication although not all forms of communication involve signification. The difference between 'non-significational' and 'significational communication' lies in the fact that signification (as we will use the term) necessarily involves an eidetic element not present in all forms of communication. Of course, it may well be that there is, in considering specific cases, some continuum between the two and that the 'threshold point' separating them may be, empirically considered, difficult to determine. But with respect to texts that we typically regard as philosophical, the threshold has already long been crossed. That is, philosophical texts do not merely communicate (though they do that too) but signify in ways in which an eidetic dimension is always operative and essential. This is the basis for my earlier claim that, while the significational systems deployed by embodied beings might not have developed out of their communicational activities, that is, that the existence of signifying systems is contingent, once they have developed they possess a certain necessity based upon their connection with an eidetic dimension. It follows that, while philosophy, as textually articulated, might not have arisen, even granted embodied beings and communication among them, once communication has become significative activity, philosophical texts become governed by a certain sort of necessity. In fact, the very *idea* of 'necessity' itself emerges only as a product of the reflection of embodied beings deploying significational systems in its production of texts.

In what follows, I will suggest, agreeing with much of the philosophical tradition, that what are often called 'logical statements' (whether made explicit or not) lie at the heart of all distinctively philosophical texts. But I will also propose, against a good deal of the tradition, that a philosophical text can never be reduced to them. Rather, the logical statements asserted or implied in philosophical texts always, and necessarily, relate, on the one hand, to what I will call 'expressive enunciations' and, on the other, to 'speculative propositions.' Roughly put, the former serve to link logical propositions to embodied being, while the latter connect them to eidetic determinations and complexes. I will say, then, that all philosophical texts involve a complex interweaving of expressive enunciations, logical statements, and speculative propositions. Put in other terms, every philosophical text is a singular way of interweaving the desires and reflective activities of embodied beings, the structural necessities defining significational systems deployed by embodied beings, and ideas that are expressed by the reflective deployment of significational systems but that are reducible to neither features of embodied being nor significational systems themselves. However, before we turn to a discussion of the elements that make up philosophical texts, we must consider an important preliminary issue in more detail.

II. COMMUNICATION AND SIGNIFICATION

I have already suggested that the production of distinctively philosophical discourses or texts is a contingent matter, that is, that it is possible for embodied beings to communicate with one another in the absence of developed significational systems. We must, therefore, first consider the differences between non-significational and significational communication, a discussion that should also help us further clarify, in a preliminary way, the meaning of signification as I wish to employ it.

An embodied being, at least from birth if not before, physically interacts with other physical objects in its lived environment, which includes other embodied beings. These interactions occur in various ways, perhaps most important, at least in the earliest phases of an organism's life, being that of direct physical contact (which includes touch, taste, and smell). The physical growth of the body of an organism is accompanied by an expansion of its sensory capacities to interact with its physical environment in a variety of ways beyond the tactile. While the 'tactile senses' are spatially limited to conditions of physical proximity, sight and hearing permit a qualitatively new sort of interaction to arise: interaction with other physical objects that are spatially (and sometimes temporally) at some remove from the immediate physical location of the body. It is especially sight and hearing that play a decisive role in constituting the 'lived environment' (as some phenomenologists have called it) of embodied beings.

However, embodied beings (both animal and human) are not limited merely to passively registering their immediate environment but actively participate in it, thereby altering it in various ways. They are capable, that is, of producing sounds that make their own distinctive additions to the environmental soundscape and physical actions, gestures, and (at a much more complex level) physical objects that become part of the visual (and sometimes also auditory) environment. Under conditions of restricted proximity, embodied beings (both animal and human) can perform actions and produce sounds that, if matched to the tactile, visual, and auditory capacities of others, can serve to attract their attention and elicit some response on their part. And since this involves at least two embodied beings, it implies the possibility of reciprocity, that the 'other' can so relate as well. Communication, in the broadest and most rudimentary sense, is just this process of effecting or influencing the current state and, usually, subsequent states or actions of other embodied beings, together with the possibility that they are capable of something similar.

Of course, this is a bare, minimal account, designed to include communication between animals as well as that between humans and animals. It does not assume, for instance, that the sort of reciprocity here is in any way symmetrical, either with respect to the means employed or the degree of influence involved. Humans, for example, certainly regularly communicate with animals, although the means humans use (verbal calls or commands, for instance) are responded to through other means by animals (perhaps physical caresses or specific behaviors). Nor is the degree of influence that humans have over animals usually matched from their side (although some cats, were they able, might disagree). Also, no mention is made here of 'information' as that which is 'communicated' (although it is central to many more formal accounts of communication). For to focus at the outset on 'information' is already to assume something essentially 'eidetic,' which confuses the important distinction between (mere) communication and signification that I am trying to draw.

If we consider communication specifically among human beings, however, we must include three additional elements as essential to the reciprocity noted above. First, communication between human embodied beings, as defined in part by desire, involves intention. That is, acts of intra-human communication, as opposed to random actions that just happen to elicit some response from other beings in the vicinity, involve some form of desire to perform certain actions designed to affect other beings in relatively determinate ways. Second, this, among other things, assumes a recognition that other human beings are, in fact, capable of interpreting my action as communicative (and not as a mere chance gesture or sound). This implies, third, that other human beings are also capable of, in turn, recognizing me as capable of intentionally communicative action. That is, it assumes a certain mutuality of recognition among human beings with respect to the activity of communication. It is this complex of desire/intention, recognition of others as 'addressees' of communication, and mutuality, from both sides, of intention and recognition that provide the basic structure of human communication and its many and complex developments.

If, as I have suggested, it is possible that embodied human beings are capable of communicating without yet signifying, what must occur for this threshold to be crossed, for 'mere communication' to become, more specifically, 'significational communication'? The answer to this requires a consideration of what is meant by a 'sign,' regarded as a particular means or vehicle of communication. We can begin with the classical structuralist account, first articulated by de Saussure and developed in more detail by others such as Jakobson, Levi-Strauss, and Barthes. A sign is a determinate and stable relation between a 'signifier' and a 'signified.' A 'signifier' is, on this view, understood as any action (like a gesture) or perceivable object (including visual images, sounds, and, in a more developed sense, spoken and written words) that causes or provokes, when presented, an associated 'mental content,' 'representation,' or 'idea.' The classical structuralist account also strongly emphasized that the relation between 'signifier' and 'signified' was entirely 'arbitrary,' that it was only conventional association, not any natural resemblance, between them that constituted the relation they called a 'sign.' It further held that both signifiers and signifieds were entirely 'differential,' that, absent any natural resemblance, the conventional alignment of signifiers with signifieds consisted of differences among signifiers reciprocally mirroring differences among signifieds. These reciprocally mirrored relations between signifiers and signifieds, i.e. signs, taken as a totality, constituted what the classical account took to be the primary object of (variously) linguistics or semiotics that they called '*langue.*' In quite strict opposition stood '*parole,*' which this view regarded as the empirical, spatio-temporal, variable, and transient manifestation of a sign-system in use or a language as concretely spoken or written. The conviction was that sign-systems, as 'differential totalities,' as '*langue,*' consisted of sets or matrices of necessary relations, the 'arbitrariness' of the connections between signifiers and signifieds notwithstanding. Any specific instance of sign- or language-use ('*parole*') was, then, viewed as entirely parasitic upon these structures for its efficacy and, of itself, could empirically disclose little of 'scientific value' about them.

Virtually every one of these structuralist theses was subsequently subjected to searching and sometimes quite vitriolic critique, especially by the first wave of poststructuralist thinkers. The view that I am developing here agrees with certain of these later critiques in denying that all communication can be explained solely in terms of signs and signification, that is, in holding that the 'sign-relation' is somehow primitive or originary. It also agrees that there are important elements of excess operating within and across significational systems that the classical account tended to regard as 'closed totalities.' Finally, from the present perspective, some of the later critics were right in questioning the classical account's strict separation between significational systems (regarded as '*langue*') and the concrete, embodied, desire-driven instances of their deployment ('*parole*').

Still, two important points insisted upon by the classical account remain significant for our project of understanding philosophy as text. First, while any significational system (say, for example, a natural language) is undoubtedly excessive to any particular instance of its deployment, and while significational systems never constitute fully closed and determinate totalities, it is also nonetheless true that there is a determinate structural core or network of relations constituting the signs that make up any such system that allows it to function as a vehicle of inter-human communication. Were all signs 'at play' at all times, no communication would be possible. More importantly, underlying this is the structuralist tenet that the concrete deployment of any significational system occurs only under certain constraints imposed by the system itself (such as the basic units available, their syntactic ordering, and rule-bound transformations). The structuralist view thus affirms the insight that, while the very existence of significational systems and, perhaps, choices among them are contingent, they nonetheless involve necessity as a feature of their own internal relations. Significational systems, that is, are contingent in their existence and conventional with respect to the specific linkages between their signifiers and signifieds, but, once in existence, present a network of necessary relations that also govern their ability to serve as means of communication in their concrete deployment.

The second thing to be learned from the structuralist account is that there is an irreducibly eidetic dimension involved in any significational system. That is, a sign cannot be reduced either to some physical object (including a written or spoken word) that serves as a signifier, nor is it identical to some signified mental content or event in the psychic life of an embodied being. Rather, a sign is a type of relation that links and mediates the sphere of physical, embodied being with that of the elemental constituents of significational systems. Signs, then, are, so to speak, the avatars of ideas and, more broadly, the eidetic realm, when considered from the point of view of significational systems. Of course, the classical structuralists themselves did not fully realize this, due to their expulsion of all empirical considerations from their theory of signification and their uncritical equating of anything eidetic with mental representations. (In this, they represented a modern, post-Kantian form of 'significational idealism,' a view shared by many others beyond the ambit of classical structuralism, including thinkers on both sides of the current 'Continental/analytic divide.') But in their basic analysis of the sign, they provided an important framework for understanding how significational communication by embodied being points toward and is necessarily connected to the eidetic realm.

I'll now attempt to bring all this together with respect to our original question about the relation between non-significative and significative communication and the fundamental alterations that the passage from the former to the latter effects. Non- (or pre-) significative communication is limited in (at least) two important ways in relation to significative communication. First, it is limited by the fact that it requires some degree of spatial and temporal proximity between the communicating parties to succeed. Second, it lacks the determinacy and stability of relations between particular communicative actions and the effects they intend, so that there remains uncertainty as to what is communicated, to whom the communicative action is addressed, and, in fact, whether the action was communicative at all. Still, non-significational communication can and does occur, both among animals, among humans, and between both, without there being any necessity for the development of significational communication out of this. Necessity enters only with the advent of significational communication, where signs emerge as stable and determinate relations between signifiers and signifieds. But these 'necessary relations,' called signs if we are speaking of the condition of signification, are, considered in their own right and as excessive to the correlation of signifiers and signifiers, the 'ideas' constituting what I have called the 'eidetic condition.' As I claimed earlier, though at that time without detailed argument, although the existence of embodied beings is contingent, and although it is also contingent that significational communication developed from non-significational communication, once this has occurred, the eidetic realm necessarily emerges.

This is immediately related to the fact that significational communication overcomes the limitations of non-significational forms of communication. Significational communication can succeed without any spatial or temporal proximity between the communicating parties. While this is especially clear in the case of written texts (as many poststructuralists have insisted), it is true even if we consider spoken language, which can be memorized and repeated at many different places and times (as were, for example, the epic poems of Homer). Further, while we can grant variances in interpretation or some 'sliding of signifiers,' it remains the case that significational communication permits a considerable degree of determination, on the part of all communicating parties, regarding the fact that communication is occurring, what is being communicated, and at least partially justified inferences about the underlying intentions.

All this means that, while philosophy is a particular type of activity of embodied beings driven by desire-as-lack in relation to their limitations in the face of excess, it appears in the form of discourses or texts only when philosophical *eros* both deploys and at the same time submits itself to the excesses of significational systems, especially spoken and written language. In so doing, however, it immediately gains entry to and engages in another realm, the eidetic, that was already disclosed to its reflective activities but now given determinate form and contours through the (in part) necessary relations governing significational systems. Every philosophical discourse or text, then, must be viewed as a complex engagement of an embodied being with the eidetic realm by deploying the resources of a significational system. Further, it is thereby a type of structured communication among embodied beings possessing its own 'internal necessity' while bearing the traces of the threefold excesses of embodied being (insisted upon by such thinkers as Nietzsche), the significational system that it deploys (as such classical thinkers as Aristotle along with poststructuralists like Derrida have reminded us), and the eidetic realm (so emphasized by figures such as Plato and Hegel). It also means that, like all significative communication, philosophical texts are, in their genesis, artifacts of their own place and time but, in their eidetic content, never limited to a particular time or place. It also implies that every distinctively philosophical text possesses its own 'inner necessity' or 'logic,' that it is never only a 'play of differences among signifiers' or a genre of aesthetic performance (as some post-structuralist thinkers have held). In what follows, I'll look in more detail at the specific features of philosophical texts that manifest these insights.

III. THE ELEMENTS OF PHILOSOPHICAL TEXTS

There are many kinds of texts, all instances of significative communication, but only a limited number of them are distinctively philosophical. Let's begin by considering three types of texts that someone, holding a different view than I'm presenting here, might regard as somehow 'philosophical': a poem (say Keat's "Ode on a Grecian Urn"), a religious work (for instance, the Gospel of John), and a scientific treatise (like Newton's *Principia*).

We can say, with respect to poetry, that, among their many rather obvious differences, what is communicated by a philosophical text does not depend on the employment of various tropes (sensual imagery, metaphor, simile, metonymy, etc.) in the way that a poem does. While philosophers do sometimes employ tropes to enhance or clarify their intentions (Plato's sun, line, and cave images, Kant's metaphor of a 'Copernican revolution in philosophy,' and Nietzsche's 'madman' come immediately to mind), these all occur within a broader context of determinate statements linked to one another in a rule-governed manner often regarded as the province of logic. Of course, we might say that a well-constructed poem is also governed by a certain sort of 'logic,' but this would already be to use the term 'logic' itself in a metaphorical sense. This is easily seen if we try (as many of us were encouraged to do in high school) to explain the 'meaning' of a poem in an interpretive essay. To reduce the tropes deployed in the poem to a logically connected set of statements attributed to the author of the poem is to erase what is most essential to the poem and transform it into what might well qualify as an instance of philosophy. For its part, while it may be true (as Derrida and others have claimed) that various metaphors or other such tropes underlie or guide the philosopher in the construction of her or his texts, the text itself, if philosophical, will involve elements—terms, discrete statements, and connections among them—that are something quite different from the tropes identified by rhetorical or literary analysis. Just as much as in the former case, writing a poem about a philosophical text (as some of my more adventurous undergraduate students have occasionally attempted) ends up destroying essential features of the philosophical text itself and transforming it into a quite different form of signification.

Two things are especially worth noting here. First, poems depend for their communicational effects on deploying features of significational systems that are intimately connected with various aspects of the experience of embodied beings, things like visual images, graphic forms, and auditory effects like rhyming, meter, and rhythm. While a philosopher might well, at certain points, engage in this as well, it will be incidental to her or his principal task. Second, and closely connected, poetry stands in a different relation to the significational system that it deploys than does philosophy. It is precisely by deploying the various ways in which a significational system exceeds any singular poetic production that permits the effective operation of the images and tropes that constitute the poem. Every poem, that is, is a singular act of affirmation of the significational excesses out of which it is constructed and thanks to which it produces its own unique effects. Philosophical texts relate to significational excess along a different trajectory. Rather than embracing the excesses of significational systems and exploiting their potentials for producing effects, philosophical texts attempt partly to limit the excesses of their significational system; to, at least temporarily, resist the 'play of signifiers' in the interest of giving some form and specificity to thought, that is, the eidetic realm. Of course, such philosophical resistance to the excessive character of signification can never be completely successful, any more than the poet can completely succeed in embracing and rendering this excess in any singular form. But the most important point here concerns their opposed trajectories: where poetry seeks to embrace significational excess by leading it back toward embodied experience, philosophy attempts to limit significational excess so as disclose the eidetic elements latent within signification, though without entirely abandoning its roots in embodied being.

Religious texts stand in an entirely different relation to the excesses of signification and hence to philosophical texts. We might begin with the first sentence of the Gospel of John: "In the beginning was the Word, and the Word was with God, and the Word was God." Here, 'the Word' is a translation from the Greek *'logos,'* a term that has a much broader meaning and set of connotations than the English 'Word' used to translate it. As has often been noted, there is no corresponding single word in English that successfully captures its range, which spans (and exceeds) such terms as 'statement,' 'speech,' 'language,' 'reason,' 'transcendent order,' and so on. We might say that what we have called the 'condition of signification,' while admittedly itself not entirely adequate, could figure as at least another term in this list. Granted this, the point I wish to make in citing this passage is that religious texts (which are something quite different than texts about religion or about personal religious experiences) tend to place signification in some primordial or originary relationship with something ultimate in the eidetic sphere. As John powerfully puts it, 'the Word' is not just 'with God' but *'is* God.' But, as we also soon learn, "The Word was made flesh and dwelt amongst us." I am not here concerned with the details or controversies surrounding 'Johannine theology,' but rather with the fact that John's (or whoever the actual author was) statements are, in some important ways, paradigmatic for understanding religious texts in relation to philosophical ones. For our purposes, the two most important points are the identification of signification (*logos*) with what is asserted as an ultimate ideality (God) and the immediate connection that is made with embodied being. The most important result is that, in religious texts like the Gospel of John, signification loses its autonomy as an actual condition and becomes, at least in its originary sense, subsumed by or absorbed into an ideality presented as the ultimate fulfillment of the fundamental 'desire-as-lack' of embodied being.

Certainly religious texts are themselves significational complexes and, like poetry, they too exploit the excessive nature of all signification (as many modern hermeneutic thinkers have insisted), but they do so in ways quite different than poetry. Where poetry acknowledges the autonomy of signification and its excesses and seeks to bring them into direct proximity with human embodied experience without any direct or overt involvement with idealities, religious texts tend to view all significational excess (including their own) as both grounded in an ultimate ideality and as a primary way in which this ideality is 'revealed' to finite embodied being. Where poetry embraces and revels in significational excess for its own sake, religious texts deploy such excess as a means of revealing some ultimate ideality to embodied being.

We can now say that philosophical texts occupy a territory that is, in some important ways, located between the poetic and religious. As I've suggested earlier, the most distinctive feature of philosophical texts is that (though admittedly with varying degrees of explicitness) they acknowledge the autonomy and irreducibility of three distinct and excessive actual conditions and present themselves as the articulation of a singular place or position where these conditions intersect and upon which their excesses exert their respective forces. As I've suggested in this section, the principal kinship among poetic, religious, and philosophical texts lies in the fact that they all recognize that excess characterizes the basic conditions with which they are engaged. This is why, among other things, poetic and religious texts can and have often offered important insights for the construction of philosophical texts. However, while philosophical texts articulate a singular intersection of the three conditions and respond to the excessive forces of all three conditions, both poetic and religious texts tend to be bi-dimensional in either suppressing one of the conditions or reducing it to another. Poetic texts tend to mute eidetic considerations in favor of exploring the interplay between embodied being and signification, while religious texts tend to identify signification with some ultimate ideality and regard it as a vehicle for relating embodied being to this ideality. Of course, because, as I've argued, the three conditions are actual and exert their excessive forces on any human activity, it should not be surprising that there can be forms of 'philosophical poetry' in which the eidetic dimension makes an appearance, or 'religious philosophy' (a type of which is theology) in which religious discourse deploys or, in part, submits itself to the structural features governing signification. For the same reason, it has often been the case that each type of text has drawn insight and inspiration from the other two without losing its own distinctiveness.

Finally, the relation between philosophical and scientific texts presents a rather different situation, one element of which is the fact that scientific texts, as an historical matter, were, at their early stages, regarded as themselves a type of philosophical text. (For instance, the full title of Newton's great founding work of modern physics was '*Philosophiae Naturalis Principia Mathematica*,' 'The Mathematical Principles of Natural Philosophy.') We can regard the two crucial aspects of the gradual separation of scientific from philosophical texts as the muting and suppression of embodied human experience as one of their essential elements, accompanied by the aim to strictly control and ultimately eliminate all excess from the significative complexes that they deploy. As to the first, it has often been observed that one of the founding ideas of modern science is that of 'objectivity.' Whatever else this may mean on its own account, it implies that modern science and its texts involve a suppression of the singular, lived, embodied experience of the scientist (summed up in the term 'subjectivity'). In its place, it installed the ideal of a 'neutral observer' and 'detached describer of facts.' As to the second, from at least Galileo and Descartes on, the extremely limited significational system of mathematics, together with a highly restrictive view of what could count as appropriate observational descriptions, came to function as the model for and genuine content of scientific discourses and texts. What it continued to share with philosophical texts was a crucial connection to the eidetic sphere. Still, its divorce from embodied being, together with its attempts to eliminate all significational excesses, also severely reduced the scope of the eidetic field with which it was otherwise engaged, leading to such philosophical critiques of natural science as those of Kant, Husserl, and the phenomenological tradition, which attempted both to reconnect scientific discourse with the lived experience of embodied beings and to locate the eidetic limitations of scientific discourse within a richer field of idealities and their excesses.

Even so, we should not lose sight of the fact that, with regard to signification and its excesses, both philosophical and scientific texts move on a similar trajectory—toward, in various ways, limiting the play of significational excess within their discourses. But we must also add that the crucial difference between them is both qualitative and quantitative. Qualitatively regarded, philosophical texts must also accommodate the excesses of embodied being, they must maintain some significant connection to lived experience in ways not relevant to scientific texts. And quantitatively, we can say that scientific texts travel further along the trajectory toward the reduction of significative excess in aiming toward their final elimination. By contrast, though the construction of philosophical texts necessarily involves arresting the play of certain signifiers (especially their most important terms and the relations among them), this must remain always provisional and its contours will vary not only among philosophers but, sometimes, within any one philosopher's various texts. Because of this, philosophy develops, both within the activity and texts of a single thinker as well as in its overall historical trajectory, in a different manner than do the sciences and their texts.

We are now in a position to distinguish and consider the basic significative elements of any philosophical text. As with embodiment, there will be three elements, corresponding to the ways in which the three conditions are registered in and exert their own distinctive forces upon signification. For reasons that will be explained in what follows, I will say that the primary significational elements of philosophical texts are 'logical statements.' These will be connected, on the one hand, with embodied being through what I will call 'expressive enunciations' and, on the other, with ideality through what I will call 'speculative propositions.' My claim, then, will be that all distinctively philosophical texts can be viewed as a complex interweaving and intersection of these three fundamental elements of signification and that the attempt to eliminate any one will destroy the distinctively philosophical character of that text.

1. Logical Statements

a. Statements

From at least the Platonic dialogues on, philosophical texts, no matter what particular literary style they have otherwise assumed (dialogues, treatises, autobiography, meditation, system-construction, etc.), either explicitly present or permit the formulation of statements within a given significational system. More than anything else, it is the set of these statements, together with the manner in which they are connected, that allow us to distinguish one philosophical text, view, or position from others. Put the other way around, a text that formulates no such statements may still be a text of some sort, but it will not be philosophical. Of course, such statements are neither the only element of a philosophical text nor, even less, do they exhaust the field of signification. But their presence in a text, explicitly or implicitly, is a necessary condition for regarding the text as philosophical. This, at least, has remained constant from Plato's having Socrates elicit definitions from his interlocutors all the way to the modern practice of studying philosophical texts by identifying or extracting from them statements that can then be subjected to analysis or critical scrutiny. The very failure of an attempt to identify such statements in a text or formulate them on the basis of the text immediately leads us to suspect that we're not, in fact, dealing with a philosophical text at all.

The first task, then, is to determine what generically constitutes a statement in the sense I am using the term here. In terms of its most generic features (and part of why I have chosen not to speak, at this point, of 'propositions'), a statement is, in the most basic sense, the significational or linguistic result of an act of an embodied being. Second, it presupposes the already established availability of a significational system (or language) that can be deployed by an embodied being. And, third, the statement must have sufficient specificity to communicate something determinate, something I've called 'eidetic,' to other embodied beings beyond its mere occurrence as a physical phenomenon like a sound or marks on a page.

More specifically, however, what can we say about the nature of statements themselves? What underlies their formulation, how can we identify them and distinguish them from other significative actions or elements, and what function(s) do they perform? Let's begin with the assumption that a statement is, in the most basic sense, a complex sign formed by the ordering of other signs (usually words of a spoken or written language) through the deployment of the resources of a significational system by an embodied being. Though I have already touched on this in an earlier section, it is well to remind ourselves again of the underlying functions involved in any sign. As a relation between a signifier and a signified, a sign involves, first, a type of identity in that it can be reiterated and recognized upon reiteration as the same sign. In this respect, it is the signifier that is most relevant. Second, the reiterative identification of a sign immediately involves the differentiation of that sign from others. To recognize a sign in its reiteration is, at the same time, to distinguish it from other signs. While the signifier continues to play a crucial role here, it is this differential aspect of the sign that underlies the associated differentiation of the signified, understood as some ideality or concept. Finally, signs are themselves (relatively) stable relationships between reiterable signifiers and the signifieds (ideas or concepts) with which they are associated. Finally, the functioning of signs as signs occurs by virtue of the structure of the significational system of which they are a part.

If a statement is a complex sign (i.e. a sign consisting of other signs as its elements, for example, a grammatical sentence made up of discrete words), then it must involve the same basic features or functions as simpler signs. We can say, then, that a statement is a complex sign that can be reiterated and recognized as the same in each reiteration; that it differs from other statements, both in its signifying units (words) and the more complex idea(s) or concept(s) that it expresses; and that (thanks, though only in part, to the differential relations of its elements) it stands in (relatively) stable relationships to other statements available within the significational system that it deploys.

We can now see more exactly how and why statements constitute the primary significational elements of philosophical texts. First, any distinctively philosophical text must either explicitly present or imply some statement (or, more typically, set of statements) that make identifiable claims or determinate assertions. It is because of this that we can either cite specific 'theses' in a philosophical text or, on the basis of the text, formulate them as assertions licensed by the text and then submit them to critical questioning. A text lacking this quality will constitute some other kind of significative communication than the philosophical. Put simply, then, philosophical texts, among other things, make specific claims or assertions capable of being extracted from the other elements of the text in which they occur and considered on their own. Second, a statement (or set of statements) made by or formulated on the basis of philosophical texts provides the basis for distinguishing between one philosophical idea or viewpoint and others. Philosophies, that is, differ in part because of the statements that they make or imply, and texts that present the same statements (or sufficiently overlapping sets of statements) will, *prima facie*, be regarded as presenting the same ideas or concepts or constituting instances of the same philosophical viewpoint. Finally, the statements serving as elements of philosophical texts stand in determinate relations both among themselves and to other statements, not in the text, that can be formulated deploying the resources of some common significational system.

To expand this last point, every philosophical text presents a finite and limited set of statements. Beginning with these finite and limited statements, we can identify or formulate, within the significational system being employed, other statements that we call 'assumptions,' statements connected to those in the text 'in retrograde,' expressing what must be claimed or asserted as a basis for the textual statements themselves. Other such statements are those that are connected 'in progressus,' the 'consequences' that follow from the textual statements. But, although statements expressing assumptions and consequences typically receive the most attention, these are not the only relevant relations even if we consider only the significational system itself, which, we must recall, is excessive to any philosophical statement or set of them in multiple ways, not just, so to speak, as 'anterior' and 'posterior' or 'before' and 'after.' For example, each of the signs constituting a more complex 'statement-sign,' taken on its own, stands in a network of relations to other signs and statements. Think, for instance, of the word 'freedom,' that not only has a long and complicated significational history but links to a multiplicity of other statements attempting to explicate it. Again, any statement in a given philosophical text may stand in hierarchical relations to other statements not included in the text itself, relations not describable by either 'assumption' or 'consequence.' Take, for example, Kant's discussion of the notion of 'system' in the section of the *Critique of Pure Reason* entitled "The Transcendental Doctrine of Method," where he describes the 'proper systematic form' of philosophy as being an 'organic hierarchy.' The main point here is that any philosophical text, even when regarded simply as one among other possibilities of a given significational system, is always exceeded along multiple trajectories delineating further relations to other statements and texts lying beyond its limits. This will be all the more so when we later consider the other conditions of embodied being and ideality.

b. The Logical Aspect of Statements

It may seem odd to some readers that I have, so far, discussed relations among statements in terms of signs and signification rather than the more usual ones of language and logic. There are several reasons for this important to the overall viewpoint that I am proposing.

First, the notions of sign and significational system are considerably broader than those of language and logic. In particular, although words are a type of sign, not all signs are linguistic; likewise, although all natural languages constitute a type of significational system, not all significational systems are linguistic. We can say, then, that a 'natural language' is a more restricted instance of a significational system (in a way, for instance, like film, where the written script constitutes only one among a number of other significational systems operating in the film—e.g. montage, 'symbolic' visual objects, the musical soundtrack, the gestures of actors, and so on). The importance of this, which will become clearer as we proceed, turns on the fact, noted above, that philosophical texts (which, traditionally at least, have been almost exclusively linguistic) must be regarded as attempts to reduce the complexity of significational systems, both generically considered as well as in relation to the specific significational system (some natural language) that they are deploying. If we regard logic (whatever else it may be) as engaged with certain stable relations among linguistic statements, then it follows that a logic of statements will always represent a way of restricting or limiting the excesses involved in signification generically considered.

Second, logic itself has, for the most part, been viewed either as a methodical way of classifying and describing certain types of 'natural connections' among statements (Aristotle and Kant, for example) or, in more recent times, formal connections among 'variables,' the 'values' or 'substitution instances' of which are themselves sentences (for instance, the 'logical calculus' developed by Whitehead and Russell). In neither case, however, do we find any very cogent account within logic itself of the nature of its basic elements, i.e. sentences. Aristotle, for example, draws on his metaphysic of substance for such an account; Kant offers a theory of judgment based upon synthetic acts of consciousness; most modern formal accounts merely invoke 'natural language' or, alternatively, certain ideas drawn from mathematical reasoning as accounts of the origins and forms of statements. My suggestion is that it is only by first viewing statements in terms of the more general notion of signification (something, perhaps, first explored by Peirce) that the 'basic units' of logic can be effectively elucidated.

Third, because of their traditional ties to 'natural languages' or a faculty of reason that is taken to govern or otherwise manifest itself within them, the various traditional accounts of logic are too restrictive to admit at least the possibility that there might be other types of stable significational relations, both more as well as less complex than those governing the relations among linguistic statements, that might be deployed within philosophy. We might, once again, think of films, computer programs, or video games, all things considerably more complex from a significative perspective than natural language, as serving as vehicles for philosophical articulation. Alternatively, as Deleuze among others has suggested, diagrams, which, in some senses at least, are less complex than natural languages, may serve as vehicles for philosophical expression. I want, that is, to leave open the question of whether the appropriate vehicle for philosophical expression is necessarily limited to spoken discourses or written texts, as traditional logic would tend to maintain. Note that I am not suggesting here that the centrality of linguistic statements for distinctively philosophical texts be surrendered, since both a film and a diagram, if philosophical, must serve as the basis for formulating appropriate sentences. I am only suggesting, once more, that natural languages and their logics are devices limited with respect to the much larger arena of significative communication.

What, then, is the role of logic with respect to the significational complexes called philosophical texts and their statements? Our earlier 'semiotic analysis' suggested that the very constitution of signs and systems of them rests upon certain invariant relations, first, between signifiers and signifieds, then among the more complex signs called statements. I suggested that, while there was no 'necessity' that significative communicational systems develop from non-significative ones, its occurrence depended upon the establishment of stable and invariable relations within signs themselves (between signifiers and signifieds) and among the more complex signs of which the former are elements. When a natural language is taken as the relevant or paradigmatic significational system in question and the stable relations in question are those obtaining among sentences, then the concept of 'logical necessity' (already itself a sort of 'ideality') serves as one way to describe these invariable connections in this limited field. However, one need only read Aristotle's logical works to see that a logic of statements can be formulated in other terms than those dependent upon some stricter idea of necessity. In any event, the main point here is that 'logical necessity,' important as it may be to any modern conception of logic, is neither a 'primitive term' nor some ultimate and irreducible feature either of the 'way things are' or even of 'natural languages.'

From the point of view that I am suggesting, then, the logical approach to philosophical texts presupposes a threefold limitation upon the excesses of signification. First, the excesses of significative communication become restricted by reducing its sphere to natural language as the traditional medium of philosophy. Second, logic further limits the relevant elements of its analytic procedures to a particular form or aspect of natural languages, that is, statements. Finally, the concept of 'logical necessity' serves both to determine what must be assumed by a certain set of statements, restrict the range of possible statements that follow from them, and rule out (by way of 'contradiction') the 'copossibility' of some statements with others. If a philosophical text, generically speaking, involves a partial and perhaps temporary putting out of play of the excesses of signification, logic serves as the primary means of accomplishing this as well as rendering its details more explicit. Just as any text, to be philosophical, must either explicitly make or provide the basis for making specific statements, it must also do so under the further restrictions imposed by logic and some attendant idea of logical necessity. As we will see, these by no means exhaust all essential features of philosophical texts, but they do serve as necessary conditions for something being regarded as a distinctively philosophical text.

One last consideration concerns the complicated question of the 'logical form' of the statements associated with philosophical texts. In the tradition, there has been a wide variety of opinion both as to whether there is some single or primary logical form of a statement (or sentence) as well as, if so, what that form might be. Aristotle, along with much of the tradition following him, privileged 'predicative' sentences of the form 'S is P,' where 'S' refers to a 'substance' and 'P' to a property or attribute linked by the 'copula' 'is.' It was such statements that provided the basis for Aristotle's syllogistic. Kant explicitly recognized three types of statements (he called them 'judgments'): the categorial (which corresponded to Aristotle's 'predicative' sentences), the conditional ('If S, then P'), and the disjunctive ('It is the case that either S or P'). Both also recognized 'negation' ('S is not-P,' which Kant further distinguished from 'S is non-P') and 'quantification,' what we would today call 'operators over predicative or categorial sentences' ('All S's are P's,' 'No S's are P's,' 'Some S's are P's,' 'Some S's are not P's). For its part, modern logic, particularly in its formalized manifestations, has offered a range of variants or configurations of these. To add to this, Hume, Kant, and others distinguished another 'deontic' class of sentences involving 'ought' instead of 'is' as the 'mediating term' of the sentence, and other 'logics,' such as 'temporal logic' and 'fuzzy logic' have more recently been constructed.

All of these developments point to two points relevant to our discussion. First, it is probably impossible any longer to identify any single form of a sentence that is primary or foundational for the sentences of philosophical texts. More important, however, this proliferation of 'logics' suggests that Aristotle's 'naturalistic' attempt to ground logic on certain metaphysical theses together with some assumptions about the relation between language and 'reality' is, for the most part, no longer tenable. Rather, with such figures as Quine, the relation seems to have been reversed: any decision about a preferred logical system implies certain 'ontological commitments' about 'the way things are' rather than the opposite, a view that echoes the sort of 'conceptual constructivism' that I have suggested. Second, a good deal of the development of multiple 'logics' in more recent times has been driven by the desire to describe and explore the structure of various aspects of natural languages that lay beyond the limits of traditional Aristotelian logic. This I take to be a further confirmation of the excessive character of signification upon which I have been insisting.

I also take all this to imply that there is no purely formal means available within logic itself for identifying the philosophical statements that occur or are formulated on the basis of philosophical texts (or, for that matter, in natural languages in general). This does not mean that there are no ways to do so, nor that formal considerations are irrelevant, only that no *formal* characterization, taken alone, can succeed in doing so. I will return to this issue in a later section of this chapter. At this point, I want to explore the ways in which the condition of embodiment is reflected in that of signification, specifically as it relates to the primary realm of philosophical statements involved in philosophical texts.

2. Expressive Enunciations

In addition to logical statements, all philosophical texts contain what I will call 'expressive enunciations' that serve to link the texts themselves with their origin in the lived experience of embodied beings. As I have been arguing, philosophical texts are, in the first instance, complex instances of significative communication among embodied beings. We should therefore expect to find traces of this as distinguishable features of philosophical texts, though we will usually not find them expressed in the form of complete grammatical sentences, as the more unified logical statements usually are. Rather, they will tend to appear as more fragmentary aspects of philosophical texts that serve to register and inscribe within the texts various 'extralogical' attitudes or orientations of the embodied author of the text toward its statements and their logical connections. They serve, that is, as a sort of benchmark (in the literal meaning of this term) attesting to the origin of the text as an artifact crafted by an embodied being. In this sense, they are 'expressive' of something about the author of the text within the overall text itself, though, as I've said, they typically will not occur as full-blown statements formulated as grammatical sentences. I attempt to mark this difference by calling them 'enunciations.'

Expressive enunciations, viewed in relation to natural languages in general, present a quite wide and varied field and any detailed study of them would likely overlap with other areas such as rhetoric, poetics, and communication theory. With regard to philosophical texts, however, there are three types that tend to occur regularly. As we will see, they correspond to the three basic functions governing signs in general: identification/reiteration, differentiation, and relation.

The first type of expressive enunciations I will call 'emphatics' (a term I first encountered in the work of Paul Weiss). Emphatics, as I will use the term, serve to identify a text or some part of it (including statements) as a result of the reflective activity of the author as an embodied being. They remind the hearer or reader that any philosophical discourse or text—however much it may otherwise assert logical statements, however distanced from the lived experience of a 'subject' it may appear, and however 'objective' it may seem—remains the product of the activity of an embodied being. In so doing, emphatics register the excessiveness of embodied being to any of its individual acts or their results. And, at the same time, they serve as indices of the fact that every text is a type of significative communication with other embodied beings, whose experience is also excessive both to the text and the experience of its author.

Though emphatics can assume a variety of forms, probably the most conspicuous is the interjection of the first-person 'I' or 'we,' usually together with either an expressed or implied 'you,' the hearer or reader. Such phrases as "I think…," "We wish…," "I hope to have…," and so on, play no role in the formulation or consideration of logical statements, yet often surround them. They do not serve to link such statements to other statements but to connect them to a self-identical though finite and limited origin. More broadly, such emphatics call attention to the intersubjective communicational context presupposed by any act of signification, including logical statements. They remind us that the objectivity, universality, and necessity characteristic of logical statements nonetheless ultimately depend upon the condition of embodied being for their very existence; that, as I have suggested (right here is another example of an emphatic!), all these are contingent with respect to their existence and dependent upon the (itself contingent) existence of embodied beings and significational communication. I might note (there we go again) that certain elements of emphatics have been highlighted by such approaches as linguistic pragmatics, speech-act theory, and 'propositional attitudes,' though the conclusions I've drawn go in rather different directions.

It is, of course, true that one can find examples of philosophical texts that rarely if ever deploy these sort of first- or second-person pronouns (Spinoza's *Ethics*, Hegel's *Science of Logic*, and Wittgenstein's *Tractatus* come immediately to mind), but if one looks carefully, one can still find such traces. In some texts, such as those of Hegel, prefaces, introductions, and commentary in footnotes serve the function of interjecting the voice and presence of the author into the text itself. We might call this 'auto-commentary,' where the author intrudes upon the work by speaking to the reader in the 'implied first-person' about statements made in the text itself (a device Hegel employs frequently in his numerous 'Remarks' on key sections of the *Logic*).

Perhaps the most pervasive indication of this intimate connection between texts and their unique origin in the activity of an embodied being is the fact that, whether the author explicitly interjects his or herself into the text or not, texts will always be ascribed to a specific embodied being as their 'author' by their readers. The *Ethics* is not just an 'objective' array of metaphysical claims, any more that the *Tractatus* is a numerically ordered set of statements or propositions. Rather, even if the author has attempted to exclude itself from the text, the reader will supply a connection to an embodied being: it is *Spinoza's* Ethics and *Wittgenstein's* Tractatus. True, we can consider the significant content of these texts as, in themselves, logical statements, but they are, at the same time, statements made by embodied beings to which we either attribute them or construct for them an authorial origin. (An interesting perspective on this point is Deleuze and Guattari's idea of 'conceptual persona' in their *What Is Philosophy?*) The main point is that emphatics, whatever form they assume, serve to identify and permit reidentification of texts and their statements by connecting them with an origin in unique reflective activities of embodied beings. While logical statements may, in some important ways, be regarded as non-spatial and non-temporal, they occur in texts that we consistently attribute to an author occupying a distinctive and limited spatio-temporal location.

Another type of enunciative expression occurring quite conspicuously in most philosophical texts is what I will call 'differentials.' While emphatics are traces of the singularity of the origin of such texts and their logical statements in embodied being, differentials introduce an element of porosity into texts that is obscured if we consider them only as logically connected sets of discrete statements. Differentials, that is, inscribe within a discourse or text the excessiveness of embodied beings more specifically (as compared to emphatics) in relation to the significational system being deployed. By breaking up and segmenting the text in various ways, they remind the reader that a philosophical text's interconnected set of logical statements stands within the broader context of the text itself, and that the text, in turn, stands under the excessive forces exerted upon it by the significational system that it deploys.

At the most basic level, neither spoken discourse nor written texts are ever some pure presentation of unitary logical statements but are inflected in manifold ways not captured in logical statements. Anyone who has studied the Greek language as deployed by Plato, for example, will immediately recognize the ubiquity of inflective words that, though never fully translatable (if at all) into Greek or any other language, color, inflect, and differentiate the meaning of statements presented within the text. Modern spoken English (especially some American 'teenspeak' variants) sometimes seems to consist more of differentials than any determinate content ("Like, ya know, I went, 'Oh my God,' ya know, I mean it was so, like, I dunno, sort of gross.") And anyone who has visited a chat room or read a teenager's 'texting' will realize how these strings of differentials have been directly translated into graphic form ('OMG,' 'TMI,' 'LOL,' :-(, ;-), and so on). Such devices communicate little, if anything, that could be formulated as logical statements; rather, they serve as a means of communicating general but vague attitudes and moods, and, perhaps most of all, simply keep the channels of communication open by filling the otherwise empty times or spaces of discourse.

Fortunately, or so most readers of philosophical texts would likely think, philosophical texts have so far avoided such devices. Still, such texts do employ their share of differentials. One of the most conspicuous manifestations takes the form of elaborate and sometimes idiosyncratic punctuation. Anyone who has read Locke or the later Wittgenstein, or has attempted to translate Kant, Hegel, or Heidegger, will immediately realize that deciding upon the sense of many passages often turns upon how one construes the punctuation marks which segment and differentiate elements of the written text. While they may, but seemingly just as often do not, assist us in identifying or formulating logical statements, what seems clear is that most of the punctuation signs themselves, though a ubiquitous aspect of the overall signifying system, play no direct role in logical statements. (Now consider just the role of the five commas in my last sentence.) Or, we might ask, what is the 'logical meaning' of a colon, a semi-colon, or (so frequent in Locke and Hegel) the dash or sometimes even double-dash? My suggestion, again, is that punctuation signs point, on the one hand, toward a differential aspect of the author's thought-processes and, on the other, toward the excessiveness of the significational system that he or she is deploying. That they can often be eliminated from logical statements or, like brackets, assigned specific and narrowly defined functions, reinforces the point that logical statements represent limitations upon the excesses of both embodied being and significational systems, in the nexus of which they originate.

I might briefly also point to certain phrases, beyond just punctuation, that seem to play a similar differential role in philosophical texts. Words and phrases such as "for the most part," "generally," "at least," "relatively," "in some sense," and some parenthetical remarks usually (see, here's another one) serve to inflect and segment the text in various ways, although they generally (see, I can't help it) play little or no role in logical statements and seem to resist any precise logical formulation.

A third type of expressive enunciation often found in philosophical texts is what I will call 'connectors.' Again, although logical statements themselves stand in determinate relations based upon a very limited and ideally well-defined set of 'connectors' or 'functors,' the expressive enunciations that I have in mind are both far more numerous and much less well-defined than these. Consider, for example, such words or phrases, so frequent in philosophical texts, as "furthermore," "moreover," "in as much as," "however," "in spite of," "accordingly," "notwithstanding," "although," and, of course (here's another one), many more. Although (see, I can hardly do without them) none of these can be assigned any precisely defined logical sense, they nonetheless (here's another) play important roles within philosophical texts. Rather than serving any strictly logical function within statements, they indicate, rather (another one), connections between and among broader segments of texts and the ideas they're attempting to express.

Were all such connectors eliminated from philosophical texts (as some over-eager editors occasionally seem to propose), it would be almost impossible to follow the train of thought or broad contours of even the logical arguments being presented in the text. Such a text would lack the sort of organic flow between and among the ideas being presented. It would, that is (another example), appear to be more a machinic assemblage of statements (even if they are presented in a way that 'shows' their logical connections) than a product of the continuous reflection and thought of an embodied being. Moreover (!), such a connector-less assemblage would make it much more difficult for the author to communicate the broader position or viewpoint that a set of logical statements extracted from the text typically point toward without exhausting it. Philosophical texts don't only present a set of assertions or claims, together with arguments elucidating their logical relations with one another and inferences as to their assumptions and consequences. They also point toward broader connections between idealities or concepts that indicate to the reader how to proceed in thinking and articulating statements from within or on the basis of an overall philosophical position or viewpoint. It is with this that what I have called (non-logical) 'connectors' assist: they disclose and instruct the reader about how the author's own thought has moved among the idealities or concepts to which the limited assemblage of logical statements only points, and they guide the reader in moving among them on its own.

As we will later discuss in more detail, the realm of ideality is excessive both in relation to the finite thought-processes of any individual embodied being as well as to any linked assemblage of logical statements. Though we encounter (non-logical) connectors within philosophical texts, they function neither as operators linking logical statements nor only as 'connective tissue' within texts. Rather, they point toward the fact that philosophical texts are, beyond their constituent logical statements and the broader textual form in which they are presented, also instances or records of an embodied being's engagement with and movement among idealities, a process that cannot be reduced either to a linked assemblage of logical statements or a specific textual construction. They remind and offer guidelines to us, the readers, that a philosophical text also presents a position or viewpoint that, due to the excessiveness of the eidetic sphere to both embodied being and signification, always harbors further possibilities for exploration.

3. Speculative Propositions

So far, I have spoken of 'statements' as central to philosophical texts rather than 'propositions.' Many influential strands of recent philosophy, including both Husserl and the phenomenological tradition as well as the positivist and Anglophone analytic traditions, have generally preferred the term 'proposition' because they wished to distinguish between the 'empirical' and contingent form in which some 'logical content' is expressed (a statement in a specific language, for instance) and the 'logical content' itself, invariable across numerous forms of expression (for example, in diverse languages). The general idea was that the statement in English, "All triangles have three sides," expresses some 'logical content' that is identical, for instance, to that of the German statement, "*Alle Dreiecken sind dreiseitig*," and analogous statements in other natural languages. While we can speak of "All triangles have three sides" as a proposition, in fact, as it concretely occurs here, it is a *statement* constructed by deploying the resources of the significational system of the English language. It is a *proposition* only when regarded as expressing some 'content' that remains identical over multiple articulations in diverse statements.

Two results important for our discussion follow from this. First, every proposition is excessive to any of the statements in which it is expressed. That is, though indefinitely many statements can express the same proposition, no single statement, or any set of them, can be regarded as the final or definitive instance of the proposition. Second, the distinction between statements, which are constructed and exist as parts or instances of a significational system, and propositions, that lack these qualities, suggests that propositions can only be eidetic. We can verbally articulate, write, and read statements; we can only think propositions on the basis of statements that serve as instances of their expression.

If propositions, viewed as a type of ideality, exceed any determinate form of signification, then it would follow that, whatever relations may obtain among them, they would also be, at least in some important respects, different than and excessive in relation to the logical relations that obtain among statements. Even more, we should not immediately assume that propositions are even discrete and differentiated in exactly the ways that statements are.

Although questions about the differences (if any) and relations between statements and propositions has been a highly contested issue in more recent philosophy beginning with Frege, the first, mostly unacknowledged, modern philosopher to frame this issue and explore its consequences was Hegel. In the Preface to the *Phenomenology of Spirit*, Hegel first called attention to what he called '*der spekulative Satz*,' a discussion that he took up in more detail in the Introduction to the *Science of Logic*.

The immediate background of Hegel's discussion was what Kant called '*Urteil*,' usually translated as 'judgment.' Kant's concept of judgment did triple duty within his overall philosophical thought. While for Kant, '*Urteil*' served as a more or less primitive term within his overall view, if we consider how he actually deployed it, 'judgment' at once indicated a mental act of synthesis, what we have called a 'statement,' and the 'eidetic content' of a statement, that is, a 'proposition.' 'Judgment,' for Kant, could function in all three senses for two reasons, both stemming from his particular version of idealism. First, Kant always regarded language as a merely empirical phenomenon that served as a transparent vehicle for conceptual articulation that, consequently, had no real bearing upon the 'logical content' expressed in it. This made any distinction between 'statement' and 'proposition' unnecessary for him. Second, Kant viewed all 'judgments' as products of 'synthetic acts' of consciousness, thus obliterating any effective distinction between mental acts and their 'logical contents.'

Hegel, anticipating a number of later criticisms of Kant's notion of judgment, began the process of prying these three elements of Kantian judgment apart. In his discussions of '*der speculative Satz*' and other writings on logic and language, Hegel first distinguished Kant's '*Urteil*' from what he (Hegel) termed '*Satz*.' From an early point in his philosophical development, Hegel (though, later, not always consistent in this) had become convinced that signification and language could not be viewed simply as a 'neutral vehicle' for the expression of some logical or eidetic content, that they exerted their own independent force upon thought and its concepts. To make this point, Hegel came to distinguish between '*Urteil*,' which he granted to Kant as the fundamental unit of *formal* logic, and '*Satz*,' which, for Hegel, indicated, at once, what we have called a 'statement' (or 'sentence') and the 'conceptual content' that it expressed. However, for Hegel, this distinction between '*Urteil*' and '*Satz*' did not turn so much on rejecting the psychologistic implications of maintaining some 'synthetic act' underlying logical judgments as it did upon the fact that judgments, as Kant (and the tradition before him) viewed them, were understood as statements of formal identity, as an 'S is P,' whatever their actual 'content' may have been. Divorcing 'form' from 'content,' formal logic, as Kant viewed it (on Hegel's account), was concerned only with the *forms* of discrete judgments and the 'external relations' in which these forms stood to one another.

The principal contrast that Hegel wished to draw between '*Urteil*' and '*Satz*,' then, turned upon a crucial difference in understanding this relation between 'form' and 'content.' Kantian judgments ('*Urteilen*'), on Hegel's view, expressed merely formal identities, indifferent to any 'content.' However, this view of judgments was untenable for two reasons. First, every judgment of the form 'S is P' implies, even as it is formally expressed, that, to the degree that S and P are different terms, S is also, in some relevant respects, not

P. That is, logical identity cannot even be stated in formal terms, much less when any determinate 'content' is substituted for its 'variables.' Further, 'S is P' also implies an indefinite and virtually infinite set of other judgments of the form 'S is not Q,' 'S is not R,' and so on. This, however, means that any view of 'S is P' as a formal identity is meaningful only on the basis of or in conjunction with an (indefinite) set of statements determining, if negatively, the 'content' of P (and hence of S).

More broadly put, Hegel's shift from speaking of *'Urteil'* to *'Satz'* as the fundamental 'unit' of logic (and philosophy as well) was, in the first instance, a shift from regarding logic (and philosophy) as merely a formal inquiry. By contrast, Hegelian logic (and philosophy) concerned not merely the formal features of thought but also its 'content.' We might say that it was a philosophical shift from 'the ways we think about things' to 'the concepts from and about which we think and speak.' When Hegel contrasts *'spekulative Sätze'* with *'logische Urteilen,'* then, I take this as a first attempt at capturing the difference between what I have called 'speculative propositions' and 'logical statements.' Put in these terms, we can say that Hegel realized two important points. First, he saw clearly, in a way that was muddled by Kant's view of judgment, that logical statements are always exceeded by the 'propositional content' that they express. Logical statements exist only as realized possibilities of some significational system, while the propositions that they express involve idealities whose connections exceed in complexity the logic governing the significational system or language in which they are expressed. Further, to call such propositions 'speculative' is to highlight both that the propositions themselves are idealities and that the concepts involved in them are excessive to any statement deploying signifiers for them.

To summarize, Hegel realized, in introducing the idea of the distinction between 'speculative proposition' and 'formal judgment,' four important points. First, there is a crucial difference between 'logical statements' and the 'propositions' that they express. Second, the former are functions of a signifying system, the latter are idealities. Third, however, speculative propositions always begin from and require, as a ground and way of access, at least some logical statements. And finally, the relations among the idealities expressed in a logical statement always exceed any particular logical statement (or set of them) in which they are expressed.

In terms of our discussion of philosophical texts, this poses the question of whether, and if so, in what form, 'speculative propositions' appear as an element of actual texts. To this question Hegel's response remained problematic. On the one hand, Hegel claimed that every logical statement (of the form, 'S is P') is, if properly analyzed, also a 'speculative proposition.' On the other, he also regarded certain statements, like 'Being is nothing,' as themselves direct expressions of 'speculative propositions.' In the end, this meant that, for Hegel, all statements were speculative, though some were so only implicitly and others explicitly. On Hegel's view, this distinction between the two sorts of statements was clearly marked. Implicitly speculative statements were themselves logically consistent but were expressed as identity statements that suppressed the differences that their articulation presupposed, differences that could be articulated in further identity statements that contradicted the statements for which they served as elucidations. Explicitly speculative statements, by contrast, were, on the face of them, logical contradictions that presupposed a broader ideality or concept that embraced the terms of the contradiction.

Here Hegel both realized something philosophically important and yet failed to appreciate some of the consequences of his view. On the one hand, by making logical contradiction central to his account, he pointed toward the excessiveness of thought and ideality to any logical statement. Contradictions, expressed in the form of logical statements, represented, for Hegel, both points where the formal logical relations connecting statements broke down or ruptured, and, at the same time, openings within (formal) logical discourse where the excessiveness of thought intervened in the order of signification. On the other hand, on Hegel's account, this intervention always took the form of constructing a new 'higher order' concept that included within itself (and, to use a term I employed earlier, 'com-prehended') the contradictory concepts appearing within the logical statements expressing them. This new higher-order concept could then be expressed as another logical statement implicitly harboring its own contradiction which, when stated explicitly, would be another 'speculative proposition.' This left Hegel with the problem mentioned above when considered at the level of texts and their constituent logical statements. On the one hand, he was forced to claim that every logical statement is, implicitly, a speculative proposition, and, on the other, that every speculative proposition is expressible as a logical (contradictory) statement. But, if this is the case, then Hegel's original insight, directed against Kant, about the fundamental difference between logical statements ('*logische Urteilen*') and speculative propositions ('*spekulative Sätze*') is undermined. This, in turn, means that, for Hegel, there is finally no way to mark the difference between the limited logical statements that occur in texts and the speculative propositions that they express and can articulate in diverse forms.

I suggest that where Hegel went wrong was in viewing logical contradiction as the only philosophically relevant way in which concepts can be related and, therefore, the only relevant way of characterizing 'speculative propositions.' Rather, we should say, to begin with, that contradiction represents only one of a multiplicity of ways in which concepts can be related within or among speculative propositions. If I say, for example, that "My cat is a mammal," one could, of course, focus upon the fact that 'my cat' is a singular embodied being and that 'mammal' is a general concept, inducing an apparent 'contradiction' by opposing the former to the latter and claiming that the original 'is-statement' implies an 'is-not-statement.' And, if one were to proceed in the way prescribed by Hegel, one would then formulate another statement, expressing another 'speculative proposition,' like "The relations between singular beings and concepts are (or constitute) the concept of 'concrete universal'" or some such. But, in considering the original statement, other features could just as well be highlighted. In one direction, we might focus upon 'cat' and 'mammal' as signs, each connected with and differentiated from multiplicities of other signs within the significational system of English. Or, in another direction, we might consider the statement as expressing a proposition that, in being excessive to the statement itself, functions within a fluid network of other concepts leading in multiple directions. We might think of Wittgenstein's 'duck-rabbit' or Descartes' 'Cogito,' or even Kant's 'transcendental deduction' as such instigators of wide-ranging thought processes. Their philosophical significance is not just that they harbor contradictions, though they might do this as well, but that they serve as beginning-points for much broader reflections involving concepts that go well beyond anything that can be fully articulated in any limited set of logical statements, even if these include explicit contradictions.

My response, then, to the original question about how the difference between logical statements and speculative propositions appears within philosophical texts is the following. As opposed to Hegel, I would claim that philosophical texts contain logical statements but not speculative propositions. By their very nature as idealities, speculative propositions cannot appear among the significational elements of texts. They can, of course, be expressed in limited and partial ways by logical statements or sets of them, but we can say neither, as Hegel did, that all logical statements are implicitly speculative propositions nor that explicit contradictions expressed as logical statements are speculative propositions in the sense I'm using this term. Rather, the order of signification and the order of ideality are, as I've been arguing all along, two fundamentally different actual conditions that are irreducible one to the other or, which is to say the same thing, excessive with respect to one another. For his part, Hegel did insist upon the difference between logical statements and speculative propositions but his own version of idealism finally undermined his ability to maintain such a distinction. In the end, ideality ended up 'com-prehending' signification, despite his various attempts to accord some autonomous role to signification.

IV. HOW TO READ (AND WRITE) A PHILOSOPHICAL TEXT

As the etymology of the term itself (think 'textile') suggests, a philosophical 'text' is the result of a series reflective acts of 'weaving together' three basic elements, each excessive in relation to the others.

First, all philosophical texts are constructed on the basis of the lived experience and desire of a finite, embodied being. They are composed at specific places and over a specific period of the author's life. This means that every philosophical text stands in a complex network of relations to other texts (usually both preceding and succeeding it) by the same author, and that all these, in turn, stand in further relations to texts by other authors, both those with which the original author was familiar as well as others exerting more distant influences. Not only does the overall thought and experience of the author exceed any given text that she or he produces, but the overall work of an author, across a series of texts, is in turn exceeded by a complex network of other cultural and historical texts and eidetic relations operating upon it.

These points are important to bear in mind for at least two reasons. First, they should warn us away from viewing any philosophical text as some completely self-contained entity or some final statement of a philosopher's views. Philosophical reflection, like series of artists' works, unfolds over time and any single work is, at most, a 'snapshot' of an evolving process of reflection. Although every philosophical text is a singularity, it nonetheless is only 'meta-stable' with respect to other texts by the same author and by those of other authors influencing it. Put simply, whatever an author may claim about a given text, there is never a 'final statement' of a philosophical thesis or viewpoint. Second, this should make it clear that no philosophical text (or set of them) can be regarded, as Hegel sometimes appeared to think, as some determinate link in an historical progression that 'sums up' all texts that preceded it and provides a platform for the next. To view a philosophical text simply as a 'moment' in some broader process overlooks both the singularity of the text within an author's work and greatly reduces the complexity of its relations to other texts. In reading a philosophical text, we can, then, neither approach it, as many scholars often do, as some entirely autonomous entity (much less some 'final statement') nor, as more historically minded readers sometimes do, merely as a paradigmatic moment in some broader historical thought process. My point is not that we can't employ either of these approaches, but that either alone or both together will fall well short of understanding the act of significative communication that the text presents.

Earlier, I suggested that the elements of philosophical texts that I called 'expressive enunciations' represent ways in which the finite origin of a text in the reflective activities of embodied beings becomes registered in the text itself. These are not merely idiosyncrasies that can be eliminated from texts but play an important, if non-logical, role in reminding us of the finitude and singularity of the text as well as in inflecting and adding nuance to its more logical aspects. In some cases, like those of Plato's dialogues and most of the writings of Nietzsche, a great deal of philosophical significance is communicated precisely by these expressive enunciations. At the other extreme, even in the case of a quite rigorous logical text like that of Wittgenstein's *Tractatus*, such expressive enunciations occur not only in the unique form in which it is organized but in the many parenthetical remarks (which often serve as a running 'auto-commentary') that he inserts throughout the text, not to mention in the occasional metaphor or analogy.

I've also suggested that the second and, in an important sense, principal element of philosophical texts are logical statements. A text that neither makes nor implies any logical statements will simply not be a philosophical text, but some other sort of work, usually some form of literature. Of course, we can interpret a work of literature (or visual art, or even music) in philosophical ways, but the philosophical text, then, is our own interpretive text, not the work of literature itself.

Several points are crucial in considering the logical statements associated with a philosophical text. First, logical statements are actualizations of a quite limited set of possibilities contained within the significational system that they deploy. They represent, that is, a simplification of the more complex network of relations among the signs making up the system (something especially clear in philosophers' frequent logical statements that define key terms). Further, in connecting statements according to the quite limited set of logical equivalences and transformations, the more complex set of relations involved in significational systems (such as a natural language) becomes further reduced. (Any student of formal logic who has struggled to translate statements in a natural language into some appropriate symbolic form will be well aware of this difference in complexity between a significative communication and a simplified logical rendering.)

The point to bear in mind in reading philosophical texts is that, as essential as it is to identify logical statements and map out their logical connections, this will always amount only to a partial understanding of the text itself. Logical statements and their linkages, while drawing upon the resources of the original significational system, are nonetheless exceeded by the significational system itself. Put in a different way, the significational system deployed by a philosophical text always exerts its own force on the simplifications introduced by logical statements and their connections. In particular, no language is ever some 'neutral vehicle' for the articulation of philosophical thought (as many philosophers seem to have assumed, among them Kant); logical statements and their connections serve merely as local and temporary devices to arrest the proliferation of other relations among signs that the significational system permits. As anyone who has attempted to compose a philosophical text well realizes, a significational system like a natural language is a two-edged sword: on the one hand, it cooperates in providing resources for the articulation of reflective activity; on the other, it must be struggled with and sometimes against in the effort to bring the reflective activity to concrete articulation. That philosophical language, especially deployed in the service of formulating logical statements and their connections, often seems unnatural or opposed to ordinary usage (a fact often registered by, among others, Kant, Hegel, and Wittgenstein), is a symptom of the struggle against the excessiveness of the significational system itself. In reading philosophical texts, then, we must acknowledge that logical statements and their connections are provisional and temporary cessation points in the author's struggle to tame the excessiveness of signification. Once again, this time for a different reason, no philosophical text, however logically rigorous, represents some 'final view' that resists any attempt at rearticulation (which, of course, is why philosophers often compose other texts attempting to articulate the same ideas).

The third element of philosophical texts is what we have called speculative propositions. I have suggested that these are not contained in texts themselves in the way that logical statements are. Speculative propositions, as I have argued, are ideal relations among other idealities (often called 'concepts'). One way of putting the relation between logical statements and speculative propositions would be to say that speculative propositions (as Hegel emphasized) present the 'movement of thought among concepts,' which is captured, though only in an arrested and distorted form, by logical statements. Speculative propositions, if we view them as the more fluid and complex relations among idealities such as concepts that thought traverses, are part (the other being the desire of embodied beings) of what gives rise to logical statements. It is the structured process of thought traversing idealities that is expressed by the author of a philosophical text in deploying the resources of a signficational system. At the same time, it is that thought process (never entirely identical with that of the author) that the text itself provokes in the reader. A text will not be philosophical for a reader unless the reader comes to move from the logical statements and connections presented in the text to the speculative propositions, their idealities, and the thought-processes relating them. In other words, an essential part of what makes a text philosophical is the eidetic thought-process of the author intersecting at some points with that of the reader. In the end, both the origin, for the author, and the aim, for the reader, of a philosophical text is, in part, the condition of ideality.

As I mentioned in passing above, the point is not that the reader somehow recapitulate the thought-process of the author; due to the excessiveness of idealities such as speculative propositions to logical statements, this will never, in any event, be possible. At the level of logical statements, we can reconstruct arguments or chains of reasoning; but the relations among idealities are more complex and multi-dimensional than this, so we can at best achieve intersections among ideas or concepts rather than any recapitulation of a thought-process. This means, first, that an essential element of any philosophical text is the eidetic thought-processes that it initiates in the reader; that is, the reader's thoughtful engagement with the text is an essential element of its being philosophical at all. But, second, all access to the eidetic sphere opened by a philosophical text must begin with its logical propositions and their enunciative inflections (and it is, in this limited respect, that philosophical texts can be misinterpreted). However, because the eidetic sphere is excessive with respect to any set of logical statements and their connections, the thought that a text provokes isn't subject to such determinate limitations. In reading a philosophical text, we already bring to the text a complex constellation of idealities and thought processes (as well as embodied experiences) and our engagement with the text serves, variously, as deflections, slowings and accelerations (as Deleuze would say), and connections and disconnections among the concepts in and through which our thought moves. We can, that is, 'misread' the set of logical statements comprising a philosophical text, but we cannot 'misthink' the eidetic processes that the text initiates.

To conclude, underlying all of this is a sort of eidetic image of a philosophical text. Anticipating the next chapter's discussion of Ideality and, perhaps, exemplifying the point that speculative propositions can be expressed discursively (though only partially), I would describe it in this way, which will also involve a good deal of 'enunciative expression.' A philosophical text is a singularity with a meta-stable structure. Its singularity is based upon the specific set of logical statements that it asserts and connects, together with the enunciative expressions that inflect it. As 'meta-stable,' it is constituted as a particular intersection of three excessive conditions, each of which exerts its distinctive force upon it. First, it distills the excesses of the reflective activities of an embodied being, existing at specific places and over a specific period of time, into a discrete though complex act of significational communication. Nonetheless, embodied desire continues to operate 'below the text' and leaves its signature upon it. Second, it deploys the already existing resources of a significational system, but places limits upon their excessive complexity by reducing signifying relations to logical statements and their connections. Still, this limitation is never complete, since the complexity of the significational system intrudes upon it at various points. Finally, it provides a determinate means of access and initiates trajectories for the movement of thought among the concepts and 'speculative propositions' constituting the sphere of ideality. However, these can and will constantly diverge from the text once they are initiated.

Beyond this more eidetic account of a philosophical text, here are three more concrete images I've had in mind at one time or another in my presentation. First, a philosophical text is something like an artificial island at the intersection of three rivers. In each of the three directions, the flow is constantly eroding the island and effort must be made to shore up its contours. Failure to attend to all three directions in its construction and maintenance will result in the collapse and ultimately the obliteration of the island. In such a case, it will be swept away by the strongest force and will no longer be an island but will become something else. Here's another. Freud claimed that the Ego was doomed to serve 'three Masters': the Id, the Superego, and the Reality Principle. To prevent disintegration, the Ego must construct and maintain means by which all three excessive psychic forces can achieve some relative equilibrium. Otherwise, the discrete Ego will be carried away toward a particular type of mental disturbance. And here's one more. In order to construct a text, I must first be driven by a desire toward the communication of my thoughts and experience. I must deploy a significational system (say English) for doing so. And, ahead of time as well as while I write, this activity will be accompanied and guided by something that I wish to communicate. My project can be vitiated in three ways (as any writer knows). Either my desire can overpower the discipline required of writing, so that I either give up the project for something else more satisfying or discover that I am only ranting or free-associating, therapeutic as it might otherwise be. Or, I can get so caught up in the complexities and intricacies of the process of writing, of finding the proper words or expressions, that I despair of ever moving forward and terminate the project from exhaustion. Or last, my ideas and thought-processes can so proliferate as I progress that the project becomes a sort of continuing though futile and never-terminating race of the tortoise with the hare. For writers of philosophical texts, it is usually this last result that poses the greatest threat; in the next chapter we'll consider the realm of ideality to see why this is so and whether this threat posed by the excessive nature of ideality need be fatal for philosophy.

DIAGRAM 5: The Genealogy of Ideality

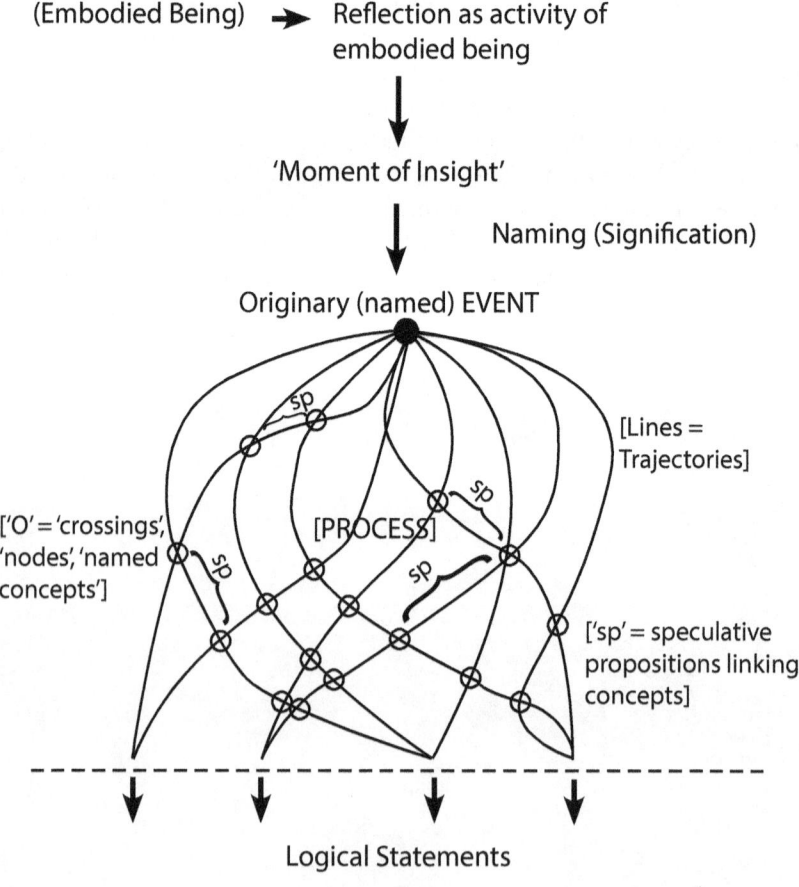

10

Philosophy as Ideality

Philosophical reflection is a special sort of activity on the part of finite embodied beings. This activity, in deploying the resources of a significational system, is expressed and concretized in texts, a type of communication with other embodied beings. Such texts express something that is excessive to them: a thought-process, viewpoint, distinctive set of ideas, or even a body of 'doctrine' (as when we speak of Platonism, Idealism, Positivism, and so on). None of these are ever fully expressible in any singular text, both because it is always possible to compose other texts expressing these in different ways and because the significational system deployed introduces its own excessive features into any text. Still, philosophical texts do provide a singular way of access to something from which they arose; that 'something' is what I've called 'ideality.' Put simply, philosophical reflection issues in texts and these texts express the concepts or ideas constructed in the process of reflection or thought.

We can summarize the ways in which ideality has appeared so far in our discussion of the other actual conditions in the following way:

1. Desire-as-lack, as a constituent feature of embodied being, impels reflection to construct or posit idealities as provisional aims, ends, or reference points. However, reflection cannot hold them stable or determinate nor can it communicate them to other embodied beings without deploying the resources of a significational system. The activity of philosophical reflection therefore issues in texts (spoken or inscribed), which are singular and always partial attempts to express the idealities with which it is engaged.

2. Idealities, considered from the point of view of the reflective activities of embodied beings, appear as thought processes that intersect at points that we typically refer to as 'concepts.'

3. Idealities, considered from the point of view of significative communication and its texts, are structures produced by thought processes that achieve expression in logical statements. However, logical statements themselves tend to suppress the eidetic thought processes from which they arise in favor of a set of formal (logical) relations among statements.

In this chapter, we will (so far as is possible) adopt the perspective of idealities. We must ask, that is, what can be said about the 'condition of ideality' in itself?

One preliminary note of orientation is needed. In what follows, I am not offering some sort of empirical description of how all philosophers, or even a single one, actually proceed in constructing and elaborating idealities. Neither am I proposing some sort of generic or '*a priori*' blueprint or model that would be normative for philosophical thought. Still less am I suggesting some sort of method for philosophical reflection. Along the same lines as the broader idea of philosophy that I've been developing from the beginning, the generation of and movement among idealities involves a field of possibilities that may be traversed and ordered in widely diverse ways. What I propose, rather, is something like what Deleuze and Guattari called an 'image of thought,' that is, a sort of schematic account of the genesis and resulting organization of the fundamental elements of the actual condition of ideality. One might also regard this as presenting a sort of matrix of possibilities that can be traversed and configured in various ways, resulting in a variety of philosophical views or positions. For this, it should suffice if I have presented the various elements involved in eidetic reflection and indicated some of the more prominent processes of movement among them. If I'm successful in this, the schema or matrix should be useful both for characterizing and comparing various actual philosophical viewpoints and warning us away from other images of thought or some of their underlying assumptions that would unduly foreclose important philosophical possibilities. (See Diagram 5)

I. THE REALM OF IDEALITY

Up to this point, I've deliberately employed 'Ideality' as a generic term to cover a wide range of more specific eidetic determinations that have occurred in the philosophical tradition. Among them would be ideas (in the Platonic sense), universals (in the Aristotelian sense), transcendentals (in the medieval sense), concepts (in the modern, especially Kantian sense), classes, sets, relations, and so forth. What they all have in common is that they (1) cannot be reduced to the reflective processes of any finite embodied being (that is, that they are excessive to embodied being), and (2) are expressible significationally, though only partially (that is, they are excessive to signification regarded either as individual statements or the significational system as a whole).

This suggests two important points. First, there is a certain differentiation at work within the sphere of ideality. Ideality, that is, possesses its own sort of internal segmentation, although this will not entirely correspond with the sort of segmentation characteristic of significational systems. Second, this account implies that there is no single ideality that must be taken as somehow 'ultimate.' Although traditional metaphysics has typically either assumed or attempted to establish the primacy or fundamentality of some particular ideality (for example, 'the Good,' 'Being,' 'God,' 'Truth,' and so forth), a point especially emphasized by both Kant in his Transcendental Dialectic and by Heidegger in his discussions of the 'onto-theo-logical nature of metaphysics,' the present view does not aim to offer yet another 'metaphysical' account, but rather an account generic for philosophy itself, whatever ideality it may otherwise assume or assert as primary.

We can formulate our task in terms of three sets of fundamental questions concerning the sphere of ideality, with the reminder, based upon our earlier discussions, that we should expect the other actual conditions to be reflected within the sphere of ideality.

1. From what do idealities issue; how do they originate? And what determines and guides their further elaboration?
2. What, from the point of view of ideality, is the relation between idealities and signification? Must all idealities be expressed or expressible within the resources of a significational system? In what more specific ways are idealities excessive to any of their concrete significative expressions?
3. How is embodied being reflected in the realm of ideality? And in what ways does ideality exceed embodied being?

1. The Event and Singularity

The term 'event' has been deployed, especially in more recent times, with a wide range of meanings. It came to philosophical prominence with the rise of modern natural science, especially physics. Rejecting the 'substance ontology' of Aristotle, modern physics, employing the formal devices of the calculus, tended to regard its basic 'object' of observation, description, and explanation as the 'event.' In fact, the idea of 'event' has, if anything, become both further developed and even more central in more recent developments in the natural sciences. Understood in this sense, anything amenable to mathematico-physical description can be regarded as an event. In one way, this view of event is too broad to serve as a philosophically productive concept, since anything that can be regarded (by physics) as existent counts as an event. In another way, it is too narrow, since it limits the notion of event solely to the physical phenomena explored by physics and other natural sciences, excluding other possibilities (mental, linguistic, historical, and so forth). At the other extreme, such thinkers as Heidegger and Badiou have deployed this term to indicate a (relatively) rare, complex, and rich experience or occurrence, involving a decidedly historical dimension, that is generative of and determining for diverse trajectories and interpretations of distinctively human import. This, however, seems overly narrow or restrictive to capture the sense of what we might otherwise want to call an 'event.'

I will employ this term in a way that falls somewhere between these two extremes. As a first pass, we can say, generically, that an event is some occurrence in the life of an embodied being (or group of them) that presents itself as especially significant in marking a point of deflection of desire, meaning, or subsequent action. In this sense, the term could include such diverse things as the birth of a child, a serious injury or illness, a marriage, a death in the family, 9/11, and, I suppose, even a World Cup final. We might then qualify the term by speaking of 'significant events' in the life of an embodied being (or group of them).

a. 'Moments of Insight'

Among such significant events, we should count a class that we might call (adapting a phrase of Heidegger's) 'moments of insight.' Some philosophers (following Plato and Aristotle) have referred to the subjective experience of such an event as 'wonder' or 'perplexity,' attributing to these the beginning of philosophy. Further, such an event is often described in terms of some visual-based metaphor (like 'insight' here): a vision, illumination, viewpoint, overview, and so on. This is revealing, since it suggests that there is a certain distance separating what I've 'seen' (something that is potentially eidetic) and my 'seeing' of it (in a particular experience or moment in my life as an embodied being). That is, although my 'seeing' arises in the course of my lived experience as an embodied being, *what* I 'see' emerges out of my reflective activities without being entirely reducible to them. More specifically, in the terms I've used earlier, we can say that such a moment of insight is (in the language of phenomenology) an intentional relation between a desire-as-lack and a eidetic correlate that appears, initially, as a relatively indeterminate and unstable 'object-correlate' serving as a possible mode in which the restless dynamic of desire might be stabilized and directed. Put in more informal terms, we sometimes say that we "have an idea," meaning not that we have any specific, nameable idea but that we've 'seen' something that focuses our desire toward further reflection and articulation.

It's important to emphasize here that such a moment of insight can occur only because embodied being is 'always already' (as the hermeneutic tradition has reminded us) engaged in reflective activities that themselves have been or can be expressed deploying the resources of a significational system.

It occurs, that is, on the basis of 'prejudgments' (to borrow a term from Gadamer) or a 'situation' (to borrow another from Badiou) provided by the anterior engagement of embodied being with signification (what Gadamer calls 'linguisticality'). However, it is equally important to realize that, although such an event occupies a temporal place within the lived experience of an embodied being, it possesses another eidetic aspect that is not reducible to any particular moment of experience, that is, that exceeds any particular temporal moment in which it is experienced.

b. Naming the Event

I mentioned earlier that a moment of insight (or, as we sometimes say, 'having an idea') is, initially at least, intrinsically vague, fleeting, unstable, and fluctuating; at first, it lacks the determinacy that would allow me even to reidentify and reiterate it. (How many times have we felt that we had a 'great idea,' only to allow it to slip away and vanish forever!) Only by deploying the resources of a significational system is it possible for this moment of insight to achieve some stability and continued existence. That is, only as significationally expressed is it possible for embodied being to identify and reiterate it, distinguish it from other possibilities, and relate it to them and other ongoing experiences. Still, the event remains excessive to any specific form in which it is articulated, even though it does not become identifiable as such until it is expressed significationally.

We can say, then, that it is only by being significatively expressed that a moment of insight becomes a fully constituted event. As such, it is a *singularity*—with respect to embodied being, in that it occurs at a determinate temporal (and also historical and spatial) point in the lived experience of an embodied being, and also with respect to the realm of signification, in that it involves a unique point of engagement of the desire and reflective activities of an embodied being with a set of determinate possibilities of a signifying system.

The event as I've described it, then, is an intersection between the experience of an embodied being, something eidetic that exceeds it, and an element of a significational system that serves to lend it some stability (that is, a combination of reiterability, differentiation, and relation). This occurs, in the first instance, when such a point of intersection is marked by a *name* that links together the reflective experience, its eidetic correlate, and a significational system of which the name is an element. (Here, as in what follows, Badiou's account of an event is very suggestive, though I utilize it in quite different ways than he does.)

On this view, what the philosophical tradition has regarded as 'metaphysical ultimates' are names of moments of insight. Terms like 'Being,' 'Truth,' 'the Good' (Plato), 'God" (Augustine among others), 'Substance' (Spinoza), 'Reason' (Kant), 'Spirit' (Hegel), 'Being' (Heidegger), and so forth, are a special sort of signifier that names a moment of insight, thereby fixing it as a singular 'eidetic event.' The important point here is that such names are essential parts of their corresponding eidetic events and are essential to their constitution. This is hardly to claim that such terms are *mere* names or words, but only to emphasize the essential role that signification plays even at the very commencement of philosophical reflection.

Such names, in constituting an 'originary event,' also anticipate and, to some degree, 'pre-select' a set of ways in which embodied being can further deploy the significational resources available to it. That is, the naming of the event, as a constituent part of the event itself, possesses a certain force or potency provoking or impelling embodied being to engage with further significational resources that the name, in a way, already anticipates. It is part of the nature of an event, we might say, to 'force' its expression, starting with its naming, through the deployment of further provisionally anticipated significational resources on the part of embodied beings.

c. Event and Signification

To summarize, the actual condition of ideality emerges against the background of free-floating and mostly inchoate processes of reflection on the part of an embodied being driven by desire-as-lack. At some contingent point in this process, there emerges a moment of insight that receives a name drawn from the already existent resources of a significational system. We say, then, that the combination of this moment of insight on the part of an embodied being, together with its receiving a name drawn from the resources of a significational system, constitutes a unique and singular 'eidetic event' or 'ideality.'

It is crucial to stress again that the emergence of such a singular ideality both lends a certain stability and reiterability to the original moment of insight and, at the same time, imparts a distinctive directionality or trajectory to its further development. To elaborate what was said above, while naming such an originary event as 'truth,' 'being,' 'God,' 'substance,' 'reason,' 'Spirit' (or whatever) is, in a certain sense, contingent, once this has occurred, different trajectories for its further development are anticipated and delineated—some trajectories for further development will be opened and others muted or excluded. This is due, in part at least, to the place that the name occupies within the broader significational system of which it is an element and the relations in which the name stands within the significational system from which it is derived. In this sense, figures like Heidegger, for instance, are right in claiming that thought beginning with 'Being' will unfold along certain lines that *can* come to constitute a distinctive and articulable history, but wrong in assuming that there is some single ideality or event underlying all possible trajectories of thought or that any given eidetic event such as 'Being' is somehow 'destined' to unfold along a single trajectory.

2. Concepts and Universality

The originary ideality, which arises when a moment of insight receives a name, serves, in the first instance, as a sort of focal point around which the otherwise chaotic and free floating activities of reflection can begin to coalesce or crystallize. It also anticipates and, to some extent, predelineates various possible trajectories along which its meaning and significance can be unfolded. However, it would be wrong, at this point, to speak of it 'determining' them. Rather, something that we could call 'determination' will gradually emerge only as the process of reflection traverses various of the possible trajectories. Again, as in the case of the original singular ideality, signification will continually intervene in the process of reflection, both opening further possibilities and directions for reflection as well as imposing certain limitations upon it.

It is just as wrong-headed, then, to regard philosophical reflection as somehow autonomous of its significational system as it is to view it as somehow merely assaying or assembling various elements of a significational or linguistic system. Rather, while reflection must borrow elements of a significational system in order to stabilize a line of thought and render it iterable, differential, and relational, it is not reducible to any of its concrete expressions. As I've already suggested, this is because both the idealities produced by reflection and the significational system by means of which they are expressed always exceed one another. That is, there is always something about an ideality (or set of them) that is not exhausted by any concrete expression (or set of them), just as there are always important features of any significational system beyond any of its concrete occurrences.

a. The Originary Event, Trajectories, and Crossings

I want now to elaborate these general points by considering more closely how these trajectories unfold and become more determinate and structured. I have already mentioned that the naming essential to the constitution of an originary eidetic event already anticipates and opens up its own space or field for further trajectories of reflection or thought. This is due, at least in part, to the fact that the name already occupies its own distinctive place within the significational system from which it is drawn. To illustrate, it makes an important difference to the trajectories following from a name if that name is 'being,' rather than, say, 'truth,' or 'good,' or 'God.' Each of these stand in quite different relations of 'proximity' or 'distance' to other signifiers within a significational system and this fact, in itself, will determine, to some degree, the trajectories that their respective unfoldings in thought will follow.

It is important to note, however, that, in considering philosophy from the perspective of ideality, we should not be mislead by taking specific philosophical texts as any indication of the actual reflective movements among idealities from which the texts eventually issue. Most philosophical texts tend to present a single trajectory of thought to the exclusion of others that were actually involved in its construction or formulation. There are, of course, rare instances, as in the case of Plato's various dialogues, Fichte's different 'presentations' of the *Wissenschaftslehre*, or Schelling's attempts to formulate diverse 'systems,' where alternative trajectories are explicitly presented. But for the most part, philosophers tend to *present* their views as if they had traversed only a single trajectory, the one portrayed in the 'argument' of the text itself. However, the realm of ideality, expressed in a text as only a single trajectory and configuration, nonetheless always exceeds any of its concrete expressions, and it is to this that we must now attend.

I want to claim, then, that, from the perspective of ideality, there are always multiple trajectories that can be traversed as unfoldings of the originary eidetic event and that the set of these trajectories will differ depending upon the naming that constitutes a given event. The initial unfolding of these multiple trajectories from a singular eidetic event occurs in a state that mostly defies any exact description, analogous, perhaps, to the 'strange period' referred to by some cosmologists between the 'Big Bang' and the emergence of sufficient material differentiation for the regularities described by the laws of physics to arise. It can only be described as a sort of 'massive contingency' or an original state of 'nomadic thought.' The most we can say about this situation is that it involves something of a largely contingent set of encounters of the activities of reflection with certain more or less fragmentary elements or regions of a significational system, both broadly set into motion and governed by the singular eidetic event. In particular, such trajectories cannot be regarded as, in any way, chains of deduction, whether formal or dialectical, from the singular eidetic event—the possibility for this, which must always be, at best, a reconstruction, will emerge only at a much later point.

As these various trajectories unfold within this situation of 'massive (though not completely random or chaotic) contingency,' various trajectories may come to intersect one another at specific points. Such a point of intersection or node can serve as the basis for the constitution of another event upon receiving a name, derived from some element of the region of the significational system deployed under the aegis of the originary eidetic event. Such a derivative named event I will call a 'concept.'

b. Concepts, the Tradition, and a New Image of Thought

My deployment of a term so prevalent, loaded, and yet controverted within the philosophical tradition calls for some comment, since it is central to the image of thought that I am attempting to develop. First, it follows from my account of 'concept' that, however otherwise they may subsequently be treated reflectively, genuine concepts are, in the first instance and without exception, events (as, ultimately, are all idealities). On this score, my account agrees, at least in part, with figures who highlight the intimate connection between concepts and thought-processes like Kant (who views concepts as acts of synthesis), Hegel (who regards them as 'nodes' or 'moments' in a larger dialectical process), and perhaps even such empiricists as Hume (who view them as emerging out of the flux of sensory impressions). On the other hand, such an account must appear, at least on first blush, opposed to the Platonic as well as nominalist traditions that regard concepts (or ideas) more as fixed structures (although I will later suggest that such a characterization might ultimately be misleading even in these cases).

Second, in claiming that concepts are not singularities but emerge from the intersection of multiple trajectories of thought, my account, I think, captures something of what Deleuze and Guattari have in mind in suggesting, in their own *What is Philosophy?*, that concepts are never simple or primitive indivisible unities but, rather, possess complex contours capable of further elucidation. On both our accounts, concepts turn out to be 'constructions' emerging from otherwise diverse trajectories of thought.

Third, a concept, on the view I've presented, cannot be regarded as some eternally existent 'object' or 'entity' nor some fixed 'transcendental function.' As we might put it, the 'meaning' of a concept can, within limits, fluctuate or morph as it is intersected by additional trajectories or in relation to further trajectories that it initiates.

Fourth, I want to insist that once a concept is fully constituted as an event, it is no longer merely some sort of 'subjective' fiction, representation, or function resident only in our minds (as it is sometimes regarded in parts of the modern tradition as well as in a good deal of popular discourse), however important a role individual thought-processes play in its construction. Rather, as I've suggested all along, once a concept is constituted as an event, especially through the naming that is essential to it, it passes beyond the merely subjective and becomes an actuality that exceeds both any thought-process of an embodied being as well as any further concrete significative articulation.

c. Concepts, Singularities, and Universals

One final point about concepts requires its own broader discussion. In the tradition beginning with Plato, concepts have often been regarded as universals. There have been various inflections of what it might mean to refer to a universal more specifically (for example, 'eternal ideas,' 'general terms,' 'natural kinds,' and so on), but they all turn on a fundamental differentiation either from things that are not themselves universals, that is, from 'particulars' or 'individuals,' or from things (perhaps other such concepts) possessing a 'lesser degree of universality.' To regard a concept as a universal, then, is immediately to define it in terms of an essential function of 'including under itself' or 'unifying within itself' other elements or 'particularities' already differentiated from it. (Plato, Aristotle, Leibniz, and Kant all tend, from otherwise differing perspectives, to view concepts as universals in this way; the Stoics, Hegel, Deleuze, and the later Wittgenstein do not.)

I want to begin to respond to this tendency to identify concepts with universals (or define them in terms of universality) by noting that, in addition to the differentiation between universals and particulars (or individuals), there is another, also relevant, difference between universals and singularities. As treated above, it is a singularity, a singular eidetic event, that first gives rise to the various trajectories from whose 'crossings' concepts emerge. Now the relation between such a singularity and the concepts arising among its trajectories can, in no way, be described as one of 'inclusion' or even 'unification,' even though both the singularity and its affiliated concepts are both equally eidetic. Still, for thinkers who view the 'universal/particular' difference as somehow primitive or fundamental, then singularities may appear as more akin to universals, as a sort of 'super-universal,' a 'highest genus,' or a 'class of all classes.' The tendency, that is, is to elide the notion of an eidetic singularity with that of a universal, to contrast this amalgamation with particulars, and then to claim that the singularity in question is a special type of concept or universal. Probably the most famous example of this, and its underlying ambiguity, is Plato's treatment of 'the Good' in the *Republic*, Books VI and VII, where the Good appears both as a generative singularity and, at the same time, as the ultimate Idea or Concept, the 'Idea of all ideas.' (Similar moves, and their attendant difficulties, can be found in Spinoza's *Ethics*, in Kant's treatment of 'God' in the Transcendental Dialectic, and, under some interpretations, Hegel's '*Geist*' or 'Absolute Idea.') Against such views, I wish to claim that the originary eidetic event, while an ideality, cannot be regarded as a concept or universal at all; even less can it be regarded as some sort of 'eidetic particular.' Rather, the actual condition of ideality can only be described in terms of three determinations—singularity, universality, and particularity—irreducible one to the other. (I would also note that this threefold differentiation corresponds, though in a quite complex way, to the three actual conditions of ideality, signification, and embodied being, though I'll leave further discussion about this aside for now.)

To return to the question of regarding concepts as universals, we can say, first, that the sort of ideality I'm calling a concept must be understood, in the primary instance, in relation to the singularity, the eidetic event, from which it issues. For instance, such concepts as 'human freedom' or 'moral action' are in no way 'universals' that somehow 'contain' or 'unify' within themselves any specific or identifiable collection of particulars or individual instances. Rather, they are constructed through the crossing of many different thought-trajectories issuing from some singular eidetic event. However, as they become developed and elaborated in further reflective processes, they may come to function as universals under which particular instances can be 'subsumed.' The main point, then, is that, while serving as a universal in relation to particulars is not a defining feature of a concept, some concepts are capable of doing so. But it is also the case that any determination that plays such a role will be a concept. So to the claim that 'concepts are universals,' I would rather say the reverse, that 'universals are concepts,' with the proviso that this not be understood as a statement of strict identity, that is, that it be recalled that the sort of idealities I am calling 'concepts' always exceed their function of 'containing' or 'unifying' particulars. At least part of this excess is due, as I have suggested, to the very different relation in which they stand to the singular eidetic event from which they issue.

d. Concepts and Meaning

It follows, as well, that we cannot adequately speak of the 'meaning' of concepts in terms either of their 'extension' or 'intension.' If we regard the meaning of a concept as its extension, we are, in effect, reducing its 'meaning' simply to its function as a universal that 'subsumes' particulars under itself. And if we view its meaning as intensional, we, in effect, nullify its possible functioning as a universal in relation to particulars, since they thereby become irrelevant to its meaning. Nor, of course, is it finally any more accurate to speak of the 'meaning' of concepts as some combination of 'extensional' and 'intensional.' Rather, if we must speak of the 'meaning' of concepts (and this in itself may not always be coherent, since on some accounts of concepts, as in certain trajectories of Plato's thought, concepts or 'ideas' just are the 'meanings' grounding the intelligibility of significative elements), we should abandon this approach in favor of indicating, on the one hand, the trajectories connecting them with their originary eidetic event and, on the other, their further unfoldings in the direction of the non-eidetic particularities involved in the lived experience of embodied beings. In the end, however, I tend to sympathize with thinkers like the later Wittgenstein and Deleuze who view 'meaning' as a term best avoided, especially in the sort of image of thought that I am attempting to describe.

3. Speculative Propositions

a. Hegel's Account of 'the Speculative Proposition'

The notion of a 'speculative proposition' was first introduced by Hegel in the Preface to the Jena *Phenomenology of Spirit* and later elaborated at several points in his *Science of Logic*. Although it is a theme that has received relatively little discussion over the years (and one that Hegel himself didn't elaborate nearly as fully as he might have), I believe that it has a central and fecund role to play in any consideration of philosophical reflection and, more broadly, within any discussion of the condition of ideality. However, it must be disengaged from Hegel's own image of thought and suitably developed for its full significance to emerge.

Hegel first introduced the notion of a 'speculative proposition' (*der spekulative Satz*) in the course of his critique of what he regarded as a pervasive 'formalism' infecting philosophical thought since Plato and Aristotle and assuming its most virulent forms in the philosophies of Leibniz and Kant. For Hegel, 'philosophical formalism,' across its many diverse instances, ultimately rested upon the long-standing assumption that all thought was governed by logic, whose invariable 'laws,' expressed as purely formal structures, were regarded as universal and normative for all thought whatever, regardless of its 'conceptual content.' At the root of this, in turn, lay the prevailing interpretation of the fundamental elements of logic, logical propositions (*logische Sätze*), as statements asserting an identity between the concepts expressed, respectively, by the subject and predicate. And, pursuing this tendency to its last hideout, Hegel faulted a particular way of understanding the copula, the "is" or "are," that links the subject and predicate in such judgments.

Now Hegel was well aware that neither Aristotle nor Kant (for him, the two most important figures in the logical thought of the tradition) ever viewed the relation between subject and predicate expressed in the copula as one of *strict* identity or logical equivalence, and he explicitly acknowledged that this type of statement, which Aristotle called 'assertoric' and Kant 'categorical,' was not the only way that two terms could be joined in a single statement. Nonetheless, his critique of 'formalism' (and all images of thought dominated by this) was based upon his view that the philosophical tradition, in assuming that all thought must be universally governed by the laws of formal logic, both privileged copulative statements as paradigmatic for formal logic and treated the relation of their constituent 'subjects' and 'predicates' principally in terms of identity, thereby suppressing the equally crucial differences between them. The result of this suppression of difference resulted in an image of thought (i.e. formalism) that Hegel regarded as static and lifeless. In the end, formalism segregated the 'forms of thought' from the dynamic processes involved in all thinking (including thought about logic itself) and reduced the processive aspects of thought to an adventitious traversal of antecedently given forms. The result was an image of thought that both failed to capture the fundamentally productive and creative aspect of thinking and rendered the essentially restless and dynamic nature of experience and being inaccessible to thought itself.

At the most fundamental level, Hegel's response to formalism involved offering a counter-interpretation of the logical copula and, following immediately from that, an alternative account of the proposition. According to Hegel, any philosophically cogent account of the logical copula must recognize that, in addition to the 'identity function' that had been privileged by formalism, a 'differential function' was also at work. The logical copula, that is, should be read as, at once, expressing both an identity of concepts or terms as well as a difference between them. For example, a statement like "A cat is a mammal" must be read as *both* claiming that the concept "cat" is 'included in' or 'subsumed by' that of "mammal," and in this sense is the 'same' as the concept "mammal," *and* that the concept "cat" is at the same time distinct, and thereby 'different' from the concept of "mammal." In other words, the logical copula must be understood as expressing *both* an identity of *and* a difference between the terms or concepts that it joins; in Hegel's terms, it must be read as expressing an "identity-in-difference."

A crucial point that follows from this is that the very understanding of a proposition or statement in this way represents an intervention of the dynamic process of thought at the most fundament level of the copula, thereby injecting a sort of movement into the heart of the proposition or statement. Even something as apparently primitive and simple as the logical copula, then, serves not merely as a 'formal operator' but, when unfolded in its full meaning, expresses the dynamic movement of thought itself. Thanks to the 'identity-function' of the copula, statements or propositions *can* always be read as expressing formal identities, but this will always remain a limited and one-sided interpretation unless supplemented by the equally essential 'difference-function' also at work therein. Further, when understood in its full significance, the copula must be viewed as expressing a movement or oscillation of thought between its 'identity-function' and its 'difference-function.' Or, to put it more broadly, the image of thought that Hegel offers us is based upon viewing thought, its concepts, and their expressions always as 'identities-in-difference,' as the dual but complementary processes of constructing identities out of differences and, at the same time, differentiating identities.

It is important to note that when Hegel refers to 'speculative propositions' as the fundamental locus of such a process, he does not intend to introduce some contrast between two *types* of propositions, 'speculative' and 'formal.' Rather, he intends to contrast two ways of philosophically interpreting the same proposition: a 'speculative' interpretation that views the proposition as expressing the movement or process of simultaneous identification and differentiation, and a 'formal' reading that focuses upon only the first and suppresses the latter.

So far, the image of thought that I am attempting to develop in considering the condition of ideality agrees with Hegel, hence my borrowing of the term 'speculative' from him. But Hegel's discussion proceeded from this point along a trajectory that I explicitly wish to avoid. According to Hegel, the 'identity-in-difference' expressed in every proposition must itself also be regarded as a 'higher' or 'more complex' identity that can be expressed in a further proposition or statement that, in turn, again requires the intervention of the process of thought in traversing the new 'identity-in-difference' that it expresses. Now in presenting this, Hegel emphatically insists that the 'identity-in-difference' expressed in every proposition is "determinate," or, as he sometimes puts it, that the crucial 'difference' involved is always a "determinate negation." This means that every proposition or statement expressing an 'identity-in-difference' (and, read as 'speculative,' all of them do) issues in another 'higher-order' statement involving a concept, indicated by the subject-term, the meaning or content of which is completely and uniquely determined by the 'identity-in-difference' expressed in the original proposition. However, this concept, in turn, must be expressed as the subject of a statement that initially expresses an identity but that proves, through the further intervention of thought, also to involve a determinate difference. Since Hegel regards this process as reiterative or recursive, his image of thought ultimately dictates that thought always follows a single, undeviating trajectory running from 'lower,' less internally complex, or, to use his term, less 'concrete' concepts and propositions to 'higher,' more internally complex, and more 'concrete' ones. While I regard the question as to why such a recursive process terminates in a final, all-embracing concept (the 'Absolute Concept' that concludes the *Science of Logic* or 'Absolute Spirit' that ends his 'Berlin System') as a serious one for Hegel, I will leave that aside in favor of a different matter more directly relevant to the present discussion.

b. Disengaging Speculative Propositions from Hegel's Image of Thought

The issue upon which I wish to focus goes back to the characterization of concepts that I presented in the preceding sections. As we have seen, one of Hegel's most fundamental assumptions is that the concepts and propositions of which they are elements, viewed either formally or speculatively, are completely determined by a specific configuration of an identity and its corresponding difference (or differences). That is, although a concept is, for Hegel, a sort of node within a broader process of thinking, and although it is internally complex by virtue of the play of 'identity-in-difference' within itself (so far, so good), it is nonetheless completely determined, and in that specific sense, a sort of equipoised and fixed *eidetic* element within a single process or trajectory of unfolding. What Hegel's account forecloses are three essential features of concepts that I have highlighted. First, concepts arise as nodes or crossings of multiple trajectories stemming from an original eidetic event. Even if that event is named 'the (Absolute) Concept' or 'Absolute Spirit,' multiple thought trajectories can issue from it and the 'nodal points' at which they cross (that is, concepts) will register within themselves the multiple differences obtaining among or implicit in the various trajectories converging upon them. That is, as Deleuze and Guattari insisted, concepts are never entirely homogenous, regular in contour, or firmly fixed but, so to speak, oscillate more or less arhythmically according to the various forces imparted by the trajectories from which they emerge. Second, concepts are, most fundamentally, events (a claim with which Hegel might also agree), but they become fully constituted as such only in receiving a name drawn from a significational system that remains excessive to the eidetic realm. Put simply, Hegel tended to regard language, at least in relation to the eidetic sphere, as a neutral and transparent vehicle for expressing concepts and thereby failed to appreciate the degree to which the intervention of language within thought exerted its own force upon the formation and meaning of concepts. Third, while Hegel recognized that the joining or unification of concepts within propositions must be interpreted 'speculatively' and not merely 'formally' (agreed), he understood this only in terms of viewing propositions as structurally identical elements (hence his emphasis, along with the formalists whom he was otherwise opposing, upon copulative statements), occupying a specific and determinate place within a single, ordered, and 'necessary' trajectory of thought. Rather, I would suggest both that a 'speculative' treatment of propositions need not limit itself only to 'assertoric' or 'categorical' propositions and that the relations among 'speculative propositions' can never be expressed by plotting them along the line of some single trajectory.

Finally, I would depart entirely from Hegel in claiming that neither the nature of concepts nor their combinations in propositions warrant us in assuming that their movement is necessitated or destined toward termination in either some movement ('upward,' as it were) toward a 'highest unity' or 'absolute Concept,' or ('downward') toward expression in the fixed form of logical statements. To use a word borrowed from Hegel that has become fashionable of late, there is a certain 'plasticity' to concepts and the speculative propositions that relate them that permits thought, beginning from any one, to move not merely along an 'up/down' axis (though it can and does do this too) but also along various equally important transverse axes or trajectories. For example, to use our earlier example, the statement "A cat is a mammal" *can* initiate a play of identity and determinate difference that leads 'upward' toward the question of a 'highest genus' and 'downward' toward statements about individual cats and their attributes, but it can equally lead 'laterally' toward a reflection about cats as companion animals of human beings, the types and differences of names that we give to various mammals, or whether cats and other mammals should be regarded as possessing 'rights.' All involve regarding this statement 'speculatively' and not purely 'formally,' all raise significant philosophical issues, and yet they move along very different axes than Hegel's image of thought would suggest.

c. Speculative Propositions as Linking Concepts

To return to our earlier discussion after this detour through Hegel, we can say that, on the image of thought that I am proposing, speculative propositions serve as the conduits through which thought moves on its various trajectories. They do this by constructing and expressing various linkages between or among concepts. Such linkages of concepts, expressed as speculative propositions, always involve, as Hegel emphasized, aspects both of identification (an 'identity-function') and differentiation (a 'differential-function'), but the resulting 'identity-in-difference' expressed in a speculative proposition need not (though in restricted cases it can) be regarded as yet another concept understood as the 'identity of (the original) identity-in-difference.' The principal function of speculative propositions in the eidetic realm, then, is not so much, as Hegel would have it, to constitute a new, though completely determinate, 'higher' concept, but to construct a network of linkages among concepts that are, in much looser senses than those employed by Hegel, the 'same' by virtue of being linked within a common network and, at the same time, different (at least in part) by virtue of the differing trajectories involved in their origination and interconnections.

Speculative propositions, then, at the most basic level, combine at least two concepts in a relation of (I would prefer to say) 'identity-*and*-difference.' However, because both of the linked concepts have their own careers outside of their occurrence in any given speculative proposition, there are always a multiplicity of trajectories for each concept along which thought can move, issuing in further speculative propositions that link them with further concepts. In this sense, we can say that the movement and directionality of thought through the conduits of speculative propositions remains open-ended. On the other hand, the fact that, in the simplest case, two concepts have already been joined in a speculative proposition does not leave the concepts wholly unchanged but becomes part of their 'career' or 'history' and inflects them in new ways which open some trajectories for further linkage and suppress others. As a result, the movement of thought in the eidetic realm, while always open-ended and never completely determinate (as Hegel would have it), nonetheless is never entirely random or chaotic. We might say that philosophical thought is always capable of 'going somewhere else,' but never 'going just anywhere.'

d. Concepts, Speculative Propositions, and Signification

So far, I have somewhat suppressed an element, crucial to the image of thought I am offering, that we must now consider. It revolves around the question of the relation of speculative propositions to signification. I have already claimed that concepts, in their most fundamental sense, are events and that they become constituted as such only in receiving names drawn from a significational system or complex. We can agree with Hegel's explicit claim in 'The Philosophy of Subjective Spirit' that "we think in names" (by which he meant names associated with concepts). But Hegel failed adequately to address the crucial fact that every name expressing a concept also, prior to its deployment in this role, occupies a determinate position within the significational system from which it is drawn. That is, the names of concepts are never *merely* 'placeholders' within the eidetic realm, but continue to impart something of their own significative force even when they have come to function as names for concepts. The same can be said of the speculative propositions within which the name-concepts occur. This reinforces the point I made several chapters ago when I claimed that each of the actual conditions of philosophy is reflected in and exerts its own distinctive force on the others. With regard to the condition of ideality, the condition of signification appears in the eidetic sphere most conspicuously in the form of names essential to the constitution of both the eidetic event proper and the events called 'concepts' that unfold from it. Let's consider, then, the effects of this intervention of the significative condition within the eidetic.

First, the fact that names, as signifiers, also stand in relations to other signifiers within a significational system means that they, of themselves, impose certain constraints upon thought. Such names, that is, can never be completely purified or emptied of their own 'significative residue' and made to function as 'pure expressions of thought' (as Hegel argued, for example, in his discussion of 'mechanical memory' in the Berlin *Encyclopaedia*). True, most philosophical concepts receive sufficient further determination in the course of their linkages with other concepts to function as 'technical' terms, but this 'technical sense' is never *entirely* severed from the significative core of its original name. In the unusual cases where this does occur, the result is either that a philosophical view becomes wholly self-enclosed and largely inaccessible and incommunicable to other embodied beings (like some so-called 'esoteric philosophies'), or it verges upon being a purely formal, mathematical-like complex (perhaps like Leibniz had in mind in speaking of a '*mathesis universalis*').

Second, however, the 'significative residue' of the name of a concept can also play a more positive role in the eidetic realm. While the entire image of thought that I am proposing is directed against any alternative that would view thinking as merely assembling, configuring, or reconfiguring significative elements or linguistic terms (a view to which certain types of 'analytic' as well as 'deconstructivist' approaches to philosophy seem prone), it is nonetheless true that the linkages among terms within a significative system sometimes (perhaps even often) serve to open possibilities for further linkages of concepts in the eidetic realm. Significative or linguistic structures can and often do, at times, serve as a resource or guide for constructing new linkages among concepts. But, it must be immediately added that such a guide is never entirely sufficient, since philosophical thought, as I've presented it, also possesses its own eidetic contours that exceed, resist, and sometimes oppose the relations resident in an existing significative complex (even, and perhaps especially, if that complex is regarded as 'ordinary' or 'natural' language).

Third, I briefly mentioned above that the condition of signification also plays a role with respect to the forms or types of linkage between and among concepts expressed in speculative propositions. While I suggested that Hegel (and much of the tradition that he critiqued) was overly limited in privileging the 'assertoric' or 'categorical' form of a proposition or statement as the principal (or, in some cases, only relevant) way in which concepts can be linked or combined, it is also true that, at the level of speculative propositions as well, the order of signification plays a dual role analogous to that which it plays with respect to named concepts. On the one hand, the types of linkages obtaining among elements of significational systems can be suggestive for and guide the eidetic processes of forming speculative propositions and linking them together in broader networks. The 'connectors' within and among speculative propositions need not be limited to the logical copula (as Hegel and much of the tradition seemed to do), but can include others such as relation, causality, implication, and so forth. (All of these equally involve an 'identity-and-difference' structure, it should be noted.) However, for the image of thought that I am proposing, an important part of the 'speculative movement' among concepts is precisely constructing novel and often complex types of linkages and combinations of concepts for which there is no exact prototype or term in a given significative complex. While concepts must possess a name, the relations among them can but need not. A large part of the novelty of such thinkers as Plato, Aristotle, Spinoza, Kant, and even Hegel lay in introducing new ways of linking concepts lacking any prototype or name within the significational complexes that they deployed, thereby, in effect, constructing new images of thought.

e. The Expressibility of Concepts and Speculative Propositions

I want now to address a question I posed at the outset of the present discussion: "Must all concepts and the speculative propositions that link them be expressible in a significative system (or in language)?" or, more generally, "If the condition of ideality is excessive to that of signification, must all idealities or aspects of them still be significatively expressible?" To these questions, I want to respond with a 'qualified yes.' Since the primary eidetic event and the concept-events that unfold from it are, as I have argued, only fully constituted as events by virtue of their naming, they are all equally expressible. The same applies at the level of their linkages in and among 'speculative propositions.' That means that all such events, including speculative propositions, possess an intrinsically significative dimension which permits their expression; none, even an originary eidetic event, are somehow ineffable, 'non-verbal,' or mysterious. However, and here's two crucial qualifications, neither the activity of thought in generating and traversing these events nor the latent or virtual trajectories open to them once they are constituted can be completely captured or are fully expressible. In the first case, the significative expression of such events will always be a product or result of reflection already having occurred; the expression, that is, will always be 'too late' or 'after the fact.' In the second case, there will always be additional linkages or thought-trajectories that have not yet been made or traversed; the expression, then, will always be at best anticipatory, that is, 'too early' or 'before the fact.' I will return to these points later in this chapter when I discuss logical statements.

f. Conceptual Networks, Philosophical Positions as Idealities, and Histories of Philosophy

Earlier in this work, I suggested that the term "philosophy" can refer equally to a certain sort of activity engaged in by embodied beings, a text or body of texts constructed from the resources of a significative system or complex , and a general position or viewpoint partially expressed in several or many such texts. In the present discussion concerning the condition of ideality, on which this last sense of "philosophy" is based, I have used the term 'network' to describe the assemblage of concepts linked by speculative propositions. I want now to claim that it is precisely such a 'speculatively' linked network of named concepts to which such terms as philosophical 'positions,' 'views,' 'doctrines,' 'systems,' and the like refer. When we speak of, say, Realism, Idealism, Empiricism, Phenomenalism, Existentialism, or, more specifically, of Aristotelian Realism or Transcendental Idealism, we are referring to speculatively linked networks of idealities (concepts) generated by an eidetic event that has made reiterable and concrete a moment of insight.

Such a way of viewing philosophy from the perspective of ideality has a number of advantages over some other possible approaches. First, it allows us to perceive and refer to commonalities and resemblances among philosophical enterprises that would otherwise escape us. That is, put in the somewhat cartographical terms I used earlier, it allows us to place various philosophical views within the 'field' constituted by the three actual conditions as relatively 'nearer to' or 'further from' one another. Specifically, the networks of concepts constituting philosophical viewpoints that lie relatively nearer to one another will possess some degree of 'overlap' of concepts and their linkages and they will tend to converge at some singular eidetic event. Second, it at the same time permits us to distinguish philosophical positions and specify their broader differences in terms of the more specific differences obtaining among their concepts and linkages, as well as their convergences toward differing eidetic events. Networks that have little overlap of concepts or linkages, and that converge toward different eidetic events, will lie relatively further apart within the field constituted by the three conditions.

Third, such an image of thought can assist us in avoiding false dichotomies between philosophical viewpoints, something that has, for example, bedeviled many discussions of 'Platonism' and 'Aristotelianism' or the 'empiricist' and 'rationalist' views of the early modern period of philosophy. Fourth, it offers the possibility of more nuanced and productive accounts of variant positions within a single historical trajectory of views such as Neo-Platonism, Kantianism, and so forth. Finally, it opens the prospect of a broader, non-reductive (and perhaps mutual) critique of and dialogue among philosophical viewpoints that avoid either the centrifugal move of turning other positions into a straw men (something that seems common in more 'analytic' approaches to philosophy) or the centripetal gesture of maintaining that, in the end, all philosophical views are 'in the end' saying the same thing (something to which both Hegel and Heidegger often seem prone).

g. Excursus: Philosophy and its History

As an addendum to this discussion, I would also claim that such an image of thought as I am proposing allows us to address, in a positive way, two related issues often raised about philosophy in relation to its history. The first concerns the question, first raised by Kant, regarding 'progress' in philosophy; the second, so central in Hegel, about viewing philosophy in terms of chronology. I'll begin with the latter. It is true that the image of thought I am proposing here is more cartological, more a matter of mapping (as Deleuze and Guattari would say) than chronological. But the very idea of chronology applied to philosophy presumes that it is appropriate to map philosophy onto a single temporal axis, so chronology is itself a form of mapping. Such an approach was attractive to someone like Hegel, among other reasons, because he rejected any view of philosophy that would see it merely as a sort of smorgasbord of various historical positions or doctrines that were external to one another and among which one could choose or 'mix and match.' Viewing the history of philosophy as one continuous narrative unfolding within a single historical chronology was taken to be the antidote to this. But, I want to suggest, this was a case of the sort of overkill or overdetermination to which Hegel and others following him in this, including Heidegger, were often prone.

Against such a view, I would make two points. First, to regard philosophy in terms of historical chronology is, ultimately, to apply an ordering principle to its condition of ideality that is entirely foreign to it. As I've suggested, the eidetic events and linkages among them that constitute the condition of ideality exceed either any particular activities of embodied being, any concrete historical expression of them in texts, or any broader ordering of either or both of these in terms of some chronology. Rather, thought processes, as they generate concepts and move among them, follow no predetermined temporal order; rather, in a sense, they constitute another order entirely, an 'eidetic order' as I have called it. Through the partial expression of such activities in texts, we can, here and now, immediately access the eidetic order of Plato, Spinoza, Kant, or Hegel and, except for certain interpretive contingencies, traversing the entire chronology of history between 'then and now' is unnecessary to understand them. This does not mean that the events or concepts are some sort of 'eternal essences,' but only that they have sufficient iterability and stability, thanks in large part to their expressibility in a signifying system or language, that we are able to retrace the trajectories, reconstruct the events, and retraverse their linkages for ourselves. In doing so, we are, in effect, reconstructing in thought an entirely different order than the chronological.

The response to Kant's question, earlier posed than that of Hegel, as to whether there can be progress in philosophy, has, in part, already been anticipated but still requires a few additional comments. In light of what I've just said with respect to chronology, if one wants to speak of the history of philosophy, it makes more sense to consider philosophy as made up of various histories rather than a single one. If one starts with a given network of concepts (say, those characterized as 'Platonism' or 'Transcendental Idealism'), it is possible to consider how that network might have expanded, contracted, or reconfigured over a certain chronological period. And it may well be that, as was the case in the period from Plato to Plotinus or Kant to Hegel, the original network of concepts may have either extended sufficiently to link with those of other networks (as, arguably happened in the case of Neo-Platonism) or reconfigured into an entirely different network (as, arguably, in the case of Hegel). But there are no grounds for assuming either that all such networks will eventually link with all others, forming some grand synthesis (such as Hegel attempted) nor that any given network will remain somehow self-contained and isolated from all others. To speak of progress in philosophy, then, is only really meaningful if some network of concepts or philosophical position is assumed and then measured against the various expansions, contractions, and reconfigurations that it undergoes over a given chronological period. Kant, for example, could fairly regard his Critical Philosophy as a sort of progress (which he, in effect, named the "Copernican Revolution in Philosophy" or, otherwise, "Transcendental Idealism") because it involved, at once, a sort contraction (in relation to the earlier conceptual network of 'metaphysics,' basically the 'rationalist' philosophy of Leibniz), an expansion (of the basic conceptual network of empiricism), and a reconfiguration of what remained from both (that is, his own Critical Philosophy). (I hardly need to note that most other such examples of progress in philosophy are not so complex or dramatic.) However, I would not say, with Kant, that his progress necessarily represented either some final 'overcoming' of, for example, Platonism, or even progress in relation to the very different conceptual network to which 'Platonism' refers. So my response to the original question is, "Yes, there can be progress in philosophy, but only in so far as it concerns some initial network of concepts considered over a specific period of time."

4. Logical Statements

a. Differentiating Propositions and Statements

In the preceding chapter, I claimed that all propositions were, without exception, idealities. In making this point, I deployed a distinction between 'propositions,' which are eidetic, and 'statements,' which are concrete deployments of elements of a significational system. First proposed in ancient Stoic thought, this important distinction has been widely utilized since at least Bolzano and Frege in the 19th century and has played important roles in the thinking of both Husserl and the phenomenological movement as well as (at various points in their thought) Russell, Moore, Wittgenstein, Carnap, and others in that tradition. In modern philosophy, at least part of the motivation for making this distinction was the conviction that Kant had created philosophical difficulties, even for his own thought, by employing the term 'judgment' (*Urteil*), which could, in various contexts, refer either to a logical statement expressing a proposition, the proposition (or 'propositional content') expressed, or the 'psychological act' either of thinking the proposition or of expressing it in language. This latent ambiguity in Kant's term "judgment" (*Urteil*) was clearly perceived by his immediate followers, beginning with Fichte. However, it was only partially resolved by their own preference for the German term "*Satz*" (as in Hegel's "*spekulative Satz*"), which, while arguably eliminating the 'psychologistic' element, continued to hover between indicating a sentence expressing a proposition and the propositional 'thought-content' expressed in a sentence.

Beyond this, there were numerous conceptual and logical reasons cited for maintaining this distinction. At least some of them turned upon what I have described in terms of the ways in which the conditions of ideality and signification exceed one another. In the case of (significational) statements and (eidetic) propositions, on the one hand, different statements (say, in different languages or as transformed from active to passive voice in the same language) can express the same proposition, while, on the other, the same statement can express different propositions when, say, the former involves words that are homonyms (like "bat," which can mean either a winged mammal or a wooden club). While there have been a few philosophers who have attempted to question or eliminate this distinction, I believe that it is sufficiently familiar and established (and is indeed required by my view of the basic conditions) that I will assume its soundness in the following discussion.

b. 'Expression' and 'Accession'

To begin, then, we can say three things. First, while there are many types of sentences that do not express propositions or only do so in a derivative way (for example, imperatives, exclamatories, interrogatories, etc.), all specifically *logical* sentences express propositions. Second, drawing upon our discussions in preceding sections of this chapter, propositions are all expressible in logical sentences. Third, in expressing propositions, logical statements serve as points of connection between the broader eidetic and significational orders. Clearly, all three points turn upon the notions of 'expression' and 'expressibility.' With regard to this, I want to ask, What transpires when a proposition is 'expressed' by a sentence and what sort of relations between the eidetic and significational realms result from this?

We can say, in a preliminary way, that a minimal condition for a sentence ('S') expressing a proposition ('P') is that the names of the 'event-concepts' involved in P occur as significational terms in S. This condition assumes both that the concepts in question have already received names due to the intervention of signification within eidetic thought-processes (see above) and that the names of the concepts are equally available, as elements of a significational system, to serve as terms or words within the corresponding sentence. We might say, then, that this condition establishes an 'identity of content' between a proposition and the sentence that expresses it.

However, another aspect of this relation between propositions and sentences immediately emerges. Not only are propositions *expressed* by sentences, but sentences also permit their corresponding propositions to be reiterated significationally and *accessed* via their corresponding sentences. So, in addition to the movement of propositions toward expression in sentences, there is always also another, opposite movement that runs from sentences to propositions. In addition to the movement of expression, there is always a counter-movement of accession. As we will see, this 'expressibility/accessibility' relation is not wholly symmetrical or, in Hegelian terms, it involves yet another 'identity-in-difference.' Put more broadly, we might say, with Hegel, that "it is the nature of thought to express itself in language" and (as Hegel would also agree) it is also the nature of language to provide access to thought. But, especially against Hegel and others who would hold that language is a sort of 'transparent medium for thought,' I would add that these two movements or relations are not 'two sides of the same coin' but differ in important ways.

c. Concepts, Propositions, and their 'Essential Remainder'

Notice that the first condition, stated above, is limited only to the 'conceptual content' of propositions and the corresponding terms of the sentences that express and provide access to them. It says nothing about the 'form' or 'order' of the concepts and their terms, that is, about the ways in which the terms themselves are related. We have seen that, in the eidetic realm, concepts are nodes of intersection of various thought-processes and are linked by speculative propositions that, in turn, link to others. By virtue of this, concepts possess a certain plasticity that permits them to function in differing ways depending upon their role within speculative propositions and their further migrations as these link with others.

However, it is precisely this quality of plasticity or malleability, both of concepts and the places that they occupy within speculative propositions, that must be stripped away in order for a proposition to be expressed by a sentence. For this to happen, several other factors or movements are necessary. First, an originally speculative proposition must be isolated from the network of linkages within which it functions; it must, that is, become regarded as a self-contained unity. In doing so, the 'restlessness of thought' (as J.-L. Nancy has called it) must be arrested, producing a stable linkage of concepts capable of expression in a sentence. When expressed in a sentence, it is precisely this 'plasticity' of concepts and 'restlessness' of thought characteristic of the eidetic realm that is left behind as an 'essential remainder' and it is this aspect that will be inexpressible within the sentence's order of signification. This means that, although every proposition can be expressed as a sentence, no expression in a sentence, of itself, permits direct access to the eidetic processes and networks within which the concepts and propositions originate and function. So the eidetic processes by which concepts are formed and linked remain inaccessible from their expressions in sentences, even as sentences continue to function as expressions of propositions. This is one reason why I have claimed that 'expression' and 'accession' are not symmetrical, that, in this case, (eidetic) propositions always exceed their expressions in (significational) sentences.

d. Significational Structures and the Basis of Logic

Once a proposition is expressed in a sentence, however, another excess comes into play: that of the order of signification. Once a proposition is expressed in a sentence, with the plasticity of concepts and restlessness of thought stripped away, its form and linkages with other sentences become determined exclusively by structural features of the significational system in which it is expressed. It becomes, that is, a '*logical* sentence.' Considered in itself, it is submitted to and classifiable as one among the limited set of types of sentences defined by the operative structures of a given significational system. Further, such structures also dictate a limited set of ways in which the sentence can be 'validly' linked to other sentences, themselves equally determined as to their 'internal' form. The determination of the internal form of sentences, together with that of the formal linkages between them that can validly obtain, constitute none other than what is called 'logic.'

At this point, we can anticipate two lines of objection to this account. First, it might be claimed that such an account of logic errs in grounding logic in 'empirical' and 'contingent' features of natural language, where the 'necessary and universal' or normative role often attributed to logic entails that its derivation be *'a priori'* or independent of such 'empirical phenomena.' (Such would be a version of, among others, a Kantian objection to my account, one also fully seconded by Husserl.) To this, I would respond that significational systems themselves *already* possess a structure that is *'a priori'* for—at least in the core sense of this term as 'independent of'—any concrete sentences that can be formed from its elements. (Kant, of course, wouldn't be satisfied with this, since he wanted to ground logic in 'Reason,' but this is, I think, another example of the sort of overdetermination characteristic of transcendental idealism in general.) Another objection might be the more robust claim that logic and its laws are to be located in the eidetic, not the significational, realm. To this I would answer that, insofar as logic is regarded as purely 'formal,' that is, to the degree that it is viewed as applying universally to all concepts or expressions of them but involves none of its own, it cannot be eidetic in the sense that I have presented this, even if it functions at a high degree of abstraction. If logic cannot be eidetic (and I'll exclude without further argument that it is some feature of the particularities characteristic of the experience of embodied beings), then it can only be located within the condition of signification.

e. Excursus: Significational Systems and 'Natural Language'

In passing, I can now clarify one reason for my speaking of 'significational systems' rather than 'language,' which one might have thought to be the more simple and natural term for what I have been describing. It is that I do not want to exclude the possibility here either that there may be alternative significational systems available to philosophical reflection or that significational systems in general can possess no more 'internal complexity' than a 'natural language.' For the present discussion, this means that I do not exclude the possibility that some formalized system of logic can function as a relevant signifying system in relation to both eidetic thought-processes and the expressions of their propositions in sentences. Nor do I want to exclude the possibility that a formalized logical system may serve as a supplement to or further aspect developed out of or in relation to a natural language. In the former case, thought involving a formalized system would be extremely limited in its scope and capacities for expression, but that is not to say that such would be impossible. In the latter case, I would say that, suitably developed, such a 'supplemented' or 'mixed' significational system might prove useful for certain philosophical purposes, as when formalized techniques of analysis are applied to arguments in philosophical texts written in a 'natural language.' Of course, it's just as likely that such a system will introduce further problems of its own, as figures like Quine have detailed. However, the main point, for which further reasons will later emerge, is that there is no need to assume that a generic account of philosophical thought or texts need limit itself to some single type of significational system, even if 'natural language' has traditionally, and continues to be, their principal medium. (As we will shortly see, there's some good reasons why this is the case.)

f. 'Logical Necessity' Limited and Affirmed

At this point, we are now in a position to respond, in more detail, to the question that arose much earlier in our discussion, that concerning 'logical necessity.' Previously, I suggested, especially in my discussion of views like that of Meillassoux, that acknowledging a general and strong notion of 'contingency' with respect to the existence of philosophy and its actual conditions is compatible with affirming the concept of 'logical necessity,' *without adopting any form of transcendental idealism*. The key lies in the grasping the fact that, while it is *entirely contingent* (in the sense that it equally well might not have happened) that conscious embodied beings exist and that they develop significational systems that permit sophisticated types of communication with one another, once these are in place, another condition appears, that of ideality. When the reflective processes of embodied beings, deploying some of the resources of significational systems, come to further constitute and traverse the realm of ideality, it becomes possible to (partially) express the results of this process in the form of sentences. Because expressing idealities in sentences submits (eidetic) propositions entirely to the order of signification and its own structural regularities, we can then describe the relations of terms within sentences and sentences among each other as involving 'logical necessity.'

Logical necessity, that is, is exclusively a feature of relations within and among sentences formed out of the resources of a significational system. Were there no embodied beings or had they not developed significational systems, there would be no *logical* necessity, only contingency. And, from the perspective of ideality, we can also say that it is entirely contingent that a moment of insight occur, establish itself as an eidetic event, and generate concepts and propositions. But once these conditions, operating together, issue in statements, then, and only then, does it become possible to recognize and refer to 'logical necessity' as an aspect of their internal structure and connections. Logical necessity, that is, is exclusively a feature of sentences and their relations based upon the structural regularities defining a given signifying system. It is applicable neither to the experience or activities of embodied beings, the movement of reflection or thought among idealities, nor the broader 'material universe' from and within which these arise. It is, in the strictest sense, always *'de dictu,'* never *'de re.'* And if it is taken as *'de re,'* this is a sure sign that some other unfounded metaphysical or transcendental idealist view is at work in the background.

Having emphasized the contingency of the existence of the conditions out of which any notion of logical necessity can emerge, however, I want equally to emphasize that, within the strict limits that I've specified, logical necessity and its attendant principles of identity, non-contradiction, and so on are as robust as any transcendental idealist or formal logician could wish. That is, the issue is not whether there can be logical necessity at all, or whether it involves principles that are (in Kant's phrase) 'necessary and universal,' but only what is its scope of application. We might think of the domain of logical necessity, then, as constituting a sort of island surrounded by an ocean of contingencies that, operating together, have permitted its upsurge. While the geography of this island possesses its own form and coordinates, and can even constitute a platform from which to survey the surrounding ocean, there is no basis to assume that its own form and coordinates, however fixed they are, can serve as a basis for mapping that which exceeds it in all directions.

g. Excursus: On Semantics for 'Modal Operators'

It follows that it is misleading and confused to regard 'necessity' and 'contingency' (or 'possibility') as two coordinate and interdefinable notions, as they are treated, for example, in some semantic interpretations of modal logic. One can, of course, develop such significative systems, but one would need to add that the sort of contingency or possibility to which logical necessity is contrasted is '*logical* contingency' or '*logical* possibility,' which is something quite different than the sort of contingency involved in the conditions from which any logical system can arise in the first place. One way of approaching this would be to point out the fact that, in such interpretations, 'actuality' (or 'the actual world') is usually treated as one member of the 'set of all possible worlds.' True, this implies that the 'actual world' is itself contingent and not necessary, but it fails to assert, as well, the crucial point that the (contingent) 'actual world' constitutes the basis for there being 'logical necessity,' 'logical contingency,' or even modal logical systems at all. Another approach would be to notice that, when such semantics for (logical) modal terms interprets logically necessary statements as 'true in all possible worlds' and logically contingent statements as 'true in some (or at least one, but not all) possible worlds,' it assumes that there is some actual and, by its own admission, contingent world comprised, at least, of embodied beings, statements (and the significational systems from which they are formed), and the concept of 'truth' such that an embodied being can assign 'truth values' to statements. If there is no such 'actual world,' or if there is but any of these conditions are lacking in it, then there would be no such 'semantics' or, for that matter, any notion of logical necessity that would require explanation.

All such semantic interpretations of necessity and contingency therefore reduce the broader notion of contingency to 'logical contingency,' treat actuality as one among other 'logical contingencies or possibilities,' and thereby obscure the very notion of 'logical necessity' that they set out to explain or interpret. What they, at most, teach us is the philosophical confusion that emerges from any attempt to approach the conditions of embodied being and ideality exclusively from the perspective of a system of signification. While such enterprises may make some gains in clarifying certain features of signification itself, they will consistently fail as productive approaches to any broader philosophical issues.

II. IDEALITY AND SIGNIFICATION

Our preceding discussion of the condition of Ideality should serve to confirm the claim I made much earlier that this condition is intimately connected, at almost every point, with that of signification. In fact, it was impossible to describe the eidetic realm without both invoking the continual interventions of signification within it or, indeed, employing the resources of a significational system in my own account. This is, of course, not a real difficulty but, in fact, exactly what would be expected if my claim about the mutual inter-reflectedness of the conditions is correct. So, much of what I said above already constitutes a discussion of the relation between Ideality and Signification. What remains to be said under this topic can be much briefer. The main point requiring further emphasis is how the actual condition of Signification exceeds that of Ideality and, more broadly, what this has to tell us about philosophical texts in relation to the ideas or positions presented within them.

1. The Intervention of Signification in Ideality

It should be clear from the preceding discussion that elements of the realm of signification intervene within the eidetic order at several crucial points. First, the name responsible for rendering an event of insight reiterable and fully constituted as an eidetic event is derived from a significational system. The same is true of the names for the thought-events or nodes of crossing trajectories that are called concepts. Signification also plays a crucial role in the movement of thought along the conduits of speculative propositions. And, finally, signification assumes an even more determining role when propositions, extracted from the networks of connections in which they stand in the eidetic realm, become expressed as logical sentences.

Even so, any significational system always remains excessive to even the most elaborated and conceptually rich traversing of the sphere of Ideality. That is, the expression of any philosophical position, however comprehensive and elaborate, remains only a limited and partial mobilization of the resources of its significational system. There is always, for any view or position, a virtually unlimited number of further logical sentences that can be formed, enunciative nuances that can be given them, examples that can be adduced, and experiential references or examples that may be relevant. To expect that any expression of a philosophical position in a text or group of them, however extensive, is capable of exhausting the relevant possibilities latent in its significational system is entirely unwarranted.

2. Excursus: Hegel and Postmodern Views

Hegel, especially as interpreted by someone like Alexandre Kojève, is perhaps the most notorious example of the philosophical aspiration (if not actual claim) to produce a 'total discourse.' Though I don't believe that, overall, this is a very productive way to read Hegel, one might begin with a thesis I've already mentioned (that I think Hegel did hold at certain points in his thought), namely, that language is, or at least can become, a diaphanous or transparent medium of thought. If we add to this another thesis that thought (or 'the Absolute Concept') must constitute a totality, meaning a complete, determinately ordered network of 'dialectically connected' concepts, then it would follow that this should be capable of expression as a text (or texts) that would constitute a 'complete speech or discourse,' to use Kojève's phrase. Of course, if we believe (as I have argued) that the order of signification always remains excessive to that of ideality, then this will seem a misguided or even perverse notion. This is worth mentioning, however, as an antidote to any idea or even aspiration that the ultimate aim of philosophy is to accomplish something like this. It is better, I think, for philosophers to remain aware from the beginning, explicitly acknowledge, and avoid presenting their thought or texts as anything more than a finite mobilization and perhaps exploration of certain limited regions of the excessive possibilities latent in any significational system.

At the other extreme, it is also possible to overestimate the degree to which the order of signification exceeds that of ideality. Several Nietzsche-inspired currents of postmodernism, especially those associated with what is sometimes called 'deconstructive strategies' for approaching texts, make assumptions directly opposite those of Hegel (or at least some of his interpreters). They hold both that language is *never*, even in its simplest instances, a 'transparent medium' for thought and, even more radically, that thought (or ideality) finally amounts to nothing but constructing texts out of significational resources in various ways. Ultimately, then, in the terms I've employed, they deny that statements ever express propositions, not because they consistently fail to do so but because there simply are nothing like what I have called propositions to express. Maintaining this, they often conclude that philosophy is just one type of written text among others and that it is differentiable from other types only by virtue of the sort of 'play of signifiers' that occur within such texts. This, however, is, in an important way, just the 'flip side' of the totalizing view of Hegel. Clearly, just as Hegel (or at least those who read him this way) was misheaded in thinking that it was possible to articulate a 'complete speech or discourse' in the face of the excess of signification over ideality, so such postmodern thinkers are equally wrong in thinking that language involves only some more or less random 'play of signifiers.' The most direct response to this is that, inasmuch as embodied beings succeed in communicating with and expressing their thoughts to others (and such postmodernists' own texts are examples of this—though, I suppose an unsympathetic reader might wonder about this as well), then it turns out that, in fact, not *all* discourse is merely a 'play of signifiers,' that at least some discourse possesses enough stability to succeed in communication. But, if this is the case, then it is fair to ask both how this can occur (via regularities of signification) and what is communicated in such instances (i.e. just what we have called 'propositions,' 'concepts,' or 'ideas'). Philosophy and its texts, then, occupy a realm that will always remain far short of any 'complete discourse' and yet are always more than mere assemblages of signifiers and the play among them.

III. IDEALITY AND EMBODIED BEING

This and the two preceding chapters have already suggested, if not highlighted, several aspects of the relations between embodied being and ideality. Here we only need to make more explicit some of the points we've already covered and this, again, can be fairly brief.

1. The Traces of Embodied Being in Ideality and its Expression in Texts

First, we've seen that idealities initially emerge by virtue of the desire-driven reflection of embodied beings who are 'always already' engaged in significative communication with other embodied beings. Were there no embodied beings, or had they not developed the capacity to communicate significatively, there would be no idealities. Put another way, the 'thought events' that are the foundation of the condition of ideality and its constituent concepts and propositions occur as parts of the conscious life of embodied, signifying beings. The realm of ideality is never some pure abstract structure wholly detached from the reflective activities of embodied beings and merely describable as a 'pre-existing' realm on its own, but always bears some trace of its origins in the experiences, desires, and reflective activities of an embodied being.

This insight must be supplemented by the fact that there is a (limited) degree of choice among the resources of a significational system involved in the naming and ways of combining the named-events called concepts. The resulting network of concepts, when expressed as a complex of logically linked statements, then provides the basic matrix for the construction of a philosophical text.

As we saw in the last chapter, however, philosophical texts are never exclusively mere assemblages of logical statements. Rather, there are other non-logical resources of a significational system, which I earlier called 'enunciative,' that enable embodied being to introduce idiosyncratic elements into the text in such forms as emphasis, inflection, nuance, qualification, and a wide variety of other devices. Such elements, then, produce a sort of presence of embodied being and its desires within the text. More specifically, they serve to contextualize or frame the logical arguments presented in a text, connect them with the idiosyncratic experiences and reflective processes from which they originated, and provide a sort of 'auto-commentary' on the logical structure of the text.

2. Philosophical Style

In my account, I have mainly emphasized the crucial role that significative systems play, by virtue of their own structural features, in rendering thought-events identifiable and reiterable and in both differentiating and combining them in more stable configurations that can be expressed as logical sentences. However, especially when we recognize the important roles that enunciative elements play in philosophical texts, we can also say that (at least some) significative systems (especially natural languages) can suggest something of the 'plasticity' and 'restlessness' of thought and provoke the reader of the text to retraverse something of the thought-processes underlying it. More specifically, while speculative propositions can only be significatively expressed in the form of logical statements, philosophical texts, especially due to their enunciative aspect, can be constructed in ways that suggest something of the more plastic thought-processes from which they originated, even if they cannot be completely reproduced in their original eidetic form. Because of this, we can also say that the thought-activities of embodied beings can, though only in a less plastic form, be suggested in a text. (Many sections of Plato's dialogues, Descartes' *Meditations*,' Fichte's *Wissenschaftslehre*, Hegel's *Logic*, Wittgenstein's later philosophy, many existential works, and much of Deleuze's writing seem particularly adept at actively engaging the reader in this way.)

If we wanted a more general characterization of this manner in which the experience, desire, idiosyncrasy, and reflective activity of embodied beings are engaged with idealities and their expression in texts, we might refer to this as 'philosophical style.' We could then say that philosophical style operates at two related levels. One aspect of philosophical style would be that pertaining to what I have otherwise called an image of thought, basically, a distinctive way in which reflection traverses thought-trajectories, encounters events, names and assembles them into linked networks. The other would be the distinctive manner in which these are expressed in statements, together with their enunciative inflections.

Viewing philosophical style as the general way in which embodied being and its idiosyncracies are engaged with idealities and their expression in texts can help account for the fact that we almost invariably recognize that the image of thought and the text expressing it is that of Plato, Hume, Kant, Hegel, Nietzsche, Heidegger, or Deleuze. This recognition is based neither solely on the specific terms employed or 'arguments' adduced, nor exclusively on some set of significational peculiarities or particular historical facts that we might infer from the text which would serve to identify them as the authors. Rather, it results from our encounter with a particular style of constructing a text that succeeds in expressing a certain style of reflection, that is, a specific image of thought. Because these, taken together, constitute a specific and characteristic way in which an embodied being engages with ideality and expresses this in a text, we are often able almost immediately to identify a particular thinker as the author of a text.

IV. CONCLUDING REFLECTIONS ON THE CONDITION OF IDEALITY

From the preceding discussion of the condition of ideality, two especially important points about the broader nature of philosophy follow. Both have been particularly vexing for any attempt to come to grips with the overall enterprise of philosophy, whether regarded as an activity, a text (or set of texts), or some philosophical viewpoint or position. I believe that it is only by recognizing ideality as an actual condition of philosophy and then considering it in something like the detail that I have here that we can pose these questions and make any headway toward responding to them. The first concerns the overall nature and coordinates of philosophical reflection, regarded as a specific type of eidetic activity; the second, the ultimate aim of such an enterprise. In other words, they concern what is means to think and write philosophically and what this aims to accomplish in the broadest sense.

1. *The Fundamental Eidetic Elements of Philosophical Thought: Event, Structure, and Process*

There is a fundamental question that was posed, in the starkest of forms, at the very origins of European philosophy; percolated under its surface, only occasionally emerging into light, through the better part of two thousand years; re-erupted with a vengeance with the German Idealists and the various responses to them in the 19th century; and continues in full force to this day. Even in the earliest times of what we today recognize as philosophy, this question had three intimately related inflections. First, should 'reality' (or whatever most comprehensive term one might choose) be regarded primarily as a structure or a process? Second, in its engagement with 'reality,' should thought be regarded primarily as a structure or a process? And third, what implications for the expression of philosophy in language (or, more broadly, a significational system) does the way in which these issues are decided have? Or, alternatively, does the nature of language or signification imply some specific way of addressing the first two questions?

If we regard Parmenides and Heraclitus as launching this set of questions, we can say that what we've come to call philosophy commenced (at least historically) with an alignment of two opposed sets of answers to these three questions. Parmenides (perhaps along with Pythagoras) responded that 'reality' is entirely unchanging structure (*statis*) lacking all process or movement (*kinesis*); that 'thought and being' must constitute a single, indivisible, 'well-rounded,' and static structure; and that only as poetry (and even then only problematically) could this be expressed. Heraclitus (as later developed by the Sophists and Skeptics) held the diametrically opposed view that 'reality' was wholly a process of constant change or alteration; that any thought that might reflect this must be equally 'kinetic'; and, at least with the Sophists if not Heraclitus himself, that language (*logos*) ultimately only reflects (if mostly in deceptive ways) this 'kinetic' nature of 'reality' itself.

In an important way, Plato's philosophy can be regarded as a series of (ultimately inconclusive) attempts both to formulate and resolve this impasse. In the end, however, Plato, at least in what proved to be the most influential version of his multiple attempts, opted for a complex resolution that involved two levels of differentiations: first, at the level of 'reality,' between that which is changeless, '*akinetic,*' and structural (*eidos*, Form, Idea), and that which is constantly changing, '*kinetic,*' and processive (at this level, particular things); and second, at the level of the soul (the locus of experience and thought), between constantly changing, '*kinetic*' desire (*eros*) and unchanging, '*akinetic*' knowledge (*episteme*). For Plato, the 'joker' in this schema remained language or discourse (or whatever other term one prefers to translate "*logos*"), which he usually seemed to treat as possessing both '*kinetic*' and '*akinetic*' features, inasmuch as its intelligibility was grounded in '*eidei*' but involved, as well, a sensory and hence '*kinetic*' aspect as concretely spoken, written, or thought. Without going further into the details of this version of Plato's view, we can say that the most important aspect of this for the present discussion is that Plato segregated structure (both in the 'reality' of the Ideas as 'Form' and in the soul as 'Knowledge') from process (sensory particulars or 'things' and desire). As almost a by-product of this, language (*logos*) turned out to be the entirely problematic place where, somehow, structure and process were interwoven with one another.

There are, however, numerous passages in the dialogues explicitly involving the notion of '*logos*'; here I will call attention to two that are especially revealing. (I leave aside many others, such as those in the *Cratylus*, the *Phaedrus*, the *Sophist*, and *Parmenides*, since they seem to involve different versions of Plato's view than the one I am discussing here.) First, at a pivotal point in the *Phaedo* (96 a ff.), Socrates offers a sort of brief intellectual autobiography, relating how, when he was young, he was initially occupied with seeking the causes of natural phenomena. Becoming bewildered with the many and diverse 'causes' cited by the earlier 'natural philosophers,' he then became impressed by Anaxagoras's notion of 'mind' (*nous*) as the single universal 'cause.' However, upon realizing that Anaxagoras made no real use of this principle but always fell back into citing a multiplicity of causes, he resolved to make a new start by examining 'the truth of that which is' as it is reflected in discourse (*logos*). (100 A) He immediately adds that "I certainly do not admit that one who investigates things by means of words (*logoi*) is dealing with images (*eikosi*) any more than one who looks at facts." Here, Plato explicitly suggests that discourse (*logos*) provides the principal access to the unchanging 'Ideas' or 'Forms' as well as to the mutable things of perception (a distinction upon which he had been insisting all along in the dialogue). If the 'battle of the giants' (Parmenides and Heraclitus) over the question of whether 'reality' is unchanging structure or ever-changing process can have a resolution, it will be sought only by examining discourse (*logoi*). But this will mean that, somehow, *logoi* themselves must have both a static or structural and a kinetic or processive aspect.

A brief sketch of how this might be is suggested, among other passages in the dialogues, at the conclusion of the *Theatetus*, the source of the later very influential 'definition' of knowledge as 'justified true belief.' (206 C ff.) To begin, Socrates explicitly asks, "What are we intended to understand by an 'account' (*logos*)?" In the course of addressing this question, Socrates suggests three possible ways of viewing a '*logos*' (which Theatetus partly summarizes at 208 D). The first is as "a vocal image of thought," which Socrates had earlier (206 D) described as impressing "an image of…judgment upon the stream of speech, like reflections upon water or in a mirror"; the second as a "the way to the whole through the elements" (constituting the whole); the third as "some mark by which the object you are asked about differs from all other things," which turns out to be a definition that combines, in a single statement, the term being defined with others specifying the different qualities that make the term's referent unique. The main point I want to make here is that Plato is suggesting that discourse (*logos*) involves, at once, a processive aspect ("the stream of speech"), a structural aspect (a "whole/

parts" relation), and what we have earlier called an "identity-in-difference" between a 'subject term' and 'predicates' joined to it.

Elsewhere, especially in the *Sophist* and *Parmenides*, Plato revisits this view of discourse from various perspectives, the main result of which is a mind-boggling set of paradoxes that emerge if we begin with this view of discourse and the assumptions on which it is based and then attempt, as proposed in the *Phaedo*, to consider 'that which is,' that is, which lies beyond or exceeds discourse, in its terms. But now, fast-forward to Hegel, perhaps with pauses to note Aristotle's treatment of logic and Kant's supplementation of Aristotle's 'formal logic' with his own 'transcendental logic.' With special reference to Hegel's notion of the speculative proposition that we have already discussed, we might say that Hegel returned to Plato's fundamental insight about '*logos*': that all discourse and thought involves both processive and structural features explicable in terms of 'identities' and 'differences.' It would follow, then, that Hegel's fundamental philosophical task was thinking and articulating the notion of a '*structured process*' (or perhaps a '*self-organizing process*') that would equally apply to thought and 'being,' ultimately revealing their 'identity' throughout the manifold 'differences' presented in experience, thought, and their mutual historical unfolding. In a way analogous to that in which physicists sometimes speak of the 'God-particle,' we might say that 'structured process' was Hegel's 'God-idea.'

Now I've already suggested, sometimes implicitly and sometimes more explicitly, why I think Hegel not only failed in this project but had to fail. In the broadest sense, this was due to the ways in which all three of the actual conditions of philosophy exceed the field that they constitute. Put more specifically, Hegel's notion of a 'structured process' was a creature spawned in the eidetic realm, nourished by a very specific image of thought that dictated that thought move only along a single trajectory, and purchased at the price of denying all the excesses of embodied experience, signification, and even ideality itself. When it came to embodied existence, its manifold forms of experience, its often chaotic movements of desire, and the 'massive contingencies' from which it emerged in the first place, Hegel foreclosed all but those aspects that could be submitted to the mono-trajectory dictated by his exclusively eidetic view of a structured process. And when it came to signification, Hegel jettisoned all but those aspects that he regarded as capable of functioning as neutral or diaphanous vehicles for the expression of thought and its eidetic determinations. Finally, when it came to the eidetic realm itself, Hegel reduced the multiplicity of possible thought-trajectories to a single, completely determined, and seamlessly unfolding structured process foreign to and undisturbed by events that might threaten to deflect it in alternative directions.

Nonetheless, Hegel, unlike any thinker before him with the exception of Plato, did manage to unearth and set in clear relief a fundamental issue of philosophy in the broadest sense. We could even view and classify the entire development of philosophy after Hegel in terms of different trajectories followed and positions taken (implicitly or more explicitly) on the question of whether and, if so, how structure and process are related and whether an additional element (or elements), unthought or foreclosed by Hegel, is required by the enterprise of philosophy.

It seems to me that the 'young Hegelians' and 'dialectical materialists' following Hegel made no headway on this but simply took over Hegel's own notion of a structured process and attempted to apply it mainly to the realm of embodied being. Nietzsche and those who have adopted some version of his image of thought (though not exclusively this group either) have tended to resolve the issue by emphasizing process and viewing structure as a sort of ephemeral by-product of it. Their principle opponents, structuralists of all varieties (including most logicist approaches to philosophy), have done just the opposite. In the middle are those who either simply haven't considered the problem, since they have refused to think (or at least talk) about the nature and aims of the overall enterprise of philosophy, or who regard the issue simply as pragmatically resolved in practice. Most productive, I think, have been those, like Heidegger, Bergson, Deleuze, and Badiou, who have, in one way or another, formulated the issue and then have realized that there is another crucial element that must be considered—what they and I, as well, have called the 'event.'

My own account both foregrounds the philosophical centrality of the notion of a structured process that occupied Hegel and maintains that a notion of event is required for any adequate characterization of philosophy. Painted in broad strokes, I have suggested that it is the desire of embodied beings impelling reflection to construct and move among idealities that is the primary locus of process. Significational systems contribute sufficient structure to thought to permit its fixation, communication, and expression. And I've suggested that, in addition to these, we must regard events as both initiating the structured processes of thought and deflecting thought among new and differential trajectories as it unfolds. Finally, proceeding in this way, I have maintained that, while this matrix of 'event-structure-process' constitutes what I've called the field of philosophy, I have resisted the broader attempt to extend it to the ways in which the actual conditions of philosophy are excessive one to the others as well as to the field of philosophy. That is, such an account does not propose that embodied being, signification, or, indeed, the 'chaosmos' itself can be viewed in terms of such an eidetic matrix and I am inclined to say specifically that the sort of excesses involved with these *cannot* be treated in this way. In fact, they cannot be treated exclusively from a philosophical perspective at all but, at most, only noted. I'll return to this in the next chapter.

2. Philosophy: 'Systemic' or 'Systematic'?

The second question upon which I want to comment concerns the aim or goal of philosophical thought and its expression. The late 17th and early 18th centuries witnessed the rise of comprehensive 'systems' of philosophy with such figures as Spinoza, Newton, and Leibniz. However, it was Kant, in the final section of the *Critique of Pure Reason* entitled the 'Transcendental Doctrine of Method,' who first elaborated the generic conception of a philosophical system that would remain the ultimate aim and Holy Grail of philosophical activity at least through Hegel. According to Kant, a philosophical system must satisfy three criteria. First, it must be based upon and developed from a 'single idea.' Second, it must be 'complete,' in the sense of including within itself all other more limited 'bodies of human knowledge.' And third, its organization must exhibit the relations of all these more limited bodies of human knowledge to one another and the relation of each to the 'single idea' on which the system is based. When satisfied, Kant maintained that philosophy would then constitute a 'system of systems.' (It is instructive that Kant specifically mentioned a biological organism as an appropriate metaphor for a philosophical system and referred to such a system as 'organic.') Though they differed about the details of what might be involved in developing such a system, the more important of Kant's immediate followers—Fichte, Schelling, and Hegel—agreed (with the exception of Schelling's later writings) on two points. First, they accepted Kant's account of a philosophical system as properly describing the ultimate aim of philosophical activity and thought and, second, they regarded the criteria he had laid down as jointly satisfiable, both in principle and in fact. As it turned out, Fichte continued to insist, through numerous and quite different versions, that the project he called a *'Wissenschaftslehre'* satisfied exactly these criteria; Schelling constructed several such systems until, sometime in the eighteen-teens or –twenties, he abandoned such projects; and Hegel, at about the same time, came (notoriously) to claim that he had, in fact, constructed the 'Absolute System.'

Now the very fact that, during this period, it proved possible for several thinkers, assuming the same criteria, to construct alternative philosophical systems should warn us that something here is amiss. To capture what this might be, I want to distinguish between two broad types of 'images of thought.' The first I will call 'systemic.' A 'systemic image of thought' will hold that Kant's three criteria can, in fact, be jointly satisfied; that, as Hegel maintained, it is in fact possible to produce such a system; and that such a system will be unique, that is, that there can only be one such system, that it will be a singularity. By contrast, a second view, that I will call 'systematic,' would hold that, while Kant's criteria remain valid as general aims for proceeding philosophically ('regulatively valid,' Kant might say), there is no reason to assume that they can *actually* be jointly satisfied by any specific philosophical construction. (I might add that one can find, within Kant's texts, passages that could be read as supporting either of these images of thought.)

It should be clear from my entire discussion that there are numerous and strong reasons for rejecting any 'systemic image of thought' and, I think, most philosophers after Hegel would agree with this. The more controversial point would be whether, once the 'systemic' view is discarded, philosophy must, or indeed can, still be viewed as a 'systematic' enterprise. In what follows, I wish to insist, against many opponents, that, with a few important qualifications, it both can and must be so viewed.

In order to do this, let's first consider the account of philosophy I have offered in light of Kant's criteria, read as supporting a 'systematic' or 'regulative' interpretation of them. First, we have seen that distinctively philosophical reflection is based upon an original moment of insight that, upon receiving a name, constitutes an eidetic event generative of multiple trajectories. I take it that this would satisfy Kant's first criteria of a 'single idea' governing a philosophical system. Then I suggested that the thought-trajectories unfolding from this eidetic event eventually interacted in ways giving rise to a network of concepts. Now, while I have insisted that such networks, when expressed, always occupy some position within the field constituted by the three actual conditions, I have equally insisted that they can and do occupy different points or regions, each involving a different combination of the 'forces' exerted by the conditions. Given such a 'pluralistic' view, what then can we say with respect to Kant's second criterion, that of 'completeness'?

First, inasmuch as every conceptual network constituting a philosophical position is, in itself, open to further development and, in relation to others, remains open to further linkages with them, no philosophical view can be regarded as 'complete'' in Kant's sense. Second, in a broader sense, due to the excesses of the actual conditions themselves to any attempt to think or express them, we cannot even frame some general idea of what it would be like to traverse, think, or express them as a totality. Philosophy, that is, is an always open-ended enterprise that by its very nature resists totalization or completion.

A rather different response must be given with respect to Kant's third criterion, that of the relation of concepts (or groups of them) to a 'single idea' and among themselves. While any conceptual network will always be open to further trajectories and linkages, its conceptual elements, by virtue of being parts of such a network, are already related both to its originary eidetic event and, in various ways, to one another. So Kant's third criteria will, in fact, be satisfied on my account.

The result is this. Any philosophical position, while never 'systemic,' will (at least on my account) always be 'systematic,' provided that we discount

Kant's second criterion of 'completeness.' But does this further bar it from being 'systematic'? First, we should recall what 'systematic' means in the sense I've introduced this term. Unlike referring to a position as 'systemic,' to speak of it as being 'systematic' suspends the criteria of completeness and, with it, singularity and replaces it with the weaker 'regulative' claim that a philosophical view only aspire to or seek completeness so far as this is possible. So there should be no inconsistency in claiming that any philosophical view or position is 'systematic,' even though none can be 'systemic.'

But what are we to say to the thinkers, representing several different philosophical traditions, who would deny that philosophy can even be 'systematic'? I believe that these can be divided into several groups. One group of objectors would be those whose image of thought derives either from Wittgenstein's turn to ordinary language but, more remotely, the broadly empiricist tradition, and those who are engaged with issues of logical reasoning, which may include the logic of natural languages or issues involving formal systems. We might gloss their view by saying that philosophy is a matter of 'problem solving' and that 'philosophical problems' originate at manifold points in the course of lived experience or thought regarding formal issues that need not be regarded as, in any relevant ways, connected with one another. They might then claim that such disparate 'problems' require no 'systematic' approach but can, so to speak, be 'taken as they come' and solved (or 'dissolved') using whatever means are at hand. To them, I would respond that this mischaracterizes what they are actually doing. As a matter of fact, their very identification of certain questions or issues as requiring *philosophical* intervention presupposes some broader network of concepts that permits such identification to occur. In general, I think most 'unsystematic philosophy' of this type *does* assume a network of concepts that, for the most part, can be described as generally 'realist' and 'empiricist.' Though some, like Quine, Searle, and Rorty, have attempted to pursue this conceptual network to its roots and articulate what is involved in it, a great deal of work of this sort is best regarded as a sort of fragment of some broader conceptual network. Just because such thinkers do not choose to make this explicit provides no grounds for claiming that, in the sense I've employed this term, they are not pursuing philosophy systematically, only that they have chosen to arrest the process of reflection and delimit it to some arbitrary point or region that they are implicitly assuming as already constituted.

A more forceful challenge to the idea that philosophy is necessarily systematic comes from figures perhaps best represented today by Deleuze but including others such as Nietzsche (depending on how one reads him), the later Heidegger, Derrida, and, arguably, Žižek (and perhaps some of the younger generation of philosophers influenced by them). A good deal of their aversion to regarding philosophy as necessarily systematic is (with the notable exception of Žižek) rooted in their opposition to Hegel. On this score,

I think making the distinction I have suggested between philosophy being 'systematic' as opposed to 'systemic' might be helpful. Even so, we must consider the views of Deleuze as representing probably the most radical challenge to regarding philosophy as even being systematic. However, if we take the image of thought that he and Guattari present in *What is Philosophy?* as organized around the notion that it is the distinctive purpose of philosophy to 'construct strong concepts,' and we look carefully at the way in which they relate this to 'planes of immanence,' I think we can see that doing so immediately involves connecting the concepts constructed with others, thus forming networks of concepts, which is at least a significant part what I mean by proceeding systematically. Indeed, Deleuze's overall thought has a distinctive architecture to it that, as he himself sometimes notes, is even capable of presentation in diagrams. While Deleuze would likely oppose my idea of philosophy requiring some originary eidetic event (something that he also contests with Badiou in a somewhat different context), I think that the real focus of his opposition would be to any view that would hold that there is some unique event (like Kant's 'Reason,' Hegel's 'Spirit,' Heidegger's 'Being,' or Badiou's 'Truth') originary for all philosophy, a point that I equally reject. In the end, then, I would say that Deleuze turns out to be one of the more 'systematic thinkers' of recent times.

I claim, then, that the enterprise of philosophy, though always open-ended and never 'systemic,' is unavoidably 'systematic' by its very nature. But I've also suggested that even the most systematically worked-out philosophy is limited by the excessive forces of the actual conditions that together constitute its field. This does not mean that there are no other enterprises or discourses that can traverse and articulate these excesses, only that philosophy is incapable of doing so (or, when it attempts to do so, does so poorly). In the next chapter, we will consider some of these discourses that constitute 'philosophy's Others.'

DIAGRAM 6: Philosophy and its 'Others'

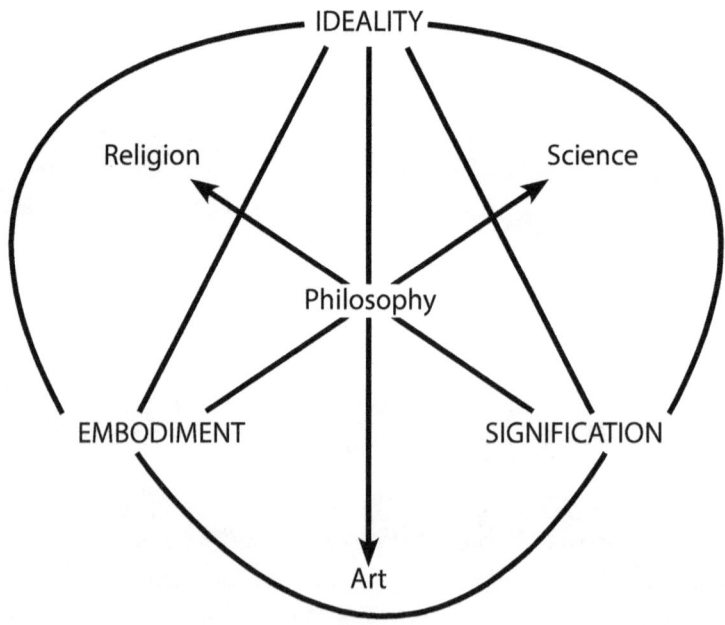

11

Philosophy and Its 'Others'

Philosophy, viewed generically, is a field constituted by the multitude of distinctive ways in which embodied being expresses and communicates the processes and results of its reflective activities. Each of its conditions—embodied being, significational systems, and idealities—is equally essential to there being philosophy at all and, if any one were lacking, philosophy would not exist. However, it turned out, though it might not have, that these conditions were satisfied. But this immediately places philosophy in a precarious and fragile situation, since each of these conditions exceeds the field of philosophy in its own distinctive ways. This isn't to say that various philosophies cannot or have not attempted to enlarge the boundaries of philosophy to include something of one or another of these excesses, but when this has occurred, one of two things (and sometimes both together) has happened. Either a philosophy imposes its own conceptual network upon certain of the excessive aspects of a condition, thereby fundamentally changing it into something that is no longer excessive; it then ends up engaging something fundamentally different than what it set out to treat. Or it attempts to bring something excessive into philosophy itself, which undermines what philosophy itself is and converts it into something that it is not.

Take, for example, the desires of embodied beings. True, philosophy itself is a product of a special sort of desire and constitutes a specific type of response to it. But, outside this (as, for example, psychoanalysis and the study of religions have emphasized), the multiple and often chaotic desires of embodied beings operate in ways wholly different from and inaccessible to philosophy's own forming and linking of concepts and their expression in texts governed, at least in part, by logic. When philosophy attempts to engage the chaotic movements of desire with its own resources, it either rationalizes them and imposes an alien order upon them, or it ends up ceasing to be philosophy and becomes something else, maybe psychoanalysis or surrealist literature. The same pattern applies when philosophy attempts to engage the excesses of signification, say, in dealing with poetry. Either it imposes some conceptual framework upon poetry foreign to it, or it becomes poetic itself and no longer recognizable as philosophy (as in the cases of some types of experimental literature or conceptual art). And when it attempts to fathom the excesses of the realm of ideality, it either reduces the situation out of which some singular originary event and its trajectories emerge to the event itself (something Hegel's 'Absolute Concept' perhaps attempted) or it becomes transformed into some sort of 'trans-conceptual' insight and discourse no longer recognizable as philosophy (as occurred with the later Heidegger).

Now I don't mean, in pointing out the intrinsic limitations of philosophy, to suggest that there are no other activities, discourses, or paths of creation or reflection that can, in fact, engage the excesses of the conditions of which philosophy is a particular type of interface. Psychoanalysis and the study of religion have much to tell us about the complexities and vicissitudes of desire; literature and the arts create and explore an open multiplicity of possibilities of signification and expression; and religious faith and spiritual practices may extend experience and thought well beyond the events, concepts, and their linkages defining for philosophy. But…*none of these are themselves philosophy*, however much they may provide materials for philosophical reflection. (I would also suggest that, for their part, when such areas draw too heavily upon philosophy, their own distinctive forces and capacities tend to become diluted and corrupted, but that's another story that I'll return to later.)

All this suggests several basic points that follow from my preceding discussion about philosophy and its actual conditions. First, philosophy must never be regarded as some sort of 'master discourse.' By its very nature, there are certain sorts of things that philosophy does uniquely and, at its best, does well. But there are other things that any philosophical attempt will pervert and violate; or, alternatively, philosophy will end up corrupting its own native abilities. Second, there are activities or types of discourse other than philosophy that do, in various ways, illuminate some of the excesses that must remain problematic for philosophy. Third, to acknowledge the integrity of these other practices or discourse is, at the same time, to affirm the integrity of philosophy itself. That is, achieving clarity about what philosophy is not (and why) is crucial in securing and preserving what philosophy itself is.

In this chapter, I want to consider the relations of philosophy with three other broad areas of human practice, thought, and discourse—religion, science, and art. Each is, in a different way, contiguous with or (to use my earlier terms) borders upon different regions of the field of philosophy. And if, as I have claimed, the conditions of philosophy are actual, that is, that they are not just productions or mere concepts of philosophical reflection, then we should expect them also to be conditions of and exert their distinctive forces on other areas of human activity as well. Finally, if the field of philosophy is constituted by a particular configuration of these conditions in relation to one another, we should expect other fields to be formed by different ways in which the conditions are configured in their own respective cases.

I think religion, science, and art are paradigmatic in this respect and, while there are certainly other possible configurations, these represent the three major broad and perennial alternatives to or 'others' of philosophy. (For this reason, it is no accident that philosophy has at times either been confused or blurred together with them or that, in some cases, philosophers themselves were able to attempt to reduce philosophy to one or another of them.) Schematically stated, the field of religious experience and discourse is constituted by a certain sort of relation of embodied being to an ideality that subjugates the forces of signification and deploys them in the service of this relation. Science functions along the axis formed by signification and ideality, suppressing the condition of embodied being. And art occupies the field formed by the interrelations of embodied being and signification, absorbing ideality, in a sort of sublimated form, into its own practices and productions. (See Diagram 6)

With respect to each of these—religion, science, and art—we will ask the following questions:

(1) What is the configuration of the actual conditions that constitute its field, what are the field's resulting contours, and how does this differ from that of philosophy?

(2) How, by virtue of this different configuration of the conditions, does this region manage to open and explore dimensions of the conditions that must remain excessive for philosophy?

(3) What does philosophy stand to gain from encounters with this field, and what limits must philosophy respect in its engagement with it?

As these questions suggest, what follows will be highly schematic and does, in no way, represent any very rich account of religion, science, art, or the various more complex ways in which philosophy connects with them. My principal aims in this chapter are only, first, to offer a very low-resolution mapping of the regions these areas occupy in relation to the field of philosophy and, second, to draw some broad conclusions from this relevant to the enterprise of philosophy. Pursuing these issues in more detail, as they certainly deserve, would involve far more than a single chapter of a work such as this.

I. RELIGION AND THE TRANSFORMATION OF SIGNIFICATION

I have used the term 'embodied being,' understood as an actual condition, as a way of capturing and expressing several crucial insights, well surveyed (though usually expressed in somewhat different terms) by some earlier philosophical views. One is that embodied beings are radically finite, that their existence extends over a given and limited span of time, and that it occupies and traverses, over its life-career, a limited region of space. This is as true of material or non-sentient things ("Beings-in-themselves," as Sartre would say) as it is of all sentient beings and of the type of sentient beings we call 'human beings' ("Beings-for-themselves"). So, in the broadest sense, all objects (and assemblages of them) can be said to be radically finite and therefore contingent in their existence. Second, among such objects are those that have become capable of recognizing, first in the physical limitations continually encountered in their movements and actions, then in their reflections upon these, that they *are* radically finite—that there are places they cannot be or go; times that preceded their birth and others that will continue after their death; and things that they cannot ever do and others that they might have done but will not accomplish in their finite lives. With respect to embodied being, we can then say that, to a sentient being aware of its own radical finitude, that which lies beyond the limited time and space through which it exists, the actions that it can perform, and the capacities that it possesses is what is 'excessive' to it. So for an embodied being to be conscious of its limitations or finitude is, at the same time, to recognize that it exists in a situation always excessive to it. And this is to say that excess is a constituent part of what we have called the actual condition of embodied being.

Within this framework of finitude and excess, we can further characterize the existence of sentient embodied being as defined by desire. Desire is the force impelling a movement of embodied being from any given, limited condition toward another less limited and more inclusive (at least with respect to the condition from which it begins). Of itself, desire, like other forces, has no pre-ordained or native directionality (as Deleuze and Guattari have argued in *Anti-Oedipus*), but it does have a rudimentary structure: it involves a sort of 'intentional relation' between desire experienced as a 'lack' and an 'object' taken as fulfilling or satisfying this 'lack' (a point that I borrow from Lacan). That is, in whatever 'direction' it moves, it evinces the same structure (there isn't any serious inconsistency between Lacan and Deleuze at least on this point).

However, we must distinguish between what might be called 'local' or 'remedial excess' and 'excess' regarded generically as constituent of the condition of embodied being. In the first case, the 'intentional correlate' of desire-as-lack is another finite object capable of, at least provisionally, satisfying the lack—food, a book, an electronic gadget, a vacation experience, or even another embodied being. Taken in the generic sense, however, the sort of excess involved in embodied being as an actual condition remains always elusive for and beyond desire-as-lack. In this generic sense, desire-as-lack remains unsatisfied and unsatisfiable, however many and extensive the local satisfactions it might attain.

The 'field' of religion comes to be constituted when the condition of embodied being, understood as desire-as-lack, enters into a relation with another condition, that of ideality. Expressed generically, this internally complex relation involves two 'directionalities' that remain in tension with one another and are never symmetrical; this is due to the different ways that embodied being and ideality stand with respect to their own excesses and thus to those of each other. I'll try to make this more concrete in what follows.

From the perspective of embodied being and its desire-as-lack, that which is generically excessive to the radical finitude of its own condition serves, in the first instance, as the 'singular generic object' that, whatever else it may be, would constitute the satisfaction of desire's lack. [In this generic sense, all religions are monotheist, even if they recognize many gods—for instance, beyond the Greek gods there was always 'nature' (*physis*) or 'cosmos,' beyond the Hindu gods, Brahmin.) That is, no mere multiplicity can serve as the generic object of desire.] Notice that embodied being does not merely 'construct' this 'generic excess,' or somehow imaginatively project it, since it is actual and a constituent part of the condition of embodied being itself. But desire-as-lack does make a contribution, since it constitutes this 'generic excess,' in itself perhaps only a 'massive multiplicity,' as the 'generic intentional correlate' of desire-as-lack.

As we saw in our discussion of philosophy, this relation of embodied being to its 'generic excess' is disclosed to it in a 'moment of insight.' It is here that signification first exerts its force, since this moment of insight becomes fully constituted as an eidetic event only upon receiving a name. However, it is precisely here that the respective relations of religion and philosophy to the order of signification begin to diverge. For, although the trajectories of both philosophy and religion commence from a primary named event (that is, an ideality), the event-constituting names are of different types. The name constituting a religious event will be a *proper name* or at least function as a proper name ('Baal,' 'Ahura Mazda,' 'Yahweh,' 'God,' 'Zeus,' 'Christ,' 'Allah,' and so on), whereas the name constituting a philosophical event will be generic or abstract ('Being,' 'Truth,' 'the Good,' 'Substance,' 'Absolute Idea,' etc.). Both types of named events are equally idealities and, once in place, immediately bring into play their own 'structured processes' together with their own distinctive ways in which they are excessive to embodied being and signification.

The fact that the names of the 'primordial events' of religion are proper names bring such events into proximity with embodied being in a way that the generic names of philosophy for such events do not. The fact that the primary ideality of a religion is constituted by a proper name immediately relates it back to the order of embodied beings which themselves possess proper names. That is, the name itself serves to constitute a sort of ideality that can both address embodied beings by their own proper names ("Go, Moses, up to the mountain," "Saul, Saul, why do you persecute me?") and, in turn, be addressed by them with its own proper name.

The constitution of an event (ideality) through a proper name (as opposed to a generic one) completely transforms the role that signification will then play in religion (as opposed to philosophy). For religion, the order of signification will no longer function as an autonomous condition imposing some of its own order of discourse (including and especially the logical) but will always function in the service of communication between the proper-named and thereby personalized ideality and embodied being, individuated by its own proper name. The principle function of signification on the part of the 'divine ideality' will, broadly viewed, be that of revelation and command, and that on the part of embodied being will be prayer and supplication. In neither case do the concepts, propositions, and statements of philosophy play any decisive role, even if they may occasionally seem to appear 'formally' in religious discourse.

Often, what is revealed in religious discourse will appear, when judged according to logic, as paradoxes, mysteries, or even flat-out contradictions. The laws of logic that operate at the level of philosophical texts therefore exert little of their force upon religious texts. This means that interpreting religious discourse or reading religious texts from the point of view of the norms of philosophical reasoning is completely to misunderstand how signification functions within them.

As I have been suggesting, the field of religion discloses much about the conditions of embodied being and ideality, the relations between desire and its objects, and the excesses involved with them that lie outside the limitations of philosophy itself. Religion is not somehow inferior to philosophy (as Plato, Hegel, and many others have held) nor is it in some way superior to it (as others like Pascal and Kierkegaard have insisted). Rather, religion and philosophy are both different and yet contiguous by virtue of their differing configurations of the actual conditions.

As a final way to illustrate this relation between philosophical and religious forms of signification, we might consider the often-asked question, "Does God exist?" The first thing to ask is what sort of discourse, religious or philosophical, is it part of, or from the point of view of which configuration of conditions is it asked? Now, in either occurrence, the word "God" names an event that constitutes an ideality, and I've argued all along that ideality is an actual condition and, as such, its concepts are also actual and can be said to 'exist.' So, understood as a generic ideality, it's true that "God exists," and saying so, so long as it's clear either that we're speaking of the primary ideality either of philosophy or of religion, should be no cause of hesitation. But, if the question is asked specifically in the context of religion, then this response won't really suffice. Here, the question is not just about "God" considered as an ideality generically named, but about "God" as an ideality with a proper name that projects the possibility of such a named 'ideal being' serving as the complete satisfaction of an embodied being's desire-as-lack (something that I suspect some people have in mind in asking me whether "I've accepted Jesus as my personal Lord and Savior.") To this, the answer will have to be, "Beyond being an ideality, God (in this further sense) might or might not exist." The conclusion, on my view, is the probably heterodox one of saying that if a philosophy employs the term "God" as the generic name for its primary event, then the statement "God exists" is true unproblematically. On the other hand, the statement "God exists," where "God" is understood as a proper name, will *only* be problematic within a religious framework and therefore only a believer can seriously doubt that God exists. [Perhaps it was something like this that Nietzsche (or at least his 'madman') had in mind in claiming that "God is dead." That is, God could only die if s/he/it was once alive, but God could be thought of as 'alive' only within a religious framework, the collapse of which Nietzsche did so much to document and hasten.]

But, one final point: what would happen if one were to insist that the question put was literally 'unconditional,' that it was intended to ask about whether 'something like a God' exists beyond or prior to the actual conditions that constitute religion and philosophy (and science and art as well), whether among the 'massive contingencies' from which the actual conditions emerge there might be something we could call 'God' or 'the Divine'? One response, perhaps post-Kantian in inspiration, would be, "This is a nonsensical question, since there couldn't be a question without the actual conditions." But this seems to me an unnecessary cop-out, despite all that I've said about the conditions. I think there are two authentic responses. One would be, "We simply can't know one way or the other, nor is there anything favoring how to decide this." That would be a position I'd call "primordial agnosticisim" and I take it as an affirmation of our relation to excess, not, as it is usually meant, as an admission of intellectual defeat. The second would be, "Since that which lies beyond the actual conditions is pure multiplicity and massive contingency, then, if we regard this 'Chaosmos' as God, we have to say that God is contingency itself" (or perhaps 'the necessity of contingency,' to borrow a phrase from Meillassoux). However, such a response, directly opposed to the usual philosophical and theological treatment of God as the singular 'necessary being,' would be neither religious nor philosophical but something 'entirely Other'—it would be as if all the three conditions, acting as a sheer multiplicity without relation to one another, were simultaneously and generically acknowledging the 'massive excess' of the 'Chaosmos.' Somehow I don't think the claim is, in itself, entirely meaningless, but it seems meaningless and empty when any finite being utters it. It's more like a song that the 'Chaosmos' hums to itself; we embodied and conditioned beings can at most catch fragments of it by silently eavesdropping.

II. SCIENCE AND THE SUPPRESSION OF EMBODIED BEING

The title of the central foundational work of modern physics, and indeed of what we have come to call 'natural science,' is *"Philosophiae Naturalis Principia Mathematica"* ("The Mathematical Principles of Natural Philosophy") by Isaac Newton. Two things are striking in its very title. First, it implies that, at the time of the founding of what we've come to call 'science,' science was still regarded as a division of philosophy. In fact, the term 'natural philosophy' continued in use well into the 19th century, only gradually being replaced by the term 'science,' as it became increasingly clear that philosophy and 'science' had gradually gone their own ways and had come to constitute two different enterprises. Second, however, Newton's title already sounds a theme decisive for this eventual divergence of trajectories for philosophy and science: it is that the fundamental principles of the enterprise (whatever one calls it) will be *mathematical*. Newton himself puts this directly when he later writes, in Book 3, that "[i]n the preceding books I have laid down the principles of philosophy; principles *not philosophical but mathematical*: such, namely, as we may build our reasonings upon in philosophical inquiries." (italics mine) The inception of modern science, then, occurs with a move by which 'philosophical principles' are entirely replaced by 'mathematical principles' that Newton explicitly regarded as non-philosophical.

What, then, was the crucial difference between 'philosophical' and 'mathematical principles' that Newton so emphasized? Most fundamentally, it involved a wholesale transformation of the functioning of signification in relation to philosophy. When Newton refers to 'philosophical principles,' he typically has in mind the sort of non-mathematical descriptions of and statements about natural phenomena first employed by Aristotle and still current in much of the 'natural philosophy' of his day. But Newton was clearly aware of and impressed by the sentiment, expressed by Galileo over a century earlier, that 'Nature was a book that was written in the language of mathematics.' If we were to 'decipher the secrets of Nature,' we must not only learn nature's language (and, in Newton's case, perhaps invent some of it) but learn to speak it fluently ourselves. As a figure transitional between philosophy and science, there remained an abundance of non-mathematical statements in his own texts (he was, in fact, quite an impressive literary stylist), and his writings were almost always set in the first person in commenting upon his own mathematical principles and demonstrations and in offering opinions on a wide variety of topics, clearly marked as his own views. However, the wholesale displacement of philosophical by mathematical principles that he championed did imply an idealized conception of signification that, in principle if not always in fact, would exclusively involve mathematical symbols and their combinations.

Of course, Newton never conceived of this ideal mathematical system of signification simply as a some sort of formal logical calculus—this idea would not emerge until much later in the 19th and early 20th centuries. Rather, Newton's overall view might be described as 'realist' in a double sense. First, he was a 'realist' in a qualified Platonic sense in that he regarded the variables appearing in his mathematical propositions as referring to precisely defined concepts—mass, velocity, momentum, force, gravitation, and so on. And he clearly realized that what his mathematical principles presented were 'idealized models' necessarily simplifying the multiplicity of factors involved in concrete situations (see, for instance, his treatment of optics). But he was also a 'realist' in an Aristotelian sense, in that he regarded the mathematical laws stating invariant relations among concepts as applying to nature itself and as explaining concrete cases that could be experimentally observed.

The main point I wish to make here is that, already with Newton (as earlier with Galileo, Descartes, and Hobbes among others), 'natural philosophy' or, later, 'science' was established as a field or enterprise, separate from philosophy, by an 'ideal' of the reduction of all signification to mathematics, interpreted as, in the first instance, expressing invariable relations among precisely defined 'concepts' (a type of 'ideality'). While Newton, and others before and after him, did have a good deal to say about the role of observation and experiment and the sort of reasoning involved in moving from these to their mathematical treatments (and vice versa), these remained issues subsidiary to the decisive separation of science (based upon mathematical principles) and philosophy (based upon non-mathematical principles). That is, the constitutive and defining axis for science was, in the primary instance, a specific configuration of the conditions of signification and ideality. (I would add that, despite occasional protestations on the part of some scientists or 'philosophers of science' to the contrary, it is finally impossible to frame any idea of science in the modern sense that does not, at some fundamental level, include some conception of mathematics and some connection of this with some sort of idealities, whether they be interpreted as 'concepts,' 'models,' 'functions,' 'laws,' or whatever.)

The constitution of science exclusively along the axis of 'signification-ideality' had several crucial effects on the relation of this complex to the condition of embodied being. First, the 'finitude-excess' structure of embodied being became homogenized by the force of some ideality like 'matter' or 'energy' (and, yes, 'matter' and 'energy,' as they function in scientific discourse, are always idealities). While we can say, generically, that every concrete instance of matter or energy is 'excessive' to every other, or that the 'totality' of others is 'excessive' to each, this converts 'excess' into a completely symmetrical relation and ultimately results in a sort of 'pure multiplicity' of monad-like points related to one another only externally. Second, a major victim of this is desire, which is, for sentient embodied beings, the paradigmatic case of the 'finitude-excess' structure. Desire-as-lack, that is, lies entirely outside the scope of science and is foreclosed by science's own eidetic-mathematical assumptions. Third, once everything excessive is removed from embodied being, it can be absorbed, without remainder, into the 'significational-eidetic' nexus, to be treated according to science's own principles and laws. Is this not precisely a description of the program of cognitive science today? (In the end, I think that what will remain elusive for cognitive science is not the 'hard problem' of representation but the 'harder problem' of desire-as-lack, that is, how something can be 'represented' as sufficiently excessive to serve as a general object for desire-as-lack.)

One important result of this suppression of embodied being and its excesses has often been referred to by the phrase 'scientific objectivity,' sometimes adding to this the concept (clearly another ideality) of 'ideal observer.' The early founders of what later became called the 'scientific method' emphasized that one of its central features was the suppression and, ideally, wholesale elimination of all aspects of embodied being that they called 'subjective,' opposing this to the 'objectivity' of science. First and foremost among these, of course, was desire. The ideal observer would function as a sort of mechanical apparatus neutrally registering the results of experiments that could be identically reproduced by other such observers and expressing the results in the wholly 'objective' significational system of mathematics. Lacking all desire and any of its corresponding excesses, the ideal observer was, in effect, the remainder produced when all the desires, events, and (non-mathematical) ideas constituting the life of embodied beings had been reduced to a cipher in the significative-ideal nexus constituting the field of science.

This suppression of embodied being, partly constitutive of the field of science, together with its operative distinction between the 'subjective' and the 'objective,' served both to alienate the realm of science from the 'lived activities' and desires of embodied being, but also to bar any possibility of grounding its own assumptions, procedures, and theories in anything more fundamental than its own working assumptions. This divorce, instigated by science itself, between science and embodied being, together with its destabilizing results, was what Husserl, in the early 20th century, came to refer to as the 'crisis of the European sciences.' His work to address this crisis, which he called 'transcendental phenomenology,' launched a trajectory of philosophical thought that would extend through most of the 20th century under such names as 'hermeneutic phenomenology,' 'existentialism,' and at least part of 'poststructuralism.' This trajectory tended to unfold under the general rubric of transcendental idealism, first announced by Kant, explicitly reinvigorated by Husserl, and widely extended by Heidegger and many whom he influenced.

From my earlier discussions, I think my position with regard to this general stance is clear: put simply, transcendental idealism, despite the express intentions of its major advocates, Kant and Husserl, ultimately succeeds neither in providing any firm foundations for the sciences, in healing the rift between embodied being and science, nor in providing any adequate account of philosophy itself. Worse, it has proven capable, in some versions, of undermining the sciences, subverting religion, coopting the arts, destabilizing the field of philosophy, and, at its most pernicious, substituting extreme ideologies, essentially mass mobilizations of desire in its most destructive forms, for all of these. Certainly we can admit that there was an original kernel of truth in transcendental idealism when it emphasized the negative effects of any complete divorce between embodied being and the enterprise of science, but we need not embrace its own path as the only alternative.

As part of the option that I have been proposing, I want now to consider a more positive view of the potentials of science, opened when science is viewed as a particular configuration of the actual conditions and placed in relation to other such configurations. In particular, I want to consider in more detail the claim I made earlier that science is capable of revealing important aspects of the excesses intrinsic to signification and ideality that lie beyond the scope of philosophy. Unlike the transcendental idealist trajectory that was one-sidedly preoccupied with the limitations of science and the violence that it does to embodied being, I want rather to suggest what the field of science is uniquely positioned to accomplish that other fields, including philosophy, do not and cannot.

Let's begin by recalling that, from the perspective of philosophy as I've described it, signification remains excessive to it, at least in part, because the words that it borrows to name its events (concepts) have relations and trajectories of their own within their signifying system. The result is that there is a kind of 'interference effect' (or, to borrow a term from Žižek, a 'parallax effect') that besets any philosophical position. Every philosophical term or concept, however deeply embedded in a network of others, continues to oscillate between its place in the network and its role in its signifying system. It is because philosophy deploys elements of an already-shared significational system that a philosophical view is accessible by and relevant to the lives of embodied beings. For philosophy, then, there is always some degree of dissonance or disconnect between ideality and signification and, for philosophy, this is a virtue (unless, I suppose, you are Leibniz or Hegel). But science, due to the direct mathematical or symbolic expression of idealities, eliminates such a disconnect. Mathematics (or a formalized logical system), that is, directly presents idealities without further interference- or parallax-effects.

The multidimensional and polysemic excesses of the significational systems of philosophy thus become mono-dimensional and univocal in formal systems such as mathematics.

As examples, it was due to such a conversion of polysemic into univocal 'excess' that allowed Cantor to develop a mathematical-based 'theory of infinities,' something that not only had no antecedent within philosophy but that would have been impossible for philosophy to accomplish with its own significational resources. Another example can be found in the formalized procedures that Gödel employed in his famous 'proof' that no formalized system capable of expressing the basic axioms and operations of arithmetic could be simultaneously consistent and complete. Finally, axiomatized set-theory, as developed by Zermelo and Fraenkel (among others) permitted long-standing philosophical paradoxes to be formally expressed and, within such systems, resolved in ways beyond anything that could be accomplished with philosophical concepts and their networks. Of course, insights resulting from such explorations of aspects of signification excessive to philosophy can and have been reappropriated and deployed within philosophy for the construction of new concepts and linkages among them, but doing so also reintroduces other dimensions of excess to that involved in their formal development.

The philosophical thought of Badiou is instructive on this point. He has referred to axiomatized set-theory as an 'ontology of the pure multiple.' However, I think this mischaracterizes what he actually does, since axiomatized set-theory (which is purely mathematical) is one thing and its *interpretation* as an 'ontology' (which is a philosophical enterprise) is something entirely different. Given that there are numerous axiomatized systems, other than set-theory, upon any of which a 'philosophical ontology' might be based, I would prefer to say that all of them represent explorations of significational excesses lying beyond the capacities of philosophy, and that 'ontology' is a special philosophical enterprise that may (or may not) avail itself of insights derived from them once they are philosophically reappropriated by 'translation' into concepts and networks of concepts.

So far, I have focused only upon the mathematical (or formalized) exploration of dimensions of signification that are excessive to the field of philosophy. I know that some might think that what I've just discussed is something different than what is usually regarded as science, but since I regard science as, in large part, defined by its 'mathematical principles,' I have been using the term in a broad sense to include mathematics and formalized systems as well. However, closer to the more usual meaning of the term, I also want to suggest that, beyond issues that emphasize more significational matters, science also illuminates areas excessive to philosophy more directly related to the excessive dimensions of ideality.

One way to approach this would begin with the reminder that the idealities of philosophy (such as concepts) are never entirely reducible either to their iterations within the reflective processes of an embodied being or to their concrete significative expressions. Further, philosophical idealities originate in a moment of insight that, when named, constitutes the primary event for all succeeding thought-trajectories. Such a primary event both constitutes and pre-delineates a field of reflection that, while always open-ended to further conceptual construction and linkage, is limited in relation to other fields (philosophical 'positions') grounded upon different moments of insight and primary events. The realm of ideality in its philosophical inflection, then, is excessive in three dimensions: first, in relation to the other two conditions; second, internally as open-ended for further conceptual construction and linkage; and third, with respect to the contingent singularity of its own primary event.

For ideality as it is inflected for science, the first sort of excess is eliminated, since, as we've seen, science suppresses both the excesses of embodied being and of signification in favor of an immediate relation between mathematical signification and ideality. However, the elimination of this first dimension of eidetic excess permits an expansion of the other two beyond the manner in which they appear in philosophy.

In the case of the second sort of excess, mathematics and formalized systems express the basic concepts of science as variables, each of which, in principle at least, can assume an unlimited number of 'values.' While the basic set of eidetic concepts with which science deals will generally be more limited in number than those involved with any conceptual network constituting a philosophical position, and while the sort of linkages between and among them may be less complex than in philosophy, scientific concepts are capable of a wider, indeed unlimited, range of variation within themselves with respect to the 'values' that the variables expressing them can assume. To put the matter a different way, while excessive variation of concepts within a philosophical position will render the position unstable and ultimately unintelligible, it is precisely by attending to the variations its basic concepts permit that science proceeds and expands. The point, then, is that science introduces and explores a sort of 'eidetic excess' unavailable to philosophy. (As an example of this, one might note the crucial and pervasive role that differential equations play in virtually all areas of science, again something without any counterpart in philosophy.)

In the case of the third dimension of excess, while, considered from a philosophical perspective, we might be inclined to say that science emerges from an eidetic event named 'Truth' (perhaps along the lines proposed in Heidegger's later work), I think that this obscures something important about the different ways that science and philosophy relate to such an eidetic event. Philosophy is based upon a moment of insight on the part of an embodied being that, when named as an 'event,' issues in a distinctive set of trajectories and remains governing for them. If there is a counterpart in science of the eidetic event of philosophy, we can only say that it would be more like the nameless decision to suppress the idiosyncrasies of embodied being (especially desire), choose in favor of a mathematical or formalized type of signification, and regard this as the unique expression of corresponding idealities, all in the interest of formulating something like 'laws of nature.' This is to say that a philosophical eidetic event like 'Truth' plays little or no actual role in the realm of science (and it's interesting to note that Newton never mentions 'Truth' as some key notion in his *Principia*).

This unhinging of science from any founding eidetic event, together with the sort of variation of which its concepts are capable, means that science possesses a degree of 'speculative freedom' unavailable to philosophy. On the one hand, as all the early 'natural philosophers' (especially Galileo and Descartes) already realized and emphasized, science would propose theses (like mountains on the moon, the mass of the sun, or the spherical shape of the earth) that would seem to contradict both the current opinions of the day and the philosophical conceptions of previous philosophers such as Aristotle. No matter (the scientist might assert) that these (or later 'black holes,' 'worm-holes,' 'strings,' or 'multiple dimensions') don't seem 'true,' and no matter that we (embodied beings) may not, even in principle, be able to observe them, we scientists acknowledge them as valid concepts because they have emerged from the mathematical variation of other of our 'concepts' that we take to be well established. My point, then, is that, from the perspective of philosophy, such 'speculative scientific concepts' exceed anything that philosophy can accomplish by its own devices. Of course, as before, upon retranslation into philosophical concepts, they may take their place within various philosophical networks and serve to expand them, but they will no longer be entirely the 'same concept,' since they will no longer exclusively be products of mathematical variation.

Beyond the excessiveness of scientific concepts, however, science is capable, through mathematical variation, of 'speculation' about that from which the conditions of philosophy themselves arise. That is, what philosophy can only refer to as 'massive contingency' or (like Deleuze) the 'Chaosmos' is open to the sort of 'scientific speculation' sometimes called 'cosmology.' To philosophy, such cosmological speculation will generally appear as foreign, epistemologically suspicious, and generally excessive, but that is because it comes from a field that has suppressed or transformed some of the conditions that are constitutive for philosophy itself. The point is that, though it may seem unexpected, science itself is capable of exactly the sort of 'excessive speculation' that Kant had forbidden to philosophy in the very interests of securing the foundations of the sciences.

Philosophy and science, then, constitute two quite different enterprises. While science, by suppressing embodied being, operates in a field that is, in a way, less complex than that of philosophy, this nonetheless also enables science to explore and illuminate some dimensions of signification and ideality that remain excessive to philosophy. Unlike Deleuze and Guattari, I think that there is more to philosophy than 'constructing concepts,' just as I think that there is more to science than 'formulating propositions' or 'expressing functions' (and, I might add, more to art than 'producing affects.') Philosophy can, of course, be enriched by the results of scientific speculation and can at times play a productive role in clarifying the contours of science itself. But philosophy and science are finally different enterprises, even if they can complement one another in certain limited ways.

As a sort of addendum in light of certain recent philosophical developments under the broad heading of 'speculative realism,' it's worth adding that the original 'flat ontology' (deriving from Deleuze) sometimes associated with this was exactly that of natural science. Already in the opposition to 'Aristotelian science,' the idea of a flat ontology, consisting of a view of the universe solely as 'matter moving in space,' was emerging. The 'flatness' in question resulted from the rejection of the ordered hierarchy of 'natural kinds and causes' upon which Aristotelian views were based. The (in this sense) flat ontology of modern science was soon translated (at least on one way of reading them) into the philosophical systems of such figures as Spinoza and Leibniz. It was Kant's transcendental idealism that introduced another, more complicated sort of hierarchical ordering, this consisting, first, of a fundamental division between phenomena (the 'world as it appears to us') and noumena ('things as they are in themselves') and, then, in the 'transcendental sphere' constitutive of the phenomenal order, of a hierarchized set of human 'capacities,' each with its corresponding 'object.' (Hegel, as usual the exception, proposed what we might call a 'spherical ontology' that, one might argue, combined the worst features of both.) Kant and most of his successors viewed some form of transcendental idealism as the privileged platform from which both to ground the sciences and to 'limit their pretensions,' establishing science as a sort of truncated, myopic, and developmentally arrested form of philosophy. While their insistence on the need for a critique of science on behalf of the broader richness of human experience and philosophy was, in some respects, important and laudable, they failed to notice that, even by the time of Kant, science had already split from philosophy and gone its own way. Rather than being the tribunal by which science must inevitably be judged, philosophy eventually found itself, within the general intellectual current called 'positivism,' being judged by science and found wanting.

As I've tried to suggest, philosophy and science are certainly related but this relation is not hierarchical; rather, they are just fundamentally different enterprises. I have tried to express this 'relation-in-difference' by pointing out that philosophy has certain capacities that science does not and vice versa. And up to a point, they are complementary, since some things that must remain excessive for philosophy can be productively explored by science and—again—vice versa. Of course, they are not completely complementary, not at all 'two sides of the same coin,' because they operate within different configurations of the basic conditions, but there are important points of intersection, some of which I've tried to suggest.

One reason for rejecting transcendental idealism as a philosophical position is that it proved incapable of accounting for this sort of relation to science. But it seems to me that the remedy for this doesn't lie in the direction of a philosophical embrace of some 'flat ontology' that reproduces, at least in part, that of science, since such a counter-move will tend to obscure what is distinctive about philosophy, just as transcendental idealism underestimated what science was capable of.

It also doesn't help much to add that such a move against transcendental idealism is 'speculative' or that is 'realist.' As I've tried to show, science itself can be 'speculative' without any assistance from philosophy; and philosophy itself, as I've described it, always has a 'speculative' dimension, even if this is in a rather different sense than that operative in science. Claiming to be a 'realist' does take a direct stand against transcendental idealism (and likely in favor of most prevailing interpretations of science) but being a 'realist' in this sense by no means, of itself, entails any acceptance of a 'flat ontology.'

In this work, I've tried to develop a view that acknowledges the 'speculative' as an essential feature of philosophy (which I also accord to science). I would argue that it is also a 'realist' view, in that none of the conditions I have discussed are in any way 'mere representations' or 'phenomena of consciousness.' However, one can be a 'realist' in a fully 'anti-transcendental idealist' sense while recognizing that there is more than a single thing that is ontologically basic. In fact, even if one asserted that 'everything is material,' there would be at least three 'ontological basics' involved: 'matter itself,' the sentence expressing this, and the concept of matter that this sentence expresses. Finally, if the core meaning of "flat ontology" is "non-hierarchical," then I would say that what I have proposed would qualify, since I have insisted that the three actual conditions are not related as a hierarchy but as three distinct but interacting forces or regions.

The main problem I see lurking under much of this is that both the notions of 'speculative realism' and 'flat ontology,' if taken as descriptions or elements of a philosophical position, tend to obscure the crucial differences between philosophy and science. As I suggested above, science is itself a sort of 'speculative realism' and its usual 'ontology' is 'flat.' So to characterize a philosophical position in the same way threatens a reduction of philosophy to science that obscures what is distinctive about philosophy (in the parallel but opposite way that transcendental idealism failed to realize what was actually distinctive about science). The attempt to oppose transcendental idealism can't succeed by adopting parts of science's own perspective unless this is accompanied by an alternative account of what is distinctive about philosophy and how it is essentially different from science. It's that sort of account that I've tried to develop.

III. ART AND THE SUBLIMATION OF IDEALITY

Embodied being is radically finite, which immediately implies that which is excessive to its finite situation. Within the activity and experience of embodied being, this relation of 'finitude and excess' is most conspicuous as desire-as-lack. In the realm of religion, a proper-named ideality functions as the 'intentional object' that presents itself as capable of satisfying this desire-as-lack; signification is thereby transformed and mustered into the service of traversing and expressing this relation. The realm of science is constituted by a dual process of eliminating the polysemic excesses of signification in favor of a univocal mathematical or formal mode of expression and suppressing embodied being and its desire in favor of science's own ideal of 'objectivity.' There remains, however, a third possibility: embodied being, with all the excessiveness of its desire-as-lack, can engage directly with signification in all its own structural and polysemic excess. We can say, then, as a first pass, that this nexus, in which desire and its excesses achieve expression by deploying various dimensions of significational excess, constitutes the realm of art.

Let's begin with desire. First, virtually anything can serve as the object of desire-as-lack—not only physical objects that are part of the condition of embodied being but also idealities and signifiers of various kinds. Desire is correspondingly unlimited with respect to the activities that it can initiate in pursuing its diverse and unlimited objects. Second, while many (if not all) of the activities of embodied beings are initiated by desire (and desire can be said, in a sense, to express itself in them), desire itself is not any of those activities but that which underlies and exceeds them, in the same way that a force (and desire itself is a sort of force) exceeds any concrete action or event that it initiates or in which it is expressed. Third, the relation between the object of desire and the activity that desire initiates with respect to that object is 'metastatic'—that is, the activity not only can follow different 'vectors' in relation to its original object but can deflect itself toward different objects as it proceeds. Finally, desire-as-lack is reiterative: it continually reproduces itself even, and especially, at every point of partial satisfaction. All of these represent ways in which desire can be said to be excessive.

However, since desire is not itself conceptual (but, as we have seen, the original basis for the construction of idealities), desire and its excessive vicissitudes cannot be conceptually described in any direct way. (Freud's *The Interpretation of Dreams* can be read as an extended argument for just this point.) Further, while desire, operating along certain specific trajectories, can serve to initiate conceptual or religious discourse, such discourse will always function under the aegis of some ideality and will therefore never be a direct but always a mediated expression of desire itself. From the perspective of fields or regions that do have idealities as part of their constituent elements, further characterization of the excessive features of desire remains largely inaccessible.

However, I earlier suggested that the condition of ideality presupposes that embodied being has already become capable of significative expression and communication. When this situation obtains, the order of signification introduces its own distinctive set of excesses different than and (relatively) independent of those of embodied being and its desires. First, the order of signification exceeds any and all 'objects' of the situation of embodied being in that it is capable of investing them with meaning by assuming them into and according them a place within a significational system. Second, however, any 'object' whatever is capable of becoming a 'signifier'—it can be a material object, a gesture, a sound, a line or color, or a spoken or written word, even, perhaps, an ideality. Third, whether a given 'object' signifies or not is a function of the ways in which it is related to other signifiers. While signification is a sort of act or force underlying the emergence of any signifier in its connections with others, it remains excessive to any of its instances or their combinations. (This is a major point made by Deleuze in *The Logic of Sense*.) Third, since any signifier possesses its capacity to signify only in relation to other signifiers, what it signifies (its 'signified' or 'meaning') will metamorphose as its relations to other signifiers are altered or new signifiers are introduced. That is, while signification produces certain structural regularities among its elements sufficient for some communication to occur, it is also a sort of force that continues to exert itself beyond any particular configuration of signifiers.

These discussions of, respectively, desire and signification point toward a certain homology or parallel between the excesses of desire and those of signification. They remain different, of course, since the excesses of desire are chaotic in a way that, left to desire's own devices, lack any basis for further expression or communication, while the excesses of signification are precisely features accompanying all expression and communication. But they are sufficiently complementary that desire-as-lack encounters, in signification and its excesses, potentials for its expression that can still, at least in part, accommodate and respect its own excesses.

We might say, then, that, for the realm of art, it is the condition of signification itself, including all its excesses and all the possibilities that they offer, that comes to serve as the 'object' of ultimate fulfillment for desire-as-lack. This is because signification, in its own excessiveness, offers the unique prospect of the direct expression of desire's own excessive nature. Desire and its excesses will always remain opaque and, for the most part, inexpressible for religion, philosophy, and science, since the idealities essential to their constitution tend to suppress desire's excesses and lead away from them in other directions. But by directly engaging signification and its excesses, desire and its own excesses can be expressed in ways not possible for the other realms. (However, that art and religion have historically been so closely intertwined is understandable, since they share in common the prospect of a complete satisfaction of desire-as-lack in ways that philosophy and science do not.)

Having characterized the realm of art as that of the direct engagement of embodied being and its desire with the order of signification, we must now consider how this relates to the realm of ideality or how ideality is reflected within the realm of art. I have already suggested that the eidetic appears within art in a 'sublimated form,' and it's this that we now need specifically to consider. With respect to religion and philosophy, we've seen that both depend upon some moment of insight constituted as an eidetic event by receiving a name (proper or generic as the case may be). To look for a similar primary event in the case of art (as Heidegger, for example, attempts in *The Origin of the Work of Art*) is immediately to subject art to something eidetic (for example, 'Being'), with the result that art becomes transformed into something like religion or philosophy (or some strange hybrid of both), thereby obscuring the distinctiveness of its own field.

What we *can* say, however, is that lying at the basis of every work of art is a moment of insight, but one that does not go on to receive a name and thereby become constituted as an eidetic event. I want to call the unnamed, unnameable, and metastatic moment of insight on which every work of art is founded an 'aesthetic notion' (something perhaps analogous to Kant's 'aesthetic ideas,' though without the transcendental baggage that he attached to these. I suggest this term because I want to emphasize that it involves something closer to perception or imagination than thought, and because calling it an 'idea' would obscure the difference between what I have in mind and something 'eidetic.' In fact, the vagueness of "notion" over "idea" or "concept" accords fairly well with what I want to suggest here.)

As I will deploy this phrase, an 'aesthetic notion' just is 'what is seen' in a 'aesthetic moment of insight.' It is, so to speak, the 'germ' or 'seed' of what may eventually be developed into a concrete work of art or series of them. For the composer, it might be a particular chord, a fragmentary melody or theme, a rudimentary harmonic progression, or even something closer to the eidetic like 'fate' or 'resignation' (though with an important qualification that I'll discuss below). For the painter, it might be the juxtaposition of several colors, an irregular line, a shape, or even an 'atmosphere.' For the poet, it might be a word, a phrase, a rhythm, or a passing mood. That is, every work of art, even one that involves a great deal of randomness or accident (or one that begins merely with 'playing around with one's medium'), becomes an artwork only when associated with some 'aesthetic notion' that it realizes.

It's important to emphasize several things about an aesthetic notion. First, an aesthetic notion is the immediate result of the desire of an embodied being focused upon something that either already signifies or can be made capable of signification. This means that the native excess of desire becomes focused or channeled toward some specific set of 'signifying objects' as possessing potentialities for its expression. At the same time, it means that the excesses of the total field of signification are delimited to a more specific region of the broader complex. An aesthetic notion, then, represents a point where desire and signification come to mutually delimit the excesses of each other. For example, a musical aesthetic notion (say, Beethoven's aesthetic notion of his Fifth Symphony) will bring a general desire to 'express oneself sonically' into relation with particular sequences and configurations of sound and, perhaps, a set of timbres of instruments producing these sounds. Or, a painterly aesthetic notion (say, Picasso's *Guernica*) would engage a desire to 'express oneself visually' with a limited palette, certain irregular lines and shapes, a large-sized canvas, and so on. There can, of course, be no clear or exhaustive description of this, but the main point is that aesthetic notions are never idealities but always involve specific materials that already are or will become significative in the work itself. Put another way, if it makes sense to say that artists 'think,' then their 'thought' is always in terms of the possibilities of expression of a particular medium and its significative possibilities.

This means that an aesthetic notion is something less than an ideality or concept but more than the concrete realization of a singular work of art. Somewhat, though only partly, analogous to a primary event in the eidetic sphere, it is an initial configuration of 'significative materials' establishing the possibility of multiple (though not completely unlimited) trajectories or lines of 'realization.' In this sense, it is (in Deleuzian terms) a sort of 'generative virtuality.' This also means that no single artwork can be a 'complete realization' of an aesthetic notion. (As Deleuze points out, this is connected to the importance of considering 'series' in art, both deliberately labeled as such by an artist as well as an artist's works considered over time.)

It is also important to emphasize that, since aesthetic notions are noneidetic and remain inaccessible to any adequate description in conceptual terms, they possess a certain fluidity or plasticity that allows them to vary and morph. In fact, the artist's actual engagement with significative materials will usually transform the initial aesthetic notion as the work progresses. Wagner, for example, attempts to document, in his memoirs, how his initial aesthetic notion of *The Ring of the Nibelungs* gradually transformed over the very long period of its completion (a case of documentation highly unusual for an artist, given the difficulty of articulating an aesthetic notion).

Finally, while some aesthetic notion will always be associated with any concrete work of art as its 'generative virtuality,' to understand (or, perhaps better, to respond appropriately to a work of art) is to achieve some sense of the aesthetic notion that was generative for it. It is, put simply, to be able, provisionally of course, to respond to the question, "Given the significative materials that the artist was employing, what did he or she attempt to accomplish?" Notice that an appropriate answer will never be some statement about the 'meaning' of the work, since 'meaning' immediately mobilizes an eidetic perspective. Certainly some (usually bad) works of art may have 'morals' or attempt directly to express some ideality, either that the artist intended or that the viewer can extract, but no discursive answer in these terms will capture what it was that made the work specifically a 'work of *art.*' Such a response ends up converting it into something that it is not and cannot be—a set of discursive or logical statements.

An aesthetic notion, then, is a form of engagement of desire with signification that functions as a virtual and mobile generator of possibilities latent within a delimited range of significative elements. We can say that any concrete artwork is a realization of one of these possibilities, with the proviso that we recall that aesthetic notions, like desire itself, tend to morph as the engagement with their 'objects' proceeds. In fact, on this view, we distinguish 'artworks' from other 'objects' precisely because we associate some 'aesthetic notion' with them. In even very extreme cases, such as some postmodern art, the difference between a mere pile of garbage and an artwork displaying the same thing can only be that one can be associated with an aesthetic notion and the other not. Of course, sometimes we just can't tell, but we can know what it would take for there to be a difference.

In what sense, then, is an aesthetic notion a 'sublimated form' of ideality? I admit that the term "sublimated" here is potentially misleading, so I want to emphasize that I am deploying it in a different sense than some that may be more familiar. Specifically, it should not be understood as implying that already existing idealities somehow enter into aesthetic notions or are expressed in works of art in some altered form (perhaps along the lines that Freud presented the 'dream work,' where 'latent unconscious ideas' undergo various displacements in becoming part of the 'manifest content' of a dream). Rather, I want to say that certain elements or features of an aesthetic notion (and, derivatively, of concrete works of art generated by it) are capable of serving as the basis for the construction of idealities. That is, one of the possibilities presented by aesthetic notions and concrete works of art is the extraction from them of idealities through the processes of interpretation and criticism. Given the possibility for such eidetic development through interpretation, we can say that idealities are 'latent' in aesthetic notions and the works of art that realize them; this is the core of what I have in mind in claiming that idealities are 'sublimated' in art. Idealities 'subsist' in aesthetic notions and works of art only as potentialities realized under certain types of interpretation.

Once such an interpretative 'rendering into ideality' occurs, however, the interplay of the excesses of desire and signification that constitute aesthetic notions and works of art become arrested and transformed into something quite different: they become concepts subject to the linkages governing these. The point, then, is that every interpretation or 'critical discussion' of an aesthetic notion or work of art is a 'two-edged sword.' On the one hand, interpretation 'reterritorializes' the excesses of the signified desire defining the aesthetic notion and artwork into a different domain, the eidetic, and it expresses itself within a significative system (usually natural language) foreign to that of the aesthetic notion or artwork. On the other hand, what is a loss for the realm of art may be a gain for that of philosophy in that the idealities constructed through the interpretation of art may offer new concepts that can find their place within and even expand an existing conceptual network. Philosophy can therefore be significantly enriched through interpretive engagements with aesthetic notions and concrete artworks, but it must remain cognizant of the fact that what art is best equipped to present—the interplay of the excesses of desire and signification—will remain ever elusive to it.

It is because of this remainder that exceeds any interpretation of an aesthetic notion or artwork that these always remain open to further interpretations. That is, aesthetic notions are 'virtual generators,' on the one hand, of concrete works of art (or series of them) and, on the other, of multiple interpretations. On this crucial point, I part ways with much of the so-called 'hermeneutic tradition' that wants to claim that, somehow, the interpretation of a work of art plays an essential role in constituting the work of art itself. Rather, interpretation is simply one possibility among others for engaging with an aesthetic notion or work of art. It may play an important role in the way we *access* an aesthetic notion or artwork, but it adds nothing essential to what the aesthetic notion or artwork accomplishes on its own and even serves to limit and obscure its native richness and excess. Put straightforwardly, in the primary instance, the possibilities presented by aesthetic notions are to be traversed and works of art are to be experienced; interpreting them by 'translating' them into a different significative system oriented by ideality is always one of their possibilities, but is in itself never what makes them aesthetic notions or works of art.

Still, it is true, in the other direction, that, in certain cases (one thinks of such figures Wagner, Schoenberg, Eliot, Kandinsky, and Duchamp and his 'conceptualist' progeny), aesthetic notions and the works of art realizing them may be preceded by or develop in conjunction with various eidetic matters ('theories' of art or artistic practice) or can even be inspired by certain otherwise independent philosophical theses or texts. But there will always be a point where desire engages directly with signification under the aegis of an aesthetic notion. It is only by virtue of this passage through the aesthetic notion and its 'sublimation' of ideality within itself that the 'art theorist' or 'philosopher' becomes an 'artist' capable of realizing certain of its possibilities in the form of concrete works of art. It is instructive that, in most of these cases of 'artist/theorists,' there is a clear division between the artworks produced and the various (eidetic) writings formulating 'manifestos,' justifications, and interpretations of their artistic activity. But the same limitations that apply in any other case with respect to aesthetic notions and artworks will also apply to the theories and interpretations of the 'artist/theorists' in relation to their own works. Artists who have themselves realized this, like Picasso or Joyce, have resolutely refused to engage in 'theory' or to comment on their own work. And many of those who have offered 'auto-interpretations' of their works have usually turned out, by general acclaim, to be quite unreliable and misleading guides.

To conclude this discussion, it may be helpful briefly to place the view I have been presenting in relation to several other well-known theories of art, usually referred to as 'realism,' 'expressionism,' 'formalism,' and 'institutionalism.'

Realism has two main variants: a Platonic and a more modern inflection. The former would maintain that the defining feature of art is the concrete expression of idealities (or even a single ideality, 'beauty'). The present view holds that, while there are certainly connections between ideality and art, not only can art never be adequately viewed merely as some vehicle for expressing idealities, but that it can do so only when the very nature of idealities are converted into something quite different and subjected to excesses foreign to them. It's also the case, I think, that such idealities as 'beauty' play no real role in aesthetic notions as I've presented this. The latter case is closely connected (if not defined by) the idea that the primary function of art is to 'represent' some independently existing reality or our perceptions of it. While I don't think that the representational function of art should be dismissed quite so decisively as a great deal of modern theory would have it, the representational view of art (however dominant it may have been in the tradition) actually amounts to a sort of arbitrary delimitation of both the excesses of desire and those of signification to a relatively narrow range of expression, often with visual (and perhaps linguistic) forms of expression in mind. It neglects both the fact that desire-as-lack is capable of taking *any* object capable of signification as its correlate (not just objects of immediate perception) as well as the multiple dimensions in which signification is excessive both in itself and in relation to desire. Despite the many possibilities opened and explored by representational art in the tradition, it is an approach that not only excludes a great deal, even the majority, of 'modernist art' but one that was too narrow to embrace even art forms already present in its heyday such as music, dance, decorative motifs, and a good deal of poetry.

Formalism is usually regarded as beginning with Kant and, even in its modernist inflections, is closely associated with some version of a transcendental idealist view. It holds that what is constitutive of any artwork is some combination of 'formal properties,' which are distinct from any particular content that an artwork might present. These formal properties, it is usually claimed, are apprehended through a special sort of 'aesthetic experience' that involves either (as in Kant) certain structural features of human consciousness or (as in later, often 'aestheticist' versions) the artwork itself. Once again, on the present view, such formal properties usually do constitute part of any aesthetic notion or artwork derived from it, but they are adventitious results, never aims in themselves, of the excessive operations of desire in engaging significative complexes that always already involve their own formal structures. As a side note, with specific reference to Kant's idea of the 'sublime' (and its extension by such postmodern thinkers as Lyotard), I would say that the 'sublime' was the principal, though far too limited, concept employed by Kant to call attention to the excesses of desire in engagement with signification. By its very nature, art of itself is always excessive in multiple directions and is therefore, on Kant's criterion, 'sublime,' not just by virtue of certain types of 'subject matter' that invoke some concept of 'the limitless' as Kant presents it.

By contrast, expressionism is the general view that the function of art is to express the emotions or, more broadly, the 'inner life' of the artist and that, by so doing, to produce certain 'affects' (to borrow a word from Deleuze and Guattari) in the viewer. (In the end, I think, their account in *What is Philosophy?* is a form of expressionism.) Expressionism, at its best, does focus upon art as rooted in desire and is often, as well, associated with the deployment of the excesses of significational complexes (for example, the use of 'non-representational color' or dissonance in music) for expressing desire's own excesses. But while expressionism agrees with a good deal central to what I've suggested, I think it remains inadequate in two important ways. First, expressionism, in most of its forms, tends to bypass anything like an 'aesthetic notion,' an originary site of intersection between desire and signification, in favor of viewing artworks as some more direct expression of desire, often viewed in the limited form of emotion (which, I think, is far too restricted a way of characterizing the excessiveness of desire). By contrast, I have suggested that it is by virtue of an aesthetic notion that the excesses of desire become sufficiently limited to and focused upon a specific set of significational elements and, correspondingly, that the excesses of signification themselves become sufficiently circumscribed to allow certain concrete possibilities to be realized in individual works of art. Second, lacking some such interface in which ideality can 'subsist' as a possibility, expressionism tends toward a more extreme separation of art and the eidetic aspects of philosophy than the present view would hold. Even in its most intensive forms of abstract expressionism, action painting, or aleatory composition, there is an aesthetic notion at work that harbors potentials for interpretation and critical analysis beyond the mere witnessing of a 'record of a creative moment in time.' Philosophy, in fact, stands to learn a great deal from such experimental or avant-garde art, but this has relatively little to do either merely with the artist's emotions or inner life or solely with the excessive possibilities of the artist's chosen medium. It concerns, rather, the aesthetic notion by which the excesses of desire meet those of signification and sufficiently limit one another so that a work (or series of works) can be generated.

Finally, a more recent development is the 'institutional' view of art. This approach basically views art as an element of a complex of social practices. An object will count as a work of art (as opposed to one that doesn't) if it fulfills a certain (though never completely determinate) set of conditions: being displayed in a museum, being the subject of interpretation and criticism, sharing certain features with other objects that are widely regarded as artworks, playing various roles in the 'artworld,' and so on. I think that the quite extensive discussions that this view has generated have shown that it is, at best, highly problematic. Here, I will only point out that, however effective such a view might be against any attempt to define art in some essentialistic way or accommodate the many novel forms that art can assume, it tells us far more about the social functioning of art than anything about art itself. Although I fully agree that 'the artwork' can have no *a priorist* definition, no necessary or even sufficient set of properties, or even be captured within some network of 'family resemblances,' there are certain actual conditions for something being an artwork. It must be produced by an embodied being (even if he or she produces the artwork through less direct means such as a digital program). It will thereby, in some way, constitute the expression of that being's desire (however heavily mediated). It will involve the mobilization of some elements, together with their excesses, of a significational system. And among its possibilities, it will be capable of interpretation and treatment within the eidetic order. This will not always permit us, in any given case, to say for certain whether a given object, artifact, or activity is 'artistic,' but it will tell us that, if it is, it will possess certain actual features that are not merely functions of its 'social context.'

IV. THE DANGERS OF ENCROACHMENTS

Religion, science, art, and philosophy are fundamentally different enterprises because their regions or fields are constituted by different specific ways in which the actual conditions of embodiment, signification, and ideality are configured within them. For the same reason, they also stand in specific sorts of relation to one another and are both complementary as well as opposed to one another in determinate ways. And by affirming that each of the actual conditions involves its own specific types of excess, we can also say that each of the four fields is capable of engaging in activities and types of expression that the others cannot.

However, due mainly to the excessive nature of desire-as-lack that operates in various ways throughout all these fields, there is always a tendency for one field to assert its hegemony over another or even all the others. While religion asserted its authority over all other realms for a long period of European history (and, at various places, still attempts to do so), it was philosophy that attempted to establish its hegemonic claims through much of modernity. Although the hegemonic pretensions of philosophy were already present in some ways in its Greek inception, this assumed a much more intensive form with Kant's transcendental idealism, eventually reaching a zenith in the philosophy of Hegel. In fact, Kant explicitly announced his intention of establishing philosophy as "the queen of the sciences" in the prefaces to his *Critique of Pure Reason*. (I've never been able to figure out what he thought the 'king' was, but maybe Kant was just more 'politically correct' than we've given him credit for: perhaps he didn't think that a true queen, and not just a 'royal consort,' needs a king.)

The Kantian 'Copernican Revolution in philosophy' officially consecrated Reason (*Vernunft*) as the supreme human faculty and regarded philosophy as its ultimate expression. Frequently employing metaphors drawn from jurisprudence, Kant referred to Reason (and, by extension, philosophy) as both the "supreme lawgiver" as well as the "ultimate court" before which all human claims must be adjudicated. Extending this metaphor, we might say that Kant's Critical Philosophy, the fundamental principles of which were those established by his transcendental idealism, issued a series of judgments concerning the claims of prior views of philosophy ('metaphysics') as well as those of religion, science, and art. The judgments came down like this. The claims of metaphysics pursued by earlier philosophy lost all 'legal standing' and were dismissed since they transgressed the limits imposed by the principles of transcendental idealism. Religion fared little better, although the tribunal was willing to entertain a heavily revised and weakened version of its claims that was purged of all mythological and metaphysical elements. The court treated science a bit more kindly, holding that its claims were legitimate but only so long as they were pursued within a highly restricted domain specified by the court's own ruling. And the claims of art were admitted as legitimate, but only when presented in the form of a brief that the court itself had written.

Under Kant's stewardship, the court of Reason functioned mostly on a case-by-case basis. That is, Kant gave relatively little attention to the relations of the claims of these areas to one another or to how the judgments rendered in one case might affect those handed down in the others. Rather, he was more concerned with ensuring that order and decorum prevailed only in their individual relations to philosophy itself and, in this respect, had little hesitation in encroaching upon their respective domains when it served the tribunal of reason's own interests. The result was that, in every case, philosophy, in the form of transcendental idealism, imposed its own terms and demands upon each of the domains that it judged. However, philosophy, as (on Kant's view) a beneficent liberal, left to each area its own legitimate sphere of 'free activity,' so long as it was conducted within the constraints imposed by Reason's tribunal.

By the time the court of Reason had passed to Hegel's oversight, however, the liberal monarchy that Kant had attempted to establish among the various areas had become destabilized by the clamor of the competing claims of its various domains both against philosophy and among one another. Hegel witnessed a torrent of historical developments, including a resurgence of religious sentiment, the rise of the Romantic movement in the arts, and the relentless advance of the sciences and their technological offshoots, all further agitated by political forces unleashed by the French Revolution, its Napoleonic aftermath, and a conservative retrenchment. Hegel sensed that the time for a new world order was at hand and he supplied its philosophical foundations by establishing a clear order of precedence, a hierarchy, among the competing claims of the various domains in a way that Kant had never considered. To begin with, Hegel made abundantly clear that philosophy was the ultimate 'system of systems' and super-domain that encompassed all others. On his view, it was only philosophy that fully deserved the name of science (*Wissenschaft*) and natural science had to be regarded as a fully subordinate, even relatively minor, department of this. Beyond natural science (and politics, one might add) came the broad domain of what Hegel called "Absolute Spirit," that he subdivided, in ascending order, into art, religion, and philosophy. Art, then, was philosophy (or 'the Concept') expressed in the 'limited and particular form' of 'sensuality.' The domain of religion subsumed all that was 'true' in art into itself and expressed this, without remainder, in the non-conceptual (and hence, for Hegel, still inadequate) symbols and language of revelation. Finally, at the apex, philosophy subsumed all the other domains into itself and expressed their 'truth' in the sole form adequate to it: the concepts of philosophy. Under Hegel's new regime, then, science, art, and religion all became viewed exclusively as expressing philosophical concepts (or Hegel's ultimate ideality, 'the Concept'), although each in its own characteristic 'defective' form. With this, the hegemony of philosophy over the other domains originally fueled by Kant's transcendental idealism was complete.

Naturally, few scientists, religious believers, or artists have been willing to sign on to such a view either of their own domains or of the relation of these to philosophy. But the complex of reactions to Hegel's view of these matters has presented a strange spectacle, rather different than might have been expected. While in most philosophical quarters, 'Hegelianism' was discredited and had become an anachronism well before the end of the 19th century, elements of the transcendental idealism that spawned it had legs that carried it well through a good deal of the 20th century. And if not in Hegel's extreme version, a good deal of the hegemonic impulse implicit in transcendental idealism persisted in many and various forms, especially various 'philosophies of'…religion, science, and art (all, by the way, owing an often unacknowledged debt to Hegel's original delineation of these areas in his system). The key issue for all of them, and one that I've continually emphasized, is that there are distinctive types of excess unique to and operative in each of these areas. For Hegel, of course, there is never any real excess outside 'the Concept' itself. But all too often, it seems, these 'philosophies of…' tend to encroach on their respective fields of study by constructing 'theories' about them that are proposed as normative for them. Philosophers of religion are often not satisfied just to map the contours of religion, but attempt to determine, in eidetic terms, what 'authentic' religious experience involves; philosophers of science have attempted to formulate a 'rational reconstruction' of the 'scientific method' to serve as some ideal to which it ought to aspire; and philosophers of art (not to mention many art critics) offer criteria for what art is and standards for judging what it should be if it is 'good (or important, or effective…) art.'

Still speaking of philosophers, one also finds a counter-move among them as well. Some philosophers (or at least those who started out as philosophers) reached a point where they decided that the only viable escape from what they came to regard as philosophy's native hegemonic impulses was to abandon the enterprise of philosophy entirely, either in favor of some more 'natural' or mundane pre-philosophical state (like 'ordinary language' or 'common sense') or one of the other regions we've discussed. The problem is that this usually produces monstrosities (in the older meaning of the term): hybrid creatures that have not completely shed the hegemonic impulses of philosophy and carry them into another region that possesses its own autonomy and may even have hegemonic designs of its own. And in some cases, when one loses one's bearings in such a border zone, the political intervenes as a ready device for reestablishing some sense of orientation. The most notorious cases of this are those of Nietzsche and Heidegger, but they are admittedly extreme examples of a general tendency one can observe at work elsewhere. As I've said before, even at the most benign, when philosophy encroaches upon other areas, it tends to warp or corrupt its own native potencies as well as deform those of the areas that it invades.

This encroachment can also occur in the opposite direction, although the results are usually less dramatic. History, and the 20th century in particular, offers numerous examples of religious partisans who have attempted to harness the latest philosophical or scientific developments to justify or strategize the dissemination of their beliefs (Scientology and 'Death of God' theology come to mind); of scientists (for instance in Nazi or Stalinist regimes) who have advanced philosophical and political views supposedly based on 'scientific principles'; and artists (like Baudelaire, Wagner, Pound, and Duchamp) who were convinced that significant philosophical and political consequences followed from their artistic practice. In almost every case, however, none of these ventures made any lasting contribution to philosophy itself and often resulted in disruptions of their own intellectual or creative practices.

At its most extreme, when a wholesale implosion of all these areas occurs, the results are catastrophic for all of them, since such a vacuum tends to revert to what is most elemental about the first actual condition: the chaos of desire-as-lack, which goes viral, reiterates itself across all possible objects and realms, and, at its worst, infects all embodied beings within its reach. Is this not what occurred in most of the great cataclysms that punctuated the 20th century?

My argument, through this entire chapter, has been that it is crucial to acknowledge, respect, and maintain the fundamental differences between the regions of philosophy, religion, science, and art. It begins with a mapping of the contours of philosophy for two reasons. The first is that philosophy, at least in recent history, has tended to be the most hegemonic of these areas, so it is crucial to understand its limitations in order guard against their breach. The second is that the field of philosophy is uniquely positioned at the interface of the three actual conditions and is therefore the only one capable of preserving the distinctiveness of each. In this sense, philosophy does enjoy a certain precedence among the various regions, but this precedence does not imply a license to obliterate the differences and dominate; rather it confers a duty to map, preserve, and protect each from encroachment by the others—and by itself.

DIAGRAM 7: A New 'Partitioning' for Philosophy

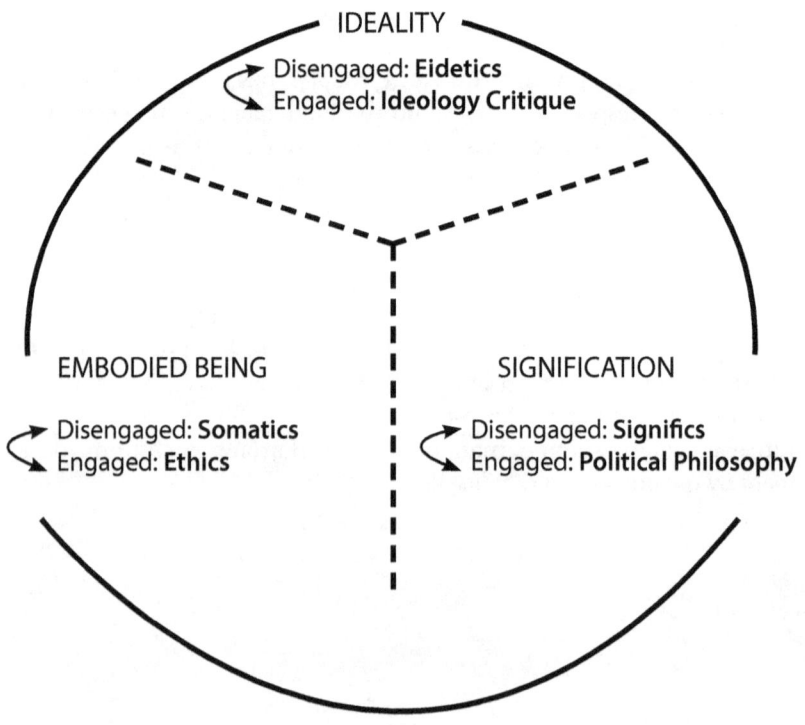

12

The Contours and Partitions of Philosophy

Beyond questions about philosophy's differences from other fields contiguous to it, there is a further issue concerning the internal differentiation of philosophy itself. One can find, in the tradition, several quite different responses to this. One, originally Socratic and Platonic in inspiration, was that philosophy is a single, seamless enterprise. A second, originally part of Aristotle's response to Plato, was that philosophy was a generic discipline divided into a hierarchy of various 'species' or 'subdisciplines' on the basis of their subject matter and the methods suitable to them. A third, more modern, view would be that philosophy is a collection of various relatively independent areas of inquiry loosely related through some network of 'family resemblances' or even by the mere fact that (often by default) they have all come to be called "philosophical" rather than something else. One way of posing this general question would be to ask whether it makes sense at all to think of the overall enterprise of philosophy as involving some 'division of labor' and, if so, what sort of division this would involve and upon what it would be based. Another way would be to ask whether the field of philosophy can be mapped at all and, if so, what sort of map would be appropriate to it?

Despite the fact that this sort of question has not been much discussed in recent times, it is nonetheless an important one. First, how this question is answered will determine, to a considerable degree, one's overall view of what philosophy itself is. Second, however, it immediately reflects, albeit at a higher order of abstraction, the basic assumptions and tenets of a given position (as with the differences between the Platonic and Aristotelian responses mentioned above). Third, it will determine, at least in part, what sort of more specific questions can be regarded as distinctively philosophical, thus serving to differentiate them from others that are not. Fourth, it will tend to channel philosophical reflection in certain directions to the exclusion of others. And finally, it may, in some cases (like Kant's 'architectonic') lead philosophical reflection in directions that would otherwise have remained unexplored. In short, it is not a question merely adventitious or peripheral to the enterprise of philosophy but goes to the heart of the very image of thought underlying any specific philosophy as well as philosophy considered generically.

I. TRADITIONAL DIVISIONS OF PHILOSOPHY

As already mentioned, the enterprise of European philosophy commenced with two opposed options. The Platonic view suggested that philosophy was a unified and seamless enterprise in which the sort of response one gave to any specific question would rest on assumptions and have implications involving the entire enterprise of philosophy itself. In direct contrast to this, the Aristotelian view was that, while philosophy was a sort of 'highest genus,' it was divisible into various sub-disciplines, each with its own distinctive content and methods appropriate to engaging it. While, throughout the tradition, the Platonic view occasionally resurfaced in various forms, especially in conjunction with the systematic projects of such figures as Spinoza and Hegel, it's probably fair to say that the Aristotelian view, that the field or discipline of philosophy could be subdivided and that a certain division of labor should prevail within it, was (and mostly remains) the dominant one.

Aristotle's division of philosophy into relatively discrete subdisciplines or fields of inquiry was based upon his realist assumption that nature itself was hierarchically ordered in terms of genus and species. The knowledge (*episteme*) of this natural order was isomorphic with it and was expressed in bodies of discourse (*logoi*) corresponding to nature's own natural divisions. Biology, for example, was the body of discourse (*logos*) concerning living beings (*bioi*). The same was true of the domain or 'genus' of philosophy.

Although one can find variants scattered throughout Aristotle's works, probably his most influential division of the whole field of human knowledge was that involving productive disciplines (the aim of which was the making of things, such as building houses), practical disciplines (activities whose end was self-contained, that is, not producing something external but 'doing them well,' in which he included ethics and politics), and theoretical disciplines (which were concerned with 'truth' for its own sake). The third, and for Aristotle highest, discipline was in turn subdivided into physics (whose objects were separate from thought or knowledge and subject to change), mathematics (whose objects were changeless but not separate from the knowledge of them), and theology (later called metaphysics, whose objects were separate from thought or knowing but changeless).

Although Aristotle himself rarely employed the term 'philosophy,' his later interpreters (often influenced by the additional complexities involved in accommodating his schema to Christian doctrine and thought) tended to settle upon a simplified hierarchical division of philosophy something like this. First in order came metaphysics (or 'natural theology,' which Aristotle himself had specifically referred to as 'first philosophy'). Next came physics (or 'natural philosophy'), concerned with the application of the principles established in metaphysics to beings in so far as they were subject to physical changes of movement and alteration. After that was practical philosophy, dealing with variable human activities that contained their end in themselves (ethics and politics). Finally, other disciplines concerned with productive activities would find their place subordinate to these. Though various figures (like Augustine, Thomas Aquinas, and Descartes) offered their own variations and interpretations of this, the basic hierarchical schema of 'metaphysics—physics ('natural philosophy')—ethics and politics—various productive disciplines (including art)' remained relatively constant. Given this general mapping of the field of philosophy, other disciplines such as biology and psychology could be grafted on at suitable points.

This general schema, loosely derived from Aristotle, remained intact until Kant's 'Copernican Revolution in Philosophy' in the last two decades of the 18th century; after that, the entire map of philosophy shifted dramatically. Kant's Critical Philosophy, and the transcendental Idealism that lay at its heart, represented nothing less than an entirely new image of thought. As Kant made clear, it involved a decisive turn away from 'things as they are in themselves' (Plato's 'ideas,' Aristotle's 'nature,' and all other such notions that followed in their wake) toward the transcendentally elucidated activities of consciousness that served as the 'grounds for the possibility' of all human experience and knowledge. With the Kantian revolution, 'ideas' were reinterpreted as synthetic functions of consciousness, what Kant called the 'categories,' and 'nature' became an eidetic construct produced by certain complex interactions among the categories when limited to the pure forms of intuition, space and time, which were themselves other synthetic functions of consciousness. More specifically, the orientation of Kant's image of thought, and thereby the entire division of philosophy that mapped it, was based not on 'the way things are' but on 'how we can claim to experience or know anything at all.' In making this transcendental turn, Kant endorsed a new image of thought for philosophy, operating within strict limits, which we might informally describe as 'doing less but doing it better.'

The first victim of Kantian critique was metaphysics, which Kant came to refer to as a 'spurious science.' According to Kant, the 'old metaphysics' (under which he included most earlier philosophy) was guilty of laying claim to knowledge of things as they are in themselves, without first asking whether philosophy is at all entitled to such a claim. Following Hume's skeptical lead, Kant decisively responded that it is not. However, in response to Hume's skepticism, Kant replied that there *are* certain types of things that philosophy *can* know, but these will only be basic structural features of our own synthetic processes of knowing. Although Kant himself did not yet use this term, it turned out that he entirely eliminated the 'old metaphysics' in favor of what became called 'epistemology,' a field never before specifically recognized as an autonomous discipline of philosophy (however much its questions may have occupied philosophy beginning with Plato). Having displaced metaphysics by epistemology, Kant then ejected physics (or what was still called 'natural philosophy') from the field of philosophy, relegating it to another field entirely, which would eventually become natural science. And since he was convinced that the principles of ethics fell within the scope of transcendentally clarified consciousness but that politics did not, he separated ethics from politics (something that had never been decisively done since Aristotle), installed ethics on an equal footing with epistemology, and relegated politics to a sort of problematic no man's land. Finally, aesthetics was promoted from being almost an afterthought to functioning as an important, but still subordinate, way in which his two major divisions, epistemology and ethics, could be related to one another.

The resulting map of the field of philosophy, based not upon some natural order but upon human intellectual capacities, looked something like this. Kant's 'highest generic term,' which he virtually identified with the field of philosophy but more specifically with logic, was 'Reason' (*Vernunft*). Reason had two divisions of equal status, 'theoretical reason' and 'practical reason.' Theoretical reason was, in its primary manifestation, identified with epistemology and practical reason with ethics. Aesthetics was assigned its own distinctive field, subordinate to epistemology and ethics, but playing an important role in providing various ways of mediation between the two major divisions. Kant did think that epistemology and ethics could be further developed into two new forms of 'metaphysics,' but he was careful to indicate that these were to be regarded as operating strictly within the limits imposed by his transcendental idealism and constituted no new fields of philosophy on their own account. It's worth adding that, if this mapping sounds familiar, it is because it's still the predominant one operative in a good deal of current philosophy.

I mentioned earlier that Hegel reverted to something like the Platonic view in one crucial way. Against Kant (and by extension Aristotle), Hegel accepted the notion that philosophy was not the sort of enterprise that was subject to division, either on the basis of some natural hierarchy or some hierarchy of human faculties. Like Plato, Hegel tended to see philosophy as a seamless whole, but a whole constituted not by some transcendent 'arche-idea' or 'original structure of intelligibility' like 'the Good' but by the ubiquitous activity of Reason itself generating concepts and linking them together ('dialectically') in a whole. In particular, Hegel rejected the Kantian map that presented the theoretical and practical spheres as divisible or separate and regarded both epistemology and ethics as limited stances or moments within the broader conceptual movement of Reason. The contourless map that Hegel finally presented placed what he called 'logic' at its apex, but this was not the formal logic of Aristotle and Kant but designated the very movement of conceptual thought that permeated the entire field of philosophy itself and every other area of human thought or experience as well. It is true that Hegel was the first to introduce such seemingly new philosophical fields as the philosophy of art, the philosophy of religion, and the philosophy of history, all of which, in other hands, subsequently became recognized fields of philosophy. But for Hegel, these divisions were ephemeral and relatively arbitrary, convenient ways to organize his academic lecture series or divide his works into sections, but no real divisions of philosophy at all. In a sense, we might say that they were just localized eddies in the overall flow of philosophical thought itself.

To conclude this historical sketch of the divisions of philosophy, let's briefly consider the third alternative I mentioned at the beginning: that philosophy is neither a seamless unity nor an articulated hierarchy but just a more or less arbitrary group of otherwise relatively autonomous enterprises collected under the common term "philosophy." This is a view that can be understood as part of the reaction to Hegel's contourless map of philosophy, together with the generally anti-metaphysical attitude of much post-Hegelian thought. If there is any theoretical basis for such a view, it was probably best articulated, at least for European philosophy, by Foucault, whose view of philosophy as a collection or 'archive' of rather diverse types of texts, each of which should be treated in its own terms, influenced many other poststructuralist thinkers. In the Anglo-American world, there has been a proliferation of 'philosophies of...' that have joined logic, epistemology, and ethics on a relatively equal footing, generally without much attempt to connect all or any of these within some larger framework. This is tantamount to the admission, characteristic of both approaches, that there is no real criteria governing what can be counted as 'philosophy' and, as I mentioned in the last chapter, has often resulted in a blurring of the boundaries between philosophy and one or another enterprise, usually at the expense of the integrity of both.

From this brief historical sketch and against the background of my earlier discussions (especially in the preceding chapter), I draw the following conclusions. First, any way of dividing philosophy that involves some hierarchical structure or 'architectonic' will tend to unduly limit and overdetermine all the more subordinate areas of inquiry. On the one hand, the questions posed at a 'higher level' will tend to dictate the form (and likely also scope) of those posed at 'lower levels.' On the other, each area of philosophy so divided will be defined in ways that suppress or eliminate the distinctive excesses that would otherwise constitute important features of their region of activity and inquiry. Second, however, any 'flat' or 'seamless' view of philosophy will tend to treat philosophy as some 'master discourse,' capable of asserting its authority over any content or field that it touches. However, I have already indicated numerous reasons why I think philosophy must be viewed as a finite human enterprise and why it is in its own best interests not to attempt to transgress its limits. Finally, the view that philosophy is merely some more or less arbitrary collection of activities or inquiries operating under a common name invites the sort of miscegenation with other fields, with their own distinctive problems and contours, which I discussed in the preceding chapter. The result is misfortune for all concerned, especially for philosophy itself.

II. PARTITIONING PHILOSOPHY UNDER A DIFFERENT IMAGE OF THOUGHT

What is needed, then, is a way of 'partitioning'—dividing the labor or mapping—philosophy that (1) is non-hierarchical, (2) accords with philosophy's natural contours, (3) respects the excesses involved with them, (4) affirms its limitations as a distinctive human enterprise or field, and (5) possesses unity sufficient (but no more) to prevent its encroachment on other areas (and them upon it). The following represents only an exploratory first pass, a sort of initial low-resolution mapping, of what such a partitioning might involve.

In the most basic sense, philosophy is a single field involving a certain type of reflective activity, texts produced by such activities, and ideas, views, or positions expressed in these texts. That philosophy involves these elements (or can mean any one of these three things) is based upon the more fundamental fact that the field of philosophy is constituted by the interplay of three actual conditions and their distinctive excesses: embodied beings, significative systems or complexes, and idealities. Because each of these conditions exerts its own distinctive forces upon the field of philosophy, that region formed by their interplay can be said to have 'contours.' By deploying this term, I mean to suggest that, while the field of philosophy is, in a sense, continuous, it can be thought of as having regions that will differ among one another depending upon the relative intensities of the forces at any specific point. In this sense, we can say that the 'contour' of a part of the field lying closer to (or more dominated by) one of the conditions will differ from other regions differently positioned. On the basis of such differences of contour, we can introduce certain 'partitions' among the various regions of the field of philosophy. We should think of such partitions not as fixed, definite, and non-overlapping divisions of the field (as Aristotle or Kant did), but as relatively adjustable, mobile, and, to a certain degree, arbitrary ways of dividing the field of philosophy—something more akin to the partitions that can be purchased at IKEA or Bed, Bath, and Beyond than to the fixed walls of a house.

Put differently, unlike a philosopher such as Aristotle or Kant, who held that philosophy had definite and fixed divisions that are articulated through a sort of hierarchical genus/species type of organization, I am suggesting that, while we can speak of partitions of philosophy, these are neither hierarchical with respect to one another nor do they form fixed domains, each with its own sets of questions, procedures, and results arrived at (relatively) independently of the others. Based upon the three actual conditions of philosophy that we have already surveyed, we can say that philosophy has three major partitions: what I will call 'somatics,' 'significs,' and 'eidetics.' (Later, I will introduce three additional types of inquiry closely related to them, but this will require further discussion. Refer to Diagram 7.)

Since the partitioning I'll suggest is clearly novel and unfamiliar, a brief preview of the more specific aims I have in mind in doing so will be helpful. We have just surveyed the three main approaches to the division of philosophy found in the tradition. The state of philosophy on this matter in the early part of the 21st century is roughly the following. While in the last couple of decades of the 20th century, a few figures (especially Deleuze, Badiou, and some so-called 'post-analytic' philosophers) have explicitly renewed the effort to articulate and defend an overall view of philosophy as a single field or discipline, almost all have also been firmly anti-Hegelian (and sometimes anti-Platonic as well). Even so, they have tended not to introduce any new divisions in philosophy, rendering their views somewhat ambiguous on this score. However, we can describe the (usually implicit) view for most other current thinkers who have not decided to throw in their lot with non-philosophical disciplines (such as cognitive science) as an unstable mixture of the second two views that I have discussed. On the one hand, epistemology and ethics (ultimately derived from the transcendental idealist approach of Kant) remain uncontroversially central areas of philosophical inquiry, sometimes supported by 'metaphysics' in a very restricted (and often, in its way, also Kantian) form. Scattered rather randomly around these are a multiplicity of other more or less acknowledged fields of inquiry (aesthetics, philosophy of science, philosophy of language, philosophy of mind, political philosophy, and so on) whose relations to the former, less controversial, fields are often rather vague and unsettled. Finally, a number of, so to speak, 'homeless questions' that, while clearly philosophical, do not fall neatly into any of these recognized areas occasionally surface. For examples of some of these, google something like "ten 21st century philosophical questions." One striking feature of most of these lists is that they are fairly evenly divided between distinctively ethical (or ethico-political) issues and others that are recognizably neither epistemological nor metaphysical. The other is that there seems to be no clear connection among the questions they list.

The partitioning of philosophy that I will present is designed to address some of these issues. First, it should make clear that epistemology (the main 'theoretical' remnant of Kantian transcendental idealism) cannot be regarded as an enterprise independent of other philosophical considerations but must be absorbed into a broader set of issues. Put more generally, epistemology, by its very nature, always begins 'subjectively,' with a knower attempting to ascertain whether, and if so how, 'objective knowledge' is possible. The partitioning I am suggesting attempts to counter this orientation as a central feature of philosophy or of one of its currently dominant areas. Second, it attempts to provide a home for some of the presently orphaned questions, according them a proper and respectable place within the overall enterprise of philosophy and placing them firmly upon the agenda for philosophical inquiry in the present century. Third, this should in turn suggest that, although I have maintained that philosophy is always a finite and limited undertaking, the ways in which it is limited are not those asserted on the basis of Kantian transcendental idealist epistemology (or its later versions) but have more to do with philosophy's relation to its actual conditions and to other fields—especially religion, science, and art. Within its own partitions, philosophy is capable of doing a good deal more than Kant would have countenanced, without violating the essential finitude of philosophy that I have emphasized. Finally, it seeks to affirm the important place of ethics and political philosophy (though not as Kant conceived them) while locating these inquiries in relation to other cognate areas (something that Kant mostly failed to provide).

1. Somatics

The partition that I call 'somatics' (derived from the Greek word for 'body') focuses upon the actual condition of embodied being and the types of excess involved with it. While, for philosophy viewed as an activity, the most important 'body' in question is what the phenomenological tradition has called '*Dasein*' (Heidegger) or the 'lived body' (Merleau-Ponty), it is fundamental to all such accounts that the body, understood in this sense, 'always already' stands in immediate relation both to other such self-conscious bodies (Sartre's 'Beings-for-themselves') as well as non-self-conscious bodies (his 'Beings-in-themselves'). We should also add a third group of sentient but non-human bodies, bodies that are 'Beings-aware-of-themselves' (but not self-conscious or fully 'for-themselves'), that is, animal bodies. Finally, circumscribing all of these types of bodies, forming their fundamental 'situation,' and existing as 'presently' excessive to them and existing both 'before' and 'after' them, is the sheer, contingent multiplicity of bodies that make up what Deleuze calls the 'chaosmos.'

This, of itself, already presents one of the most important, but also difficult, set of issues that the partition of somatics must confront. First, how is it possible that a sheer, contingent multiplicity of bodies was capable of dividing into discrete 'sets' at all? Second, how could certain of these sets achieve a degree of internal complexity sufficient to constitute discrete 'things' or 'objects'? How, then, could some of these things or objects achieve a degree of internal complexity sufficient to constitute living organisms? And, how could certain living organisms become capable of being, first, conscious, and then sufficiently self-conscious, such that they were capable of such enterprises as religion, science, art, and philosophy? Of course, since excessive elements enter at each point, what somatics can respond at any juncture will be limited, first of all by the fact that all such questions are posed from the finite perspective of embodied beings. So it is true, as Kant claimed on different grounds, that somatics is capable of posing questions that it will never be in a position to answer with finality. But it is also true (an option not open to Kant) that, at such points, mathematics and science may provide models and approaches that can enrich somatics on this score (though bearing in mind the 'translation' that will inevitably be involved).

We might note that it was with such questions that certain parts of metaphysics, especially cosmology, were formerly occupied. The main problem was that metaphysics usually formulated such somatic questions in an eidetic mode, thus subjecting them to a conceptual regime that obscured many of the actual complexities of the questions and rendered science incapable of offering any assistance in their conceptual speculations.

At a more local level involving specifically embodied conscious and self-conscious beings, there are issues associated with their relations to the various 'objects' that they experience and with which they deal. To begin with, as the phenomenological tradition (and especially Merleau-Ponty) has highlighted, physical objects are always perceived by embodied beings 'perspectivally.' Because of this, physical objects are always excessive to embodied being in that what is revealed of them from the limited perspective of an embodied being at the same time conceals other of their features. But, even more, while embodied beings may view an object from multiple perspectives (say, by moving around it), there is no finite set of perspectives that, added together, would constitute the 'full givenness' of the object itself. Objects, then, always remain excessive to embodied being (and embodied beings to them as well, if the object itself also happens to be conscious).

These ubiquitous excesses, however, do not prevent embodied being from dealing with objects 'practically'; in fact, they constitute important dimensions of this. Heidegger's discussion, early in *Being and Time*, contrasting an object experienced as 'present-at-hand' (as a 'mere object,' which can become an 'object' for epistemology, among other things) and one encountered as 'ready-to-hand' (as playing some meaningful role in the practical experience and activities of embodied being) has provided important insights regarding embodied being's relation to tools, its broader 'world,' and ultimately crucial philosophical questions (explored by Heidegger himself and many others) concerning both the excessive possibilities as well as dangers inherent in the 'technological framing of the world.' It's worth mentioning that the 'philosophy of technology' has been one of those orphan areas of philosophy, mentioned above, that should assume an important place within the partition of somatics, which may also serve to link its questions to others from which it has often been separated.

Further, conscious embodied beings encounter both non-sentient objects as well as other conscious embodied beings as objects, the multiplicity of which constitutes a sort of rudimentary though still always excessive 'world' for embodied being. However, since any conscious embodied being is also an object for other such beings, there is, even merely at the perceptual level, a sort of 'multiplication of excess': not only are others excessive to me, but I am equally excessive to them. I can never 'see myself as others see me,' nor can they 'see me as I see myself.'

However, it should not be thought that any sort of 'symmetry of excess' prevails here, since every self-conscious embodied being (as psychoanalysis so resolutely affirms) involves its own distinctive form of internal complexity apart from, but related in various ways to, its being as an object for others. In other words, every self-conscious embodied being is, at the same time as being an 'other' to other such beings, also 'other' to itself (which psychoanalysis formulates in terms of the 'unconscious' and various 'topologies' derived from it). Incidentally, it is only when formulated in this way, somatically, that it becomes possible to acknowledge the intersubjective excesses that are systematically eliminated by such eidetic treatments as Hegel's famous 'master-slave dialectic.'

It is here that desire-as-lack comes into play as the restless and excessive force that continually both connects sentient embodied being to some objects, both sentient and non-sentient, and, at the same time, disconnects it from others. When formulated in such somatic (and not eidetic) terms, the excessiveness of desire itself, together with the excessiveness of its objects, can be seen to underlie both sexual relations and broader social and political groupings of self-conscious embodied beings. It also has the potential of revealing connections among the different ways that desire and its excesses operate that have often remained obscure or opaque when treated in more restrictive and reductionistic eidetic terms, like those of more traditional epistemology or political theory.

What will, perhaps, prove in the near future to be one of the most urgent set of questions, though until now one of those orphan areas I mentioned earlier, concerns those surrounding the nature of 'life' itself. While recent advances in the biological sciences have shed significant new light on questions of the origins and functioning of organic life as well as upon the conditions for regarding something as 'living' or 'sentient,' serious somatic philosophical questions remain regarding the actual application of such scientific concepts, such as in arguments concerning abortion. Beyond this are other philosophical questions now being raised by new biotechnologies involving cloning, stem-cell research, and ultimately the production of new and until now unknown life-forms. And in perhaps the near future lies the discovery of new non-synthesized 'extraterrestrial' life forms. Whatever complex issues this may pose, among them will be important philosophical questions that will not be merely epistemological but will require the breadth and orientation of a somatics.

2. Significs

In an earlier chapter, I suggested that there is an important distinction between mere communication, of which many (if not all) embodied sentient beings are capable, and distinctively significative communication, a capacity possessed by only self-conscious embodied beings (humans and perhaps some higher primates). The main point was that it was possible for embodied beings to exist and communicate without signification, the second actual condition of philosophy (and other cognate areas), emerging. However, once signification has developed, there is a sort of necessity attending the further emergence of the third actual condition, that of ideality. Ideality, that is, is already implicit or latent in the actual condition of signification.

There are ways other than through signification in which the set of issues associated with this has been approached. Two prominent alternatives begin from either natural language or formal logical analysis. However, I have preferred to start with insights offered by the version of the broader enterprise of structuralism called 'semiotics' or 'semiology' for several reasons. To approach such questions by a study of natural languages (linguistics) starts from a position whose focus is too narrow to encompass a good deal of what I have in mind. Certainly any natural language involves a highly complex set of basic elements, structures, and principles; it may be that natural language is a (or even *the*) paradigmatic case of a significative system; and it is true that natural language has traditionally been the favored and almost exclusive medium of philosophical expression. However, it is not the case that natural language is the most complex of such systems, for example, when it is embedded within a broader significational complex such as a film or video game. Further, while a natural language certainly has ample areas of excess (as much modern communicational, literary, and rhetorical theory has affirmed), it is by no means certain that the sorts of excesses characteristic of natural languages exhaust those associated with other types of significational systems. Such considerations are, I think, sufficient to favor the semiological view of regarding natural language as only one type (important as it may be) of the broader field of signification. As for formal logical analysis (e.g. axiomatized set theory, formal semantics, or transformational grammar), these either aim to simplify and reduce the complexity of natural languages even further or they focus upon certain mathematical phenomena that are significational systems considerably less complex than natural languages.

The present approach involves three notions crucial for our discussion, each associated with its own set of excesses. Taken together, these go a considerable way toward mapping our partition of 'significs.' (I refer the reader to Chapter IX for a fuller account of signification; here I am mainly concerned to highlight some implications of this discussion for the partitioning of philosophy.)

First, the fundamental notion underlying the semiotic or semiological approach is that of the 'sign,' an idea with its roots in Aristotle and the medieval 'theory of intentions' and developed in various directions by Peirce and Saussure (among others) at the beginning of the 20th century. On the standard account, a sign is regarded as a relation between a 'signifier' and a 'signified.' Saussure, in particular, tended to think of a signifier as some perceivable or observable 'object' (it can be a physical object or an attribute of a physical object) that is related to a 'mental object' (an image or idea). With regard to this relation, which itself constitutes the sign, Saussure emphasized that the connection between the signifier and the signified is 'arbitrary,' that is, that it not based on any natural resemblance between the two (neither the sound of 'cat' when spoken or the written word 'cat' bear any resemblance to an actual cat or the image of a cat in my mind).

A sign, even regarded in this most basic sense, is already a locus of several excesses. First, in order for there to be a sign at all, some object must either be constituted as a signifier or be selected from among other signifiers already available. This 'object aspect' of the sign immediately suggests that desire-as-lack, embodied being's most fundamental relation to objects, is already at work here. As mentioned before, any object whatever can become an object of desire. But the very fixture of desire upon an object as its 'intentional correlate' already selects it from the always excessive multiplicity of other objects and constitutes it as a potential signifier capable of functioning as one element of a sign. (Psychoanalysis refers to this 'signific investiture' of an object as 'cathexis.') Further, since there is no natural relation between signifieds and signifiers, the connection between an object of desire, functioning as a signifier, and its corresponding signified must also be supplied by the further extension of the force of desire. What is signified by desire's object/signifier is some further movement of desire itself by which its object/signifier becomes invested with meaning or significance for it. This can, of course, be, as Saussure thought, a 'mental image' associated with the object/signifier, but it can, as well, be some strategy for the active appropriation of the object, some other object (a word, gesture, or a feature of the object), or something eidetic that is not merely a 'mental image' of an object. As Peirce already recognized before Saussure's analysis of signs, the realm of signifieds available to any signifier is also excessive. A sign, then, is a relation, constituted by desire, between a signifier and a signified, where both 'relata' are excessive to the relation itself and each is capable of further elaboration by the restless movements of desire.

The second fundamental notion of semiotics is that signifiers and signifieds, and hence the signs formed by their relation, are 'differential.' That is, just as desire-as-lack involves a sort of selection or preference (though often not a conscious or intentional one) among an open and excessive set of potential objects available to embodied being, the investiture by desire of an object as a signifier also immediately serves to differentiate that object/signifier from other objects, which might also be, at another time or for another's desire, constituted as signifiers. Correspondingly, the potential signifieds corresponding to any object/signifier also become differentiated among themselves. Fully constituted signs emerge when the innately restless activity of desire connects elements of an open set of signifiers with elements of an open field of signifieds in ways that allow these *relations* (signs) to be reiterable, differentiated one from the other, and also related to one another in various ways.

The constitution of signs is itself, therefore, a work or product of desire involving a double set of differences—differences among object/signifiers and differences among the signifieds with which they are connected in signs. To take a simple example, if one desires to produce a 'stop sign,' it is first necessary to select both among the possible shapes (round, square, hexagonal...) and colors of an object (green, yellow, red...), and the particular type of action that is to be regulated (go, turn, proceed with caution, stop...), and then establish (in this case, by law) a connection between a particular shape and color and a specific type of action. But the establishment of this relation between shape and color, on the one hand, and a specific action to be regulated, on the other, is itself excessive to its elements. In this case, the connection could be established in a different way, for instance, by reinforced habit, or indoctrination, or persuasive advertising. The point is that there is a sense in which the constitution of the sign-relation is excessive to the elements of the sign involving the signifier and the signified. While it is true that, given specific 'scopes' for signifiers and signifieds, the excess of desire becomes more limited and focused, there still, within these limits, remains space for the further expression of desire.

The third fundamental notion of semiotics is that of a 'significational system.' A sign is a (relatively) stable relation between a differential order of signifiers and a differential order of signifieds. However, signs themselves, once constituted, are reiterable, differential, and related to one another. As such, they come to form (relatively) stable significational complexes or systems made up of 'relations of relations.' Saussure, for example, distinguished discrete instances of the use or deployment of signs (say, in gesturing, speaking, or writing), which he called '*parole*,' from what he regarded as the more or less 'closed differential totality' of signs which he referred to a '*langue*.' The difference was roughly that between acts of speaking or writing a language and the language itself that is being spoken or written. If we attend specifically to the latter, some of the ways in which linguistic signs (always a relation) are in turn related to one another can be expressed in such forms as a diagram, matrix, or set of rules presenting certain structural features of a significational system. (Logic would be one example of this, ranging over the complex signs called 'statements.')

However, as made clear by later semiotic thinkers like Roland Barthes, who were less focused on more narrow linguistic questions, there are multiple significational systems beyond natural languages for which it is also necessary to distinguish between concrete instances of their deployment and the overall system of possibilities from which these are drawn. Because of this, any concrete instance of signification may involve the interaction of and mutual inflection by such multiple systems of signification, even if, for any given example, one may be dominant. Moreover, as both Peirce and later Barthes made clear, already constituted signs can themselves assume the role of signifier or signified in 'higher order' processes of signification. Indeed, much of philosophy itself (not to mention religion, science, and art) involves exactly such iterative significational processes of ordered complexes of signs ('named concepts,' for instance) that are linked to others at higher degrees of complexity, variously exchanging places as signifiers and signifieds (as when we speak of 'Ideas' in a Platonic sense or 'Categories' in a Kantian sense).

This consideration of signs as elements of differential complexes or systems has important implications for desire. While desire plays a pivotal role in the constitution of signifiers and their linking with signifieds, the resulting signs, in forming a (relatively) autonomous significative complex or system with its own distinctive structural features, eliminates some of the excesses operative in desire's initial operation. As Saussure indicated, while the relation between signifier and signified is 'arbitrary' (and thus excessive on both sides), once such relations are established and signs assume their place within a system of differences, the excesses of desire become, at least in part, delimited and directed along the vectors inherent in any given significational system. As I mentioned in the case of art in the last chapter, the engagement of desire with an existing significational system serves to (in part) limit the native excesses of desire, focus them, and provide a conduit or vehicle for their concrete expression. We can say, then, that there is an important respect in which desire is subjugated by (or perhaps 'sublimated' within) a given significational system. Further, it is only within an already constituted significational system that desire can be expressed and communicated to other embodied beings. (This is the aspect of structuralism missed by much of the poststructuralist critique of it.)

However, as I noted above, the actual condition of signification comprises an open multiplicity of significational systems, each involving its own set of sign-elements and distinctive differential relations among them. The excesses of desire that are, to a considerable degree, foreclosed upon the formation of significational systems, are reproduced in new forms within the differences and incommensurabilities obtaining among the multiplicity of significational systems. For example, Richard Wagner, in *The Artwork of the Future* as well as in his artistic practice, envisioned a new form of art that would deploy a number of otherwise independent significational systems (music, poetry, acting, painting, architecture, stage design, and so on), exploiting the various types of excess native to each, to achieve novel types of expression of desire. If we think (as we probably should) that Wagner overstated his goal of producing a '*Gesamtkunstwerke*,' a 'total work of art,' we should at least credit him with having recognized the excessive possibilities for desire's expression offered by new forms of excess resident in the interstices among different significational systems.

In addition to desire's more direct relation with the condition of signification, we may recall that there is another more indirect or mediated way in which desire engages with signification: the eidetic realm of thought and its expression in philosophy also originates in desire-as-lack. As I suggested earlier, the eidetic events and the event-concepts generated from them also draw upon already constituted significational systems for names that render them reiterable, differential, and relational. To date, philosophy has limited itself almost exclusively to natural languages for its expression. However, given the multiplicity of significational systems within the condition of signification, there is no reason why philosophy might not express itself in other ways than in natural language although, even so, the importance of logical statements in philosophical expression will likely persist as a sort of baseline or terminus of other forms of expression. In particular, I have in mind such media, more complex than natural language and usually deploying additional significational systems, as film and video games. To date, such significational complexes seem to have served as more concrete and experientially rich presentations of existing eidetic complexes or philosophical views, but it may well be that they will eventually issue in novel philosophical insights or views. Whichever turns out to be the case, these extensions of philosophy beyond texts composed in a natural language attest both to the excesses of the condition of signification beyond the eidetic as well as to the necessity of recognizing the importance of embodiment and desire in the activity of philosophy itself.

To summarize, then, we can say, first, that the partition of significs should absorb that of the current fields of philosophy of language and logic as limited parts of itself. Based upon the much broader and inclusive notion of the sign, it would be, in some ways, coextensive with what has, to date, been call 'semiology' or 'semiotics.' However, it would acknowledge (along with such figures as Barthes, Lacan, Kristeva, Deleuze, and Leclerc) the importance of desire (and hence embodied being) as an originary and integral element of the condition of signification. Like some poststructuralist critics, it would emphasize, at every level of investigation, the importance of distinctive types of significational excess, but it would affirm, with the structuralists and other such views as those of Habermas, Foucault, and Althusser, the degree to which significational systems, in their (relative) autonomy, are both essential to meaningful human communication and yet also serve to channel, subjugate, and distort desire. In this sense, significs would also comprise part of what has formerly been called social theory or even political philosophy. Finally, significs should especially attend to new forms of expression and communication that emerge within the differences and excessive interstices of existing significational systems, exploring their implications for and impact upon both the desire and lived experiences of embodied beings and upon the ways of constructing concepts and their networks in the eidetic realm.

Whatever directions this project may take, it will finally rest upon the conviction that signification constitutes a realm different than and irreducible either to that of the multiplicity of objects encountered by embodied being and its desires or to the ideas (relations, meanings, concepts, or networks) expressed in the process of signification. Of course, just as we should expect, the conditions of embodied being and ideality are reflected in that of signification, still signification is an autonomous realm of activity and expression that is neither reducible to nor exhausted by either or both together. The order of signification therefore has a sort of life of its own relatively independent of that of either the lived experience of embodied beings or the thought-processes of the eidetic sphere, though influencing both in profound ways. It is upon this basis, then, that I am proposing a partition of philosophy called significs.

3. Eidetics

While the partitions of philosophy I've called 'somatics' and 'significs' involve a quite extensive revision of traditional divisions of philosophy, 'eidetics' will probably seem more familiar. This is, in part, because the first two aim to establish a place, within the overall enterprise of philosophy, for novel and important philosophical developments dating from the last two centuries or so. It is also partly because, beginning with Plato, many of the most influential currents of philosophy have explicitly affirmed or at least assumed that 'ideas' occupy a realm sufficiently independent of the concrete experiences of embodied beings and the significative media in which they are expressed to permit them to be considered on their own account. Forerunners of what I am calling eidetics are therefore numerous and include Plato (especially the *Sophist* and *Parmenides* as well as many sections of other dialogues), Aristotle (in certain sections of the *Metaphysics*), some of the medievals (especially Duns Scotus), Leibniz, Kant (in his theory of categories), Hegel (most notably in his *Science of Logic*), Frege, Peirce, Meinong, Husserl (especially his *Ideas*), parts of Deleuze, and Badiou (*Being and Event* in particular). Eidetics therefore has more of an established philosophical pedigree than do somatics and significs.

The problems involved with providing an overview of eidetics as a partition of philosophy are therefore somewhat different than those involved with the other two. To begin with, it will be especially important to clarify exactly how what I am proposing stands in relation to other previous approaches that would clearly count as eidetic.

In the view I've been presenting, I take three assumptions as now established. First, ideality (and the elements and processes that it comprises) is an autonomous 'actual condition,' irreducible to those of embodiment and signification. Second, however, it does stand in certain specifiable relations to the other two actual conditions, which are registered in various ways within it. Third (and this is perhaps the most controversial assumption), the realm of ideality involves processes of construction that generate (relatively) stable structures. That is, the basic elements of the condition of ideality (what I have called 'concepts'), their connections within propositions, and propositions' own linkages among one another, are structured products of the process of reflection or thought. To summarize, the condition of ideality is constituted as an open set of structures constructed by thought-processes motivated by a particular type of desire working in conjunction with the resources of a significational system or complex.

While eidetics (as I am using this term) does agree with Platonist approaches that also affirm the autonomy of the eidetic sphere from the particularities of lived experience and the forms of its significative expression, it insists that 'ideas' (like those of Plato) are not some 'eternally existing essences.' Instead, we should say that they would not 'exist' at all without the reflective and expressive capacities of embodied beings. And although the realm of ideality can, when deployed in certain ways, provide a framework for organizing and classifying the objects encountered in the lived experience of embodied beings, it does not somehow 'exist in or among' them nor is it, in the first instance, 'abstracted' from them, as Aristotle would maintain.

Neither do idealities in themselves express certain necessary logical features of the 'world,' as Leibniz and, later, the early Wittgenstein would claim, although they can appear to do so if we begin with their expression in logical statements rather than the processes of their own genesis.

The account of concepts underlying eidetics does agree with Kant's form of transcendental idealism in holding that they are the precipitates of what might be called 'synthetic processes' and that these latter can, in turn, be regarded, *in the specific sense of 'independent of experience,'* as '*a priori*.' But it entirely rejects the further transcendental idealist assumption that their being '*a priori*' also entails that any denumerable set of fundamental concepts (i.e. 'categories') are 'necessary' either logically (as specific constituents of any 'rational thought'), transcendentally (as structural features of the experience of rational beings), or metaphysically (as somehow constitutive for anything that can be regarded as a 'world' or 'universe'). Hegel, in a much broader way than Kant and probably more than any other thinker before his time, did recognize that concepts were structured precipitates of a broader process of thought ('dialectical logic') and attempted to embed them within the lived experience of embodied beings (his version of 'phenomenology'). However, Hegel offered what ends up being a 'super-transcendental idealism' that attempted to eliminate all excess from concepts, experience, and also signification by viewing them all as elements of a single eidetic process, 'the Concept.' Husserl's approach, another self-confessed form of transcendental idealism, explicitly sought to ground concepts or ideas in the 'synthetic processes' of consciousness and (later) 'lived experience' (and devoted considerable attention to signification), but he regarded philosophy as a sort of 'presuppositionless self-grounding' rather than an enterprise contingent upon a set of actual, and not merely transcendental or 'consciousness-based,' conditions, each excessive to the enterprise in its own distinctive ways.

In a sense, Chapter X, on Ideality, was itself an initial foray into and mapping of the basic contours of the partition of eidetics, so I won't retrace it here in any detail. Rather, it will suffice to indicate several important problems, questions, and, in some cases, directions for further inquiry that the earlier discussion suggests.

a. The Central Issue of Eidetics: Structured Process

The generic notion of a structured process is fundamental to any attempt to present, explain, or defend a constructivist view of idealities. Although it was present from the very beginning of European philosophy, it was Hegel's philosophical view that brought this issue squarely to the fore for all later philosophical thought. Now the notion of a structured process is intuitively clear and familiar. When we brew a cup of coffee, drive a car, observe a play in a game like football, watch a dancer in motion, speak a sentence, sing a song, or add a column of numbers, we are immediately engaged with a structured process (or set of them). In fact, we might even say that what we call 'the world' consists of an open multiplicity of structured processes. The problem arises when we come to describe or analyze structured processes. In the 17th century, the calculus was devised with the explicit aim of formulating the multiplicity of structured processes comprising 'nature' in precise mathematical terms. Soon after, beginning especially with Kant, philosophy also had to engage this task with its own devices if it was to remain abreast of developments in the natural sciences and secure its own integrity by shedding light on the basically dynamic nature of experience and the world. While Hegel might fairly be regarded as the first (though thoroughly idealist) 'process philosopher,' an entire movement subsequently arose whose aim was to reflect upon and describe structured processes beyond the limitations of Hegel's idealistic stance (a movement that included such figures as Bergson, Whitehead, and more recently Deleuze). However, any such *philosophical* (and, one might add, mathematical) attempt to describe and analyze structured processes (which will include any 'constructivist' view of concepts) must inevitably confront a fundamental problem.

We know, intuitively (so to speak), both that every structure is a result or precipitate of some process and that no process is identifiable or accessible except through the structures that it produces. A process that produced no structure would be mere chaos, just as a structure that did not arise from some process would, quite literally, be unthinkable and inarticulable, at least for any finite, temporal being. In other words, we know intuitively that structure and process are fully co-equal elements of anything that we can experience, express, or think. But embodied experience, as finite and temporal, simply *is* an immediate and continual unfolding of structured processes. Further, its expression and communication are themselves processes that draw upon structural features of significative complexes in producing discretely structured statements. So, although it is possible to distinguish acts (processes) of expression and communication from the structures operative within them (as the structuralists did), there remains a kind of equipoise between process and structure (something that the structuralist emphasis on the latter tended to obscure). Put in other terms, for the condition of signification, structures are 'virtualities' that require processes in which they are 'actualized,' and every act of expression or signification is a deployment of some 'virtual possibility' of a signifying complex.

However, the condition of ideality, at least as interpreted from a constructivist perspective, presents a special problem in this respect. On the one hand, thinking, which must be regarded as a type of process, produces concepts, connects them with other concepts in propositions, and links propositions together forming broader networks of concepts. On the other hand, however, it is precisely because the sole function of thought is constructing concepts and their linkages that thought, as it were, empties itself into its products without apparent remainder and its processes seem to disappear into the structures that they produce. By contrast, this is neither the case for the lived experience and desire of embodied beings nor for significative communication. In the first instance, it is the very nature of desire-as-lack to be incomplete and Protean, to confront a multiplicity of potential objects that remains always excessive to it and induces further activity on its part. Further, every significative expression of desire is always partial, both respect to further expressions and to the significational system that it partially deploys.

For the condition of ideality, however, a divorce seems to occur between the structures produced by the activity of thinking and the processes of thought which produce them. While desire is itself a sort of restless and unceasing process, and signification involves activities that can always be continued in further acts of signification, thinking tends to terminate and become fixed in the concepts and their linkages that it produces. This means that structure almost inevitably dominates the eidetic sphere, leaving the process of 'further thought' as an inarticulable (or at least 'not-yet-articulated') remainder. When, for example, we 'grasp' or 'understand' a philosophical view or position, we automatically tend to think of this as a structure or network of concepts that we apprehend and, because it has no other means of articulation than this structure itself, we simply pass by or ignore the fact that this structure or network is also a product of thought-processes. This, by the way, is true of virtually all of the historical examples of eidetics that I mentioned earlier: eidetics has been regarded almost solely as an inquiry about conceptual *structures*, ignoring the fact that these structures are products of processes, thereby, in turn, ignoring or suppressing the processes themselves.

The central task of the partition of eidetics that I am proposing will be, at the least, to formulate explicitly the problems involved with this bias toward privileging structure in the sphere of ideality and, so far as possible, to redress this imbalance. We might say, put directly, that the partition of eidetics that I am proposing would deal not only with *what* has been (or can be) conceptually thought, but equally with *how* thinking proceeds in generating concepts, their networks, and ultimately philosophical views or positions. It's worth mentioning that this is by no means a matter of the 'critical thinking,' understood as the cultivation of certain reasoning skills, that has become prominent in recent years; rather, it is itself a serious and fundamental philosophical engagement with what might be called 'speculative thinking.'

However, there are intrinsic limits to what we might expect such an eidetics to accomplish. Like the other partitions, eidetics must acknowledge and confront its own distinctive types of excesses. Perhaps the most important dimension of excess for eidetics is precisely the fact that the processes by which any concept, network of concepts, or philosophical position is constructed will always remain excessive to the products themselves. And this problem is recursive. That is, it will not suffice for eidetics to aim at producing some 'meta-account' of the processes of 'speculative thinking,' since such an account can itself only be yet another structural complex that must again confront the same issue. Instead, eidetics must explore and deploy various devices or strategies that permit it both to map conceptual structures while, at the same time, highlighting and elucidating the processes by which they are constructed. In what follows, I will briefly note a few of the strategies deployed in my earlier discussion of ideality in Chapter X as illustrations of this.

b. Events

The notion of an event is, I think, essential to any project of eidetics (and one mostly lacking in the philosophical tradition). To speak of an 'event' is to refer to something that is, in its most fundamental sense, at once a process and a structure. Events happen, take place, or appear along the trajectory of some broader process or set of processes that we might call (borrowing from Badiou) a 'situation.' However, they are not merely the process or situation itself but a specific, reiterable, differential, and relational punctuation or node of a broader process (or processes). As such, events have a determinate structure, but one that immediately spawns further processes and trajectories that follow from their occurrence. In a way, then, we can say that an event is the fundamental and paradigmatic case of a 'structured process.'

c. Concepts

Any constructivist view of ideality must maintain that concepts are themselves a type of event. While concepts (or 'ideas') can (and, in the tradition, usually have) been treated as a special sort of 'object' (an intellectual, mental, or non-physical one), this tends immediately to emphasize their structural features at the expense of the thought-processes that generate or reiterate them. Calling them 'objects' also tends, due to the intervention of signification, to oppose them to 'subjects,' which is, presumably, the locus of activity or process (a tendency that can be traced directly back to Kant and his transcendental idealist viewpoint). While the language of 'subject' and 'object' may be suitable for certain areas of the partition of embodied being, it is wholly unsuited to that of eidetics, especially on a constructivist interpretation, that must insist that concepts are ultimately events—neither 'objective structures' nor 'subjective processes' but unitary 'structured processes' that have consequences in generating other 'structured processes.'

d. Propositions

Likewise, propositions are linkages of named-events (that is, concepts). In insisting that every proposition can be viewed either 'formally' or 'speculatively,' Hegel meant to suggest both that every proposition has a determinate logical structure and that every logical structure is, at the same time, the precipitate or product of a broader process. However, instead of assuming ahead of time the contrast between a 'formal' and a 'speculative' interpretation of propositions (probably derived from Hegel's continued acceptance of certain tenets of transcendental idealism), a constructivist eidetics would prefer to say that propositions are themselves 'higher order events' involving linkages among other 'lower order events,' that is, concepts. It is not that propositions are first given as formal structures and then rendered speculative by the activity of thought, as Hegel's discussion seemed to suggest; rather, propositions are events to begin with that, under certain conditions provided by signification, can be regarded and dealt with in terms of their structure, that is, formally. Like the concept-events that they link, proposition-events also have 'consequences' (as well as 'antecedents'), but they do so not *because* the operations of the 'laws of formal logic' prevail in the eidetic sphere but, rather, because propositions can be (partly) expressed in discrete statements, the purely structural relations among which the 'laws' of formal logic, derived from features of a significational system, govern. In a strict sense, then, formal logic does not form part of eidetics at all but finds its proper place in the partition of signification.

e. Networks

I suggested in Chapter X that we should think of philosophical views or positions as complex networks of linkages among speculative proposition-events, which are themselves linkages of concept-events. The networks that make up philosophical views or positions are, in the most fundamental sense, large-scale sets of 'named events' (concepts and propositions) that, due to the intervention of signification, can be expressed in terms of ordered structures. For a constructivist view, however, it is important not to identify a philosophical position exclusively with the structure of its conceptual or propositional network. A philosophical position is, rather, a sort of open generator of further possible concepts and linkages. In a sense, we might say that every philosophical position is a 'virtuality'; to grasp or understand it, it is necessary both to (at least in part) retraverse its trajectories and reconstitute its structures, but, just as important, to know how to extend it 'speculatively,' how to think both with it and beyond it. This is, in fact, one important way in which process reasserts itself in what might otherwise be regarded as a structure.

Particularly since the digital revolution, the notion of 'network' has emerged as a central area of investigation. Latour has deployed this notion to reconceptualize 'the social,' but I believe that the notion is equally important for a constructivist eidetics. In particular, Latour has also warned against regarding networks merely as formal structures linking some sort of otherwise monadic and independent 'units,' insisting, rather, that they are merely the 'structural face' of what is otherwise a dynamic set of processes (or events?) involving 'actors' that are themselves involved in processes of interaction.

Deleuze and Guattari, in *A Thousand Plateaus*, considered networks from a different perspective, distinguishing between 'arboreal' (or 'tree-like') and 'rhizomic' (or 'root-like') types of what I am calling 'networks.' With respect to eidetics, specifically as a partition of philosophy that I am proposing, we might say that the network of concepts and propositions that make up a philosophical viewpoint or position has certain characteristics of both. On the one hand, I've suggested that philosophical positions develop from an originary event that issues in certain trajectories. In a certain sense, the further development of concepts along these trajectories can appear 'arboreal.' However, such trajectories are always diverse, often overlapping, folding, and open to further conceptual construction and linkages in multiple directions. Instead of the contrast between a tree and something like grass or weeds, perhaps the appropriate metaphor for a philosophical position, as a third option, is a special sort of tree, an aspen, that also involves a rhizomic structure: although an aspen can sprout from a single seed, as it grows above ground, it also produces a rhizomic root complex underground that spreads and, at various points, produces further aspen trees above ground. An aspen, then, is, at once, a tree, a rhizome, and, eventually, an expanding colony of trees joined by a common rhizomic complex.

I mention such ways of regarding the sort of networks that are philosophical positions only to illustrate both that this notion has already begun to influence philosophical thought and to indicate one of the sorts of issues to be confronted by an eidetics. Beyond this, eidetics will likely have a good deal to learn of use to its own project from reflections on communicational and cybernetic networks, from cognitive science's study of neural networks and 'parallel processing,' and from emergent mathematical and logical descriptions of networks, including 'fuzzy' and 'multi-valued logics.' These will, of course, require retranslation into philosophical terms, but, in the process, eidetics should, in turn, prove to have insights to contribute to them as well.

III. ENGAGED THOUGHT: ETHICS, POLITICS, IDEOLOGY CRITIQUE

1. From Disengaged to Engaged Thought

The partitioning of the field of philosophy that I have just described involved a distinctive directionality that we might call 'centrifugal.' That is, it required that we traverse the field of philosophy in a way that attempted (in a provisional and flexible manner) to view the three actual conditions as separable from one another and, so far as possible, to regard them as standing apart from one another. Doing so, however, meant that, in order to identify, differentiate, and describe the partitions, we occupied a position within the midst of them without adopting a specific stance *within* any one of them. When, for example, we described the partition of somatics, we were holding it apart from the other conditions and mapping it without adopting a particular position within it. And even if we happened to prefer a specific 'position' with respect to embodiment, it would be one among a variety of possible positions whose claims we would have to acknowledge even if our preferred position differed from them. Operating 'centrifugally,' then, we might describe our own position as 'mappers' of the contours or partition of an actual condition as 'disengaged' from it. To speak of such an attitude of philosophy as disengaged is neither to claim that it is 'disinterested' (as if the mapping is a matter of total indifference or detachment) or (in some meanings of the term) 'objective,' but is intended only to register the fact that, from a 'disengaged' perspective, we are temporarily suspending questions about and influences of the other conditions in favor of a focus upon one among them. It also does not assume that all the more specific possible positions that one might adopt regarding one of the conditions are 'equally valid' for us, only that all be regarded as possible positions (any more than all of the towns on a certain region of a map are equally desirable destinations—but they *are* possible destinations and deserve inclusion on the map).

There is, however, another attitude that philosophical reflection can adopt, one that I will call 'engaged.' To begin with, an 'engaged attitude' can be described as 'centripetal.' That is, rather than separating the partitions and their defining actual conditions, it involves an explicit acknowledgement of all the actual conditions and their forces and it positions itself with respect to all of them. In so doing, an engaged attitude involves occupying a specific position with respect to the three actual conditions and their excesses. It takes a stand, so to speak, with respect to the actual conditions at a certain point and judges other possible positions as different from and no longer as equally viable alternatives to its own. Even more, an engaged attitude interprets other possibilities in terms of its own stance and will thereby map them in relation to it. In this sense, it does not merely differentiate other positions but differentiates them in relation to its own position. Finally, an engaged attitude will imply and can often issue in ways of acting, signifying, and thinking that will configure the basic conditions in specific ways that can refine, enhance, and extend its own position in multiple directions.

The contrast between disengaged and engaged philosophical attitudes (or perhaps 'modes') corresponds, to a certain degree, to the long-standing distinction that the philosophical tradition has drawn between theoretical and practical philosophy or, more generically, between theory and praxis. It originated with Aristotle, who deployed this distinction (among other things) to divide philosophy into theoretical disciplines such as metaphysics, mathematics, and physics, and practical disciplines like ethics and politics. Kant provided his own transcendental idealist version of this distinction, and a corresponding division of philosophy, by distinguishing between 'Theoretical Reason' and 'Practical Reason,' holding them to be the two sole and mutually exclusive divisions of philosophy. However, despite the appearance of continuity between Aristotle and Kant, there was a crucial difference between the way in which each made this distinction. For Aristotle, and most of the tradition following him up until Kant's Copernican Revolution in philosophy, 'practical philosophy' (at least where ethics and politics were concerned) always involved an engaged attitude while 'theoretical philosophy' was disengaged. For instance, Aristotle's *Nichomachean Ethics*, or so the tradition has it, was formulated as a sort of 'handbook' of advice for living well for his nephew (and presumably anyone else who might find it valuable). While he mentioned numerous views in the process, it remained clear that Aristotle was concerned to offer a 'preferred position,' not just a smorgasbord of possible alternatives from among which his reader might indifferently select. The same was true of his *Politics*.

By contrast, Kant's 'Practical Philosophy,' as an investigation into the rational bases of moral principles and the actions that followed from them, was addressed to generically 'rational beings' and purported to provide the theoretical basis for any principles and actions that could qualify as moral. Kant, in effect, transformed what had previously been 'engaged practical philosophy' into another mode of 'disengaged theoretical philosophy.' Of course, certain practical consequences for the principles and actions of 'rational beings' followed from Kant's 'Practical Philosophy' (telling the truth, keeping promises, and so on), but he regarded these as logically entailed by his theoretical (that is, disengaged) analysis of principles and actions rather than something arising from his own engaged attitude. Just as Kant's transcendental idealism prevented him from inquiring, in his theoretical philosophy, about the actual conditions for the possibility of philosophy itself (and not just of experience and knowledge), so it barred him from asking, in his practical philosophy, about the conditions for the possibility of there being such things as actions or ways of life based upon principles at all.

2. The Partitions of Engaged Philosophy

I want to suggest, then, that the actual conditions likewise provide a framework for a kind of partitioning of philosophy pursued from the attitude of engagement. The three partitions I propose are those of ethics, political philosophy, and ideology critique. However, given the nature of engagement as I have described it, the overall project will be 'centripetal' rather than 'centrifugal,' that is, it will involve not an attempt to hold the three actual conditions apart but one that will continually ask about the ways they are or can be configured within an engaged attitude. Put in other terms, philosophy in an engaged mode will have, as its main concern, taking a stand with respect to how the desires of embodied beings can be optimally harmonized with types of signification and communication within the context of a conceptual framework that involves ideals that might govern the lives of embodied beings in communicative interaction with one another.

Kant's transformation of what had before always been an engaged attitude in ethics into a form of disengaged theoretical philosophy had a significant effect on the way in which this was often subsequently pursued. It suggested, first, that the major task of ethics was to 'objectively' determine the various meanings of moral terms and appropriate 'methods' for relating them, then to outline the set of 'ethical positions' based upon them. From here, one might then select among these alternatives according to some 'rational criteria' or 'method.' (The former was later sometimes called 'metaethics,' the latter 'normative ethics.' Henry Sidgwick's *Methods of Ethics* served as a *locus classicus* of such an approach and still remains influential in much current ethical thought.) The main point is that this approach tends to subordinate an engaged to a disengaged attitude when considering ethical issues, thereby obscuring the bases upon which distinctively ethical (as opposed to theoretical) questions arise in the first place—as specific points of intersection among embodied beings and their desires, their significational interactions with one another, and principles or ideals that do or should govern them.

We can formulate a sort of paradox with respect to this relation between disengaged and engaged attitudes toward ethics (and, by extension, political thought and ideology critique) that is, in some ways, analogous to those that arose, in our earlier discussion of the 'analytic *a posteriori*,' with respect to the three actual conditions of philosophy. Suppose, as Kant's 'theoreticizing of practical philosophy' suggests, that we approach an 'ethical issue' from a disengaged attitude. We will then formulate a differential array of ethical positions and actions following from them. This will then require a 'rational' selection of one among them (or perhaps some hybrid of them) as the genuinely 'ethical alternative.' The paradox is that, once we have made this choice, the other 'alternatives' turn out *not to be genuinely 'ethical' options at all*, but only possible (non-ethical) alternatives serving as means by which the 'genuinely ethical alternative' is differentiated. (Anyone who has read some of Plato's more 'Socratic' dialogues will immediately recognize this problem together with its 'solution'—that Socrates always approaches ethical issues from an engaged attitude to begin with.) The point is that, analogous in some ways to the actual conditions of philosophy we considered earlier, the very formulation of 'ethical alternatives' from a disengaged attitude both presupposes the very condition (an engaged attitude) under which any situation can be regarded as 'ethical' to begin with and, at the same time, suspends this attitude in its disengaged formulation of various 'alternatives.'

I conclude from this that, at least as a philosophical matter, ethical reflection (as well as political philosophy and ideology critique) always and only issues from an engaged attitude; that is, it is the actual engagement of an embodied being in a situation that first provokes ethical reflection and any attempt to shift to a disengaged attitude undermines the very grounds upon which ethical reflection itself is based. This does not mean, however, that ethical reflection is somehow completely arbitrary or relative, since, like the disengaged attitude, it also proceeds differentially. But the engaged attitude differentiates alternatives in relation to its own engaged stance rather than as a mere multiplicity of 'equally valid' options in relation to one another. And such an engaged stance remains always subject to response and critique on the part of other embodied beings with different engaged stances, with their own processes differentiation and sets of positions defined in relation to them. So while there is no single position that is 'morally right' in some '*a priori*' sense with regard to any situation, an embodied being must be engaged in a situation in order for it to provoke moral judgment and, perhaps, action at all.

This is, I think, the true weakness of the practical philosophy that is associated with Kant's transcendental idealism: in a way similar to that in which his theoretical philosophy fails to ask the further question about the actual 'grounds (conditions) for the possibility' of philosophy at all, his practical philosophy fails to recognize the actual 'grounds (conditions) for the possibility' of there being such a thing as 'ethics' at all, that is, in terms we've been using here, the engaged attitude. More specifically, while Kant does provide a '*theory* of moral judgment,' he never clarifies (nor raises as a problem) the situations, and conditions constituting them, within which his theory (or any other for that matter) would apply. Just as does his transcendental idealist theoretical philosophy, his practical philosophy leaves us with an idealized 'rational being' deciding, according to abstract formal principles, about 'ideal types' of actions in completely generic situations.

So far, I have introduced the engaged attitude as the actual basis for there being such a thing as an ethical question, situation, or course of reflection, that is, as a feature of embodied being, which is, so viewed, the 'subject' of ethics or, perhaps better, 'ethical subject.' But disengagement and engagement are also modes of philosophical involvement with the other actual conditions as well. Political thought or philosophy also presupposes and is based upon an attitude of engagement, though, in this case, it is an engagement with significational structures and complexes that influence and affect the relations of embodied beings with one another. Parallel to the case of ethics, it is possible to adopt a disengaged attitude toward the condition of signification. Such a theoretical attitude toward this condition has issued in a number of disciplines that are often grouped together as the 'social sciences.' Depending upon what aspect of signification is highlighted, there are, for example, the disciplines of linguistics, ethnology, sociology, and political science. However, by considerations similar to those in the case of ethics, political philosophy is differentiated from these in that it is based upon an engaged attitude. Political philosophy (as opposed to political science, for example) does not merely study political processes or enumerate alternative types of political organization but assumes a location with respect to the significative processes and institutionalized structures that make up the field of politics and takes a stand with respect to them. However, political philosophy does not simply assert its own position but, like ethics, it acknowledges others and differentiates them in relation to its own engaged stance. As such, it remains open to response from other engaged stances with other sets of differentiations. Political philosophy is therefore always both engaged and yet open to further interaction with respect to ways of configuring the significational processes and structures that constitute 'the political.' Of course, it is possible to be engaged, sometimes extremely so, and yet to foreclose this openness to other positions; this, however, would not be political *philosophy* but rather a type of politics or propaganda. Hitler's *Mein Kampf*, for example, is not, in any sense, a work of political philosophy but an extreme example of a certain kind of politics, propaganda, and ideology unhinged from anything philosophical.

A similar situation obtains with respect to the engaged attitude in relation to eidetic formations. Marx and Engels were right-headed in suggesting, in *The German Ideology*, that every philosophy must be regarded as an 'ideology.' However, the present account would claim that this is somewhat misstated. Philosophical reflection, operating within a disengaged attitude, produces networks of linked concepts or ideas that, when articulated from or appropriated by an engaged attitude, constitute 'ideologies' (in the specific sense that I am employing this term). An ideology, then, is exactly an eidetic complex as it functions within an engaged attitude. The claim of Marx and Engels remains valid *for them*, however, since they insisted from the beginning that philosophy was always a matter of engagement and, consequently, all philosophical positions were, from that point of view, ideologies. Still, they failed to acknowledge another attitude that would be disengaged and hence non-ideological—a point later made, on different grounds, by subsequent thinkers in their own tradition such as certain members of the Frankfurt School and Althusser. [With respect to the latter, however, I would not claim that there is some 'position outside ideology'; rather, every philosophy (including 'scientific materialism') can be regarded and function as an ideology within an engaged attitude, though there is no 'necessity' involved in assuming such an attitude.]

A set of considerations, similar to those in the cases of embodied being (ethics) and significative complexes (political philosophy), applies to eidetic complexes deployed by or regarded from an engaged attitude (that is, as 'ideologies'). In particular, an engaged attitude, by its very nature, takes a stance with respect to ideologies and locates itself among other possible positions. As in the engaged partitions of ethics and political philosophy, it 'occupies its position' through a process of differentiating itself from other possible engaged positions, other ideologies. It is this process of differentiation with respect to its own engaged position that I refer to as 'ideology critique.' As in the cases of ethics and political philosophy, ideology critique is neither some disengaged assaying of 'ideological possibilities' from some position 'outside ideology,' nor does it establish a situation where all alternatives except its own are 'ideological.' Rather, an engaged attitude with respect to the eidetic realm is itself always ideological but it defines and establishes its own position through critique, the process of differentiation from other possibilities that presupposes continued engaged interaction with them. To say, then, that an eidetic complex or philosophical position is 'ideological' is not, in its most fundamental sense, pejorative; all such complexes or positions just *are* ideological inasmuch as they involve an engaged attitude, whether the position be mine or someone else's.

3. The Centripetal Nature of the Engaged Partitions

Let's now return to the earlier claim that the partitions of engaged philosophy—ethics, political philosophy, and ideology critique—are 'centripetal' rather than 'centrifugal.' Rather than (provisionally) holding the forces exerted by the three actual conditions and their excesses apart, as does the disengaged attitude, engaged philosophy involves bringing them together and occupying (or 'territorializing') a specific space defined by their intersection. This means that every space or position of any philosophical reflection conducted in an attitude of engagement will always involve a convergence of ethical, political, and ideological forces, whether explicitly acknowledged or not. That is, every genuine (which means engaged) ethical view—say, a position with regard to what is good and evil, right and wrong, or desirable and undesirable with respect to embodied beings and their desires—will be bound up with a position with regard to their significative and communicational interactions and the institutions based upon them, and with some eidetic complex ('ideology') that provides the terms, aims, and principles under which embodied beings interact with one another. The same can be said of positions regarding political matters and ideologies. Political thought always has ethical implications for embodied beings and is associated with a particular conceptual complex that regulates the significative interactions of embodied beings. And every ideology has implications for the desires and actions of embodied beings and the significative and institutional structures within which they function. Put simply, then, every instance of engaged philosophy will involve ethical, political, and ideological considerations and this will be the case whether a given position explicitly acknowledges this or not. Put more affirmatively, we might say that the force of any engaged position of philosophy will depend upon the degree to which it manages actively to bring the three actual conditions into productive relation with one another, and its cogency will consist in the degree to which it is explicit about this and is able to differentiate itself from other possible positions and articulate these differences.

4. The Engaged Partitions and Their Excesses

An issue crucial to this entire discussion that I have suppressed until now concerns the fact that, as in the case of the actual conditions regarded from a disengaged attitude, the partitions of engaged philosophy also involve their own distinctive dimensions of excess. Of course, given the way we've approached these partitions, a certain type of excess has already been tacitly acknowledged—since, as engaged, ethics, political philosophy, and ideology critique always involve occupying a position and differentiating it from other alternatives, any engaged position will always be exceeded by other possibilities, both explicitly acknowledged as well as 'unthought' or 'not yet thought.' But beyond this sort of excess generically involved in engaged philosophy, there are others whose roots lie in the excessive nature of the actual conditions themselves and which have special relevance to their respective engaged partitions. For ethics, it is the excessiveness of the desire of embodied beings that continually threatens to undermine and dissolve any attempt to regulate (or self-regulate) it by 'moral principles.' For political thought, it is the excessive nature of significational complexes that threatens to destabilize and subvert any attempt to restrict them to limited 'institutionalized' structures. One of the main effects of the excessiveness of signification is (to borrow a term from Habermas and the later Frankfurt School) 'systematically distorted communication,' a disruption of the very basis upon which any functional political or legal structure rests. And the excesses of the eidetic sphere, both with respect to its primary events and conceptual networks, tend, in the engaged mode, to provoke a congealing and hardening into determinate dogmatic structures of what is, even for an ideology, an essentially open set of processes and virtualities.

5. Universal Principles or 'Rules of Engagement'?

This leads us to a final, and for much of the philosophical tradition, decisive question: Does the approach to 'engaged philosophy' that I've adopted imply or suggest anything like clear, universal, or (in some sense) necessary ethical or political principles or firm grounds for preferring one ideology to another? There are (at least) two considerations involved in a response to such questions.

First, we might formulate a counter-question: Is philosophy itself, engaged or not, the sort of enterprise from which we could fairly expect the sort of 'absolute answers' that such questions seem to anticipate? The answer to this is straightforward and it is a threefold 'No.' No, because there is no clear or final point of demarcation between limited desires and their excesses for embodied beings. No, because the excesses of signification militate against any final form in which such principles might be stated. And No, because the eidetic sphere and its concepts are open processes always subject to further linkage, expansion and revision. More generically, No, because the excessive nature of the actual conditions of philosophy itself bars philosophy from any fully 'universal' or ultimate account of the conditions 'as they are in themselves.' This, however, does not mean that there can be no such 'ultimate principles,' 'claims,' or 'truths'; the question itself is not empty or meaningless. Such 'ultimate principles' do have a place in religion in the form of 'divine commandments'; science and mathematics may well make certain 'truth claims' within the limits of their various fields of inquiry; and art, perhaps, presents us with singular and perceivable 'absolutes' or affects. But such universal or necessary principles will not and cannot be produced by philosophy as a finite and contingent enterprise based upon three actual conditions, each of which exceeds philosophical reflection in its own distinctive ways.

There is, however, a different and more affirmative way to approach the question posed above. Rather than asking whether the enterprise of philosophy is capable of producing universal or 'morally necessary' principles of action, political right, or ideological critique, we might ask, instead, if our account of the field of philosophy, especially in its engaged attitude, suggests certain general 'rules of engagement' that, if followed, will tend to maintain and hold open the field and, if violated, will tend to undermine and subvert it. Put in other terms, is there something intrinsic to the nature of philosophy that suggests an ethics, politics, and ideology of philosophy itself? Let's consider each of the conditions and their distinctive types of excess in relation to these three engaged partitions.

a. Ethical Rules of Engagement

As we have seen, there are at least two major types of excess defining for the condition of embodied being. First, the very existence of embodied beings is contingent and dependent upon a very specific coalescence and configuration of 'cosmic events' excessive to it both as anterior to and as sustaining for it once it has emerged. Second, once it exists, embodied being continually exceeds itself due to the force of its own desire-as-lack. Without the continued operation of the physical conditions that give rise to and support the physical life of self-conscious embodied beings, there would be no self-conscious embodied beings and hence no philosophy. And without a certain level of (partial) satisfaction of desire-as-lack, no philosophy could arise, even if embodied beings continued to exist.

This suggests that any engaged attitude of philosophy with respect to embodied beings (ethics) must, at some point, concern itself with or reflect a concern for the physical and biological environment that supports the sentient and self-conscious life of embodied beings. An engaged ethical view that either regarded preserving the environment that supports the life of embodied beings as irrelevant or advocated policies or actions that would tend to destabilize or destroy it would be self-undermining and nihilistic.

Further, the very existence of philosophy requires not only the mere physical existence of embodied beings but their 'flourishing,' enabled by limiting some of the excesses of desire-as-lack and channeling it toward human communication and ideality. Any engaged ethical position must therefore involve or reflect some form of balance or reconciliation between an embodied being's 'traversal of desire' (to borrow a phrase from Lacan) and constraints upon it sufficient to allow the possibility for significative communication with other embodied beings and the emergence of eidetic complexes from this process. The ancient Greeks were partly right in claiming that a certain degree of 'leisure' was necessary for the practice of philosophy, but, perhaps, should have delved more deeply into the conditions required for a situation of 'leisure' to obtain. These would involve, beyond the satisfaction of basic biological needs, at least some level of security from suffering inflicted by other embodied beings, an anticipation that there is some connection between the 'traversal of desire' and its satisfactions, and a space and time in which this can unfold. We might say, then, that such things as dire poverty, deliberately inflicted suffering, and physical and psychological oppression are the enemies of engaged philosophy, whatever form it might otherwise assume. Again, a position that held otherwise would negate its own conditions of possibility and could not be genuinely 'ethical.'

b. Rules of Engagement for Political Philosophy

The actual condition of signification (or, more precisely, significative communication among embodied beings) involves its own excessive features. With respect to its engagement in political philosophy, three dimensions of excess are paramount. First, as we have seen, every significative system or complex exceeds any instance (or finite set of instances) of its deployment. Second, there are always, beyond any significational complex, others (equally excessive to any of their instances) that interact and deflect one another at various points. Finally, both any given significational complex and the various significational complexes different from it proliferate and metamorphose through the events constituting their deployment. But the crucial point for engaged political philosophy is that this interplay of significational complexes and their excesses are never merely 'objective' structured processes but are results of and, in turn, have consequences for the physical being, desires, and communicative lives of embodied beings.

Political philosophy takes a stand in the midst of these complexes and their excesses. Of course, we might have spoken of 'political institutions' instead of 'significative complexes,' but this would tend to emphasize structure at the expense of events and processes as well as to artificially segregate embodied beings and the 'institutions' within which they 'function.' Viewed in the present way, we can say that the primary mode of engagement of political philosophy with signification, communication, and its excesses involves occupying a position (and differentiating it from others) where the interaction of significative complexes (along with their excesses) can function to support productive communication and the conditions necessary for this among sentient and conscious embodied beings.

While there certainly have been and are institutions, polities, and political activities that challenge such a stance, political *philosophy* is possible only by acknowledging and sustaining its own 'conditions of possibility.' This means, first, that it assume and maintain an open field of possibility for significative communication among embodied beings, without which there could be no place for it itself to take a stand. Second, since it cannot take a stand apart from differentiating itself from other positions, it must, at least to that degree, acknowledge and respect other stances or positions in contrast to which it differentiates itself. Third, it must remain open to the 'virtualities' latent within the significational systems within which it operates. That is, political philosophy must remain open to the prospect of historical change, even (and especially) if not anticipated by it. And, finally, it must, so far as possible, resist 'communicative distortions' produced by non-philosophical political activity such as propaganda, hate-speech, or torture. Again, while this view admittedly settles relatively little with regard to such traditional questions of political philosophy as the 'best form of government,' rights, liberty vs. coercion, and so on, it does suggest certain broad conditions in the absence of which we pass beyond the realm of political *philosophy* into 'mere politics,' tyranny, or terror. Acknowledging, maintaining, and respecting these general conditions, which are, after all, the very conditions of its own existence, is the most that the enterprise of engaged political *philosophy* can do.

c. Ideological Rules of Engagement

I have claimed that every disengaged philosophical position, as a network of concepts based upon a originary event, becomes an ideology when occupied in an engaged attitude. Ideology is therefore not a term of opprobrium applicable only to the views of the engaged stances of others; rather, it merely describes some position of any engaged attitude. However, we've already indicated two ways in which networks of concepts are excessive.

First, they are always open, in multiple directions, to linkages with further concepts. Second, they tend to appear as structures that suppress or divide themselves from the thought processes that produced them and further link them with other concepts and propositions. The basic problem to be confronted in ideology critique is either forgetting or attempting to eliminate these two forms of excess, and this is true both of one's own 'ideology' and that of the 'ideologies' differentiated from one's own. The pejorative sense of ideology comes into play precisely when one takes one's own ideological stance as some fixed set of propositions or views, regards others in the same way, and then ignores or suppresses the possibilities of further processes and events that may reconfigure one's own view and those of others. As a matter of engaged philosophy, ideological critique obscures or negates its own origins and conditions when it proceeds in such a way. This is especially so when (as Badiou so emphasizes) philosophy, especially in the form of an ideology, asserts itself as some 'master discourse,' dominant for or stating some 'privileged truth' for all other philosophical positions and other enterprises such as religion, science, and art.

The point is that there is nothing in the nature of philosophy, even and especially in the eidetic realm, that supports any idea of totality, closure, finality, or necessity (other than the 'necessity' limited to logical elements of significational complexes). Any philosophical view or ideological position is a finite, limited, and essentially open enterprise—a sort of 'virtual generator' of concepts, propositions, and discourses, as I expressed it earlier. Among the historical names of its originary event is that of "truth," but so naming such an event is itself contingent and differentiated from other possible (and historically actual) names. Philosophy, therefore, is not and can never constitute itself as 'the Truth,' either for other positions or views or for other enterprises. Rather, it exists only as a virtual field of possibilities and disappears in any attempt to reduce or collapse this field. If there are rules of engagement for ideological critique, then, they are tolerance for a diversity of other positions, openness to self-critique, and resistance to any notion of totality or closure. Of course, philosophers have sometimes transgressed these rules, but in so doing they have also left the field of philosophy and become theologians, prophets, poets, or apologists for science.

6. The Endgame

In summary, then, philosophy, whether disengaged or engaged, is not capable either of producing universal or necessary truths, grounding absolute moral or political principles, or constructing some final and closed position by which all others can be finally judged. This is because philosophy is itself entirely contingent and dependent upon three actual conditions, each of which exceeds it in its own distinctive ways. What philosophy *is* capable of doing is identifying, differentiating, and relating those conditions, and recognizing the fact *that* they exceed it and clarifying some of the ways in which these excesses are registered within its own field. This can suggest some 'rules of engagement' with respect to ethics, political philosophy, and ideology critique. These, however, cannot be regarded as anything like universal or necessary principles, but only as conditions tending to support and sustain the otherwise contingent existence of philosophy itself. Of course, one could always ask, one step further on, "Is there some value in philosophy itself, such that we should seek to support or continue it?" And the only genuine answer, in this endgame, would be, "That itself is a paradigmatically philosophical question and assumes the very conditions that it seeks to question."

Concluding Considerations and Questions

As I suggested early in this work, philosophers have devoted a good deal of attention to how one begins to think philosophically or to compose a philosophical text. However, explicit discussions of how philosophical texts end are rare, if they can be found at all. Of course, there are some memorable endings to philosophical texts that come to mind: the 'myth of Er' that concludes Plato's *Republic*; Spinoza's discussion of 'blessedness' in the final book of his *Ethics*; Kant's assertion, in the final paragraph of the *Critique of Pure Reason*, that it may be possible, "before the end of the present century...to secure for human reason complete satisfaction in regard to that with which it has all along so eagerly occupied itself, though hitherto in vain"; Hegel's invocation of 'the Absolute' at the end of several of his works; and Wittgenstein's concluding sentence in the *Tractatus*, "What we cannot speak about we must pass over in silence." But about the only conclusions we can draw from such endings are that they somehow 'fit' the text that they conclude and that they often anticipate further texts, either by the author him- or herself or by readers responding to the text that has 'ended.'

These two points will guide the ending of the present text. First, I'll try to articulate, in broader terms than I've usually employed so far, what I take to be the overall significance of the image of philosophy that I have proposed. And second, I'll attempt to address a few recurrent questions that have been raised in previous discussions with colleagues and students over several years. Beyond this, I leave it to my readers to critically assess what I've offered here. Please feel free to respond or contact me at jsurber2010@gmail.com.

I. THE NATURE AND 'VALUE' OF PHILOSOPHY

The most important points I've tried to make about the overall enterprise of philosophy are these:
1. Whether regarded as a distinctive type of activity, a body of texts, or a position or view expressed within them, philosophy is always a

contingent, finite, and limited enterprise.
2. Philosophy is also, in all three of its aspects, an essentially open undertaking; it is simply not the sort of thing to which notions of 'closure' or 'finality' can apply.
3. Both of these rest upon the fact that there are real or actual conditions, not merely thought or posited by philosophy itself, without which philosophy would not exist at all.
4. *That* philosophy has these conditions can be recognized, acknowledged, and 'known' by philosophy, even though philosophy's 'knowledge' of the actual conditions 'in themselves' is always partial and limited.
5. To say that there are actual conditions of philosophy implies both that they exceed that which they condition in distinctive ways and that these excesses nonetheless affect and are registered within philosophy, both generically and in any particular philosophical view or position.
6. The actual conditions of philosophy are also the actual conditions of other human enterprises as well, though they are configured differently in each.

Philosophy can therefore be regarded generically as a 'field,' bounded and defined by the actual conditions and occupied by an open multiplicity of 'positions,' both realized and possible. This also means that particular philosophical views or positions can be 'mapped' with respect to where they are located with respect to the actual conditions, that is, with respect to the way in which the forces of the conditions and their excesses are configured and reflected within them.

Given the contingency of philosophy's very existence and the fact that its conditions remain always excessive to it, we can say that every attempt to think philosophically or express this activity is an intrinsically fragile and uncertain undertaking. One thinks or writes 'philosophically' (or should, in any event) with full awareness, from the beginning, that one's view will ultimately take a position among a multiplicity of others, both already actual and yet to be articulated, and that, however much concentration and effort one devotes to this, the result will never achieve a 'full disclosure' of the conditions that make it possible or a 'final accounting' of any other theme to which it addresses itself. To borrow some terms made popular (or unpopular, depending upon one's view) a few years ago, even the most skilled and elaborate philosophical undertakings will swim in the ocean of both 'known unknowns' and 'unknown unknowns' constituting the excesses of philosophy's actual conditions. Put in other terms, any philosophical undertaking will always be able to pose questions (or have questions put to it) that it itself cannot answer and it will remain unaware or ignorant of other matters about which (at least at any given point in time) not even a question can be (or as yet has been) formulated. Given this intrinsic fragility and uncertainty of philosophy, it is, perhaps, no wonder that philosophy has been seriously pursued by so few in comparison with the many other undertakings pursued by embodied beings.

However, because of the very fragility and uncertainty of its results, the pursuit of philosophy is also, in a sense, heroic. Proceeding without the consolations of religious faith, the certainty of a truth-guaranteeing method, or the satisfactions of self-expression in a singular material artifact, the would-be philosopher sets out on a quest to secure a 'place' and construct a 'dwelling' from materials that, left to their own devices, threaten to overwhelm and engulf her or him in the chaos of contingency. Whatever part of the terrain of the field of philosophy it territorializes, every philosophical 'position' represents, as Deleuze would say, a 'roll of the dice,' a willingness to engage in an uncertain enterprise and to accept the consequences of the result of the roll. Philosophy, therefore, is heroic in the sense that it commits itself, in the face of massive obstacles and odds stacked against it, to construct, express, and territorialize a habitable place, in full knowledge that this place itself is limited and can only be temporary—and that it and all other places will ultimately return to the chaos of contingency.

If the existence of philosophy is contingent, if it does depend upon conditions independent of and excessive to itself, and if it is incapable of producing any final reconciliation among them, then what, one might ask, accounts for its resilience and what is its 'value'? At one level, we could just as well ask the same question of religion, science, and art (and any other human enterprise for that matter) since they, too, depend upon the same actual conditions: the existence of embodied beings, significational complexes, and ideas expressed through them. In this broad sense, we would probably have to answer along the lines of the old 60s quip, "Life is strange, but compared to what?" That is, there can be no real answer to the question of the 'value' of human enterprises (or 'humanity' itself as a species) since it is precisely within such enterprises (and their primary events) as philosophy, religion, science, and art that notions of 'life,' 'humanity,' and 'value' emerge in the first place. They 'have value' precisely because they generate it. Any other relevant stance or basis for the comparison that such a question presupposes is lacking—or, rather, it is just the chaos of sheer multiplicity.

But, at a more restricted level, we might ask a different question: What is distinctive about philosophy among other human enterprises that constitutes its own 'value' or 'significance'? To respond to this, we should first observe that the configuration of the actual conditions in the case of philosophy, more so than that of philosophy's 'others,' is that of sentient human life itself. Religion, science, and art all represent particular and, so to speak, 'subtractive' configurations of the actual conditions and their excesses that, for philosophy as well as human life, appear and exert their forces in their full difference and distinctiveness. In some important sense, 'before' there was *homo religiosus*, *homo scientificus*, or *homo creator*, there was *homo philosophicus*. I do not mean to imply by this that religion, science, or art are, as human enterprises, in any way 'inferior' to philosophy nor that they are somehow 'defective' responses to human life as defined by the actual conditions. I only mean that philosophy recognizes and accords an autonomy to all the actual conditions and their excesses that the other realms only do in part. Religion, science, and art are, each in its own way, effective and enduring human responses to an actual situation defined by the three conditions and their excesses, and they constitute and open up their own distinctive fields of human activity and creation. But, no more than in the cases of philosophy and conscious human life itself, they would not exist without the three actual conditions. What is distinctive about philosophy, and what accounts for its proximity to conscious human life itself, is that it must recognize and take a position among these conditions in their full state of differentiation, relation, and excess.

To return to the beginnings of philosophy, I think Socrates and Plato had something similar in mind when, in their occasional discussions of the different 'kinds of life,' they suggested that the 'philosophical' was the 'best.' Though these discussions sometimes resulted in a hierarchy (though different ones at various points), I think the salient point was that the 'philosophical life' is always the 'best' because it most accords with the full range of human potential, viewed as the interactions among what they regarded as the 'actual conditions,' that is, *eros*, *logos*, and *eidos*. For them, it was the philosopher who, at once, recognized that there were these three conditions, was aware of the excesses associated with each, and attempted to locate his or herself among them at points where each could be given its due. But for Socrates and Plato, discovering this situation was none other than the most fundamental human project itself. And because of this coincidence between the aim of philosophy and that of a 'life worth living,' it made sense for the philosopher to enter the *agora* and engage others who, for a time at least, came to engage in 'philosophy' too. What Socrates' 'midwifery' ultimately demonstrated was that all with whom he engaged—religious zealots, tyrants, aristocrats, sophists, even slave boys—were, to some degree or other, already 'philosophers *in nuce*.' And they were so because they were conscious human beings in the process of negotiating the three actual conditions that, together, constituted the texture of human life prior to any further decisions about how these might otherwise be configured.

Of course, Socrates and Plato would likely not have agreed that any of their own actual conditions, or even the enterprise of philosophy itself, was ultimately contingent. But, in an important way, the very acknowledgment of this contingency raises the stakes involved in defending and cogently articulating what philosophy is, how it differs from other cognate enterprises, and why it remains important for the 'value' and 'meaning' of human life. There are hints in the dialogues that Plato might have, but apparently didn't, compose a dialogue called 'The Philosopher' to follow those called 'The Sophist' and 'The Statesman.' Perhaps he felt either that it couldn't be done or that he didn't need to compose it. However, I think that, within certain limits, we *can* say what philosophy is (and is not). And, in the face of the very serious and sustained threats to philosophy and human life of the last century, we no longer have the luxury of avoiding this question. For to defend and secure philosophy as an enterprise is, ultimately, to establish and preserve what it means to be human, especially in a situation where we cannot but acknowledge the ultimate contingency, and possible annihilation, of both.

II. SOME FINAL QUESTIONS

The following questions have been posed to me by philosophical students and colleagues, as well as by others with little formal acquaintance with philosophy. In keeping with my view that philosophy is an always open and often unpredictable undertaking, I'll restate and respond to them in what is clearly a contingent order.

Aren't you advocating a sort of 'relativism'?
I would agree with this up to a point. But we need to be clear about what this question really means. First, what's the alternative to 'relativism'—'absolutism'? 'dogmatism'? 'necessitarianism'? But I've maintained that, given the conditions for there being philosophy at all and hence philosophy's own contingency, no philosophical view can be expected to produce either 'absolute truths' or some final position that can displace or vanquish all others. So to say that any particular philosophical position is 'relativistic' is almost tautological, since the alternative isn't a possibility for philosophy. However, the actual conditions of philosophy, while 'contingent' in their own occurrence, are, *for philosophy*, not relative but 'absolute' or 'necessary' in the sense that, were they not to obtain, philosophy itself would not exist. So we could say that philosophy, generically speaking, is 'relative' to the actual conditions, and that particular philosophical views are 'relative' with respect to one another, while affirming that there are actual conditions 'necessary' (and hence not 'relative' in the former senses) for philosophy to exist in either the generic or more specific senses of the term. Viewed in this way, while the position I've advocated is 'relative' to other possible views or perspectives and 'relative' with respect to the actual conditions, it is not 'relative' inasmuch as it acknowledges or registers the necessary grounds for its

own existence. But, it has to be immediately added that the same can be said of any other position within the field of philosophy. I might add that the very idea that philosophy might be capable of producing 'non-relativistic truths' probably comes from confusing philosophy with other areas, especially religion or science, where such an idea might make sense. But if we understand what philosophy is and does, we'll see that that's just not the sort of thing philosophy is equipped to do and 'relativism' will not appear as a serious charge against any particular philosophical position.

But what about the claims you make about the actual conditions themselves? Don't they count as 'absolute' or as 'necessary truths'?

This is what my earlier discussion of the 'analytic *a posteriori*' attempted, at least in part, to answer. I suggested that claims like "The existence of embodied beings is an actual condition of philosophy" is 'necessary' in the very specific sense that its denial (of the 'subject term' when stated in this form) entails a 'performative contradiction,' something like the 'Liar's Paradox.' To deny it presupposes the (contingent, hence *a posteriori*) *fact* that there is an embodied being that is capable of both stating the sentence and its negation. This doesn't mean that the existence of embodied beings is itself necessary, but it does mean that, given the existence of embodied beings, any sentence denying their existence is 'performatively' self-contradictory (and a contradiction is one form of a 'logically necessary,' hence '*analytic*,' statement).

The important point, however, is that 'analytic *a posteriori*' statements involving embodied beings, language or significative complexes, or idealities (that is, the actual conditions of philosophy) constitute a special and limited class. They are neither merely 'logically necessary' (because they involve existential claims) nor merely 'empirical' (since their denial is contradictory). They are also not 'synthetic *a prior*,' as Kant understood this, since they have to do with real as opposed to conceptual or categorical conditions. Their distinctiveness can, perhaps, best be captured by saying that, while they are not logically necessary statements as they stand, they are constituted as necessary only 'performatively,' that is, when we attempt to deny them. This reflects the fact that, unlike other types of logical statements, they *already* function as designating the real or actual conditions for any statement expressing them. So, in answer to the question above, we can either say that they are 'necessary statements' but that their 'necessity' is different from that typically employed in formal logic, or we can say that, as they stand, they are not 'necessary statements' but can be seen to be such in the 'event' of their denial. On either account, such statements can't be counted among those that would provide evidence, one way or the other, that my view is either 'relativistic' or 'absolutistic' in the usual senses in which such terms are employed.

What about 'truth,' then? Doesn't philosophy have some special relation to 'truth,' or some general aim of expressing 'truth' or making 'true statements'?

This question, taken broadly and not just as a matter of formal logic, really concerns the constructivist view that I developed in my discussion of ideality (Chapter X). On that view, 'truth' is one of the names involved in the constitution of an 'originary event,' an ideality. It is not the only possible name for such an event—among others are 'the Good,' 'God,' 'Substance,' 'Object,' 'Reason,' 'the Absolute,' 'Freedom,' and so on. While a good deal of the philosophical tradition has proceeded from 'truth' as its originary event (as Heidegger has shown), and while 'truth' may (and often does) appear as a concept-event within the trajectories issuing from other primary events, it is not an 'essential' or 'defining' ideality for philosophy. Plato, Hegel, Nietzsche, the later Wittgenstein, Derrida, and Deleuze provide ready examples of philosophical activity that, for the most part, proceeds without 'truth' playing an originary role. Of course, there is a special relation to 'truth' for any philosophy for which it is the originary event, but it is in no way defining for either the condition of ideality or philosophy itself.

It's worth remarking, as well, that, even in philosophical views where it does function as an originary event, the ways in which distinctively philosophical statements are 'true' are entirely different from those in which other types of statements (for example, logical or empirical statements) are 'true' (as has often been pointed out). Of course, some philosophers, such as the positivists, have claimed that philosophical statements are 'meaningless,' that there is no distinctive class of such statements to which a 'truth value' can be assigned. I would prefer to say, rather, that, under the regime of 'truth' as an originary event, philosophical statements must be regarded as meaningful and that their 'truth' consists in the singular way that they enact and reflect the convergence of the actual conditions of philosophy and their excesses.

Does your view imply that all philosophical positions, as occupying specific locations in the field of philosophy, are equally valid or important?

This is a fair though difficult question when put to a view that regards itself as 'pluralist' in orientation. To answer it, I think we have to distinguish between a view merely counting as philosophy (that is, being locatable as a 'point on the map') and the 'force' or 'intensity' with which it 'territorializes' its position or region (to borrow some terms from Deleuze, who borrowed them from Nietzsche). Simply to count as a philosophy, a view or position must be locatable with respect to the three actual conditions and their excesses as differentiated or standing apart. Different 'subtractive' configurations of the conditions will determine fields other than that of philosophy.

The problem is that philosophical views lacking sufficient force or intensity will have a tendency to allow the actual conditions to reconfigure and they will thus migrate or slide across the boundaries separating other fields from that of philosophy—they will, sometimes very subtly, take on the characteristics of religion, science, or art.

So the question becomes, "What constitutes the 'force' or 'intensity' of a philosophical view or position?" There are many factors involved here, so I'll just mention several of the most important.

First, a philosophy's capacity to be explicit about its engagement and location with respect to the three actual conditions is important. I have suggested that all views that can count as philosophical involve them, but some are more explicit about this than others. Plato's entire philosophy (at least on my reading) unfolded as an attempt to be explicit about the relations among *eros*, *logos*, and *eidos*. Descartes framed his philosophical project in terms of *res cogitans*, *res extensa*, and God as the guarantor of 'true judgment.' Kant explicitly distinguished and explored the differences between and relations among sensibility, understanding, and reason. I'd conjecture that this very explicitness about what are ultimately the actual conditions of philosophy has a great deal to do with the force and intensity of their philosophies and why we still return to them rather than to so many others.

A second consideration concerns how a philosophical view or position recognizes, reflects, and deals with the distinctive excesses of the actual conditions. We might say that a philosophical position or view is more forceful or intensive to the degree that it develops or constructs ways in which to register the facts that embodied existence is restlessly desiring, signification or language obscures in its very act of expression, and thinking is an ever-expanding process of conceptual creation. Put the other way, philosophies that tend to reduce embodied being to some conceptual 'definition' or 'material nexus' (like the brain), proceed as if language is a 'neutral vehicle' of thought, or view thought as the production of some fixed 'categorial structure' tend to lack force or intensity (although, as I discussed earlier, there can be cases where a great deal of intensity can be concentrated in the way a philosophy deals with one or two of the conditions at the expense of others, as was the case with Nietzsche and Hegel).

Third, philosophies gain in force or intensity to the degree that they succeed in differentiating their own position from those of others. This involves a willingness to engage the full force of other views and then articulate one's own in relation to them. Philosophies that tend to turn other views into 'straw men' or fail to engage them at all tend to lack force and intensity.

Finally, the force or intensity of a philosophical view depends, in part, on how fecund or open it is to further expansion and development, not only by the philosopher herself or himself but by others beginning with it. More forceful or intensive views present conceptual networks that continue on in new and unexpected directions, suggest new forms of expression and signification, and offer new and enriched views of what it means to be a finite embodied being. It is no accident that the most forceful and intensive philosophies have spawned new and unanticipated trajectories that are often named after their starting-points: neo-Platonism, neo-Aristotelianism, neo-Kantianism, and so on. It is the force or intensity of the parent-philosophy, not its 'Truth' in some transcendent sense, that accounts for this.

Given how you ended the first section of this chapter, do you regard philosophy as 'humanistic' or 'anti-humanistic'?

I think that this whole debate, probably launched by Nietzsche and running through most of the last century, has been confused and misleading. The main reason is that 'humanism' (and therefore 'anti-humanism' as well) has several different (and sometimes opposed) meanings, among which the discussion has tended to migrate. How one responds to this question will depend upon the meaning of the terms implied in the question itself.

In one important sense, opposing 'humanism' and 'anti-humanism' is shorthand for the question concerning the 'ontological status' of human being in the broader context of the universe, whether 'humanity' as a biological species occupies some privileged place in the 'order of things.' I would hazard that this question is more about the difference between certain religious tenets and certain scientific theories and is really not posed in precise enough terms that philosophy can or need adopt a position one way or the other.

Another sense, more relevant to philosophy, concerns whether human being, regarded, especially in the modern tradition, as 'subjectivity,' provides the inescapable beginning and continuing reference point for any further action, discourse, or thought. On this score (with regard to the philosophical movement known as existentialism), Sartre famously asserted that 'existentialism is a humanism' and was countered by Heidegger, who claimed that 'existentialism' (and philosophy in general) was not a 'humanism' inasmuch as its primary concern was the 'question of Being' and not just 'human being' as the tradition had understood this. In such cases (as well as in the more methodological based affirmations of 'anti-humanism' among, for example, certain neo-Marxists, structuralists and post-structuralists), 'anti-humanism' was never meant to imply anything more than some claim about the inadequacy of taking 'subjectivity' as some absolute baseline for philosophical or, in some cases, scientific inquiry. In this sense, perhaps philosophically important but otherwise innocuous, anyone who (like myself) rejects 'subjectivity' (especially in its transcendental idealist versions) as some ultimate philosophical reference point can claim, without apology, to be 'anti-humanist.'

However, again thanks to Kant to some degree, when 'subjectivity' is linked with the possibility of ethical or moral concerns, claiming to be 'anti-humanist' can seem equivalent to endorsing 'amorality,' 'immorality,' or even 'nihilism' (Nietzsche's influence is clear here). Put more broadly, if we deny that 'man is the measure of all things,' or if we are 'true to the earth,' then it seems to follow that there is no 'measure' for human action, that 'everything is permitted' (*'Alles ist erlaubt'*), and we have no grounds for responding to the Shoah or the Gulag. The philosophical problem here is really a simple logical *non-sequitur*: such nihilistic 'anti-humanism' with regard to ethical or moral issues in no way follows from the 'anti-humanist' claim that 'subjectivity' is an inadequate basis for philosophical (or, for that matter, scientific) thought or discourse. This doesn't, of course, necessarily imply that morality, ethics, or politics need be 'humanistic' in some earlier sense, as some environmental thinkers have recently reminded us. But it should, at least, warn us against attempting, as transcendental idealism did, to forge some firm or 'necessary' connection between broader philosophical issues and moral, ethical, or political claims alleged to follow from them.

So, to respond directly to the original question, inasmuch as my view rejects 'subjectivity' (transcendental or otherwise) as some ultimate foundation of philosophy, affirms that there *are* actual conditions for philosophy all excessive to 'human being' or 'subjectivity,' and that they (and hence philosophy itself) are contingent (in the sense that they might not have obtained and that the enterprise of philosophy might not have existed), my view is, in the second sense mentioned above, 'anti-humanist.' But, I would immediately add that, as the human enterprise most coincident with and reflective of the human situation with respect to the actual conditions, my view (and any other genuinely philosophical view) can be regarded, in this specific sense, as 'humanistic.' Beyond this more generic point, I have also suggested that, in its engaged modes, philosophy also has an interest in securing and preserving the conditions of its own existence: the continued existence and flourishing of embodied beings, their free and (so far as possible) undistorted communication with one another, and the openness of thought to further proliferation and expansion across multiple trajectories.

Your view seems ambiguous or confused on a crucial issue at the center of much recent philosophy. Should your view be regarded as 'metaphilosophy,' one among other philosophical positions, or perhaps even 'non-philosophy'?

I'll begin with two very straightforward claims: The view I've articulated is all three, and every other position that can be regarded as philosophy is as well (whether implicitly or explicitly). Obviously, if we can make sense of the second claim, the first directly follows from it, so I'll begin there.

Philosophy, as I've described it, always involves a 'differential situating' among its actual conditions and their excesses. As situated and differentiated among others, every philosophy can be regarded as a (relatively) determinate 'position.' However, every philosophy, because it engages, registers, and reflects the actual conditions of philosophy as a generic enterprise, also at least implies (if it does not make this explicit) a 'meta-philosophy,' that is, a generic view regarding what philosophy itself is apart from any differentiated positions within its field (including its own). (I think here of Duchamp's claim that every artwork, whatever its medium, content, or theme, is, at the same time, a definition of art itself.) Finally, inasmuch as the actual conditions are excessive both to philosophy generically regarded as well as to any particular philosophical position, every philosophy is already situated within that which is only partly accessible and articulable by philosophy itself, that is, within 'non-philosophy.'

However, if things are as straightforward as I've just suggested, it's fair to ask why it has appeared to some recent thinkers, and I have in mind especially Deleuze, Badiou, and Laruelle, that there is something important at stake here. This will provide an occasion for some further differentiation of my view from other recent alternatives. The issue originates in a conviction shared by all three thinkers that philosophy must be 'immanent.' Though itself a highly problematic term, this notion probably emerged from the thought of Spinoza, Hume, and, probably most of all, Nietzsche's sustained and forceful critique of all ideas of 'transcendence.' It expresses the general conviction that philosophy, as a human and finite enterprise, is not, and can never be, entitled to invoke or claim knowledge or experience of something that is beyond or 'transcendent' to it, whether this be 'eternal ideas,' some absolute or eternal being, a 'principle of sufficient reason,' or 'transcendentally necessary' grounds or foundations.

This conviction about the 'immanence' of philosophy suggests (at least) three options with respect to the question that we are considering. We might claim that, at the most fundamental level, all philosophies are 'immanent,' and any claim to 'transcendence' (either on their own behalf or from the point of view of other positions) is simply a result of misunderstanding, mischaracterization, or ignorance about the enterprise of philosophy in which they are engaged. The problem here is that, if all philosophies are actually 'immanent,' then it doesn't really add anything to claim that they are, so there's no real issue here. It's just a matter of providing a proper reading of them that reveals this. The second is that some philosophies (say, the three figures I mentioned above, and their 'immanentist' predecessors) are 'immanent' but there are others that are not (say Plato and Kant). But what, then, makes the two types of philosophy different? Is it just that one group affirms that they are 'immanent' and the other denies it or explicitly claims that they are 'transcendent' (or 'transcendental')? But the question is not what a philosopher thinks or says about his or her view, but whether it is, in its basic claims and procedures, 'immanent' or 'transcendent.' Finally, one might claim that all philosophies are 'transcendent' and that those that claim to be 'immanent' misunderstand or misrepresent their own views (and those of others). This is the same situation as the first view, only reversed, and what is required is, again, a proper interpretation or strategy.

Admitting that this and what follows is a schematic gloss of a much more complex discussion, I suggest that the first view is roughly that of Deleuze, the second Badiou, and the third Laruelle. While Deleuze does suggest, in *The Logic of Sense*, that there are philosophies of 'height,' 'depth,' and 'surface,' his numerous interpretations of various traditional figures, which he describes as (politely put) 'taking them from behind,' are designed to reveal that they are actually 'immanentist' and that their own idea (if present in them) that they make 'transcendent claims' is a sort of delusion or misstatement about their own view. Badiou, by contrast, does think that there is an actual difference between 'immanent' and 'transcendent' philosophical views. The difference lies in whether a given philosophy attempts to 'produce truth' or true statements and to develop an 'ontology' to support this, or whether it regards the 'production of truth' as occurring elsewhere (politics, love, or poetry) and 'ontology' as the domain of some non-philosophical discipline (in his case, mathematics in the form of axiomatized set theory). Finally, Laruelle is very explicit and insistent that all philosophy, as philosophy, is 'transcendent,' whether a given philosopher admits this or not. In response to this, he proposes another discipline or 'science' called 'non-philosophy' whose aim is to disclose the limits, conditions, and suppressed assumptions of philosophy generically considered as well as of any particular philosophy.

So here are the consequences: either we must be able to inhabit and interpret any philosophical view in a way that reveals its 'immanence'; or we must be able to construct a notion of truth and an ontology supporting it outside the enterprise of philosophy but still relevant for it; or we must establish a position 'outside' (or 'alongside') philosophy that will permit us to describe the basic features and limitations operative in all philosophy, but of which philosophy itself is unaware.

Now philosophies that regard themselves as 'immanent' tend to reject any notion of a 'metaphilosophy' on the grounds that it would presuppose some position or standpoint, outside of and 'transcendent' to philosophy, from which philosophy itself could be generically regarded. On such a view, 'metaphilosophy' would either be just another philosophical position among others (and hence not really a '*meta*-philosophy'), or it would be something other than philosophy (and hence not a 'meta-*philosophy*' at all). However, if it is merely one philosophical position among others, it is in no better position to claim anything about philosophy generically considered than any other position, so this resolves nothing. 'Philosophers of immanence' must therefore either (like Deleuze) maintain and attempt to show that all philosophies are, properly interpreted, 'immanent,' or (like Badiou and Laruelle) adopt a position with respect to philosophy, generically considered, 'outside' or 'alongside' philosophy itself.

The problem with the first (Deleuzian) strategy is the following. On the one hand, it must grant that it is at least possible for some philosophy to be 'transcendent' if there is to be any point in showing that a given philosophy is, in fact, 'immanent.' On the other, on what can only be called 'metaphilosophical' grounds, it has already decided that philosophy generically considered, and hence all particular philosophical positions, are 'immanent.' So we can say that this strategy fails to avoid adopting the very 'metaphilosophical' stance that its own 'immanentism' rejects.

The second type of strategy avoids adopting a 'metaphilosophical' stance either by occupying a position within an existing field (or fields) other than philosophy (Badiou) or attempting to establish a new discourse other than philosophy, i.e. 'non-philosophy,' that unfolds 'alongside' philosophy (Laruelle).

The problem in the first case (Badiou) can be put in the form of a dilemma. Either the chosen field (say, mathematics) is relevant to philosophy, generically considered, or it is not. If it is not relevant, then it has no implications for philosophy and no gain is made with respect to characterizing philosophy or its conditions. Or, it does have consequences for philosophy, but this can only be if the 'results' of the mathematical discourse is 'translated' into and presented in terms expressing concepts that are distinctively philosophical (and not purely mathematical). But this simply constitutes another philosophical position among others. As such, it tells us nothing about philosophy considered generically.

The second of these options (Laruelle) does not have the 'relevance' and 'translation' problems of the preceding view, since this strategy explicitly takes philosophy, generically viewed, as its 'subject-matter' and deploys philosophy's own terms in ways unfamiliar to philosophy that amount to a sort of 'hyper-deconstruction' of philosophy. The problem here lies in deciding about the claim that this 'science' of 'non-philosophy' is not itself philosophy. Since Laruelle insists upon the 'immanence' of his own project, we cannot think of his 'non-philosophy' as some form of 'metaphilosophy.' But might 'non-philosophy' still turn out to be another, albeit novel, philosophical position among others? In order for this not to be the case, we would have to accept the fundamental premise of 'non-philosophy' that philosophy itself can be regarded as an enterprise sufficiently determinate and bounded to permit adopting a position 'alongside' it without thereby becoming it. I think the history of philosophy speaks against this, since, throughout its history (and I especially have in mind Kant's Copernican Revolution) philosophy has developed precisely through new images of thought arising 'alongside' preceding ones. In the case of Kant, we could fairly say, I think, that, if we regard philosophy, prior to Kant's Copernican turn, as equivalent to 'dogmatic metaphysics' (as Kant himself does), then his Critical view is 'non-philosophy' with respect to it (a point made in so many words by some of Kant's more conservative and recalcitrantly 'dogmatic' contemporaries). The point, then, is that Laruelle's 'non-philosophy,' however different it may be from philosophy as pursued in the tradition, must nonetheless take its place among other philosophical positions and cannot avoid doing so. The reason is that, in asking about the conditions of philosophy of which philosophy itself is unaware, it is doing precisely what philosophy, at its most forceful and intensive, has always done—as I've suggested all along, such a gesture is paradigmatically *philosophical*.

Now I can expand my initially terse response to the original question. First, while my view agrees with the 'immanentism' of the figures I've discussed in the sense that philosophy, as a limited human enterprise, cannot, by its own devices, establish 'transcendent truths' or 'universal and necessary' concepts or propositions, it is capable of acknowledging *that* there are actual conditions of its own existence, *that* these are excessive to it, and articulating some of the ways in which these conditions are configured within as well as exceed it. One could then say that the actual conditions are both 'immanent' to philosophy itself and yet, as excessive to it, they 'transcend' philosophy. Since every particular philosophical position is defined by the specific way in which it distinguishes and relates these conditions, every position both attests to the actuality of the conditions for philosophy generically considered and instantiates their 'relation-in-difference' in a specific form. In this sense, every particular philosophical position is also, at least implicitly, 'metaphilosophical' in enacting or instantiating the three actual conditions that together constitute the field of philosophy generically. We can also arrive at the same result by considering that every specific position is constituted as a 'location' in the generic field of philosophy by differentiating itself from (at least in principle) all other positions within the field. That is, the specificity of any position presupposes a 'virtual totality' (or 'field') of other positions whose differences from it constitute its own distinctiveness. Finally, we can say that the field of philosophy exists alongside (or, perhaps better, in the midst of) 'non-philosophy' in two different senses. On the one hand, the actual conditions, as excessive to philosophy's very existence and accessible to it only in part, are, quite literally, 'non-philosophical,' since the fact that the conditions obtain or not is independent of philosophy's existence and has nothing to do with philosophy's own activities. On the other, the actual conditions can be configured in other ways than they are in philosophy, producing other 'fields'—among them, religion, science, and art—that are themselves other than philosophy (that is, are 'non-philosophy'). So, once more, on the view I'm suggesting, every particular philosophy is also, at least implicitly, a 'metaphilosophy' and it stands in relation to 'non-philosophy' in the forms both of its own conditions and their excesses as well as of other fields produced by their configurations different than that of philosophy.

Does philosophy have a future?

Had you asked me this question fifteen or twenty years ago, I would have hesitated and then offered a 'guardedly pessimistic' account. But, as I indicated in the Preface, I think we've been witnessing a sort of philosophical renaissance since, perhaps, the final decade of the last century. I think there are a number of things that have contributed to this, part of which, as philosophically inconsequential as a mere calendar date may seem, was the anticipation and dawning of a new century as well as a new millennium. Over the last century, philosophy really was, as Hegel said, the reflection of its epoch in thought. The last century witnessed what can only be viewed as several major overt attempts of the human species to annihilate significant parts of itself and the invention or intensification of several other more covert, though potentially even more deadly, mechanisms that could eventually result in mass extinction. Philosophy quite faithfully reflected these suicidal tendencies both in its overt efforts to erase itself, like those of the positivist critique, Wittgensteinian 'dissolution,' poststructuralist 'deconstruction,' and 'eliminative materialism,' and in its promotion of covert tendencies to blur or eliminate the boundaries between itself and its 'others.' However, as the century drew to a close, one noticed, first, scattered realizations that most of the major 'anti-philosophical' trends of the preceding century had exhausted themselves and, then, the emergence of explicit efforts to defend the enterprise of philosophy by engaging in new discussions and constructing novel images of what philosophy might be and do, chastened and steeled by the misadventures of the preceding century. Further, by regarding its past from the perspective of millennia and not just centuries, philosophy also began to realize its deep connections with its own history as well as with large-scale historical trends that it could continue to ignore only at its own peril and that of the human species as well.

Despite these reassuring signs in the realm of philosophy, however, we should realize by now that its future depends upon certain conditions that are excessive to it. Philosophy will have no future if natural, environmental, or deliberately produced catastrophes eventually destroy the material conditions for the existence of embodied beings or their flourishing beyond the threshold of mere physical survival. Its future will be rendered uncertain, if not impossible, if significative communication among embodied beings becomes suppressed or irremediably distorted by political violence operating either as brute physical force, propagandistic conditioning, or the institutionalized control of communications media. And it may be seriously disrupted by the development of future bio-, psycho- and cyber-technologies that manipulate, alter, or suppress our very capacities for experience and creative thought. An important aspect of the enterprise of philosophy in the future will involve its adopting an engaged attitude in identifying, critiquing, and countering these threats to its own existence, which are, at the same time, threats to the existence and flourishing of the human species itself. If such resistance does not originate in philosophy, it is difficult to see from whence it will emerge.

Assuming that such catastrophes can be avoided and that philosophy begins to fulfill its renewed promise, it is fairly certain that philosophy in the future will look, in some important ways, quite different than it has in the past. Probably the most obvious and significant source of potential change at the moment is the 'digital revolution,' which is certainly still at an early stage. It is no accident, I think, that Kant's 'Copernican Revolution in Philosophy' and its almost immediate impact occurred just at the time when printing was becoming mechanized, making it possible inexpensively to publish and circulate large numbers of books and journals in a short time to a broad and diverse readership. The possibilities opened today by digital communications are already apparent in the growing popularity of blogs, chatrooms, digital journals, and websites, where philosophical ideas can be disseminated and discussed almost in 'real time' in a sort of 'virtual agora.' New forms for the dissemination of composed philosophical works are also emerging, with the advent of self-publishing, 'open publishing,' and content downloadable on such devices as Amazon's Kindle, all at least partly uncoupling the dissemination of ideas from commercial interests and the authority of their 'recognized experts,' who have tended to perpetuate their own views and preferences and suppress those of others. The development of other digital media such as 'art installations' and video games have also begun to expand both general interest in philosophical issues and the types of media that may be deployed for the significative communication of philosophical issues and ideas. In some ways, all of these digital developments will tend toward the proliferation of philosophical ideas and a sort of democratization (perhaps, on the downside, with its attendant 'qualitative levelling'). In any event, for better or worse, we can certainly expect the future of philosophy to look very different from what it has previously with respect to its media of communication.

The effects of the digital revolution on our sense of being embodied beings and the structure, channeling, and proliferation of desire has already become a topic for philosophical reflection and debate. However, it is also worth noting that concepts and models of thinking based upon digital and related developments, such as 'diagrams,' 'networks,' 'fractals,' 'nonstandard logics,' and various aspects of 'artificial intelligence' have already found their way into the eidetic sphere as well. I think we can fairly anticipate that this influence will continue.

Finally, perhaps under the heading of wild speculation or 'unknown unknowns,' what will be the consequences for philosophy and its present images of thought if (as some scientists believe to be not only possible but likely in the next century) new non-synthesized life forms are discovered that are radically different from anything presently known to us, or (still possible but less likely) some sort of significative communication occurs with intelligent non-terrestrial beings? And what if they have developed something comparable to philosophy as we know it? Or what if it becomes possible to synthesize an embodied being, complete with a 'brain,' the capacity for significative communication, creative thought, and an entire repertoire of emotions and desires? Or, what if time travel or 'teletransportation' becomes practicable? The stuff of science fiction at present, of course, and one might well think that philosophy has enough on its agenda at the moment not to waste too much effort on such speculation. But, with the ever-accelerating pace of technological development, it will not be surprising if some of the questions these developments raise find a more respectable place within the enterprise of philosophy than previously. Again, I would add that such 'excessive matters' can only be productively confronted and considered from the perspective of an enterprise aware of its own actual conditions and open to the types of excess involved with them. Neither religious faith, artistic expression, or scientific theorizing will suffice, though all may have something to contribute—no, the most fundamental issues will find their place within the field of philosophy or not at all. And for this among many other reasons, it is urgent that we ask and respond anew to the question, "What is philosophy?"

www.ingramcontent.com/pod-product-compliance
Lightning Source LLC
Chambersburg PA
CBHW022050160426
43198CB00008B/176